D0481574

Whores of the Court

Whores of the Court

THE FRAUD OF PSYCHIATRIC TESTIMONY AND THE RAPE OF AMERICAN JUSTICE

MARGARET A. HAGEN, PH.D.

ReganBooks
An Imprint of HarperCollins*Publishers*

HarperCollins books may be purchased for educational, business, or sales promotional use. For information please write: Special Markets Department, HarperCollins Publishers, Inc., 10 East 53rd Street, New York, NY 10022.

FIRST EDITION

Designed by Laura Lindgren

Library of Congress Cataloging-in-Publication Data

Hagen, Margaret A.
Whores of the court : the fraud of psychiatric testimony and the rape of American justice / Margaret A. Hagen. — 1st ed.
p. cm.
Includes bibliographical references and index.
ISBN 0-06-039197-9
1. Evidence, Expert—United States. 2. Forensic psychiatry—United States. 3. Psychology, Forensic—United States. I. Title.
KF8965.H34 1997
347.73'67—dc21 96-52972

97 98 99 00 01 ❖/RRD 10 9 8 7 6 5 4 3 2 1

This book is dedicated to the countless people in this country who devote themselves to helping others see more clearly: in particular to the journalists and reporters who spend endless hours sitting on hard benches in courtrooms and rooting through transcripts in dusty files so the rest of us can have some idea of what really goes on in our country's halls of justice, especially to Dorothy Rabinowitz of the *Wall Street Journal*, and to the psychological professionals—scientists and clinicians—who devote their lives to "lighting up the massive obscurities in which we move," especially the late Dr. Gert Heilbrun, who helped me light a number of candles in the dark, and Professor Sigmund Koch, who did his lifetime best to guide psychology onto rational paths.

. . . may Your deep brilliance light up
the massive obscurities in which we move.

Teilhard de Chardin

CONTENTS

ACKNOWLEDGMENTS

BECAUSE THE GESTATION PERIOD for this book was so long, I owe a significant number of people a debt of gratitude for their support, encouragement, advice, and enthusiasm.

My greatest thanks are owed to John R. Silber, former President, now Chancellor, of Boston University, for supporting my attempts to turn outrage into action, and, in support of that goal, for introducing me to his agent, Gerald Gross of Palmer and Dodge.

It is not possible to thank Gerry enough for all he has done for me. Without his good sense, knowledge of the publishing world, and patient guidance, this book would have remained a promissory note.

I am deeply grateful as well to Judith Regan of ReganBooks for sharing my vision of what's wrong with having psychological hired guns in the legal system and for bringing this book to fruition. Without her commitment and her extraordinarily gifted and dedicated staff, this book would be a much lesser version of itself.

Todd Silverstein, my fine and unflagging editor at ReganBooks, deserves a great deal of credit for helping me envision and create a much better book than was evident in the first draft he read. It goes without saying that all the weaknesses that remain are the responsibility of the author alone and persist despite the best efforts of the people at ReganBooks to eradicate them.

I am deeply grateful to Boston University for supporting me on the sabbatical leave that gave me the freedom to begin the reading and research required to write this book. I am grateful to the university also for the extraordinary assistance granted by the excellent library staff, particularly at the Pappas Law Library.

Without the assistance of James Ravitz, a student at Boston University School of Law and my summer research assistant, I would no doubt still be peering confusedly at the arcane abbreviations of American legal letters. His help in ferreting out and interpreting cases was invaluable. I am likewise grateful to Mary Perry, researcher extraordinaire, who helped me with every kind of legal question that came up. I could not have done it without her.

To my chairman, Henry Marcucella, who read and reread with unremitting patience and on-target criticisms and suggestions what must have seemed like endless versions of the manuscript, I can only say that very few academics are as fortunate as I in their chairman.

Special thanks also are due to Elizabeth Loftus, professor of psychology at the University of Washington, national expert on eyewitness testimony and memory, a first-rate experimental psychologist, and a very dear friend, for her limitless patience in reading the succeeding versions of this book, for catching my errors, and for encouraging me all along the way.

I thank also various friends and colleagues who read and encouraged and cheered me on when the way seemed interminable, especially Susan Milmoe, my old editor at Cambridge University Press; Karen and Kay Maloney; and Eamon Dunworth.

Lastly, I wish to thank the members of the International Psychology and Law discussion group on the Internet who responded so quickly and so helpfully to seemingly random queries for citations on every possible matter touching on forensic psychology. Their intellectual generosity was impressive and invaluable.

INTRODUCTION

THIS BOOK WAS ORIGINALLY INSPIRED by that most banal and most questionable of motives—personal outrage.

In the summer of 1993, in Seattle, my older brother was sued for $3.4 million in a civil case alleging psychological injury.

There was no evidence as such in this case. The trial itself consisted of a parade of half a dozen psychological experts of various types, all declaiming that the plaintiff suffered from one mental disorder or another and that the disorder—with all the attendant negative effects in her life—had been caused twenty years earlier by the accused, my brother—a person whom none of them had ever met.

The defense consisted of another witness parade of experts, this time experimental psychologists, all arguing that memory does not and cannot work as the plaintiff claimed, that psychoexperts have no special expertise at all in verifying such claims, and certainly no expertise in determining the historical cause of a current psychological condition.

I had heard of such lawsuits before, of course. Who has not? But as they had not directly touched the life of anyone I knew, I paid them no more attention than did the other experimental psychologists busy with teaching, research, and writing. My own area of research is visual perception, particularly issues of art and geometry. That has nothing at all to do with theories of the repression and recovery of traumatic memory.

After my brother's trial—he did win, if anyone can be said to win after being subjected to such an appalling accusation, at a defense cost totaling some $90,000—I began to take a closer look at the activities of my clinical colleagues in the world of law. I found that they were everywhere with their fingers in every half-baked legal pie cooked up by the wildest of imaginations. What a shock.

While I and my academic research colleagues were sleeping, our entrepreneurial clinical colleagues had infiltrated the American justice system like kudzu taking over every inch of lawn and garden. This book is an attempt to weed them out, root and branch.

Margaret A. Hagen
Boston, November 22, 1996

I

Whores of the Court

Psychologists as De Facto
Triers of Fact in Our Justice System

> In February 1992, [Eileen Lipsker] came to the Fairmont Hotel ballroom in San Francisco to explain the process of her memory return and her testimony at the trial to the American College of Psychiatrists. Afterward, the psychiatrists, including some of the most distinguished members of the profession in this country, crowded around Eileen. They believed her, they told her. They admired her. They felt intense compassion for her ordeal. At first, Eileen's big light-brown eyes looked doubtful. But along came another psychiatrist, and another, and yet another. With each one of their congratulations, Eileen brightened a bit. And soon she was glowing like the moon.
>
> Lenore Terr, *Unchained Memories*, 1994

THE PSYCHOLOGY-BASED COURT CASE

One afternoon in early 1989, Eileen Franklin Lipsker, a young American mother, gazed deeply into her daughter's dark eyes and fell directly into a nightmare twenty years past. The merest accident of expression in her daughter's eyes brought Eileen face-to-face with another child, long dead, brutally murdered in California in 1969. With the vision of the dead child's face as the key, a whole vault of terrible memories of that long ago death became unlocked in Eileen Franklin's mind and she began to remember, slowly at first, but then faster and faster, what her mind had fought so hard to keep hidden from view—that as a child herself she had witnessed the murder of her little friend, Susan Nason, at the hands of Eileen's own father, George Franklin. When these long-repressed memories were fully recovered and Eileen knew what she had, she also knew what she had to do. She brought before the legal authorities in California her memory of that terrible trauma from so long ago.

On November 28, 1989, the police arrested George Franklin and charged him with the murder of nine-year-old Susan Nason twenty years before.

There was not much direct evidence in this case. Susan's body had been found eight weeks after the murder in a rather remote wooded area. The material details of the case were widely published in the media—that Susan's head had been crushed by a rock, that she had worn a silver ring on her finger, that she was found lying not far from an old mattress—but at the time of the crime, no circumstantial evidence tied any particular individual to the crime and no eyewitnesses came forward.

Twenty years later there was still not much evidence other than Eileen's recovered memories. She said her father committed the murder; he said he did not. No one else saw anything. Eileen claimed that the trauma of witnessing the horrifying murder of her little friend had been so great that she repressed the memory for all those years and then, quite inexplicably, recovered it twenty years later.

Given the lack of physical evidence and the heavy reliance on psychological claims in this case, it is not surprising that in Franklin's trial for murder the bulk of the "evidence" presented was the opinion of experts—psychiatrists and psychologists—concerning the repression and recovery of memory, and the consequent reliability of Eileen's accusations against her father. Dr. Lenore Terr, a California psychiatrist, was the prosecution's principal witness in explaining to the court the obscure psychological phenomena the jury had to consider in weighing the case against George Franklin.

The prosecution's case rested on certain psychopolitical assumptions that have become popular in some segments of the mental health community. It is assumed that children who experience terrible trauma, like witnessing murder or experiencing sex abuse, often suffer, like some Vietnam vets, from post traumatic stress syndrome. It is also said that one of the most common features of this stress disorder is the loss of the memory of the precipitating traumatic event—what psychiatrists call "repression" of the traumatic memories—because the mind seeks unconsciously to protect the person from having to reexperience the trauma in memory. Lastly, it is assumed that repressed memories can be recovered in the proper conditions, usually in the context of therapy, but perhaps through an accidental triggering as in Eileen's case.

These psychological assumptions and countless others like them—lacking any scientific basis but embraced unquestionably by their adherents—over the last twenty-five years have crept insidiously into our legal system, into legislative bodies and courtrooms all over the country.

In George Franklin's case, the judge and jury accepted as scientific fact Dr. Terr's testimony regarding trauma theory, repression, and recovered memories; they took as truth the startlingly assured statements of this psychological expert about historical facts and mental mix-ups, and her confident explanations of the way the mind works. On November 30, 1990, based on the word of his estranged daughter and the testimony of this expert psychological witness, George Franklin was convicted of murder and sentenced to life in prison.

Dr. Terr writes that when Elaine Tipton, the prosecutor, asked several jurors after the trial what led to their decision, "She told me that a number of them said my testimony had convinced them. I learned something from that: sometimes hypotheticals are just as compelling as specifics" (Terr 1994, p. 58).

Did George Franklin murder Susan Nason? Was Eileen really so scared by the awful event she witnessed that she immediately lost all memory of it, continuing to pal around happily with her father as before, riding around the state unconcernedly in the same vehicle where she supposedly witnessed the assault on her little friend? Can a memory really be blown out like a candle in an instant, only to be relit by accident twenty years down the line? When Dr. Terr lectured the courtroom in California on the mysterious operations of the mind that would permit just such a sequence of events to transpire, should the court have accepted what she said as reliable truth?

All over America today, psychological professionals like Lenore Terr are climbing confidently into the witness box to lecture judges and juries on just such matters: how the mind works, how memory works, what a trauma is, what effects trauma has on memory, which memories are trustworthy and which are not.

With nothing else to go on in most of these trials other than the word of the psychoexperts so confidently testifying, it is crucial that we know the answer to these questions: Do all these hundreds of very expensive experts really know what they are talking about? Can the rest of us trust them? Can we rely on what they tell us to be the last word in scientific knowledge about the workings of the mind?

Alas, no. Psychology's takeover of our legal system represents not an advance into new but clearly charted areas of science but a terrifying retreat into mysticism and romanticism, a massive suspension of disbelief propelled by powerful propaganda.

Thanks to the willingness of judges and juries to believe psychobabble with scientific foundations equal to horoscope charts, babble puffed about by psychological professionals with impressive credentials, what we've got now are thousands of self-styled soul doctors run amok in our courts, drunk with power, bedazzled by spectacular fees for the no-heavy-lifting job of shooting off their mouths about any psychological topic that sneaks a toe into a courtroom.

The demand is great, the supply is huge, and the science behind it all is nonexistent. But the reality does not matter.

With the passage of well-intentioned and broad-reaching social welfare and safety net legislation over the last decade buttressing Americans' willingness to buy into any claim made by a certified psychological professional—not just claims about trauma and memory—our legal system today generates a virtually unlimited demand for psychoexpert services while the psychoexperts display an equally unlimited willingness to service those demands.

Lenore Terr sound-alikes are echoing around the country in hundreds of courtrooms in various types of trials both criminal and civil. Thousands of psychological "experts" confidently—and expensively—inform judges and juries, patients, plaintiffs and defendants not only about how memory works—as in the Franklin trial—but how the mind itself works, how the personality is formed, what aspects of character and behavior can be changed and how to go about it, as well as what wrong was done, when and how it was done, who did it, how much responsibility a party bears, and whether and when said party can be rehabilitated. In the civil realm, psychoexperts determine for the courts the nature and extent of psychic injury, disability, and discrimination; the presence or absence of abuse; and the relative fitness of parents.

The result is what has all too clearly become the rape of the American justice system.

A Mental Devil Made Him Do It

> The man who stabbed the daughter of state Sen. Arthur Dorman 16 times in February did not know right from wrong at the time, making him guilty of the crime but not criminally responsible, a Howard County circuit judge ruled yesterday.
>
> Gary C. Moncarz was found guilty of murdering Barbara Susan Dorman, his girlfriend of about a year, but Judge Dennis M. Sweeney ruled that Moncarz suffers from a severe mental illness that prevented him from understanding his actions.
>
> Moncarz, 42, a former accountant, was remanded to the custody of the state Department of Health and Mental Hygiene until he is deemed no longer a danger to society or to himself.
>
> State's Attorney Marna McLendon said psychiatrists will determine when Moncarz can be released but that he likely will spend a long time in an institution. (Francke, *Baltimore Sun*, August 27, 1996)

In criminal trials, we have competing teams of psychoexperts analyzing the accused, first to tell the judge whether the defendant is competent to assist in his or her own defense; then, if the defendant is found competent, the defense hires another raft of experts to testify that competent or no, the defendant is mentally disordered in some way and so should be found not guilty by reason of insanity, or, if not completely insane, his or her criminal responsibility should be considered less due to some diminished mental capacity or state of mind.

"He cannot understand the charges against him. She couldn't tell right from wrong. He couldn't distinguish fantasy from reality.

She couldn't control her actions. He is the victim of an irresistible impulse. He was traumatized by the war. She was in a flashback. He suffers from an incapacitating mental disorder. She has a psychological disease. It's not his fault because he wasn't taking his medication."

A mental devil made him do it.

> Che Rashawn Pope reportedly said five words before he pulled the trigger of the gun he was pointing at 17-year-old Sadrac Barlatier in Mattapan Square.
>
> "This is your time, man."
>
> Pope, 18, has been charged with first-degree murder in the October 11, 1995, shooting. His defense attorney is considering arguing that Pope . . . killed because he is afflicted with "urban psychosis" from living in an environment made "toxic" by exposure to gangs, poverty, fatherless families, drug use, teen-age pregnancy and violence. (Ellement, *Boston Globe*, October 14, 1996)

In old mystery stories, motives were assumed to be simple and the detective always asked first, "Who benefits from this crime?" That was yesterday. Today the psychiatrist asks, "Who traumatized this perpetrator?"

Psychological explanations invoked to get people out of impossible situations are much like the deus ex machina solution to irresolvable plots in ancient plays. When all the characters are inextricably knotted up with no hope of resolution in sight, suddenly the god descends from the heavens and takes everything in hand. And, like deus ex machina and all other good dramatic devices, psychological resolution tales require considerable suspension of disbelief to operate effectively.

What we want today is not retribution but the understanding that is the heart of a compelling narrative. We want a good story, preferably a classic tale if not an epic drama. We are no longer willing to judge the conduct of others as good or bad, because we no longer believe that the individual is actually responsible for his or her own conduct.

Lately, in Massachusetts, we had the tragic and senseless murder of a brilliant young student at Harvard by her female roommate, who then committed suicide. The press was full of psychological experts speculating that this appalling action was caused by cultural isolation disorder or school stress disorder or rejected friendship disorder. Not one expert suggested that the fault lay with the murderer herself. Why not? Have we lost all belief in personal responsibility for good and bad?

Modern psychology, permeating our culture and our legal system, has convinced the larger society that responsibility for behavior belongs to the background and context in which it occurs, not to the individual performing the action. We believe that people act—when they act badly—for reasons that are essentially written in their history and outside their control.

Rehabbing Rapist Killers

This is also the reason that so many Americans are so ambivalent about punishment for crime. We vastly prefer the idea of rehabilitation over punishment, especially for criminals who can make even the remotest claim to victim status. Thus we have, despite any evidence of effectiveness, judge after judge sentencing criminals of every dangerous description and degree to so-called treatment programs.

When O. J. Simpson pled "no contest" some years back to the charge of beating his wife, he was sentenced to psychotherapy. Cellular psychotherapy. He did it by telephone.

In 1975, Officer Matthew Quintiliano, a policeman in Connecticut, was sentenced to therapy after he killed his first wife. He was cured by the wonders of modern psychotherapy in three months and was freed. He married again and subsequently killed his second wife.

Why do we, the public, go along with psychotherapy as a sentence? Because it goes right along with the idea that no one is really responsible for his or her own actions. We are all victims of outside malevolent forces. Criminals are not bad; they are damaged. Since society caused the damage or allowed it to happen, society should repair it. Rehabilitation has long been a component of the criminal justice system, so rehabilitative psychotherapy fits well as a natural extension of that idea.

Does it work? Can psychotherapy really rehabilitate wife beaters and murderers and rapists and drunks and druggies? Our current method of measuring effectiveness is to ask psychotherapists if psychotherapy works. Mostly they say yes.

They are wrong. Even for what is probably the most important question—"Will this guy kill or rape again?"—the forensic clinician is correct in his or her predictions no more than one third of the time.

Constructing the Psychological Child

The demonstrated incompetence of forensic clinicians at seeing into the souls even of their own patients has not stopped the legal system from granting them terrifying power, not only in criminal domains but also in any and all cases involving children as defendant, victim, witness, or subject of some adult dispute.

When a fifteen-year-old, 220-pound "child" in Massachusetts is accused of stabbing the neighbor lady ninety-six times, unto death, it is the court-ordered psychological evaluator who counsels the judge whether the young man should be tried as a child who can be rehabilitated or as a man subject to a man's punishment for a man's crime.

When ten- and eleven-year-old boys drop a five-year-old child to his death from the roof of a fourteen-story building, it is child specialists who peer with mental telescopes into their histories and into their futures and tell the judge what caused this terrible behavior and what can be done to fix the boys so it will not happen in the future. The courts accept this counsel from the highly paid professional because they think they have no choice. Our courts accept at face value the claims of all these entrepreneurial experts that they understand what goes wrong with children and they understand how to fix them.

They don't.

Psychological professionals also claim to have special skills that allow them to detect unerringly what is in the best interests of a child. They tell our courts who will be the better parent, who is too crazy to have custody of a child, whether moving from one place to another will disturb the child's mental health, and whether the child was abused by one parent or another.

Are mental health professionals any more knowledgeable than you or I about whether a child has been abused in the home? About whether the child is better off removed from the home? About whether the child will grow up better under Mother's custody or under Father's? Of course not. How could they be? There are no special secret tests for any of the factors that child clinicians claim are so crucial to their so-called professional opinions.

It is essential for the future health of American children and their families that all these professionals be forced to lay their cards on the table so that everyone, parents, prosecutors, and judges alike, can see what an empty deck they are dealing from. The system is a farce and it perpetrates awful injustices.

My Mind Has Fallen and It Can't Get Up

Like family law, the entire arena of civil litigation also has experienced a huge increase in the testimonial activities of the forensic clinician. The modern proliferation of mental disorders has provided a veritable bonanza for entrepreneurial psychologists, not to mention their associated attorneys, not only in traditional injury and liability tort cases but also in disability and discrimination claims.

How does it work? Simple. Hire a psychoexpert to come into court and testify that you are damaged invisibly—mentally, emotionally, psychologically—that you suffer from one of the hundreds of psychological disorders "recognized" today. Then you have two ways to go. In a straight injury claim, your expert can testify that your psychic injury was caused by the trauma you experienced at the hands of your neighbor, your employer, or an unfeeling institution. In a disability claim, the expert must testify that your employer or a public accommodation discriminated against you by refusing to recognize or make reasonable accommodation to your disability. In both cases, you require much money to repair the injustice.

A typical case is that of the employee fired from a radio station in Washington state for offensive on-the-job behavior, who recently was awarded $900,000 by a jury for a discriminatory firing and for the psychic injury done to her by the discrimination. Her poor job performance, according to professional opinion, was produced by a mental disability and therefore occurred entirely outside the realm of personal responsibility.

Psychological disabilities, not incidentally, can be diagnosed only by trained professionals whose word cannot be credibly disputed by anyone other than another trained professional. No mere layperson can hope to match or, God forbid, criticize the diagnostic skills of the clinical psychological professional.

The cost of the needed treatment, the psychotherapy, is always included in the requested compensation in civil injury trials. Thus you have therapists testifying that yes, it is absolutely crucial that this plaintiff receive plenty of expensive psychotherapy for her disorder. Having therapists testify about the need for psychotherapy is about as smart as answering an insulation ad that promises Free Analysis of Your Home's Heating Efficiency.

They Say This Is Science

In criminal trials like that of George Franklin, in which the psychoexpert Dr. Terr created a completely novel and entirely hypothetical model of the operations of mind and memory, and sold it to the jury as science—science!—and in the innumerable civil trials over just about everything, we now have countless psychoexperts shamelessly regaling the courts with their personal opinions about the workings of the mind and behavior, which they have wrapped in the trappings of science through nothing more than a liberal sprinkling of jargon and some fancy-sounding titles and credentials.

That the courts accept expertise on the experts' own valuation of it reflects desperation as much as acceptance. Our courts—we, the people—need help to understand past behavior, to control present actions, and to predict who's going to do what kinds of awful things in the future.

Common sense tells us some things. We believe that the older guys get, the less likely they are to rape anyone. We believe that if guys knock around one woman they will knock around another one, and if he hits you once he will hit you again. We believe that most men who beat up on their children in a real nasty way do so much more than once. We know that most killers don't kill more than once in a lifetime—which makes rehabilitation of murderers a kind of funny concept—and we know that the older a guy is, the less likely he is to be violent. (He is also more likely to drive slowly and to wear a hat.)

We also know that all these little factoids gained from our own experience, newspapers, movies, and television are unreliable, the best-we-can-do, unscientific beliefs that don't give us absolute security or predictive accuracy. What's to say that this particular seventy-five-year-old man won't knock your head in with a baseball bat and rape you? Who's to know if this other guy wasn't so horrified by his hitting his wife once that he'd kill himself before doing it again?

We want more certainty than that provided by rules of thumb, and we want more safety than that provided by our own limited experience. Thus modern Americans will embrace almost any psycholegal theory or claim that highly paid and highly arrogant experts spin on the witness stand. We and our judges are blinded by jargon, fancy-sounding credentials, and fancy degrees.

Does it drive all of us crazy to live with the myriad uncertainties that arise because the field of psychology is in its infancy and simply unable to answer—sometimes unable even to address—so many of the questions in our justice system for which definitive answers are desperately needed? Perhaps so. But relying on pseudo-experts who are simply not up to the job the courts demand of them will not further the cause of justice in this country. It will just make the whole system and the whole society sicker.

For all forensic psychologists who work one side of the courtroom or the other, the job is lucrative. However, the idea that much of professional psychology's move into the courtroom has been motivated by simple economic interest is not really all that alarming. Money is a motive we can all understand. As a society, we are used to people willing to do anything to chase a buck, and we understand them.

But we also must wake up to the fact that the present and growing dominance of psychology in the courtroom poses a graver danger to society than simple monetary corruption. Much of the present marriage of psychology and the law has been cemented by a virtually impregnable arrogance and institutionalized in both law and legal practice, and that is a scary thought indeed. Both the public and the practitioners themselves have been seduced into believing the pseudo-experts' bunkum, have managed to get that bunkum written into law, and have effected a wide acceptance of a crucial judicial role for the bunkum artists as well.

TWO ROADS DIVERGED—EXPERIMENTAL AND CLINICAL PSYCHOLOGY

The public and its legal system do not know that the psychology that holds such sway in their legislative chambers and courtrooms lacks any scientific foundation because most of the men and women who make up the scientific and academic discipline of psychology have kept their mouths shut about what's going on. The experimental scientists have clung to the mistaken belief that the practice of psychology in the public domain is the territory of the clinical practitioners. The scientists felt that if they didn't step on the clinicians' territory, the clinicians wouldn't step on theirs.

Who are the scientists and who are the clinicians among the different varieties of psychologists? The scientists, the experimentalists, are researchers who study perception, language, learning, cognition, and memory, mainly. The clinical types are the practitioners who focus on personality as well as on so-called abnormal behavior. Another way of saying this is that the experimentalists don't see patients; the clinicians do. (That's why they are called "clinicians"; they go to clinics to see patients.) Also, the clinicians don't do experiments; the experimentalists do, sometimes in laboratories and sometimes in the real world. Of course, these divisions aren't clean. There are people who study personality, for example, who do real experiments; there are learning theorists who see patients; and so on. But in general, the two divisions hold well enough.

The split into clinician/practitioner versus scientist/experimentalist also holds across the various psychological subdivisions of academic clinical psychology, professional psychology, psychiatry, counseling, and psychiatric social work and nursing. In each subdivision, the majority of the practitioners are clinicians untrained and inexperienced in scientific research; the minority were actually trained in or actively engage in science.

For social workers and for psychiatrists and psychiatric nurses in medical educational settings, the situation is even worse than for conventionally trained Ph.D. psychologists. In these fields, there is not even the rhetorical expectation that the future practitioner will be broadly educated in psychological theory and research.

(In this book, I will use common terms for psychological practitioners working within the realm of the justice or legal system—psychiatrists, psychologists, social workers, or other—whatever the particular education and training, unless that background is relevant to understanding or evaluation of some point.)

THE BIG LIE

Experimental psychologists know that the education commonly possessed by licensed mental health care providers, whatever their background and training, is woefully inadequate to the job demands. They know too that with the present state of psychological knowledge, there are severe limitations on what *any* education could provide to the most diligent student. No education on earth today can be held to give an adequate account of how the mind works, how personality and character are formed, or what can be changed and how.

Psychology is a science in its infancy. With the best will in the world, it could not today meet the demands and expectations placed on it even by patients in need, much less by the legislative and judicial systems of the country. The entire psychological community knows all of this, at least the scientists do, and most of them ignore it.

The psychology establishment has nevertheless permitted the tenets and practices of clinical psychology to be incorporated into our laws and our courtrooms, knowing full well that they are untested, untestable, profoundly unscientific, and not even generally held to be factually true. We have allowed the courts and the public to confuse the methodology and findings of scientific, experimental psychologists with the practice and interpretations of clinicians. We have allowed so-called clinical psychological experts we know to be utterly unequal to the task to presume to take over the roles of judge and jury as finders of fact in American courtrooms.

We know forensic psychology's massive infiltration of the judicial system has been wrong. But, because of the takeover, the prestige and the power experienced today by members of the psychological community—experimentalist and clinician alike—are unprecedented in history. Who can blame the ever-reaching branches of psychology for succumbing to temptation?

THEY MUST KNOW WHAT THEY ARE DOING

There has been another critical factor driving what must seem to the public like almost criminal negligence on the part of the profession of psychology: Many experimentalists would argue that because numerous troubled people seem to find in therapy the help they need, it is not just permissible but perhaps even desirable to ignore its complete lack of scientific foundation. This has been a grave error, with wide-ranging consequences for the field of psychology and the public alike.

"Hey, he cured me. He must know what he's doing, so I'm sure he can cure other people." It seems reasonable, doesn't it? I was better off after my time with the psychiatrist, so I assumed that the psychiatrist must have made me better. It follows that he must have known about what was wrong with me psychologically, what caused it and how to fix it, doesn't it?

No. The effectiveness of a therapeutic approach in treating a disorder is logically unrelated to the validity of the therapist's theory of causation of the disorder.

How can that be? Let us see.

2
Psychopathological Science

Clinical Research

> The most insidious thing about bad science is that it can afflict even some of the more intelligent, methodical, and honest members of the scientific community. The reason is that it appeals to a broad element in human nature, not just to vices but to some virtues as well.
>
> Peter Huber, *Galileo's Revenge*, 1993

LEAPING BEYOND THE DATA

> I'm in bed with Ann. We're making love. She teases me, and I get my feelings hurt. I don't know why, but I hate her for teasing me. So we stop making love, and we each turn away from the other and go to sleep. Now I'm sleeping. I began to dream. In the dream I'm in bed with Ann, just like I really am, and we're making love, and she begins to laugh at me, to make fun of me. And suddenly I realize she isn't really Ann, she is my mother, in disguise somehow. And I'm in bed fucking my mother! And she's laughing, saying, "I finally got you. I finally got you!" And I'm so ashamed, so embarrassed, I just start hitting her to make her stop. (Barber 1986, pp. 56–57)

This dream was related by a young man, John, who had been arrested one night for beating up his girlfriend, Ann, although he claimed to have no memory of the event. Even though Ann did not press charges, John decided to seek help from a psychotherapist.

The therapist, Dr. Barber, chose dream analysis and hypnosis as therapy techniques. His weekly instruction to John was, "Some night this week, and I don't know which night will really be best . . . but some night this week, you will have a dream. This dream will be interesting to you, and will tell you something you need to know about your life right now. As soon as the dream ends you will awaken, and you will remember the dream vividly as you write it down so you don't have to memorize it. And you can bring in your notes about the dream next time." The therapist directed John to have amnesia each week about all of this dream instruction business.

Finally, after numerous sessions in which John would relate his dreams under hypnosis, he came in with that supposedly highly revealing dream about having sex with his mother and his girlfriend that "explained" why he beat up Ann.

> In the days that followed that dreamwork, John began to remember bizarre and painfully confusing incidences of sexual seduction by his mother. . . . His view of his own sexuality, and of his terrible need for both control over and distance from women, was also undoubtedly rooted in these early experiences. . . . Memories of the actual torture of being locked in the dark closet [one of his punishments for not satisfying his mother] made clear how John had developed his dissociative capacities. (Barber 1986, p. 57)

"Dissociative capacities" is the phrase John's doctor uses to describe John's ability to beat up women and remember nothing about it afterward.

So, after a short time, John was completely cured, terminated therapy, and became engaged to be married—to a girl we hope is luckier than Ann.

Quite an impressive little story, isn't it? Is it true? Who could possibly know?

WITCH DOCTOR FALLACY

Consider this example: In a mythical tribe, a person who behaves in a way that leads him to be labeled mentally ill is tied to a stake, burned, and beaten. During this procedure, the witch doctor dances around the stake rattling his gourds until the patient's behavior improves. The witch doctor believes that the patient is possessed by a spirit and the purpose of the treatment is to scare the spirit the hell out of the body. If the symptoms of many people who receive such treatment quickly disappear, and given this kind of treatment one can imagine that it is highly likely that they will, then one could conclude that the witch doctor's treatment is effective in curing mental illness.

If we assume that the positive outcome—disappearing symptoms—supports the witch doctor's theory of psychopathology, then we are in the rather difficult position of having to accept a theory of demonic possession as the cause of mental illness, the common primitive explanation of bizarre behavior. We must conclude that the witch doctor knew what was wrong with his patient, knew what caused it and how to fix it.

Most modern Americans would not accept that conclusion. The witch doctor may believe he has cured his patient; the patient may believe he was cured by the witch doctor. But the rest of us know that there are many possible reasons for the improvement in behavior, despite the beliefs of both doctor and patient, and we are not about to conclude that the witch doctor has any special knowledge of mental illness at all.

We can see that the effectiveness of therapy is logically unrelated to the validity of the therapist's theory of mental illness when we are presented with the witch doctor scenario, but in the case of modern psychotherapy we often forget it.

In the case of cancer, we don't usually make this logical error. Although there are now successful treatments for some cancers, and significant advances in understanding the origins of cancer, very few patients will assert that their oncologist knows all that could be known about cancer.

Why the difference? Why do we go the witch doctor route with psychotherapy but not with cancer therapy? Part of the answer is that in most types of mental illness there is no independent, corroborating measure of mental illness except for what the patient says and does. This is not true of cancer patients. The patient can feel great, go to work, and still have cancerous tumors that can be observed in a number of ways. Whatever he or she may say, the patient has cancer and the doctor knows it. The harder it is to verify independently the disease process in medicine, the more likely it is that medicine will fall into the same witch doctor trap as psychotherapy.

We have no direct, objective indicator of mental health. We can't measure the mind. And because mental functioning cannot be measured directly and objectively, psychotherapists are boxed into the corner of believing the patient, and the public falls into the trap of believing our witch doctors. The clinician has no way to verify independently what the patient says, and the public has no way to verify independently the clinicians' assertions about mental life.

All of us, patients, clinicians, and public alike, are willing to accept the occasional success in therapy as evidence that therapists are experts in causation of mental disorders and in general psychological functioning. Our belief is quite understandable.

That the general public confuses psychology's hit-or-miss success in making people feel better as evidence of a comprehensive understanding of general psychological functioning is not a new observation, although it is much overlooked these days. And the fundamental inadequacy of psychology as a science is not a new issue.

What *is* new is the extraordinary depth and extent of the acceptance, as a *science*, of the principles and practices of clinical psychology by the older institutions of our society—by courts and police, by judges and juries, legislators and policy makers. Our legal system has been told that clinical psychology is a *scientific* discipline, that its theories and methodology are those of a mature science, and our legal system has believed it. Given the deplorable state of the "science" of clinical psychology, that is truly unbelievable.

THE IDEAL OF SCIENCE

Science is an ideal. Some people would say that it is so much an unreachable ideal that it is a fiction. That is not true. That so many fail so often in so many ways does not change the nature of their endeavor.

What is it that the people engaged in science are trying to do?

They are trying to acquire knowledge about what things exist and how they work. What distinguishes scientists from other seekers after knowledge is their belief in and practice of a specific methodology for seeking truth.

Scientific methodology is essentially controlled observation of how some aspect of the world changes when some other factor is added or removed, increased or diminished in quantity. Scientists make predictions about what lawful changes will take place under what circumstances. The accumulation of these tested laws of change—of cause and effect—makes up the knowledge base that is the body of scientific theory. Through the testing of predictions—hypotheses, in scientific jargon—under carefully controlled conditions, the theoretical body of scientific knowledge is built step by step.

Control in the experimental testing of predictions is essential because it is impossible to know what you are seeing if too many things are going on at once. The goal of science in the experimental testing of predictions is to reduce the number of things "going on" to a controlled and observable level so that the results obtained can be reliably attributed to a *particular* cause, not to any of a number of uncontrolled and unknown factors.

But what makes science so powerful is a second trait that it has. Science exists independently of the scientist. While any individual scientist may claim to see something or to think that he or she is seeing a certain pattern, such a finding is not considered valid until anyone—skeptic, friend, or foe—can achieve the same results in an independent experiment of his or her own. The findings discovered through observation in one laboratory must be replicable in another laboratory. Data measured and gathered by one instrument must be the same as data gathered by another similar instrument. And thus the objectivity comes not from an individual practitioner but from a system that demands consistent and repeatable results.

Objectivity and replicability depend too on reliable instrumentation. Data attributed to the scratch on the lens of a lab scope are not the findings of science. Objectivity and replicability depend as well on commonly held assumptions, consistently defined terms, and clearly defined phenomena. When researchers cannot even agree on what they are trying to observe and measure, it is impossible to engage in the systematic testing of hypotheses and the logical buildup of coherent theory.

Science depends on its practitioners to play by the rules and to be absolutely honest about both their successes and their failures.

What distinguishes a scientist from any other seeker after truth is exactly this. The scientist can be and often is wrong. A real scientific theory tells you, in effect, "If the theory is right, then this particular thing ought to happen under these certain conditions. If it doesn't happen, then the theory is wrong." If a theory cannot be proven wrong in its predictions, then it is not science.

This is not to say that every scientist faced with incontrovertible evidence that his or her beloved theory is wrong will trash the old without a qualm and embrace the new. Some philosophers of science even claim that a field changes only when old scientists die off and younger ones come forward to view the evidence with less biased eyes.

In clinical psychology, however, the imperviousness to factual challenge is not just the don't-bother-me-with-facts mulishness of a few stubborn graybeards, it is a legacy handed down from generation to generation.

CLASSICAL CLINICAL JUNK SCIENCE

Clinical psychology is classic junk science.

In his 1993 book *Galileo's Revenge: Junk Science in the Courtroom*, Peter Huber defines the term so:

> Junk science is the mirror image of real science, with much of the same form but none of the same substance. . . . It is a hodgepodge of biased data, spurious inference, and logical legerdemain, patched together by researchers whose enthusiasm for discovery and diagnosis far outstrips their skill. It is a catalog of every conceivable kind of error: data dredging, wishful thinking, truculent dogmatism, and, now and again, outright fraud. (pp. 2–3)

There are a great many ways to do science badly, and the junk science that makes up the bulk of the body of "knowledge" of clinical psychology manages to exemplify every one of them. The myriad failures of psychology as a science are not at all surprising, considering the roots of modern clinical practice. It is impossible to understand the essence of clinical junk science without a cursory understanding of clinical "science" as practiced by the principal founding father, the great man himself, Sigmund Freud.

What "scientific instruments" did Freud use to gather the data to build his theory of the healthy and unhealthy development of personality, with its psychosexual stages, Oedipus complex, castration anxiety, penis envy, Id, Ego, Superego, defense mechanisms, and the unconscious mind? Well, he analyzed his patients' dreams, he listened to their little slips of the tongue, and he asked them to freely associate to various words he gave them. That's it. The patient talked. Freud listened. A theory was born. And it grew, and it grew, and it grew.

The "instrument" for gathering data and building theory used by Freud and his cohorts and followers and by nearly all clinicians today was and is "clinical intuition."

Coitus Interruptus

Freud gives a nice example of using intuition to develop his version of scientific truth when he explains how he discovered in a patient of his the connection between depression, sinus pain, constipation, and coitus interruptus.

This patient had quite a few children. He was troubled intermittently with anxiety, various aches and pains, and, well, constrictions, in his sinuses and bowels and lower back. The pattern of their coming and going was a mystery. Suddenly the symptoms ceased altogether. Finally Freud discovered that when the patient's wife was pregnant, she permitted him to ejaculate in the customary way, but when she was between pregnancies and unenthusiastic about commencing another, she insisted on coitus interruptus. This, according to Freud's brilliant reasoning, caused the patient's system to back up physiologically and psychologically, inducing the various blockages here and there. The prescription for his cure, then, was obvious, if somewhat inconvenient for his wife. (Freud was surprisingly literal in his metaphors, prescribing both cocaine and nose surgery for other blocked customers.)

It is beyond foolish to ask whether "research" of this order can properly be characterized as objective, replicable, or generalizable. The ordinary standards of scientific methodology don't even come into play. Likewise, it is futile to ask whether Freud's intuitions were falsifiable. Freud's intuitions were freely supplanted when new intuitions seemed to him to be more plausible. And there is no reason whatsoever to expect any other "researcher" employing the intuitive interpretive methodology to have the same intuitions as Freud. "Objective intuition" is an oxymoron. Likewise, whatever "generalizability" and "replicability" there may be for such work resided entirely within Freud's own head.

Freud's collected works, occupying some two linear feet of library shelf space, provide hundreds of examples of his clinical intuition at work building the pseudo-science of clinical psychology. They provide *no* examples of the objective testing of falsifiable hypotheses under carefully controlled conditions of observation producing replicable, generalizable results. None. In Freud's work, there is not one scintilla of what any respectable scientist would call science.

As the twig is bent, so grows the tree.

CLINICAL JUNK SCIENCE TODAY

Have things changed in clinical psychology? Are the instruments modern clinicians use any better than those of Freud?

No, they are not, and nothing has really changed.

Like Freud before them, in place of data gathered or theory built by any instrument even remotely scientific, today's clinical practitioners offer the courts and legislatures—not to mention their patients and students—their clinical intuitions about how the mind is formed and how it functions, about psychological injury or guilt, about repression and recovery of memory, about trauma and the unconscious, dangerousness, parental fitness, child welfare, competency, rehabilitation, or any psychological thing under the sun.

The Miss Marple Approach

In common parlance intuition means the kind of knowledge gained from experience with people that is very hard to put into explicit words: "I've seen a lot of clients like that, and after a while, you just get kind of a feel for it."

Intuition is real. Of course it is. It's exactly the kind of knowledge a good cop is using when she feels suspicious of the way two guys are standing together on a street corner. It's the knowledge an experienced teacher uses when he "smells" a plagiarized term paper. It's what Agatha Christie's Miss Marple relies on when she says that weedy little fellow reminds her of old Tom's son down at the garage, who always made his repairs just a little weaker than they should be.

We all use intuitions like these in our daily lives. But we do not permit police officers to arrest people for looking vaguely suspicious;

universities do not permit professors to flunk students unless the plagiarism can be proved; and even Agatha Christie supplemented Miss Marple's unfailingly correct intuitions with a bit of material evidence. We should require at least as much restraint in the exercise of clinical intuition by psychological practitioners when they hand the court a professional report, or mount the stand to testify. Perversely, we require less.

How Did Dr. Terr Know How Eileen's Mind Worked? Consider, for example, the source of evidence Dr. Lenore Terr used when she testified about the functioning of Eileen Franklin's mind at her father's trial for murder.

Did Dr. Terr undertake controlled observation of Eileen's mind? Well, be fair, how could she? She did what all clinicians do. Eileen Franklin Lipsker told Dr. Terr a story and Dr. Terr created a wonderful theoretical interpretation of Eileen's account of her claimed experiences.

Did Dr. Terr have any way of judging whether what Eileen told her was true? Of course not. How could she? Dr. Terr got the "information" about what and when Eileen forgot and what and when Eileen remembered from Eileen herself. That's where clinicians always get the evidence for their "theories," except, of course, when they analyze dead people.

What about logical consistency within the story itself? There isn't any. Dr. Terr said that Eileen had repressed the terrible traumatic experiences of her childhood, but in fact Eileen claimed to remember many events in her abusive childhood, including numerous things about her violent drunken father, who beat his wife and children. And yet she forgot the murder.

What about the physical facts of the case? Many people took the apparent eyewitness-type detail as evidence of Eileen's general veracity, while defense attorneys tried to argue that all the details about the crime that Eileen claimed to have recovered with her unrepressed memory had been published in the popular press at the time of the murder and were available to anyone, eyewitness or no. However, the accuracy of the physical details reported by Eileen is irrelevant to establishing the validity of the psychological claims about repression and recovery of memory.

Eileen Franklin Lipsker may have seen her father commit murder or she may have seen someone else commit the murder or she may simply have heard about it, read about it, dreamed and fantasized about it. I don't know. But neither does Dr. Lenore Terr.

The psychoexpert presenting a creative interpretation of a claimant's story is authenticating that story, corroborating it, vouching for the veracity of the story without a scintilla of data gathered from anywhere but the claimant. What's the point? To tell the court that the claimant is a truthful person? How would any psychological expert know that? Clinicians are not lie detectors. They are no better than any judge or jury at distinguishing truth from falsehood. Besides, lie detection is not supposed to be the function of an expert psychological witness in court. The psychoexpert adds nothing to the claimant's testimony except a fraudulent veneer of authenticity that is utterly misleading and entirely out of place in any courtroom.

Grandmother Riding a Broom Consider the case of Richard and Cheryl Althaus of Pittsburgh, whose sixteen-year-old daughter one day accused them of sexual abuse. Dr. Judith Cohen of the Western Psychiatric Institute and Clinic at the University of Pittsburgh diagnosed the girl with post traumatic stress disorder brought on by sexual abuse. How could Dr. Cohen possibly know that the allegation of past abuse was true with such certainty as to warrant a diagnosis of PTSD? Retrospective clairvoyance?

> Miss Althaus also claimed that her grandmother flew about on a broom, that she had been tortured with a medieval thumbscrew device, that she had borne three children who were killed and that she had been raped in view of diners in a crowded restaurant. (Associated Press, *New York Times*, December 16, 1994)

In her defense of her diagnosis, Dr. Cohen "argued that her job had been to treat Miss Althaus, not investigate the patient's accusations" (Associated Press, *New York Times*, December 16, 1994).

No investigation. No corroboration. No physical evidence that any of these highly unlikely events transpired. No questioning, even about the multiple pregnancies and murdered infants? No curiosity, even about granny on the broom or the thumbscrews or maybe which restaurant had the floor show? This is really nuts. The good news is that a jury recognized that it was nuts.

> A jury awarded more than $272,000 today to a couple and their teenage daughter who had joined in a suit charging a psychiatrist with failure to evaluate the girl's accusations of parental sex abuse. The parents, Richard and Cheryl Althaus, had been arrested and charged with sex abuse before their daughter, Nicole, recanted. They won $213,899 in their malpractice lawsuit again the psychiatrist, Dr. Judith Cohen, and the Western Psychiatric Institute and Clinic at the University of Pittsburgh. . . . When the verdict was read today, Mrs. Althaus closed her eyes, sighed and held her husband's hand across their daughter's lap. Miss Althaus, smiling, said afterward, "I'm going back to college." (Associated Press, *New York Times*, December 16, 1994)

This refusal to seek corroboration of the patient's claims is clinical junk science in its most common form.

You cannot validate a clinician's intuitions with more intuitions, and you cannot validate what a patient says with what a patient says. However consistent or plausible the story is does not touch on the matter of truth, on accuracy and reliability.

Selective Amnesia and the Solar Phallus Man

Peter Huber, writing on the similarity between the layperson's willingness to believe in prophetic dreams and the pseudo-scientist's discovery only of data that confirms his or her theory, says: "Selective amnesia, a pick-and-choose economy with the truth, has a remarkable power to make the dreams that do occasionally come true seem important. In a similar manner, great catalogs of data that don't track the hoped-for results can be explained away before they are ever recorded in the laboratory notebook" (1993, p. 28).

A truly hilarious example of pick-and-choose research occurs in a current dispute over the theoretical work of Carl Jung, who is, along with Freud, one of the founders of psychoanalysis. He developed and popularized the theory of the collective unconscious. According to this theory, we all have buried deep down in the mind common myths and "archetypal" images, a sort of race memory of the human species.

> One basis for Jung's theory . . . is a case known as Solar Phallus Man. This man, a patient at the Burgholzli Mental Hospital in Zurich, where Jung was a physician until 1909, claimed to have seen a vision of the sun with a phallus. The image, Jung contended, came from the ancient Hellenic mystery cult of Mithras, a pagan god associated with sun worship.
>
> Over the years, Jung used the case as a proof of the theory, arguing that the man could not have known about Mithras and so must have derived the image from deep within the collective unconscious. (D. Smith, *New York Times*, June 3, 1995)

But a modern Jung scholar, Richard Noll, claims that the patient was simply familiar with popular books of the time on the subject and that Jung knew this and lied to the psychological community when he hid this fact from his followers.

This is a notable dispute because it so closely echoes the controversy over alien abduction fantasies raging around Cambridge, Massachusetts, these days. Abduction proponents argue that the alleged abductees tell remarkably similar stories and have somehow been insulated from the popular sci-fi culture that saturates America. QED, they were all abducted by Martians.

How can anyone, in good faith, take such "data," subject them to the interpretation of clinical intuition, and treat them as "evidence" to support a "theory"?

Flashbacks, Trauma, and Vietnam Veteran Killers The most extraordinary aspect of clinical research when considered from a scientific point of view is its imperviousness to the complete absence of material evidence considered indispensable in any other endeavor that claims to be a science. One such courtroom favorite is the flashback. Vietnam veterans who hear the radio station traffic helicopter overhead suddenly see themselves back in combat, crouch down, and take cover. Seized by a flashback, these suffering vets load up rifles and blow away the wife and kiddies under the misperception that the family is the enemy.

The public likes flashbacks because they have such dramatic power and fit in so well with currently popular theories of memory. However, is there actually any evidence at all that flashbacks exist? No. The existence of authentic flashbacks presupposes that memory works like a video recorder, storing perfect, unalterable records of life's experiences in the mind. When a flashback occurs, the patient puts the video machine on rewind and then hits the play button. Zoom. Back again to the enemy-infested jungles of 'Nam. Sounds perfectly plausible, doesn't it?

Well, no. In fact, everything we know about memory suggests that flashbacks are impossible. We have no video recorder between our ears. There is no evidence that the "tapes" of life's events, whether traumatic or otherwise, are stored in little vacuum packs in the brain, waiting in pristine condition to be replayed as needed. Memory is selective, destructive, reconstructive, alterable, distortable, dissolvable. No videotape. No film. Not even a handwritten diary. There may indeed be people whose hallucinations, fantasies, or nightmares carry a powerful sense of déjà vu, but a sense of familiarity carries no seal of authenticity.

Nevertheless, professional trauma experts can be found who will claim straight out that the nightmares often are exact replicas of the traumatic event. What an extraordinary assertion! Just trying to imagine the evidence necessary to make such an astounding claim quite stuns the mind. My video player must be jammed. How could anyone claim to know that your nightmare is an *exact replica* of your experience of twenty years ago?

Does the lack of evidence for the existence and operation of flashbacks stand in the way of clinicians specializing in trauma hiring themselves out to explain to the courts about the delusionary authenticity of flashbacks? Indeed not.

> A Louisiana court, using a M'Naghten modified insanity test, acquitted a former Marine of murder in State v. Heads. The accused had experienced extensive combat as a point man in long-range reconnaissance patrols in Vietnam. After returning home he suffered a flashback following a stressful marital breakup and killed his brother-in-law. . . . Heads, reportedly perceiving his brother-in-law as a Viet Cong, pulled a rifle from his car, shot the victim through the eye and then "stalked the ranch house as though it were a straw hooch." The defense convinced the jury that Head's combat flashback had destroyed his ability to distinguish right from wrong. (Davidson 1988, p. 425)

Evidence for such intuitively compelling psychological phenomena is not necessary. All that is needed is for a well-credentialed expert witness to climb onto the stand and present this gobbledygook with sufficient authority and a lot of scientific-sounding jargon, and who is going to demand some petty little thing like scientific proof of what is said? It is distressingly easy to confuse a compelling narrative with self-evident truth.

> Great novelists, for example, are wonderful at explaining human behavior, or at helping us seem to understand the underlying motivations and actions of individuals. . . . Although a reading of *Hamlet* may seem to reveal great insights into human nature, the play by itself does not constitute scientifically validated knowledge. (Ziskin, 1995, p. 85)

Tests, Tests, Tests

Intuition is the most frequently and widely used tool in clinical psychology, but it is not the only weapon in the forensic clinician's armamentarium. Clinicians who work for institutions of various types, like hospitals and universities, and those who testify in court or provide reports to the courts on various matters usually buttress their clinical intuitions with a slew of figures from what are known in the trade as assessment instruments.

The purpose of these tests is to blind judges and juries with science, but a quick look at the standard instruments used to gather data for court-ordered evaluations and in clinical research should give the most credulous pause.

✓ ***MMPI and the Inkblot Test*** Essentially two types of nonintuitive instruments are used for assessing psychological functioning, so-called objective tests and projective ones.

Objective tests are pencil-and-paper tests in which the person being assessed answers any number of multiple-choice questions about various topics. The most widely used and the most generally respected of the so-called objective tests is the Minnesota Multiphasic Personality Inventory (MMPI), designed in the 1940s by Starke S. Hathaway and John C. McKinley. The test asks 550 true-or-false questions about people's attitudes about religion and sexual practices, their perceptions of health, and their political ideas, as well as information on family, education, and occupation.

The basic idea underlying both objective and projective tests is that the answers on the tests give away people's most secret psychological pathologies when their answers mirror those of patients with known diagnoses. The logic is simple. Depressed people supposedly give answers A, B, and C to questions 1, 2, and 3. You give answers A, B, and C to questions 1, 2, and 3. Voila! You are a depressive. Perfectly straightforward.

Generally, the questions were specifically designed to lack what is called content validity, so as not to give away the nature of the mental illness being assessed. Hathaway and McKinley thought that a test of depression that asked a bunch of questions like "Do you feel low a lot of the time?" was a dead giveaway both about what was being tested and about what the expected answer was for that question. They wanted a test that could not be scoped out easily by those taking it.

This design was compromised somewhat by the inclusion of questions designed to reveal symptoms supposedly known to be exhibited by certain supposedly well-defined groups of mentally disturbed people, but the balance of the test items were not obviously indicative of some kind of pathology. Answers on the MMPI are said to reveal hypochondriasis, depression, hysteria, masculinity-femininity, paranoia, hypomania (excitability), psychopathic deviancy, psychasthenia (irrational fears and compulsive actions), schizophrenia, and social introversion (withdrawal). There is also a scale that is supposed to detect truly savvy test takers who are just faking it.

Projective tests—the second big category of so-called psychological assessment instruments—are usually pictures (sometimes words or sentences), either meaningful or not, that supposedly stimulate the test taker to tell the tester some sort of revelatory story about what he or she sees in the picture.

The most famous of the projective tests, the inkblot test, was developed in 1938 by Hermann Rorschach, inspired by earlier so-called tests of imagination. As Anne Anastasi explains in her classic *Psychological Testing*, "projective techniques are regarded by their exponents as especially effective in revealing *covert, latent, or unconscious* aspects of personality. Moreover, the more unstructured the test, it is argued, the more sensitive it is to such covert material" (1970, p. 494).

There are ten Rorschach cards, five black-and-white and five colored. The client-patient-plaintiff-defendant is asked to go through the cards and discuss freely what he or she "sees" while the tester asks questions. The Rorschach, "unstructured" as it is, lacks any content validity at all.

What's wrong with using these putatively "scientific instruments" to measure enduring personality traits like paranoia or serious mental illnesses like schizophrenia?

Basically, they do not do the job. They *cannot* do the job. As instruments to measure the psyche, they are useless.

Just what, exactly, do we suppose that people labeled as suffering from a particular kind of mental illness have in common other than the category label? For the testing approach to work, the people who serve as the definitive representative groups for the making of the test must all truly have the same kind of mental illness, and that illness must manifest itself in uniform ways across all or nearly all of the patients.

Not even the fairly straightforward category of depression can make that claim—what most depressed people have in common is that they say they are depressed—so where does that leave the other hundreds of mental diagnoses used today?

There are *no* studies showing that, for example, one hundred people with, say, Diagnosis #10 give the same answers to the 550 questions on the MMPI or the same bird-butterfly-blood responses to the inkblot test. Not only would establishing so many consistent patterns of responses across all the mental diagnoses available have been an extraordinary amount of labor, it would never have worked out whatever the effort expended. Why not?

The logic does not hold water.

Even if we were to grant against all the evidence, just for the sake of discussion, that all or most of the persons categorized with a certain diagnostic label *do* actually show the same symptoms, does it follow logically that they also share views on religion, sexual practices, politics, and health as asked on the so-called objective MMPI? No. Of course not. And what sort of thinking or logic dictates that schizophrenics or depressives or obsessives or whoever all feel the same way about the color red or the use of detail or "negative" space or whatever as required by Rorschach scoring systems?

Or, vice versa, that a great many people answer religious or political questions in common ways, or see one particular inkblot as looking like a butterfly, says nothing at all about their possible mental illness or lack of it, about their schizophrenia or depression, or their degree of compliance or contrariness or whatever. Why would it?

The logic underlying the use of psychological tests to diagnose people with unknown problems—that everyone with a certain type of mental illness resembles everyone else in the labeled group, right down to their feelings about the pope and the president, the color red, cannibals, and butterflies—is foolish on the face of it and empirically false.

In fact, the authors of the MMPI gave up the original attempt to use the test to diagnose various kinds of mental disorders almost before the ink was dry on the first edition.

Anastasi explains, "[W]e cannot assume that a high score on the Schizophrenia scale indicates the presence of schizophrenia. Other psychotic groups show high elevation on this scale and schizophrenics often score high on other scales. *Moreover, such a score may occur in a normal person*" (1970, pp. 445–46; italics added).

In a nutshell, that means that the most widely used instrument for testing personality in America has a theoretical foundation that is pathetically weak.

Was the MMPI, then, simply abandoned as hopelessly not up to the job? Oh, no. Of course not. Remember, clinicians are the people who think sinus problems are caused by sexual practices. The current routine is to take persons with similar profiles across the nine scales and then try to find something else in their lives that correlates with their MMPI profiles. By the end of 1995, there were over nine thousand such *published* studies. That means that for just about any profile a person displays in answers to the MMPI, the clinician can probably find some study somewhere that correlates the profile with *something*—low self-esteem, perhaps, or maybe cigarette smoking or eating disorders.

Are these profiles meaningful? Oh, no. They are not even reliable. In fact, the reliability of MMPI code types falls apart after two weeks. Two weeks! From one-third to one-half of subjects tested didn't even have code types in the same diagnostic grouping on tests given two weeks apart. This is supposed to be a test of the enduring makeup of the personality? It is not completely unreasonable to suppose that adults might respond in much the same way from time to time on items questioning their religious or political beliefs, for example, but they don't. Numerous studies show that for normal college students, more than half show different profiles even when tested again only one to two weeks later. For psychiatric populations, the percentages who stay the same are even lower. After a year, the stability is laughable.

Undeterred by what others might see as crippling logical and empirical problems for both objective and projective tests, testing advocates slog ahead with revisions, elaborations, and embellishments of both objective and projective tests—especially the MMPI and the Rorschach—blinding the rest of us with a blizzard of code words and scoring systems.

The courtroom doubter—attorney or judge—bold enough to challenge the validity or reliability of these tests will in turn be challenged, "Well, what about the brand-new, state-of-the-art, high-tech, computerized scoring system, eh? Doesn't that answer your objections?"

The answer is "No, it doesn't." It can't and it won't until the tests acquire a theoretical foundation and empirical reliability and the diagnostic categories themselves achieve some degree of solidity to give a firm foundation for their measurement. Until that day arrives, the truly bewildering expenditure of intellectual effort to pump air into a dead horse will remain just that. It is sad and puzzling that so many excellent minds pass their time in just this exercise.

Neither clinical intuition nor any of the countless psychological tests currently in use and endlessly under development can possibly be held to be scientific instruments capable of providing precise and reliable data about the structures and functions of the mind, normal or abnormal, in general or for individual cases. It is laughable and downright fraudulent to pretend otherwise. It is inconceivable that any scientists would tout such "instruments" as the tools of their trade.

I Had a Case Like That So There Must Be Many Like That

Not only does clinical research routinely fail to control for innumerable extraneous factors outside the researcher's agenda, it nearly always also fails to observe the most basic of conditions for ensuring that results can be generalized—choosing a sample that is truly representative of the people to whom the researchers want to generalize their findings. In the most common kind of clinical "research" the clinician "studies" only one individual, or sometimes a few, and then generalizes the "findings" to an indefinitely large number of other, unknown persons.

What is wrong with that?

Let us say that you had never before encountered the dog breed Bouvier. Let us say that the first Bouvier you encounter has blue eyes. Do you then conclude that Bouviers have blue eyes? Of course not. But in time you see another and another and another Bouvier, until you have seen ten such dogs and each and every one of them had blue eyes. Would you not then conclude that Bouviers generally have blue eyes? Of course you would. Who would not? But, at the same time, you know perfectly well that you might be wrong. It might be the case that 99 percent of Bouviers have brown eyes and you just happened to have encountered ten examples of that minority blue-eyed strain.

Because we are all aware that our personal experience is limited, even when we have seen a number of instances that support our hypothesis, we retain some doubt about our conclusions. In science, the attempt is made to reduce and quantify the doubt by sampling randomly from among all those Bouviers in the expectation that a random sample makes it more likely that the dogs seen will resemble those in the whole population of Bouviers more closely than would a sample based on nonrandom personal experience. In most clinical research, random sampling to reduce uncertainty and increase generalizability is not even an issue. Clinicians often generalize from single instances, from samples of *one*.

What a Single Instance Means Other than the fact that the accumulation of reliable scientific knowledge cannot proceed based on the ungeneralizable intuitions of individual practitioners about individual cases, what else is wrong with depending on case studies of actual patients?

Let us say that you are an American who has never known anyone Vietnamese. You know a fair amount about the Vietnamese because of our shared history, but you have never known, personally, an authentic Vietnamese person. It happens that you hire one to do some computer programming for your business. So you get to know the guy a little. And you notice that he has some priorities, or values, that are different from yours. Different religious practices. (He's Catholic.) Different attitudes about sex. (He's chaste.) Different work habits. (He works like a crazy Vietnamese boat person grateful to be in America.) Different sense of family. (He sends most of the pittance you pay him back to Vietnam to support his mother and father.) And different life goals. (He wants to reunite his family and make them proud by succeeding in computer science.) So he's rather different from you.

What do you conclude from your relationship with this guy about Vietnamese people in general? "Nothing" is the conservative, scientifically correct answer, but that is bull. You conclude that it is very likely that most or at least many Vietnamese are like this guy you've hired. Why would you conclude that from just one guy? Well, why not? Why would you conclude that the guy you met is the wild card in the deck? You wouldn't.

We think people will be normally distributed. That if you grabbed a thousand guys off the street and measured their heights, say, most of the guys would fall in the middle and the farther you got away from that middle—like up to seven feet or down to five—then the fewer and fewer guys there are going to be. Most people are average; most people fall in the middle of whatever you are measuring. If I ask you what are the chances that the next man to show up at some party you're at is over seven feet tall, you're going to say it's damned unlikely unless you're hosting a Boston Celtics' party. We expect people to be average. When we meet the first person in our experience from some unknown bunch of people like the Vietnamese, we expect him to be average, to be typical. It's far and away the best guess, is it not?

It is far and away the best guess, but it is by no means a sure bet.

Tigers and Quicksand Is it sensible or foolish to generalize from a single experience? Say you meet your first tiger and it growls at you and charges, and you barely escape with your life by slamming the door of the cage shut just in time. How smart would you be to leave the cage door open and just stand there when you encounter your second tiger? Not smart. Not smart at all. If you survived the mauling and having your arm bitten off, people would say to you, "Just how many tigers do you have to meet before you get the idea?" Because one should have been enough. You should have learned. How many times do you have to step in quicksand before you get the idea?

The same logic holds for the case study. If I meet one Catholic, chaste, hardworking, and so on Vietnamese fellow, then there are probably lots of Catholic, chaste, hardworking Vietnamese family men out there, right? Sounds good, doesn't it? It certainly works well enough for tigers and quicksand.

What's wrong with applying the same "logic" to people? First off, it doesn't matter if you're wrong about the quicksand or the tiger. A conservative approach to both cannot hurt you. Nor can it hurt anybody else. In fact, it might well protect you. When it comes to people, however, instant generalization has a big downside. Even if your prototypical Vietnamese was a good guy, generalizing from him to all Vietnamese leads only to witless stereotyping of millions of highly individualized people. And you're going to be real disappointed when the next Vietnamese computer programmer you hire steals your software ideas and skips town with a Protestant prostitute. When people ask you why you trusted this guy, are you going to say to them, "Well, I knew another Vietnamese man once and he was a great guy"? You can't say that; you would sound too stupid.

You know, we all know, that you cannot generalize from one individual to all individuals who are members of a group, because there is no way to guarantee that that individual is the most representative—the average—of the group. To make a reliable generalization to the whole group, one would need to study the behavior of many, randomly selected, and, one hopes, representative members of the group.

In every science, the ability to generalize your findings depends on the quality of your instruments, but it also is only as good as your sampling techniques. If we get a good sample, we can trust the generalization. Generalization is still dangerous, even with a good sample, especially when we try to apply it to a single unknown individual, but it is not so completely crazy as generalizing to millions from a *single* example.

For these reasons, no one with any scientific respectability would argue that the case study has any research usefulness at all except to stimulate thought. Good ideas for research can be found in individual cases; research itself cannot. It is just inexplicable, then, that clinical psychology continues to publish hundreds of such cases each year in professional journals and to use them as teaching materials in class.

Double-Blind and Double-Sighted Even good science has its pitfalls. One of the most pernicious is the unconscious agenda. This is often called the Rosenthal Effect after Robert Rosenthal, who demonstrated its operation in some fairly important social science studies. Because the effect is so well-documented and so destructive of any claim to objectivity, researchers long ago devised a procedure for obviating those effects—a procedure routinely ignored by clinicians engaged in their pseudo-science.

The Rosenthal Effect is simply the effect of expectations of both researchers and subjects on the outcome of experiments. If the researchers who give sick patients little pink pills to make them better believe that the little pink pills *will* make them better, and if the patients believe that as well, better the patients will get. And this is true whether the little pink pills contain penicillin or white sugar. You get the effect you expect to get. Any properly designed experiment uses "placebos," little pink pills that really *are* sugar for half the patients, and real pills for the other half, and neither researcher nor patient knows who is getting what. That's called a double-blind experiment.

What you get in clinical psychological research is double-sighted experimentation. Both the clinician and the subject—often a patient—expect to see the same thing, and see it they do. Wonder of wonders. Aren't clinicians taught how to do research in graduate school?

Actually, many clinicians in academic departments and their graduate students often do make stabs at doing "research" beyond the case study. They grab a batch of college sophomores and give them three or four questionnaires and then look to see if there is any relationship between answers on one questionnaire and answers on another. For example, they might first ask students to fill out a questionnaire on family history with lots of questions about maltreatment, then ask the same students to fill out one on how they feel about themselves, and then another on how they feel about the relationships in their lives. Researchers expect those students who report having rotten families and childhoods to also report feeling rotten about themselves and rotten about the personal relationships in their lives. Amazing. They do.

Any participant in one of these studies would have to be completely brain-dead to miss what the researchers are getting at with their questionnaires. They are suffering from face validity overload. The hypotheses in the so-called studies are transparent to both the participants and the researchers. This kind of double-sighted research is so common in academic departments, it is almost the prototype for today's clinical doctoral dissertation.

Strange too is the complete lack of any effort to make sure that all these questionnaires—there are thousands of them, with new ones being created every day—actually have anything to do with reality. They only ask people to "report" things as they see them. There is no cross-check to see if, for example, families reported to be abusive were truly abusive. The only subject matter for such "studies" is the question of whether students—or patients—are consistently negative or positive when asked about a number of related issues. This activity gets people Ph.D.s in clinical psychology but it sure as heck isn't science.

Shape Shifting in Clinical Junk Science

If we look at the most basic of issues in the definition of a science—common terms used in a consistent way—we find that even that most trivial of requirements is not met by clinical psychology. Definitions of concepts are so fluid, ever-changing with the whim of the speaker, and so utterly without any substantial basis that it is impossible to prove any claim, no matter how inconsistent with any other claim, to be wrong. As soon as any reasonable logical or evidentiary challenge is launched, the psychofact shape-shifts, assumes a new form, and heads off into unknown territory.

I Can Explain, It's a Different Kind of Gravity Dr. Lenore Terr, the psychological expert who was crucial to the conviction of George Franklin for the twenty-year-old murder of nine-year-old Susan Nason, gave us an illuminating example of definitional shape shifting as she prepared for the Franklin murder trial and provided a perfect illustration of why clinical methodology, theory, and claims should not be welcome in our courts.

Long before she ever met Eileen Franklin Lipsker, Dr. Terr had become famous through her interviews with the children who were kidnapped, school bus and all, in Chowchilla, California. These kidnapped children showed no evidence of repression following what seemed to have been a very traumatic situation—the children were kidnapped in their bus, driven into a pit, and buried underground with an air vent to keep them alive. As reported in Terr's book *Too Scared to Cry* (1990), the children had *not* been traumatized out of their wits during the misadventure, had *not* repressed their memories of the events, and even years after, they were quite capable of fairly clear and complete recall.

Now, this is not a great surprise. In fact, many people—even far too many young, vulnerable, defenseless children—remember their traumatic experiences all too well. Many of these people would welcome the opportunity to put out of their minds forever horrible memories of months or years of war, torture, or imprisonment, but cannot do so.

Yet here we have Eileen Franklin claiming that the death of her friend Susan was a memory so horrible that it remained hidden from her mind's eye for twenty years. How could that be? What made Eileen's trauma so special that it wiped out her memory?

Dr. Terr explains, "There were great differences in the wholeness of retained memory between the Chowchilla kidnap victims and Eileen Franklin Lipsker. The Chowchilla group consistently remembered everything. Yet Eileen started to repress on the very night of the day she witnessed her best friend's murder" (1994, p. 11).

How is Dr. Terr going to explain away this huge discrepancy? It would be like explaining why dropped apples sometimes rise up into the air instead of falling down to the ground. How could that happen?

Easy. It is a different kind of gravity.

> After I met her, I realized that Eileen was what I had defined as a *Type II* trauma victim—a repeatedly traumatized child. She had always remembered, for instance, that her father was an unpredictably violent alcoholic—this she had not forgotten. . . . Moreover, Mrs. Franklin was hospitalized a couple of times for mental illness. The illness memories too might have been frightening. All this would have added up to make

> Eileen a child well rehearsed in terror—a child prone to losing the memory of an ordeal.
>
> These experiences were probably frequent enough and awful enough, in fact, to have allowed Eileen to develop the knack for automatic repression. By the time she was eight years old, she had no doubt practiced "forgetting" so often she could repress when she really needed to. Children who go through a number of terrors protect themselves this way. They are able to muster massive defenses against remembering, because this is the only way they can get through a frightening childhood. (Terr 1994, pp. 11–12)

You might think that Dr. Terr is saying that it will be easier for you to remember a single instance of rape if you have experienced only one than it will be if that instance is just one among dozens. She is not. Dr. Terr means that somehow an automatic mechanism of unconscious forgetting is triggered when you are the victim of *multiple* instances of abuse and not when you are the victim of only one or a few episodes. She is saying too that the traumatic amnesia is highly selective, applying in Eileen's case not to episodes of violent and unpredictable paternal violence, or to displays of maternal mental illness, but only to Susan Nason's death and some other unspecified but no doubt repeated traumas more horrible than drunken assaults but less horrible than murder.

This creative view of the mind is interesting, but it does leave all people who have survived the Holocaust, or other long-term hideous experiences like war, slavery, torture, and imprisonment, and who remember it, in a rather odd position. Dr. Terr is suggesting either that such experiences were not horrible enough to be traumatic and thus cause amnesia through repression, or that somehow most of the millions of people who find themselves in such situations are just generally pretty resilient.

Whether George Franklin killed Susan Nason is not as important as the misleading psychobabble poured out to make sense of Eileen's story. To account for Eileen's denial of memory of her traumatic event, Dr. Terr had to create a convoluted story that turned her previously held views on memory and trauma inside out. Fluid definitions like that are clever but they do make cross-examination of psychoexperts impossible. Changing definitions case by case and expert by expert makes any claim about the effects of trauma consistent with every other claim. And if we ever encounter a case that doesn't quite fit, we can create Type III traumas, and Type IV, and so on. There is no logical, theoretical, or empirical impediment.

Dr. Terr took this nonsense into court. Dr. Terr got a man convicted of murder on the basis of her clinical intuition, buttressed and complemented by her selective perception of the interesting story her client told to her. It was no problem at all with a theory so insubstantial and research that is no more than the intuitive biases of its expositors.

An old chestnut of a graduate school joke says that the B.S. degree stands not for bachelor of science but for "bull shit," the M.S. for "more of the same," and the Ph.D. for "pile it higher and deeper." The endlessly metamorphosing concept of traumatic repression is an excellent example of this process.

What kind of a theory could possibly be assembled on such a quicksand foundation?

Diagnosing the Foundations of Clinical Psychology Describing clinical psychology as "soft science" is flattering the field; it is as soft as a grape. Consider just the shocking but indisputable fact that it is rare to find agreement across clinicians or clinics on the results of psychiatric evaluations, on the basic mental diagnosis itself so central to countless criminal defenses and claims of psychological injury.

In the United States, diagnoses are usually based on the *Diagnostic and Statistical Manual* of the American Psychiatric Association (APA). Generally, everyone—every psychiatrist, psychologist, clinical social worker, psychiatric nurse, psychotherapist, and counselor—is supposed to use this diagnostic manual.

The first *Diagnostic and Statistical Manual* came out in 1952, followed by a revision in 1968; the DSM-III appeared in 1980, and was followed by its own mini-revision, the DSM-IIIR in 1988. In 1994, we got the DSM-IV, some nine hundred pages long, covering 374 mental disorders.

The authors of the new DSM-IV claim that the sets of symptoms—what they call "criteria sets"—that are supposed to be used to determine a particular diagnosis were arrived at by consensus. That sounds like an impressive, almost scientific, level of agreement among clinical practitioners until you see what these psychiatrists mean by consensus.

By consensus, they mean that the members of work groups assembled sets of symptoms for the various diagnoses by simply including *all* the symptoms championed by numerous different practitioners, turning the combined list into a Chinese menu multiple-choice test. Consequently, the manual directs that a particular disorder should be diagnosed if the patient shows one symptom from column A, two from column B, and one from column C. This inclusive approach certainly took care of any little niggling disagreements about which symptoms belong to which disorder, but it represents a pretty distorted view of the word "consensus." It's like saying that one hundred people agreed on what to have for dinner by the simple expedient of ordering everything on the menu. Consensus, my foot!

A new National Institute of Mental Health analysis of some 34,000 patients diagnosed with depression revealed that the majority do *not* suffer most of the "classic" physical symptoms of depression: unexplained fatigue, insomnia, poor appetite, restlessness, unusually fast heartbeat, constipation, or weight loss. Where patients do claim to experience a symptom such as "eat less than I used to," the only indication that that is true is the patient's say-so; there is no accompanying weight loss. Even among the most severely depressed patients, some 10 percent show no physical symptoms at all.

What this study shows is that clinicians reach their diagnoses for reasons of their own, just as they did before the publication of the new nine-hundred-page manual. Perhaps each diagnostician has his or her own favorite symptom of depression or schizophrenia or whatever—the tidy little symptom checklist is nothing more than a sham. The sham gives both the patient and the public alike the illusion that the mental disorder diagnosed is on another reality plane than the telltale behavior when indeed the disorder is often nothing more than a single "symptom" itself.

It is undeniably true that in the diagnosis of a medical condition such as cancer physicians will certainly disagree over which symptom has the strongest association with a particular diagnosis or which is most indicative of a certain prognosis, but that a test for breast cancer, for example, would be no more than a cobbling together of a bunch of oncologists' varying opinions is unthinkable.

How did the authors of the diagnostic manual arrive at all those 374 different categories of mental disorders in the 1994 manual?

Consensus again. Disorders and symptoms went into the book if the various co-authors for the different sections of the manual agreed that they should. Sometimes that meant as many as sixteen people agreed, sometimes as few as five. The APA calls this "consensus." Whatever it is called, it has nothing to do with agreement among the tens of thousands of psychological practitioners out there in the field.

(That politics and passionate lobbying have since the first edition played a not insignificant role in determining which "mental disorder" gets into the book and which stays out is undeniable and has been the subject of several books, including Kirk and Kutchins's *The Selling of DSM*, 1992, and Paula Caplan's *They Say You're Crazy*, 1995.)

Given their farcical "empirical" procedures for arriving at new disorders with their associated symptom lists, where does the American Psychiatric Association get off claiming a scientific, research-based foundation for its diagnostic manual? This is nothing more than science by decree. They say it is science, so it is.

Clinical psychological practitioners simply do not mean by "science" what real scientists mean. And they never will without a drastic change in the foundations of their discipline.

We Can Explain Everything Science is evaluated as science not solely by its definitions and methodology—where clinical psychology fails spectacularly—but also by its explanatory adequacy—where it truly excels. Clinical psychologists, from Freud to the present, provide us with wonderfully plausible and comprehensive explanations of any and all aspects of human behavior. Of course, so do novelists.

We must be wary of any theory that explains too much. If virtually anything that could possibly occur can be "explained" by the theory as well as any other, even opposite, occurrence, then that explanation is not scientific because it is unchallengeable and irrefutable.

Pretend you are a male patient of mine. Assume that I assert that your classic seductive relationship with your mother, your alienation from your weak and distant father, and the symbolic structure of your dreams, along with the strongly feminine character of the literary career you have chosen, clearly tell me that you are homosexual. You say, "I am not! I have a happy wife and seven children!" I reply, "So what? You are just defensively overcompensating for your homosexuality."

Anything a patient says, anything at all, can be found to have a coherent psychological interpretation despite an apparent surface contradiction between what is said and the interpretation. You cannot prove clinical psychological theory wrong in any respect. If you deny my clinical explanation, or if aspects of what you tell me are inconsistent with the explanation, then I have only to invoke mysterious psychological mechanisms to ride right over you.

How are you going to prove that I, your therapist, am wrong? You can't. Anything you say about your life and how you feel is perfectly consistent with my interpretation. Since, by definition, you have no access to your unconscious mind, who are you to dispute my claims about your unconscious? Good luck trying it.

Neither the patient nor anyone else, in or out of a courtroom, can falsify the claims a clinical professional makes about the working of the mind. Without observation of the phenomena of interest or their reliable indicia, testability is impossible. If testability is impossible, then falsifiability is moot.

THE STATE OF THE ART

The Unicorn Argument

Court cases, by their very nature, involve agendas. The goal of testimony—scientific and otherwise—is always to make some point for one side or another. That objectivity of all testimony—scientific and otherwise—takes a serious beating in court is not really very surprising.

What is truly astonishing, however, is when the absence of scientific evidence that harm did *not* occur is taken as evidence that harm *did* occur. For example, some of the attorneys for the silicone breast implant plaintiffs claimed injury by arguing that research has *not* proved there is *not* a connection. That's beautiful. Although not all that common in medical argument, it is an extremely popular tack in the claims made by clinical psychologists.

It is what I call the Unicorn Argument.

For example, I might say, "There's no such thing as unicorns." You say, "Of course there are unicorns. They are always kissing virgins." "No," I say. "I have looked everywhere and cannot find a single unicorn." "You have not looked everywhere, and even if you did, the unicorns were one step ahead of you." Stymied, aren't I? You must be right. There are unicorns all over the place just beyond the edge of my vision.

The silicone lawsuits aside, it is very hard to find any reputable scientist who would make the Unicorn Argument even in the silent recesses of the heart. It is fundamentally counter to scientific reasoning. The scientist believes nothing unless it is proven to be true. "I will *not* believe in unicorns unless you can prove to me that unicorns exist." The unicornist believes everything unless it can be proven absolutely to be false. "I *will* believe in unicorns until you prove to me that there are none."

Clinical psychologists regularly lay claim to beliefs on the grounds that they have not been disproved. But it is not possible to prove that something does *not* exist simply because you failed to find it. There are many possible reasons for your failure, only one of which is the nonexistence of whatever it is you are looking for. There are many possible reasons that people in a study do not behave as expected other than the one the researchers hold to be true.

But true believers will die believing in unicorns. Actually, true believers will continue to believe even in the face of incontrovertible evidence against the belief. Everything, after all, is subject to interpretation and reinterpretation. With the right frame of mind, there is no such thing as incontrovertible evidence.

This outlook on life makes perfect sense in what are properly considered "matters of faith." It doesn't make sense in the training or practice of scientific professionals, psychological or otherwise, and it does not make sense in our courtrooms. You cannot allow Miss Marple on the witness stand to argue for the existence of unicorns. It does violence to logic and terrible damage to real people's lives.

Astronomy and Astrology

Almost since its inception, clinical psychology has been subjected to the same criticism: It's not a testable science; it's a secular religion disguised as a science. And, since the first utterance of this presumably crippling criticism, the defensive reply has been, "Oh, you academics are always saying that." It is time to drop the charge that clinical psychology is nothing more than a secular religion. It has always fallen on deaf ears and it will continue to do so.

A more telling comparison likens clinical psychology to astrology and experimental psychology to astronomy. The names of the two fields are similar, but they have nothing more in common than an interest in the stars. They do not have common aims and their methodologies could not be more dissimilar. Moreover, astrological practitioners do not usually claim that either their general "theories" or the interpretations of an individual's astrological portrait are scientifically based.

Nevertheless, astrology, like clinical psychology, is a comprehensive and coherent system for the interpretation and prediction of human behavior. Also, like clinical psychology, astrology is taken very seriously by a large number of people—whose identities are often quite surprising—who claim that it illuminates and guides their lives.

Astrology is widely accepted as true by believers in astrology, just as much of clinical psychology can be said to be generally accepted by believers in clinical psychology.

It is entertaining but absurd to imagine our courtrooms filled with astrologers testifying that Leos would never commit murder when the sun is in Jupiter or that Capricorns make better parents for Virgos than do Geminis. Very few adherents of astrology would attempt to get astrological interpretations, in general terms or for specific individuals, accepted in court as expert testimony. (Or would they?)

Moreover, despite the millions of horoscope readers and customers of psychics, society will not let astrologers bring their articles of faith into our courtrooms as expert testimony. Society as a whole maintains that there is some important difference in the quality of beliefs of astrologers and astronomers and in the credibility of true believers and scientists, a distinction that is crucial for our justice system to maintain.

Yet we not only tolerate but welcome testimony from clinical psychologists that, like astrological interpretation, is built on nothing more than faith.

It is profoundly disturbing that clinical psychologists are themselves unable to maintain this critical distinction between fact and belief, between astronomy and astrology, as their testimony on the witness stands in courtroom after courtroom shows. How can educated people so blind themselves to the reality of their own belief system?

The Problem of Psychology

All professionals who identify themselves as psychologists share a common problem: They cannot study what they so desperately want to study, the structures and functions of the mind. They don't want to be philosophers who create elegant logical arguments about the nature of the mind, the nature of reality, and relations between the two. Oh, no. Philosophers get no respect these days. If you go to a party and say that you are interested in whether there will be a sound if a tree falls in the forest and there is no one around to hear it, your fellow party guests will walk away mumbling under their breath, "Get a job."

In today's America, psychologists must be *scientists*. But, alas, they are scientists with no direct access to their subject matter and not a hope in hell of ever getting one. What *experimental* psychologists do, most of them, is compromise. If they wish to study an inaccessible mental process like what little babies pay attention to out in the world, for example, they define "attention" in terms of something that they can actually measure, like the amount of time the babies spend looking at one thing or another.

That makes every research psychologist vulnerable to the same criticism: You aren't measuring what you say you are measuring. You can't measure what you want to measure and you are making great inferential leaps from what you are actually measuring—like babies' looking behavior—to what you wish to measure—like babies' attention. You want to make a description of some mental activity using the building blocks of physical activity; from these shabby clay bricks you are attempting to build a cathedral of glass.

It's a point well taken.

I think it is the general impossibility of arriving at a verifiable account of mental activity that leads so many clinical psychologists into cutting the tie to physical observation altogether. If we are always stuck making these great inferential leaps from the carefully controlled studies of physical behavior to the mental processes underlying those behaviors, if we have no way of guaranteeing that the leaps are in any way producing an approximate model of the mental activity of interest, then to hell with it.

HOW CLINICIANS DEFEND JUNK SCIENCE IN COURT

It is bewildering but true that despite the incessant claims that clinical psychology is a science with its findings soundly based on scientific methodology, clinicians challenged in court often revert to a flat-out denial of the status. Often, when challenged in court about the lack of scientific evidence for their claims, clinicians will reply that they are *not* scientists, they are *artists*, and that they are not interested in numbers or groups because they deal with individuals. They claim that science is irrelevant and unnecessary to their conclusions.

In addition, they launch ad hominem attacks on the scientific experts themselves. Dr. Lenore Terr in the Franklin case referred to experts on the scientific study of memory as "outsiders."

The ultimate courtroom put-down of the scientific researcher by a cross-examining attorney is, "You have never seen a patient, have you? So how would you know?"

Lenore Terr describes the use of this tactic in the Franklin murder trial:

> As Elaine [Tipton, the prosecutor] had anticipated, Elizabeth Loftus [an experimental psychologist from the University of Washington] eventually also appeared for the defense. She testified that her misinformation experiments served as proof that repressed memory can be changed in the process of intake, storage, or retrieval. But Elaine was ready for Dr. Loftus, and on cross-examination quickly received an acknowledgment from her that she was not a clinician and did not ordinarily use children in her research. (1994, p. 57)

That seeing patients almost constitutes prima facie evidence of the *inability* to give scientifically accurate and reliable testimony doesn't enter the minds of anyone in court. But it should. It must.

Miss Marple is testifying in our courts. Miss Marple is writing "psychological" reports for our judges. Miss Marple is telling our legislators how to write law to match up with Miss Marple's intuitions about how the mind works. This farcical state of affairs cannot continue. The larger society has already begun to believe the courts mad, and a society that does not believe in its system of justice is a doomed society.

3
Three Kinds of Liars

History of the Forensic Psychology Industry

When there is no evidence of validity of psychiatric evaluation regarding a particular legal question, it should not be assumed that the evaluations can be made accurately. Rather, when evidence is lacking, the assumption should be that psychiatrists cannot make such evaluations accurately, especially in view of the general findings that validity of diagnosis is usually very low wherever it has been tested.

Jay Ziskin,
Coping with Psychiatric and Psychological Testimony, 1995

MENTAL AND EMOTIONAL DISTRESS

[Richie] Parker, 19, drew national attention after pleading guilty on January 13, 1995, to felony first-degree sexual abuse in a case in which he was charged with forcing a 14-year-old freshman girl to perform a sexual act on him in a stairwell of Manhattan Center High School. Parker received five years probation. . . . Parker is undergoing treatment and counseling for sexual abuse.

He settled an $11 million civil suit with the victim last June 15. . . . Parker's victim said she suffered "severe and serious physical and psychological injuries including sexual assault, fear of contracting AIDS, and Post-Traumatic Stress" as a result of the attack. (Reid, *Orange County* [Calif.] *Register*, March 26, 1996)

The tort business is a billion-dollar industry in America. By 1980, some five million lawsuits were being filed annually in the United States. Whether that number has increased, decreased, or stayed the same is a matter of some contention, but whatever the actual numbers it is clear that psychology has played a huge role in expanding both the variety of possible claims and the size of possible awards.

The American system of justice, of course, has long recognized intangible damage like mental and emotional distress in personal injury cases, and American juries have a long history of adding emotional damages onto the damages incurred to one's income by, for example, defamation of character or invasion of privacy. So in most standard tort cases today, claims for mental or emotional distress or psychic damage that causes loss of the enjoyment of life's activities are now routinely tacked onto claims of personal injury resulting from any of the innumerable accidents and incidents for which the blame can be laid at someone's door.

Psychology's contribution is to add several hundred new "injuries" that can mean either the loss of much of the enjoyment of life or even the loss of one's mental health.

Damages for the loss of enjoyment of normal life activities are called "hedonic" damages. According to Walter Olson in *The Litigation Explosion*, "total estimates of hedonic damages have ranged from $450,000 to $13,400,000 in 1989 dollars" (Olson 1991, p. 171). That is a lot of money just because you are not having any fun anymore, but it is nothing compared to what you will get if your mental health itself is directly damaged.

> An early California case involved a suit by a woman who was involved in a trolley car accident. As a result of that accident, the plaintiff alleged that she engaged in over 100 illicit sexual experiences. The California jury awarded her $50,000 for the mental distress associated with her trauma. (Gordon 1976a, p. 3)

Today, according to Jury Verdict Research, Inc., damage to your mental health is worth one hundred times what loss of ability to satisfy your hedonic desires pays.

In the United States, in the mid-1970s, there was just one million-dollar personal injury award per week, on the average. In 1990, there were 735 million-dollar personal injury verdicts awarded, and 750 million-dollar verdicts were awarded in 1991. Nearly every one of those verdicts included a component for psychic injury, for damages for noneconomic injuries.

And just who do you think is going to make the claim for you that you do indeed suffer from a psychological injury worth $11 million in compensation? The professional forensic clinician, of course. Who else?

> In cases of personal injury, the psychologist can explain to the court and the jury the personality changes that the allegedly injured individual has undergone as a result of the injury, the problems the injury has created in his family life, and how such injury affects his vocational adjustment in the future. (Gordon 1976a, p. 3)

You might take the stand and claim that since you were struck by the falling ladder, you are unable to work or to sleep and you have shattering nightmares in which you relive the trauma of the injury and envision your three children naked, hungry, and shivering, begging on the street with bowls, but this is going to sound a whole lot more convincing if Dr. V.I.P. Harvard tells the court that in his professional opinion, you suffer from the serious disorder of post traumatic stress syndrome.

Many experts will go even further, particularly in claims of post traumatic stress disorder, and not only will diagnose you but will pinpoint for the judge or the jury the actual cause or agent of the trauma that you claim to have suffered—e.g., the dangerous falling ladder. Only another expensive psychoexpert could argue that your expert is wrong.

It is clear that what used to be the well-guarded province of the prosecutor or judge or jury—the determination of what wrong was done, who is responsible for that wrong, and what the compensation should be—are now all decisions that belong, in fact if not in law, in the realm of the professional psychologist. Professional psychologists have claimed a unique competence to assess such mental damages, and the public believes their claim.

How did we get to such a state of affairs? How did we come to the point that we have literally handed over to a bunch of entrepreneurs the determination of injury, not only in standard tort cases but even in cases of discrimination and disability?

It was pretty much inevitable given the evolving history of psychology and the law in the criminal domain. That the tort psychological-injury market has become the exclusive realm of the trained psychological professional follows right along with the medicalizing of legal competence and insanity and the consequent cornering of that market by the psychologists.

A quick look at the Byzantine history of interactions between psychology and the law will make their present misalliance, if not acceptable, at least comprehensible.

EXPERTS, STEAM ENGINES, AND EXPERIMENTAL PSYCHOLOGY

> Gentlemen of the jury, there are three kinds of liars: the common liar, the damned liar, and the scientific expert. (Foster 1897, p. 169)

Experts on nonpsychological matters have long enjoyed access to the witness chair with their testimony subject to much wrangling about its admissibility and utility. The basic ideas that evolved over time were that expert testimony should be admitted whenever it will assist the judge or the jury, or when the matters before the court are beyond the experience or the understanding of the judge or jury. So an expert on steam engines, for example, could be called into court to explain to the jury the workings of such engines and the conditions under which they were likely to blow up. The jury, having been educated about steam engines, would then reach its own conclusion about the claimed negligence in the particular case before it.

For psychological expert witnesses, the experimentalists and the clinicians followed two very different paths to today's prominent role in our courtroom.

EXPERIMENTAL PSYCHOLOGY EYES THE WITNESS

Experimental psychology's ventures into the legal expert witness business began inauspiciously in 1908 with the publication of Hugo Munsterburg's work *On the Witness Stand.* Professor Munsterburg, brought to Harvard from Germany by William James, the father of American experimental psychology, argued that law would benefit greatly if it embraced the findings and techniques of experimental psychology about such matters as attention, memory, and perception, particularly as they address questions of eyewitnesses' accuracy and reliability. Many outspoken and outraged lawyerly defenders of the status quo replied to Munsterburg with withering contempt, but the barn door was irrevocably cracked open.

Munsterburg had been a student in the laboratory of Wilhelm Wundt, who had founded the first experimental psychology laboratory in the world in Leipzig, Germany, in 1878. By the turn of the century, German psychological researchers had been actively engaged in studying real-world problems and applications in perception and memory for two decades.

Among the best known of the German researchers was William Stern, who conducted what he called "reality" experiments, simulations of real-life situations, to examine the reliability of eyewitnesses under more or less natural conditions.

The classic example involves the staging of a quarrel between two students in front of a class. One student draws a revolver on the other. The teacher stops the staged incident and then questions the class about the events that they just witnessed. Over and over again, the results are the same. The eyewitnesses to the incident are in serious error about every aspect of the witnessed event, including what words were spoken and the type of weapon used.

Munsterburg's book summarized and extended the European studies for the American public. It also attacked American lawyers for their close-minded response to psychological science. That was a political error.

> The time for such applied psychology is surely near. . . . The lawyer alone is obdurate. The lawyer and the judge and the juryman are sure that they do not need the experimental psychologist. . . . They go on thinking that their legal instinct and their common sense supplies them with all that is needed and somewhat more. (Munsterburg 1908, p. 21)

Perhaps it was the tone of Professor Munsterburg's book as much as its content that produced such a withering response from the American legal community. John Wigmore, who was later to publish the classic *Wigmore's Code of the Rules of Evidence* (1935) and *The Science of Judicial Proof* (1937), published a scathing satire of the book, pointing out both methodological errors and the inapplicability of much of the research to actual legal proceedings. In particular, he noted that despite errors in the testimony of witnesses, jurors hearing those witnesses nevertheless come to conclusions that are in accordance with the facts of the case. Reasoning that the outcome of the case is of far greater concern to the legal system than the perceptions or memories of witnesses, Wigmore dismissed Munsterburg's reported researches as irrelevant.

During the 1920s and 1930s a revival of interest in law and psychology occurred and a number of books appeared, nearly all by lawyers. The past focus on the perceptions and memories of witnesses was joined by an interest in the psychology of crime and the "criminal personality."

> All was quiet on the psychology-law front during the 1940's. There were scattered studies on the usual topics of witness testimony, evidence rules, and criminal behavior, and simulations of jury decision making were introduced. On the whole, this work did not add significantly to what had been done before, and provoked no response from the legal profession. (Loh 1981, p. 671)

BURGEONING OF EXPERIMENTAL PSYCHOLOGY IN COURT

> A critical development in the modest expansion of the role of experimental psychology in the legal system took place in the 1950's through psychologists testifying in cases involving the impact of pretrial publicity, and civil rights.
>
> Research psychologists had developed reliable techniques of conducting surveys with samples that began to approach being truly representative of the population relevant to the

> survey. Results of the surveys began to show up in trials where defense attorneys might use them to show that their clients could not get a fair trial in a particular locale because pretrial publicity in newspapers, news clips and magazines had so biased the potential juror pool against the defendant. (Woodward 1952, p. 447)
>
> In 1961 the Supreme Court put the seal of approval on the methodological competence of such research surveys and reversed a conviction because of pretrial publicity in Irvin v. Dowd, 336 U.S. 717 (1961). In the famous case of Sheppard v. Maxwell, 384 U.S. 333 (1966), the Supreme Court reversed Sheppard's murder conviction based at least in part upon the Court's acceptance of the reliability and methodological soundness of surveys of the effects of negative pretrial and mid-trial publicity. (Loh 1981, pp. 672–73)

A dozen years earlier, in 1954, a crucial case was decided with lasting implications for the parties to the case, for society as a whole, and for the future of the forthcoming marriage of law and psychology in the American justice system. Not quite a first date, this case was surely a turning point in the relationship. Since then there has been no going back.

This case was the landmark school desegregation case. Employing the "findings" of psychologists, part of the case was built on the foundation of the famous "Brandeis Brief." In 1908, Louis Brandeis (later to become a Supreme Court justice) had argued persuasively that conclusions of social scientists should be considered when evaluating the merits of limiting the workdays of females. His presentation laid the groundwork for the crucial *Brown v. Board of Education* case argued before the U.S. Supreme Court in 1954.

In that case, Kenneth Clark, an experimental psychologist from Harvard, assisted by thirty other psychoexperts, submitted an amicus brief to the Court, alleging that supposedly scientific evidence showed that a segregated school system had ill effects on the personalities and academic performance of black children. The Supreme Court cited as the modern authority for these findings Clark and other social scientists.

Legal scholars argue about the relative weight the Court gave to the scientists' "evidence," many claiming that, whatever the public perception, it was slight, but there is no doubt that the Pandora's Box of psychological expert testimony was now open and showering its contents across the land. This occurred despite what Wallace Loh, past dean of the law school at the University of Washington, described as yet another "swift and caustic" reaction from the legal community. Legal experts pointed out the methodological shortcomings and unjustified inferences of the work cited by the psychoexperts in the *Brown* case, and described the findings, quite rightly, as more common sense than science. They reacted about as enthusiastically as their turn-of-the-century counterparts had to Professor Munsterburg's efforts.

But the tide was turning in America against racial segregation, and the Court and the public alike moved with the tide. And the Court and the public alike wanted a scientific basis to justify what was, after all, a major change in American political opinion. Clark and company gave it to them.

It is interesting that in a recent column in the *New York Times* addressing the issue of ethnic dormitories at Cornell University, Clark cited no scientific evidence at all about the injurious effects of such living arrangements on the hapless students but merely quoted the Supreme Court in stating that "separate educational facilities are inherently unequal" (Clark, *New York Times*, April 1, 1995).

The response of the legal community to psychologist Clark's Brandeis-style brief was so negative that experimental psychology generally avoided excursions into the legal arena for more than a decade following the *Brown* decision. In the 1970s, the floodgates opened. Do-gooders from the sixties blossomed into professionals with a cause in the seventies, and experimental psychology was ready to aid the cause. Classic research on witness reliability was refined and replicated with more sophisticated methodology and with a renewed sense of its critical application to important social problems—like maintaining an equitable, color-blind justice system.

By the middle of the 1980s, experimental psychologists were testifying all over the country—wherever the judge would allow it—on the confusions and distortions of memory that result from various police interrogation techniques, and the serious difficulties witnesses encounter with cross-racial identification.

Notwithstanding Wigmore's historical criticism of their applicability, German-style "reality" studies had become by the 1980s the paradigm for research on eyewitness reliability in the United States. According to Wallace Loh in a March 1981 *Michigan Law Review* article, "they are repeated so often that the findings are no longer considered novel" (p. 661).

> In a modern version of the reality experiment, the videotape of a mugging was broadcast on the nightly news of a major television station in New York City. It was followed by the showing of a lineup of six suspects, and viewers were asked to call in with their identification of the mugger. Less that 15% of the 2000 respondents correctly identified the assailant, a rate no better than random selection. (Buckhout 1975, p. 7)

Experimental psychological research of this type was and is carefully conducted according to strict principles of sound scientific methodology. Testimony presenting the findings of such research does not involve the expression of the personal opinions or intuitions of the experimentalist. It is not even necessary to have as an expert witness the person who actually conducted the research because, like all sound scientific work, this research is easily replicated in any laboratory by any scientist and the findings are readily available in the published psychological literature.

The major argument over this type of testimony was whether it interfered with the judge's or jury's role as trier of fact in deciding whether a witness's identification of an alleged criminal was reliable. It is true that most of the research consists of demonstrating the effects of various factors that make memory *less* reliable, like stress, leading questioning, passage of time, violence, misleading photo IDs, and biased lineups, so most expert testimony on the topic does consist of casting doubt on the reliability of eyewitnesses. It would be highly unusual, however, for any experimental psychologist testifying about research on the perception, attention, and memory of witnesses to offer any decisive opinion about the accuracy of a particular individual's testimony.

The purpose of such expert witness testimony offered by experimental psychologists is, like that of the expert witness on steam engines, to explain the scientific findings about the reliability, accuracy, and malleability of memory due to various factors and the conditions under which memory is likely to fail.

In addition to research on memory and factors affecting witness reliability, experimental psychologists presented research in court on issues like confusion allegedly caused in consumers by brand names or product packaging that is similar to that of competing products. Robert Gordon in "The Applications of Psychology to the Law," from a 1976 issue of *Law and Psychology Review*, reports that Coca-Cola sued Chero-Cola in 1921 for such alleged trademark infringement, the Spring Aire Mattress Company sued the Sleep Aire Mattress Company for the same reason, and Frito Lay Corn Chips sued Ajax Potato Chips for making bags that allegedly bore a strikingly similar appearance to its own product's bags. In all such cases, careful scientific studies are run with representative consumer samples and the findings are presented to the court and the jury.

Some research is conducted just for the sake of research—for the sake of acquiring knowledge about cross-racial identification, for example, or the effects of "weapon focus" on eyewitness testimony—and it gets introduced into trials because the information it provides happens to be helpful to the finders of fact. But some research is "special purpose" research conducted just for the litigation at hand. On confusability of specific products, it is the second kind of research that shows up in court.

With the exceptions of the researchers on mental confusion over similar commercial products, the small band of eyewitness testimony researchers, and their colleagues involved in the development and refinement of survey and other measurement instruments, few experimental psychologists ever ventured outside their laboratories and into the courtrooms.

For the clinicians, however, it was another story. They came directly into the American court system through the wide open door of legal insanity and mental state of the accused at the time of the crime and at the time of the trial.

DANIEL M'NAGHTEN AND THE FORENSIC CLINICIANS

In 1843, in England, Daniel M'Naghten, while attempting to assassinate the prime minister of England, accidentally shot and killed the prime minister's secretary. M'Naghten suffered from delusions and thought that killing the prime minister would eliminate the source of his oppression. He successfully pleaded an insanity defense, claiming that he did not know right from wrong, a test that "had its origin in 16th century England, where judges enunciated a test of criminal responsibility which was premised upon the knowledge of good or evil" (Burke and Nixon 1994, p. 10).

Following this case, the insanity defense was reformulated, resulting in what is known today as the M'Naghten Rule, which focuses on the accused's understanding and knowledge, stating that an accused should not be held criminally responsible if he was laboring under such a defect of reason, from disease of the mind, as not to know the nature and quality of the act he was doing, or if he did know it, he did not know that what he was doing was wrong.

The M'Naghten case was also quite important because, according to the American Psychological Association's Richard Rogers, it was one of the earliest cases that allowed expert testimony on the issue of insanity as a defense in a criminal trial (1987, p. 840).

Today, medical specialists in psychopathology flood into our courtrooms as legal criteria both for insanity as a defense and for mental incompetency to stand trial evolve and proliferate, increasing in subtlety and complexity.

Until the 1960s, in America, medical psychiatrists—not Ph.D. psychologists or any other kind of mental health professionals—had the exclusive right to provide expert "medical" testimony on the issue of insanity as a defense in a criminal trial, although judicial decisions in 1940 (*People v. Hawthorne*) and in 1954 (*Hidden v. Mutual Life Insurance Company*) had permitted clinical psychologists with sufficient education and experience to testify as experts on mental disorders and their causal connections to criminal or tortious conduct. This changed in 1962 with the appeal of the landmark case of *Jenkins v. United States*.

The trial court had ruled, "A psychologist is not competent to give a medical opinion as to mental disease or defect. Therefore, you will not consider any evidence to the effect that the defendant was suffering from a mental disease or a mental defect . . . according to the testimony given by the psychologist" (*Jenkins v. United States*, 1962, 307 F.2d 637, 638 n. 1).

The United States Court of Appeals for the D.C. Circuit reversed the lower court and remanded for a new trial. The court ruled that the evaluation of relevant competence was up to the trial judge and was not a straightforward matter of medical training.

Giving as examples electricians who could testify about the effect of electrical shock on the body or an optometrist knowledgeable about symptoms of eye disorders, they wrote:

> The kinds of witnesses whose opinions courts have received, even though they lacked medical training and would not be permitted by law to treat the conditions they described, are legion. *The principle to be distilled from the cases is plain: if experience or training enables a proffered expert witness to form an opinion which would aid the jury, in the absence of some countervailing consideration, his testimony will be received.* (Miller, Lower, and Bleechmore 1978, pp. 119–21)

That was in 1962. Today, every state permits clinical psychologists to join their psychiatric brethren as expert psychological witnesses on insanity and competence.

Mushrooming Psychological Experts in the Legal System

> The broadening of admissibility of expert psychological testimony occurred during a time of increased professionalization (e.g., state certification and licensure), rapid growth of mental health professions, and formulation of legal doctrines of insanity consistent with modern psychiatry. An extensive literature on the professional and legal aspects of the role of psychologists in court suddenly mushroomed. (Loh 1981, pp. 672–73)

Today we have just about anybody who sets up as a so-called therapist confidently mounting the witness stand as a psychological expert to pronounce diagnoses, prognoses, and needed courses of future therapy. Given the state of the art of mental diagnosis and treatment, the credentials of the "experts" do not, in fact, make any difference, but it is nevertheless astonishing to hear so great a cacophony of self-styled yet societally accepted experts all testifying about how the mind works, what goes wrong with it, and how this relates to guilt and responsibility, competence and insanity, diagnosis and the effects of disorders on individuals, not to mention needed future therapy.

Professor Loh is right about the concomitant mushrooming of forensic psychology and the developing formulation of legal doctrines of insanity away from the idea of good and evil and toward the philosophy of modern psychiatry. The legal profession is still reeling from the 1980 publication of the ambitious third edition of the diagnostic manual of the American Psychiatric Association. Earlier versions of the manual were inconsistent, piddling little efforts at systematizing and regularizing the diagnoses of mental illness. The third edition—the DSM-III—was something else altogether with its hundreds of different diagnoses with fancy-sounding names, critical symptom lists, and up-to-the-minute timely relevance. It was to the DSM-III that we owe today's glittering *variety* of "diminishing" diagnoses—those mental conditions, temporary or chronic, that somehow magically diminish a person's responsibility for whatever heinous act he or she committed, decreasing the crime with which the person is charged or weighing in the defendant's favor when it comes to sentencing.

CORNERING THE CRAZY MARKET

Since determination of competence and the use of insanity defenses of one form or another are hardly new to the American legal system, there was nothing particularly remarkable about employing professionals in psychopathology to express their opinions of the psychological functioning of accused criminals. However, with the increasing and inexorable medicalizing of psychological problems, it seems inevitable that our courts will eventually take away altogether from the layperson the right and the duty to judge another person's competence or insanity in a criminal case.

Two recent court decisions have gone a long way toward handing the task completely over to the professionals who claim that they are so much better qualified than the rest of us to make these hard decisions. *Hunter v. Massachusetts* (1995) established the necessity of professional psychological examinations for the accused, and the more recent Supreme Court decision in *Cooper v. Oklahoma* (1996) established the illegality of sending an accused person to trial if a psychiatrist says the accused is too nuts to assist in his or her own defense.

Given the farcical and highly contentious procedures of clinicians for reaching mental diagnoses, handing determinations of competence and insanity entirely over to their charge can bring nothing but a further distortion of common sense in our justice system.

The same psychologizing of the law with the subsequent distortion of both sense and justice has been occurring in the civil courts as well as in the criminal justice system.

Damages paid out in tort cases due to psychological injury have reached dizzying heights, and not only in the usual personal injury realm but in the modern arenas carved out by today's governmental social policy decisions.

SOCIAL BETTERMENT THROUGH FORENSIC PSYCHOLOGY

The United States has a decades-long history of providing both for the economically disadvantaged and for those who are unable to work due to accident or disability. It should come as no surprise that recent social legislation, as well as amendments of older acts, now include—like tort law—a whole raft of mental disorders that qualify as disabling and, as such, as subject to compensation and to protection from discrimination.

Two such pieces of social legislation—spiritual siblings in their psychological compass and passed within a year of each other—are the Civil Rights Act of 1991 and the Americans with Disabilities Act of 1990.

The consequence of such well-intentioned psychological state-of-the-art legislation has been to flood our courtrooms with mental health providers of every stripe and degree.

Civil Rights Act of 1991

In 1991, Congress passed the Civil Rights Act, amending Title VII of the Civil Rights Act of 1964, which had prohibited discrimination by employers of fifteen or more employees on the basis of race, color, religion, sex, and national origin. Sexual harassment was considered a form of sex discrimination. Under the original act, an employee could recover damages for back pay or future pay (or reinstatement in the job), but not for emotional pain and distress. Because of the 1991 changes, wronged employees today can recover compensatory damages for emotional pain, suffering, inconvenience, mental anguish, loss of enjoyment of life, and other nonpecuniary losses, in addition to wages due and/or reinstatement, any or all of which may be caused by discrimination or sexual harassment.

Simply, this means that Congress has agreed that racial and sexual discrimination or sexual harassment can cause mental anguish that can, by the tiniest stretch, be classified as a genuine mental disorder. Mental anguish can easily be certified as a disorder by a trained mental health professional and enhanced in degree for the purposes of trial by the addition of a formal, perhaps Latinate, label from the DSM.

Sexual harassment is interesting because it, like the psychological damage it causes, is often imperceptible to others, or exists only in the mind of the harassed. This does not mean that the mental effects of harassment are any less real than the bodily effects of physical assault, but it does raise, once again, the troubling question of whether it takes an expert psychologist to identify them.

> A Connecticut woman has sicced a [federal civil rights] lawsuit on a judge she says brings his skirt-chasing dog to a Danbury courthouse where the pooch harasses women with "offensive nuzzling." . . . "Kodak [the dog] acts like a high-testosterone male," said Nancy Burton, who said the out-of-control canine only hits on women wearing skirts. But the judge [said] that Kodak is a female. (Delfiner, *New York Post*, September 25, 1996)

Americans with Disabilities Act of 1990

The American with Disabilities Act was passed the year before the Civil Rights Act of 1991 and is, in its psychological provisions for determination of injury and compensation, much the same as its sister legislation. Congress, in passing the ADA, however well-meaning in intent, essentially passed another full-employment bill for psychological professionals.

The ADA prohibits discrimination in the workplace and in places of public accommodation against the disabled, be they physically disabled or mentally ill. Since, as we have seen, there are several hundred ways of being mentally ill, all requiring the skilled eye of the trained psychologist for diagnosis, it should be clear that employment opportunities for clinicians in discrimination litigation are vast. Not only can the clinician diagnose just about anyone with some kind of mental disorder, but he or she can also be called upon to testify that the discrimination suffered by the victim in the workplace has produced still more mental trauma likewise worthy of compensation.

GELT WITHOUT GUILT AND THE LAW OF LIMITLESS DEMAND

When the clinical employment opportunities provided by the ADA are added to those opened by the new Civil Rights Act, and all these new jobs are added on to the old Social Security Administration base of workers' disability and compensation claims, the job prospects are dizzying. Throw the Child Abuse Prevention and Treatment Act for the children into the pool, with its ever-increasing demand for more and more professional child psychological evaluators, and it becomes clear why the supply of mental health providers in this country has been growing exponentially to meet a constantly rising demand.

The concepts of government-legislated social betterment and a social safety net for the less fortunate have a long history in this country. Given the general psychologizing of the whole society, it was inevitable that mental betterment and mental health safety nets would eventually take their places alongside their older physical counterparts. It was inevitable too that mental health professionals would be produced in great numbers both to implement and to augment these strides forward toward social betterment.

Add the numbers of the forensic clinicians employed in the social welfare domains to those already laboring in the vineyards of competency and insanity, alongside those experimentalists venturing into the courtroom on occasion to assist the trier of fact in understanding the present state of scientific psychological knowledge about attention, perception, and memory, and we have a subset of mental health professionals that itself defines a whole new profession—the professional forensic clinician.

In an apparent violation of the fundamental law of economics, as the supply of mental health providers grew, largely through expanded licensing of diverse professionals, the demand grew as well. The psychoexperts educated their nonpsychological fellows to recognize a need for psychological expertise where none before had ever existed. And more and more forensic psychology types were hatched out of our schools and licensed to meet that demand, and they, in turn, agitated for more of the same.

At the present time, it is not clear where the growth will end. There is still plenty of room for more well-intentioned legislation to improve the lot of the ordinary citizen. Perhaps in response to the high level of domestic violence in this country Congress will pass a version of the Child Abuse Prevention and Treatment Act for women, requiring that all suspected domestic abuse be reported and evaluated by trained psychological professionals. It is not such a crazy idea considering the present system of handling cases in which violent men pose a clear danger to the women in their lives and, often, the family members of those women.

In a recent case in New York City, an eighteen-year-old woman, Danielle DiMedici, allegedly was killed by her ex-boyfriend after numerous well-documented attacks and threats, including a kidnapping. The man allegedly had threatened a dozen family members in addition to Ms. DiMedici. The *New York Times* reported:

> It was far from clear whether any amount of official intervention could have deterred Mr. Parker, a convicted felon and drug dealer apparently obsessed with Ms. DiMedici, who was pregnant with his child. Officials from the [Brooklyn] District Attorney's office said yesterday that Ms. DiMedici and a dozen family members also threatened by Mr. Parker would probably have been moved out of the city by the end of this week. (Kennedy, *New York Times*, September 18, 1996)

A dozen people would have been moved out of the city to accommodate a man threatening to harm them? It is kind of hard to imagine that the entire family of the President of the United States, for example, would have been moved out of Washington, D.C., because some man threatened them with harm. Perhaps a Family Abuse Prevention Act for Adults is overdue. If one does come to pass, it would certainly keep the psychological professionals fully employed well into the next century, especially if "psychological" abuse were included in such an act.

SOCIAL LIBERALISM AND WOMEN'S LIBERATION

The American liberal tradition has long held that the individual without the sheltering arm of the community is a frail creature helplessly buffeted by the cruel and capricious winds of fortune. Liberal thinkers believe that the citizen must be shielded not *from* the government but *by* the government, in the same way a benevolent father shields his child from danger and even risk. From this perspective, both decision-making power and accountability lie solely in the hands of the paternal government, since the childlike individual citizen is incapable of accepting the burden of either.

There are two types of liberals, those who see themselves as making up the shielding government and those who see themselves as needing government protection from responsibility for the conduct of their own lives. Liberals in the first group quite naturally see just about everybody else as belonging to the second, a large but necessarily stratified group. One's position in the hierarchy of the needy is of course determined by the degree of success experienced in life: the greater the success, the lower the position, on the "to each according to his needs" principle.

Thus, black Americans and Hispanics rank higher on the needy scale than do white Americans, while children rank higher than women, who, naturally, rank higher than men. (There are liberals who rank Asian Americans among the needy, but not many; it is too hard to reconcile their evident success with their numerous disadvantages.)

For decades, liberal thinkers have found allies for their position among economists and philosophers, but with *Brown v. Board of Education* in 1954 they got something more. They got science. Against all odds, clinical practitioners convinced much of the legal community that psychology was a science and that psychology's beliefs could be accepted and proffered in court as scientific findings.

The law is, of course, a principal tool of social policy implementation, addressing as it does fundamental issues of type and agency of injury and degrees of accountability for action. With ethics and economics, and now the *science* of psychology behind them, the liberal agenda of partitioning out legal responsibility in accord with the hierarchy of perceived neediness was greatly advanced.

Traditional Freudian-style clinical psychology, however, would have been of no use to liberals. With its focus on the healthy development of the strong, independent, and principled male, there was no scientific apologia available in the theory to explain rankings on the hierarchy of need. It is impossible to imagine Freud arguing before the Supreme Court in favor of either black plaintiffs or white defendants on the issue of mental health and segregated schools.

No, a major change in the whole theory of personality development was required before the allegedly "scientific" clinical psychology would make a useful weapon in the liberals' arsenal. Oddly, and somewhat unexpectedly, that major change was a direct result of the infusion of a specific brand of feminism into clinical psychology in the 1970s.

Arrested Feminism

In both law and clinical psychology, the growth of the number of women in the ranks has been exponential over the last few decades in this country. From 1950 to 1967 approximately 3 to 5 percent of law students were women. In 1980 that number had risen to more than 30 percent. In 1995 it stood at over 50 percent.

For the psychologists the picture is similar. In 1980 about half the first-year doctoral students were women; by 1990 that number had risen to two thirds. In programs granting only master's-level degrees, the figure is 70 percent. For the academic year 1992–93, in master's programs, over 40 percent of the faculty are female, and in doctoral programs, it is a little over one third. In 1976, women received just over 31 percent of all Ph.D.s in clinical psychology. By 1990 they received over 58 percent. (Among academics the picture is quite the opposite, with males making up 70 percent of today's departmental faculty and women 30 percent.)

Today, the majority of the 75,000 American clinical psychologists and 45,000 psychiatrists are women. Most of these people have obtained their licenses in the last twenty-five years, in the years since the modern renaissance of the women's liberation movement. That the vast increase of the number of women in the mental health profession coincided with the boom years of the women's liberation movement has had significant consequences for the interface between psychology and the law.

Consider, for example, how Judith Herman, a Harvard psychiatrist well known in the fields of incest and recovered memory, explains the personal and professional history of writing her 1992 book *Trauma and Recovery*:

> This book owes its existence to the women's liberation movement. Its intellectual mainspring is a collective feminist project of reinventing the basic concepts of moral development and abnormal psychology, in both men and women. . . . The day-to-day practice that gave rise to this book began twenty years ago with the formation of the Women's Mental Health Collective. . . . The collective is still my intellectual home, a protected space within which women's ideas can be named and validated. (p. ix)

The underlying logic of women's liberation went like this: Sex is political and politics is about power. Power relationships are either equal or unequal. Power inequity is bad. In our society, men have more power than women, so all sexual relationships between men and women are unequal power relationships, with women on the weaker end. This is bad.

The program resting on this platform of reasoning had two basic stages: First, men and women must recognize the inequities through a careful process of consciousness raising, a process termed "navel gazing" by its rude disparagers. Second, men and women must strive to equalize power—the men through broadening opportunities for women and the women through ambition, action, education, and hard work.

No single characterization can possibly do justice to a group so large and diverse as the tens of thousands of clinicians practicing today, but let me hazard the generalization that a great many of the women clinicians, coming of age as they did during the flowering of women's liberation, are feminists, and so are a not insignificant number of the men. The feminists among them can be divided into two radically different groups.

The first group might be called the Fully Developed Feminists, the women (and simpatico males) who recognized the inequities in traditional roles and strove for years to equalize the power and the responsibilities. They studied for years for advanced degrees, labored to establish professional practices, and today, along with millions of their "sisters," struggle to satisfy the competing demands of work, family, friends, and their own needs.

The second group consists of the Arrested Feminists. These are the clinicians who wholeheartedly embrace the idea of woman-as-exploited-and-dependent while utterly rejecting the plan for her liberation and independence. It is not that Arrested Feminist clinicians have a better plan; it's simply that the need for one escapes them.

Arrested Feminists don't like or trust men: either they have been hurt by them, or they believe most women have been hurt by them, and the excess of pity they feel for female victims of men has been both blinding and immobilizing. The situation is much like that of partners in a marriage trapped by the pain of old wounds, unable to leave the recounting of past grievances long enough to see any future together. Pain, rage, and compassion have led these clinicians to rewrite the traditional Freudian script of life into the dysfunctional family model we have today.

The Dysfunctional Family Model of Life and Society

In the traditional Freudian formulation of the psychodrama of life, the father was properly villainized for scaring the hell out of little boys, but he got off scot-free when it came to the psyche of little girls. The Arrested Feminist version features the eclipse of the bad mother's starring role and the rise of an old villain—the castrating father—in a horrifying new form, the Father Rapist.

Over the last dozen years or so, the father as rapist has come to play the leading role in the psychodrama of life on both the familial and societal levels, as scripted by modern feminist clinical psychology.

According to modern theory, psychological life begins with pathogenic interactions between the Father Rapist and his sexually—and otherwise—abused children. In the natural course of development, these abused children grow up to become Abuse Survivors and Battered Women who will be wives to the next generation of Father Rapists. Mother in this scenario is a long-suffering, saintly soul who is helpless to protect herself, shelter her children, or change her life in any way. Thus has current clinical theory transformed the roles of husband and wife and father, mother, and child into a truly hideous domestic scene held to be ubiquitous, if not universal, in America today.

Arrested Feminist clinicians and their attorney counterparts apply this same model of the family to society as a whole, seeing the physically and mentally disabled as well as the societally disadvantaged as metaphorical abused children of a sick society. This point of view has produced both compensatory legislation and a whole new genre of criminal defenses in the last decade based on the toxicity of urban life, television, and racism.

It should be clearly understood that dysfunctional family theory incorporates the philosophical assumptions of the women's liberation movement in a form so severely truncated that it amounts to a perversion of the movement's most fundamental goals. It is tragic that much of what arouses the ire of the self-styled anti-feminist, and fills the pages of the media, is this distorted, profoundly nonfeminist, picture of what women are and what they can be, but so it is.

THE AMERICAN PSYCHOLOGICAL TRADITION

It is very important to the understanding of the success of this distorted view of family and society to realize that the dominant therapeutic tradition in American psychology always has been, basically, navel gazing; it has never been one of urging clients to change direction, take charge, or effect life change through positive action.

Just as there are two kinds of liberals, those who see themselves as dispensing help to the needy and those who see themselves as in need, so too are there two kinds of arrested clinicians: those who see others rendered powerless by abuse and in need of a sympathetic witness to their pain, and those who see *themselves* as victimized and irrecoverably injured by men or by the white, male-dominated society.

Both do no one any favor by their views. The witness bearers expend their energy attempting to bind up the psychic wounds of their clients while absolving them of any responsibility at all for the conduct of their own lives, while their paralytic fix on abuse and powerlessness guarantees endless wound licking.

Clinicians who see themselves as having been personally exploited or abused, raped physically or metaphorically, are in grave danger of seeing both their clients and society through the prism of their own terrible experiences. A clinician who sees herself as an adult abused child is dangerous indeed. If she cannot get past her own anger, then she cannot move past the stage of focusing on exploitation, oppression, and powerlessness. She will remain trapped in the impotent exercise of railing against fate, and she will inevitably trap her clients in the same flailing state.

Both types of clinicians, however, do very well financially with today's miscegenation between law and psychology—a relationship as inevitable as the confluence of two rivers running into the same valley.

VENALITY, PERJURY, AND BAMBOOZLING

There are approximately 850,000 lawyers in the United States, with about 40,000 new ones being hatched out of our law schools each year. The ratio of lawyers to the general population today is twice its historical average. Lawyers have to eat. Lawyers have to pay the mortgage, club dues, and greens fees. Psychologically hyped cases are a gift from heaven—or from the state and federal legislatures controlled by lawyers.

Psychologists have to eat too. Psychology, like law, has been a growth industry over the last three decades, with an exponential increase in numbers of Ph.D.s, and M.D.s in psychiatry, as well as in numbers of graduates in social work and counseling increasing tenfold since the mental health initiative launched by the federal government under President Kennedy's administration.

With less cynicism, I should note that various legal scholars like Wallace Loh and Laura Kalman point out the vital importance of the legal realist movement in this country from the 1920s to the 1960s in effecting diametrical changes—in a significant number of minds—in the conceptualization of the interactions between law and politics. That such changes would create a natural receptivity to the arguments of the socially concerned and proactive psychologists was inevitable. Legal history is considerably outside the scope of any expertise I might claim, but the interested reader is referred to the work by Kalman (1996) in the reference section.

Attorneys' and psychologists' common interest in forensic psychological issues and assessments has spawned a number of organizations devoted to the practice and development of the area at the nexus of law and psychology. The American Psychological Association has a special division of its membership open to both psychologists and lawyers, and both groups of practitioners have swelled the ranks of the American Psychology-Law Society, active since the mid-1970s.

In addition, a dozen new professional journals have found their way into productive print since the early 1980s. We have the *American Journal of Forensic Psychology*; *Law and Human Behavior*; *Law and Psychology Review*; and the guide for the up-to-date litigator, *Advances in Forensic Psychiatry and Psychology*.

The increase in the number of books devoted to the topic of law and psychology published over the last twenty years has been phenomenal, including everything from handbooks for testifying as a witness to guides for performing evaluations for the courts and perspectives on the international scene. The world is growing smaller. There is even a book on how to sue your parents if you recover memories of abuse while they are still alive.

Forensic psychologists and litigators belong to common chat groups on the World Wide Web, where forensic clinicians advise one another on techniques and procedures for assessment, report writing, and testimony, and where attorneys looking for a forensic clinical specialist in one area or another can advertise for help.

Bold forensic clinicians have their own home pages on the WWW, listing their areas of expertise, like child custody determinations or psychological distress in employment litigation.

Clinical evaluators, most of whom were trained over the last twenty-five years in programs steeped in the nouveau dysfunctional family model of life and society, determine in some 50 percent of juvenile cases whether the "youth" can be rehabilitated as a child or is beyond youthful redemption and must stand trial as an adult. Parental fitness was evaluated by court-appointed and parent-hired custody clinicians in about one quarter of the 125,000 disputed custody cases last year, with a cost in expert witnesses approaching $100 million.

In some 2 to 10 percent of those disputed custody cases, an allegation of child abuse was made and the determination of the reality of that claim dropped into the willing hands of the paid clinician. Estimating about ten thousand such cases annually, the added involvement of social workers and child protection workers would likely triple the usual per case expert psychological witness cost of $3,000. That means that the child evaluation specialists in these cases are raking in an additional $60 million a year.

Nationally, outside the arena of the divorce court, there were, in 1992, some 2.7 million reports of some form of child abuse in this country, each and every one of which must be evaluated by a trained professional, usually a team. Even assuming that all the investigators are state workers with a considerably lower hourly wage than their counterparts in standard custody disputes, the time involved in home visits, interviews, consultations, and report writing must come to at least twenty hours per child. At a very conservative $20 an hour including benefits, that works out to $1.08 billion. And that is a ridiculously low figure because it doesn't even include such little matters as overhead and transport.

Thousands of treatment specialists with expertise in youth rehabilitation, alcohol and drug abuse, domestic violence, and even serial murder and rape also feed out of a trough that never empties as judge after judge, court after court attempts to solve the intractable problems of escalating crime and personal irresponsibility. There are at least two thousand rehabilitation treatment programs for "troubled" youth in this country, costing over $30,000 per youth, annually, to treat. With an average of about one hundred youths per year "treated" in such programs, that amounts to a staggering cost of some $6 billion. Of course, it may not seem so staggering if you are on the receiving end of it. Some two thirds of the costs of these programs are for staff.

In addition, thousands of well-paying job opportunities are created for clinical psychologists as reams of new legislation are passed that is designed to protect the weak, aid the handicapped, and level the playing field for all. It is estimated that some 500,000 personal injury, disability, and discrimination claims reached the trial level last year. With an average of three forensic psychological experts per trial, at $200 an hour for an average of about five hours each, the cost to plaintiffs and defendants of expert psychological witnesses in such trials is about $15 billion.

Today, self-styled forensic psychological experts testify on almost every conceivable criminal, judicial, civil, and legislative issue that touches on human behavior and mental functioning.

According to William Foster in the 1897 *Harvard Law Review*, Prof. John Odronaux declared in 1874 that:

> There is a growing tendency to look with distrust upon every form of skilled testimony. Fatal exhibitions of scientific inaccuracy and self-contradiction cannot but weaken public confi-

dence in the value of all such evidence. If Science, for a consideration, can be induced to prove anything which a litigant needs in order to sustain his side of the issue, then Science is fairly open to the charge of venality and perjury, rendered the more base by the disguise of natural truth in which she robes herself. (Foster 1897–1898, p. 170)

It is the psychological community as a whole that has laid itself "fairly open to the charge of venality and perjury." The clinical psychologists are responsible because they are indeed rendered, as the Victorian scholar above remarked, "the more base by the disguise of natural truth in which" they robe themselves. The experimental psychologists are equally guilty by their sin of silence, by their failure to strip away from the clinical charlatans and greedy frauds of the field the trappings to which they truly have no claim.

It is very important in evaluating the basis of clinical psychology's claims to scientific expertise to have a clear understanding of what actually goes into their education and training. We will look at that in the next chapter.

4 Learning to Read Tea Leaves

Growing the Forensic Psychology Industry

William Miller and Reid Hester . . . summarized all the studies in which alcoholics were randomly assigned to inpatient or outpatient treatment. Some of the inpatient programs involved prolonged stays in institutions devoted to radical changes in lifestyle, beliefs, and attitudes. But there were no differences in outcomes between inpatients and outpatients, nor did Miller and Hester find any relationship between the length of treatment and outcome. In fact, nothing worked better for alcoholics than a minimal treatment involving detoxification and one hour of counseling!

Robyn Dawes, *House of Cards*, 1995

WHAT FORENSIC CLINICIANS ARE TRUSTED TO DO

On July 19, 1996, David Lynn Cooper, a 33-year-old former mental patient, was arrested after Wheat Ridge police discovered the nude, mutilated body of his daughter Renee inside his home.

The 10-year-old girl had been stabbed and sexually assaulted.

Last week Cooper was charged with her murder, sexual assault and abuse of a corpse.

> Cooper had been released from the supervision of the Colorado Mental Health Institute at Pueblo just four months ago.
>
> He was ordered to the hospital by a Jefferson County district judge in 1992 after he was found not guilty by reason of insanity in a knife attack on his father. While there, Cooper told therapists that his father was also known as Jimmy Hoffa. Cooper was diagnosed with schizoaffective disorder, court records show.
>
> A judge released him from state hospital supervision in March on condition that he continue taking anti-depressant and anti-psychotic medications and remain an outpatient at the Jefferson County Center for Mental Health. He is now in jail under a suicide watch. (Cortez, *Denver Post*, August 1, 1996)

The people of these psychologized United States, and their judges and legislators, along with their fellow citizens in states all across this country, entrust the evaluation, diagnosis, and treatment of those judged "criminally insane" to psychological professionals who have bamboozled the justice system into believing that they are up to the task. Our whole society—with the occasional pocket of sane disbelief here and there—from the Supreme Court to the legislators, to judges and juries, to the public itself, all believe that bona fide psychological experts, credentialed by their training, their degrees, and their licenses, know better than the lay public how to evaluate competence to stand trial, how to judge intention and motivation in the commission of crime, how to determine what a rehabilitation program should be and who can benefit from it.

We trust the psychological professional to tell us how the court system should treat children as victims or witnesses; how to determine who should rear a child and who is unfit; how to determine if a child has suffered from abuse that leaves no physical trace; how to assess when anyone, child or adult, has suffered some psychic injury or is suffering from mental or emotional distress brought on by physical injury, discrimination, or harassment; when they have been so disabled by psychological injuries suffered on or off the job that they can no longer work and are in need of employer accommodation or government-provided support.

COURSES PSYCHOLOGY DOES NOT KNOW HOW TO TEACH

Police, attorneys, judges, juries, and lawmakers expect psychologists to tell them if one man will rape again, if another man is a danger to himself, if a child should be returned to her family, if an individual is too "crazy" to be held responsible for her actions, whether this person is lying, whether that one has real memories or false ones, whether that child was molested and who did it.

How would the psychologists know? There are no courses in graduate school that answer these questions. Call any graduate school in the country and it will be happy to send you a course catalog and you can see for yourself that there are no such offerings. They don't teach them over in the psychiatry department at the Harvard Medical School either, not that this lack keeps their resident experts off the witness stand. Go to the library and see how many books and research articles you can find for a class on "When Men Should Be Held Responsible for Murdering Their Wives." You are going to have a mighty short reading list for that class.

Well now, if important questions about wife murderers—or serial rapists or truth telling or the rehabilitation of children—are generally left unanswered in the formal, academic training of future clinicians, what *do* the students study? They take classes for two or three years and write doctoral dissertations, so they must be studying something.

THE BOULDER MODEL OF CLINICAL PSYCHOLOGICAL EDUCATION

The programs of study vary, of course, from psychiatry to psychology to social work, to the different types of counseling, and they vary by type of school or institute as well, so it is impossible to make a short and simple description that covers all of them, much as one might argue that the differences among them are trivial. So I will use what is supposed to be the best—American Psychological Association–approved Ph.D. programs in graduate departments of psychology in universities—to illustrate what is probably well above average in the formal training of the future clinical practitioner.

Many of the most respected graduate programs in clinical psychology follow what is known as the Boulder Model of the clinical psychologist as a "scientist-practitioner." This is especially true for schools that claim to value the role of science in the education and practice of clinicians. The idea is that students will be taught not only to perform diagnostic assessment on patients and to implement courses of treatment for them but also to regard *scientific research* as an integrated part of their professional lives, not just as students but in their practice after graduation. What do students in a Boulder model program study?

Diagnostic Courses, or How to Tell What's Wrong

If you can't come up with a diagnosis, you can't send a bill. So it is obviously important that students be taught how to tell if someone is suffering from any of the hundreds of disorders cataloged by the American Psychiatric Association in its bible, the *Diagnostic and Statistical Manual.*

Of course, there is not sufficient time in three short years for detailed study of all the literature on the existence and treatment of the myriad of billable disorders and their dozens of symptoms. It would be impossible. Remember, there are some four hundred problems and disorders, each with a number of putatively distinguishing symptoms that can reveal themselves in tricky disguises. Students just can't memorize all this material, and in any case, clinicians believe that it is really not the sort of material one can learn from a book.

Any number of practitioners will assert that diagnosis is more an art than a science, and that, as such, it is best learned in the field at a master's knee. The success of this approach should be apparent to all upon contemplation of the conflicting diagnoses routinely offered by testifying psychoexperts at any criminal or civil trial involving a dispute over someone's mental state. After all, it is not surprising that different artists make different forms from the same raw clay. Different masters reveal different truths.

Therapy Courses, or How to Fix What's Wrong

In addition to courses on how to diagnose what's wrong with the patient, clinical graduate students take classes in how to fix these problems. Depending on the school, students can take various courses in marital and family therapy, child therapy and practice, group dynamics and therapy, and women and psychotherapy, and numerous classes on the developmental, behavioral, cognitive, systemic, and supportive approaches to therapy.

The variety is astonishing given the general ineffectiveness of all of them as treatment methods except behavioral therapy, which most schools don't offer.

Some students—the distinct minority—take the few science-based classes in psychopharmacology and neuropsychology offered in clinical curricula designed to teach students to tell if the patient needs drugs or how to tell if the patient is brain-damaged.

It is sad but true that graduate courses in psychopharmacology and neuropsychology, as well as courses in behaviorism—the most scientifically grounded of all the offerings in clinical programs—are taken by the smallest numbers of future practitioners. Because of this, it is in the areas of neuropsychology and psychopharmacology that psychiatrists may have the educational edge over the psychologists and other non-M.D. mental health practitioners. Psychiatrists are more likely than psychologists to have received training in the diagnosis of known brain disorders and in the efficacy of psychotropic drugs and to be up-to-date on advances in these fields. It is more likely, but it is by no means certain. Psychopharmacology is especially problematic because the whole area of treating mental problems with drugs changes so drastically from year to year, with new drugs being developed all the time and research studies constantly reshaping what is known about the older ones. Psychiatrists—whatever their initial training—will be no more informed than psychologists unless they also actively keep up in the field.

The ideal training of scientist-practitioners would require that students be exposed to all the varieties of therapy, learn all there is to know about their theoretical and research underpinnings, know the literature on their relative effectiveness, and, consequently, approach their own clinical practice with the same critical sense.

But in practice this is impossible. No one studies all the possible varieties of course offerings in clinical programs of study. Such a dedicated soul would never graduate. Besides, clinical graduate programs usually have a single philosophy or general approach that shapes the specific course of study they offer. One program might emphasize the Freudian approach while another is strongly committed to the systemic or familial approach to therapy. It would require a truly enormous graduate department to offer courses in all the existing varieties of therapeutic approaches—they proliferate like rabbits—and a profound change in attitude to require that students be able to evaluate the relative effectiveness of all these different varieties. Clinicians do not approach their own practices in this objective light and they do not teach therapy this way either.

It is inevitable that the scientist-practitioner model runs into trouble as soon as we get into teaching therapy. Although an assumed reliance on science for their expertise is supposed to distinguish clinical practitioners from all the frauds and hacks, astrologers and motivational seminar experts, teacher-practitioners are in the business of handing on their *own* approaches to clinical practice, not somebody else's approach. It doesn't really make much sense to ask someone to teach a psychotherapeutic approach he or she sees as useless. No one would do it. It would be like asking for a strictly academic approach to the teaching of a religion. The objective, scholarly approach is fine for an intellectual classroom experience—say, for an undergraduate class in comparative religion—but nobody trains priests that way. Who would ask a Jesuit seminary to train Buddhist monks?

The goal of any graduate program in psychotherapy is to train students, from the best possible point of view according to the lights of the faculty, how to diagnose and help fix what's wrong with men, marriages, families, children, groups, and women. In America the approach is frequently some modern derivative of Freudian theory usually described not as "Freudian" but as "psychodynamic." Psychodynamic means "more or less Freudian because we believe in the importance of early experience and family relations and lots of sexual motives but we don't really know that much about Freud in a scholarly way."

Lest anyone believe that the Freudians are dying out or waning in influence, note that in the 1985 National Survey of Psychotherapists, 48 percent of psychologists reported that their principal orientation was "psychodynamic." The next highest finisher was "eclectic," with 25 percent. "Eclectic" means Freudian with a little something else sprinkled in. For psychiatrists—medical school graduates—the percentage of Freudians was 54 percent, with "eclectic" a distant second at 28 percent.

These numbers mean that almost three quarters of practicing psychologists and 82 percent of psychiatrists see themselves as more or less Freudian, and it is this legacy that they, as teachers and supervisors, will pass on to their students.

Moreover, given the appalling lack of scientific evidence for the effectiveness of any of the therapeutic approaches other than behavior modification, how could therapists be expected to teach courses in scientifically validated therapy? There ain't no such animal.

Politically Correct Courses

These days, graduate students also take courses on political correctness. In many departments, the basic required PC course is titled something along the lines of "Race, Class, and Gender" or "Psychology of Social Oppression." In Massachusetts, the latter is a required course for licensing. For reasons I don't want to explore, African Americans are usually the teachers for this class.

PC courses teach students the politically correct handling of patients and illnesses from minority America and from other cultures. They are also designed to indoctrinate students with the modern version of the psychodrama of life that clinicians use to characterize the relationships between white majority culture and minorities, between American culture and third-world culture, as well as relationships between men and women and between parent and child. They all have heavy political agendas.

Is the clinical position on all these issues *only* determined by political bent? Well, yes. It has to be. There is little or no research, little or no scientifically based knowledge to teach the students in classes such as these. The only possible content of such classes is political.

Of course, it may be argued that, to some extent, all professional education consists of a mix of indoctrination into the profession and education about its substance, but clinical psychology, lacking as it does any substantial knowledge base, has no choice but to rely on political indoctrination to make up the bulk of class material.

That these indoctrination classes are political does not mean they are uninteresting. I'd like to sit in on a "Women and Psychotherapy" class, for example.

I would like to, but I can't.

The Secret Stuff of Clinical Courses

Clinical courses on diagnosis and treatment are usually closed to anyone but clinical students. The content of the courses the clinical students take are closely guarded secrets. They must be. Broad dissemination of the material covered in the courses and open admission for graduate students of all academic stripes would not only demystify the clinical courses but would subject them to the same degree of academic rigor—and respect for the standards of science—as any other graduate courses. Amalgams of rhetoric and religion, most clinical courses would dissipate in the thin air of reason.

What would become of the initiates if the rites of initiation were open to the public? A priesthood without mystery is a priesthood without authority. The authority of psychotherapists is absolutely essential if they are to maintain the enviable position of power in law, medicine, and education they occupy today. Who would let persons with no authority decide that a serial rapist is cured, that a murderer will kill no more, that a killer was forced into the act by childhood sexual abuse? What government or insurance company would let persons with no authority bill them for millions of hours of "therapy," for billions of dollars of treatment? Surely not my government or insurance company. If clinical psychology is to maintain the fiction that it knows what it is doing with respect to all these difficult issues, a mantle of secrecy over the content of their courses is essential.

Kneeling at the Distant Feet of the Master

Most professors who train clinicians would probably agree—although not perhaps for the same reasons—that you can't teach the subject solely in a classroom setting. So, beginning the second year, much of the future clinician's time is spent actually doing psychotherapy under supervision.

This is the guild model of learning. The student is an apprentice to the master. Each week the student sees a patient for individual therapy, or two or three (or nine or ten, depending on the program), and/or a therapy group, and then meets with the supervisor to discuss each case. The supervisor gives the apprentice the benefit of his or her years of experience in practice, helping with interpretation and making suggestions for therapy.

The guild approach to learning a craft has a long and honorable history. It is too bad that the clinicians' claim to have adopted this method of training is a fraud. A true apprentice works in the master's shop, observing the master, copying the master, being shown on the job how to dovetail the joint or calibrate the instrument. In a psychotherapy apprenticeship there is darn little observation on either side. Indeed, it is seen as repugnant—perhaps even unethical—to "force" a client to be observed by the trainee's supervisor while revealing intimate secrets. Supervising the dovetailing of the joints of the soul apparently can be done at second hand.

The psychotherapy supervision experience no doubt gives rise to the extraordinary willingness of therapists to diagnose both people they have never seen and people they have seen only briefly.

Dr. Richard Restak, a well-known neurologist who has written eleven books, was quoted in the September 1996 issue of *Esquire* magazine as saying that President Bill Clinton displays all the symptoms of someone suffering from narcissistic personality disorder. "It's characterized by the Diagnostic and Statistical Manual of Mental Disorders as, among other things, a pervasive pattern of grandiosity, a need for admiration, a belief that he or she is special or unique, and a haughtiness or arrogance," says Restick. "If this doesn't describe Clinton, I don't know what does. . . . [Narcissistic personality disorder] is not something that you're real happy that someone of Clinton's power has" (Restick 1996, p. 34).

It must be at the feet of the master that clinical apprentices acquire the clairvoyance that makes the psychoanalysis of unknown people possible, along with the extraordinary confidence that so often accompanies it.

Hoist with Her Own Petard

Recently the *Boston Herald* reported on a rape trial in which the defense attorney got the alleged victim to admit that she had been raped before. Since the clinical psychological community in its present feminist manifestation insists that sexual abuse is a trauma, that means, necessarily, that all abuse victims are traumatized. Traumatized means that they are damaged psychologically. In other words, they are nuts.

A psychoexpert at the rape trial then testified that this unfortunate, previously raped woman may well have been experiencing flashbacks to the first rape during the act of intercourse under dispute in the present trial. The defendant wasn't really raping her; she just thought he was because of her flashbacks to an earlier rape. Pretty clever defense, don't you think? It worked too.

The expert *did not even examine the woman* because his clairvoyance made that unnecessary (Mulvihill, *Boston Globe*, June 30, 1994).

The Psychological Autopsy

The outer limits of unsubstantiated omniscience are truly reached, however, with the psychological autopsy. I mean the psychological diagnosis of dead people. Freud paved the way by analyzing historical figures like Leonardo da Vinci, who had no contemporaries alive to complain about whatever unflattering characterizations Freud may have reached. But his modern counterparts analyze the recently dead.

Insurance companies frequently write life insurance policies that pay off only if the death is not a suicide, or not a suicide within a certain number of years, or they pay double benefits if the insured individual dies from an accident rather than an illness. Many cases arise in which the insurance companies dispute the beneficiary's claim that a death was not a suicide. To prove that the death of the insured was a suicide—absent any note—the companies call forensic psychologists onto the stand to testify that old George was depressed, off his feed, sleeping poorly, and just in general exhibiting all the characteristics of your typical suicide.

Who needs evidence when you've got clairvoyance?

Substantive Content Areas of Psychology

The scientist-practitioner model of the clinician assumes that the practitioner is firmly grounded in the scientific foundations and current findings of modern scientific psychology, but in reality, clinical graduate students and medical students can go right through school to their professional degrees without ever encountering, much less mastering, the meager body of knowledge that makes up the findings of one hundred years of experimental psychology—the substantive content of psychology.

Clinicians can and do practice with virtually no education about normal people's perception, cognition, language, learning, social skills, or group behaviors. A psychotherapist specializing in children can be graduated with almost no knowledge at all of how normal children perceive the world around them, how normal kids think and speak, how normal children learn about friendship and how to behave in school.

With no grounding in knowledge of normal behavior, would-be experts on abnormal behavior are turned out and turned loosed on the world.

INDOCTRINATION AND EDUCATION

How can this be? If the American Psychological Association and many, many graduate programs are committed to turning out so-called scientist-practitioners with a solid, broad knowledge of psychology, what goes wrong?

What goes wrong is exactly what goes wrong in trying to be objective about approaches to therapy. Therapy cannot be taught as a science when it is taught by current practitioners to future practitioners, and wannabe healers have little incentive to be interested in anything other than how to accomplish that goal. You cannot expect young seminarians who are burning to ease the pain, heal the wound, lighten the load, and illuminate the way, both for the injured individual and the bewildered society, to take a course on the biological foundations of cognition.

Students with a genuine scientific bent, the ones who really want to try to understand how the mind works or how the brain works, or the interaction between brain and behavior, quite often take such classes. They also take classes on what we know about the nature of thought, and computer modeling, and the structure and functions of language, and the behavior of animals, and many other topics for which there is both a sound research base and a means of expanding that base. Yes, this also includes some zippier-sounding areas like the structure of groups, and the effects of stress on learning, or a neurophysiological model of "trauma." Science is not a matter of area; it is a question of attitude, of approach to study.

But, sadly, in psychology as in related fields, there is almost an upside-down relationship between the size of the research base and the immediate social welfare applications of the findings. Psychology can tell you a great deal about the picture perception of both pigeons and people, but not much about whether a child should be returned to his mother; a great deal about how to train a rat to walk around its cage carrying its tail in its mouth, but not much about whether this woman was actually sexually abused as a child; a great deal about the stages of language development in children, but little about how best to educate the great numbers of children who are failing in our inner city schools.

Who can blame future clinicians for avoiding most of the research-based courses? These classes are incidental to the healing of most wounds, they are irrelevant to the saving of souls. It is no surprise that psychotherapy practitioners fail to learn the pathetically limited scientific body of knowledge that makes up the field of contemporary research psychology.

Moreover, most of their teacher-practitioners share their view. This is obvious when you look at the transparently flimsy requirements for demonstrating comprehensive knowledge of the field of psychology. Graduate students quite rightly conclude that the clinical establishment itself holds cheap such scientific knowledge as psychology does have.

STATISTICS AND RESEARCH COURSES

The same self-defeating, anti-real science message is conveyed to clinical students in the required courses on statistics and research design. Clinical students may be required to take these courses, but for the vast majority of them, these courses simply don't "take."

The situation is very much like that of teenagers and alcohol. We adults are quite understandably concerned about the abuse of alcohol by young people in high school and college. We are worried about their ability to study, the dangerous situations they get themselves into, the stupid and quite harmful things they do when drinking. So what do we do? We tell them not to drink at all. We tell them alcohol is bad, that it impairs judgment—not to mention motor skills and memory—that responsible young people do not drink alcohol. Then we go home and have a vodka martini while we put on dinner, drink a $20 bottle of wine that we buy by the case with the meal, and if the day has gone well, we reward ourselves with a small cognac. We drink beer at ballgames and knock back champagne at weddings. Apparently, adults believe that while drinking they are invisible to people under the age of twenty-one. Or else they believe—and expect young people to believe—that a magical transformation occurs on the twenty-first birthday whereby alcohol becomes a good thing—kind of like wine into water—and a child becomes a responsible adult. No wonder we have such success with youth abstinence programs.

It's the same with clinical research. Telling wannabe clinicians they are to be scientists, we push them into statistics and research design classes. At the same time, the "research" material they are assigned to read in class consists largely of the Miss Marple pseudo-research of case studies and questionnaires. Students read books and articles selling them viewpoints and approaches to diagnosis and treatment that are based on studies so shabbily designed that they could be used in a research class only as examples of what *not* to do. It's amazing the students don't go crazy. It is the classic "Do as I say, not as I do." It can't work. Students, like the rest of us, live their lives in monkey-see, monkey-do mode. They don't pay $15,000 a year to be taught by schizophrenic role models.

SCIENTIST-PRACTITIONERS

So where does that leave our Boulder Model of the scientist-practitioner? About where you would expect it. Down the tubes of impracticality. For this approach to work, both the teacher-practitioners themselves and the students would have to genuinely embrace the model. Both teachers and students would have to adopt the skeptical attitude of the scientist, not the believing frame of mind of the priest. They cannot do that. They see themselves as priests, and what does a priest want with statistics, research methodology, or cognitive biology?

Certainly there are some teachers and some students—even those who actively practice psychotherapy—who wholeheartedly embrace the role of scientist-researcher-clinician. This is particularly, but not exclusively, true of those whose interests lie in the more biological branches of psychology. These clinical psychologists often specialize in neuropsychology or psychopharmacology or epidemiology, or even in traditional behaviorism. As scientists, they know they can be wrong and often are. They do not share the mind-set of the do-gooder priest healers, nor do they partake of the willful ignorance so common among psychotherapists. The trouble is, we just don't have enough of these people.

In clinical fields, there must be ten priests for every scientist, or is it one hundred?

THE TRAINED CLINICIAN

Since the knowledge base is completely missing for nearly all the decision tasks undertaken by forensic clinicians, it should come as no surprise that some 375 separate studies combined in a meta-analysis show that extensive training in psychotherapy, with years of postgraduate education and years of postdoctoral experience, has absolutely no effect whatsoever on one's effectiveness even as a basic therapist for garden-variety mental and emotional problems (Smith and Glass 1977, pp. 752–60).

The only transfer of knowledge from master to apprentice that realistically can take place in the psychotherapy guild is that of belief structure and attitude about the power of psychotherapy—indoctrination. Budding young therapists *must* come to believe in their expanding powers. Why else would they stay in the program?

Graduate and professional training programs in clinical psychology fail because the task they have set for themselves is impossible. Besieged by unmeetable demands from legal and institutional authorities, buffeted by political pressures, handicapped by the minute size of the actually verifiable body of scientific knowledge in psychology, and faced with the insurmountable problem of bestowing on what is fundamentally a religious sect the veneer of a scientific enterprise, with the best will in the world the programs could not turn out the kind of product the public demands. It just isn't doable. Nevertheless, it is undeniable that there are a great many well-meaning people involved in this fruitless enterprise. If it weren't for the truly dreadful effect their endeavors have had on our legal system and on society as a whole, it might be possible to feel some sympathy for them.

Clinicians—M.D. psychiatrists and Ph.D. psychologists especially—have assumed a burden of explanation and of healing that is so far beyond not just their own abilities but the capabilities of human knowledge today that it is amazing they don't all die from an attack of hubris. But, as is clear from the ever-growing numbers of clinicians in ever-increasing variety, overweening pride is not fatal.

LICENSING

Starting in the early 1970s the various psychological factions struggled to expand state licensing for mental health providers beyond the sole reach of medical psychiatrists. Year by year, field by field, the imprimatur of licensing gradually embraced psychologists, counselors, psychiatric nurses, and then social workers in an ever-broadening authentication of mental health workers, each certified by his or her state as an authoritative, bona fide source of mental health expertise.

The experimental psychologists generally watched this rage to get licensed—to get legitimized—by the state as a genuine, certified mental health provider without much interest.

Many of us ignored our ambivalence about the implicit claims to competence and efficacy involved in governmental prescription and limitation of psychological licensing and we obtained our own licenses to practice psychology and to present ourselves to the public as registered psychologists, counselors, and mental health practitioners. At the time I thought the licensing movement was nothing but an attempt to restrain trade and increase income for license holders, but the consequences for society were far broader than that.

Licensing created a group of practitioners, of bona fide experts, certified by the state as possessed of special knowledge and training, the fruits of which can legally be made available to the public for a fee. The state has agreed that we have something of value to sell. Now, not only the self-interested profession but the government itself is involved in the conspiracy to delude the public.

Of course, no one admits that. In fact, the professional organizations represent licensing as a measure to *protect* the vulnerable public, not to scam them further.

PROTECTING THE PUBLIC THROUGH CONTINUING EDUCATION

For example, as part of its ongoing, if almost completely ineffectual, effort to protect the public from the ignorant or out-of-date clinician, the American Psychological Association requires that every licensed therapist take twenty-five hours of APA-approved continuing education courses every other year.

What kinds of courses might those be?

Breathing Through Your Genitals

Two of my colleagues participated recently in a workshop on the psychology of sex, designed to keep them up-to-date and in synch with modern psychotherapeutic trends. The workshop leader wanted the participants to get in touch with their bodies, to bring all the different parts and functions of the body closer together. I have no idea what that means, but students were instructed to "Breathe deeply. Deeper, deeper. Breathe through your genitals!" I'm not sure how well my colleagues mastered this exercise because they both broke out in giggles at this point in the story, but I'm sure the experience was valuable.

Aqua Genesis

Below, Steve Moen, the defendant's attorney in a 1993 personal injury trial in Seattle, is asking Kate Casey, the plaintiff's therapist, to explain to him, *on the witness stand*, the meanings of various extracurricular "trainings" listed on her résumé.

Attorney: In addition to your background in substance abuse, Ms. Casey, you've had some additional trainings. I'd like you to explain some of these types of mental health trainings that are mentioned on your vitae and in your testimony also. What is Aqua Genesis?

Therapist: Aqua Genesis is a technique using water as the context in a hot tub to help people to, uh, recall prenatal and preverbal experiences. (*Mateu v. Hagen*, 1993)

Here the judge, Dale Ramerman, asked Ms. Casey, "One was prenatal and what was the other"? She replied, "Preverbal experiences." Either not hearing or not understanding, he said, "Preverbal?" She explained kindly, "Preverbal. Before the age of nine months."

The attorney then picked up the questioning again and asked the clinician, "Is it your understanding that in the process of Aqua Genesis memories can be recovered from both the prenatal and the preverbal periods of one's life?" She replied, "Yes."

She said, "Yes." And we have proof that she is right.

In the dialogue below is actual testimony from this same civil injury trial in which the plaintiff is explaining to the defense attorney how this therapist took her back in time so that she remembered what it was like to be in the womb.

The attorney asked her, "What can you tell me about prenatal work?" The patient/plaintiff told him, "My understanding of that is they have you reenact some events. So prenatal would be maybe some experiences you had prenatally that were very difficult." The attorney said very politely, "Can you give me some specifics as to what your experience was in that?" The plaintiff replied, "I remember—the specific piece that I remember doing was remembering having a very tough time breathing. Feeling really suffocated, really tight." In an attempt at clarification, the attorney asked, "What did that have to do with the prenatal state?" She said, "That's what I experienced in the womb prenatally." Still pushing for clarification, the attorney asked gently, "Can you describe for me specifically, though, in the therapy context, the connection with your prenatal state and what you were doing in therapy? Can you just give us kind of a view of how that therapy worked? I'm asking you to describe what happened." The patient/plaintiff replied, "You reenact being in the womb. And I said I remember feeling I had a hard time breathing and a suffocating feeling."

The judge said then, "Let's take a five minute break or so" (*Mateu v. Hagen*, 1993).

In the course of her "therapy," this patient, who became a plaintiff in a recovered memory suit, came to believe such foolishness because of her trust in the training and knowledge and authority of her therapists. That is unforgivable.

BIRTH TRAUMA AND BODY MEMORY

Attorney: You have some training with Dr. Emerson, William Emerson, on treating pre- and perinatal trauma. Can you describe that a bit?

Therapist: Hm-hmm. This particular work focuses on Birth Trauma and helping children, in particular, in this training to release some of that trauma that is stored in the Body Memory.

Attorney: What do you mean by Body Memory?

Therapist: I mean that anything that happens to us, particularly of a traumatic experience, becomes stored in the body. It's done through activating the adrenal glands. It's done through a particular tensing. It's done through the release of adrenal, so that our body, in essence, has a shock, has a reaction to the traumatic experience that becomes locked in our bodies in certain ways. (*Mateu v. Hagen*, 1993)

Although on a first hearing this has a decidedly goofy sound, it can be proven to be true in a matter of moments. Like so. You can't consciously remember learning to walk or to talk, can you? No, of course not. But you can walk and talk, can't you? What about riding a bike? Isn't it true that you always remember how to ride a bike even if it's been years since you tried? How can that be? Simple. You have stored the learning in your Body Memory. QED. It is stored in the permanent part of your body, of course, not in the renewable parts like your skin or your hair. Or your muscles, or tissues, or cells or . . . What did she say? "It's done through the release of adrenal." Well, no doubt.

Attorney: Now, obviously, in the prenatal state the human being has no vocabulary or speech, right?
Therapist: It's my belief that they don't. [Cautious little doggy, isn't she?]
Attorney: And so if a prenatal memory is recovered, how is it expressed?
Therapist: It's usually expressed through the body, through a body position. If one is an adult or a baby it may be expressed through crying. (*Mateu v. Hagen*, 1993)

It might seem that prenatal memories have a rather restricted range for their expression but perhaps subtlety of interpretation is required. The reality of such memories is undeniable, right? After all, it is frequently reported that victims of violence curl up into the fetal position. Well, what else could that possibly mean? One rather intriguing question does arise. What, exactly, does a fetus have to be upset about? It's cold? It's hungry? Bored? What kind of traumas are encountered in the daily life of the fetus, anyway?

Both therapists and patients who become involved in these folie à deux techniques believe absolutely in whatever trendily plausible story is sold along with them. It never seems to occur to them that there are countless other possible explanations.

Transactional Analysis

The crucial importance of prebirth experiences is taken as an article of faith by many modern therapists, as is the vital role played in adult life by the inner child, the progeny of Eric Berne, the founder and promulgator of transactional analysis.

He explains it so:

> Each individual seems to have available a limited repertoire of . . . ego states, which are not roles but psychological realities. This repertoire can be sorted into the following categories: (1) ego states which resemble those of parental figures (2) ego states which are autonomously directed toward objective appraisal of reality and (3) those which represent archaic relics, still-active ego states which were fixated in early childhood. Technically these are called, respectively, exteropsychic, neopsychic, and archaeopsychic ego states. Colloquially their exhibitions are called Parent, Adult and Child. (Berne 1964, p. 23)

Technically, this is called psychobalderdash, but it is entertaining, and Berne's books are rather fun pop psychology tracts, especially the one entitled *Games People Play*. Bewildering and alarming is that transactional analysis, which has nothing but a rhetorical reality, is among the more *substantial* of the continuing education offerings in modern American psychology.

More bewildering, and certainly more amusing, is the fact that:

> Borrowing from pop-psychology classics of the 1960's and 70's like *Games People Play* and *I'm OK–You're OK*, the official [Texas] state gun-class curriculum requires that applicants for a gun permit know about the three "ego-states" said to exist within everyone: the parent, the child, and the adult. To minimize the risk of gunfire in any dispute . . . move the verbal encounter toward resolution incorporating as much win-win strategy as possible. . . . "'Adult to adult' is very de-escalating." (Verhovek, *New York Times*, November 8, 1995)

Ah, well, however touchingly simplistic the psychoexperts' injunction to act like an adult when you have a gun in your hand, it is rocket science compared to age regression.

Age Regression

As Ms. Casey explained in her testimony to Mr. Moen: "My belief is that within us we all carry different ages that we've been in the past.

And so in an age regression . . . they get in touch with that part of them that recalls being [a prior age]" (*Mateu v. Hagen*, 1993).

Get in touch with your self at prior ages? What a great idea. Talk about the inner child! If Ms. Therapist is right, you've got a whole one-room schoolhouse in there! We might think of this—technically—as the Onion Theory of Development. Think of yourself, I mean yourselves, as forming in sequence like the rings of a tree or the layers of an onion. When you want to be three years old again, you can, with the help of a trained therapist, just peel off the newer layers and pop out that rosy-cheeked three-year-old. Or you can work on uncovering the fresh-faced twenty-year-old who lurks within your many-layered orb.

Do you only carry one inner child per year? Or one every six months, or what? It would be helpful if these psychological theoreticians would spell out the details of their theories a little more clearly for the rest of us.

Dr. Margaret Bean-Bayog, the Harvard psychiatrist whose medical student patient killed himself after what was later seen as a scandalous course of treatment, was accused of using age regression to turn her patient into a child again and to make him believe that she was his mother. It is interesting that she pointed out in disgust that the field of psychology was entirely incapable of successfully employing the techniques that she had putatively used to destroy her patient's mental health. Whatever other mistakes she may have made, she was certainly right about that.

Despite the absence of any substantial, scientific content in these so-called continuing education courses, the number of such offerings available—certified by the American Psychological Association as appropriate for mental health practitioners—is huge and growing. It is a lucrative business.

Ericksonian hypnosis? Well, at the Massachusetts School of Professional Psychology, for $895 you can learn Ericksonian hypnosis in four weekends plus three supervision sessions. And you get seventy continuing education credits! That will keep you up-to-date for five or six years.

Not interested in hypnosis? Well, how do you feel about the "Psychology of Investing," also offered at the Massachusetts School? For $369 you can "explore the psychological meaning of investing in our culture. Using Kohut's concept of selfobjects and Winnicott's ideas about potential space, we will understand investing as one cultural activity that occupies the potential space between individual and society." Yes, indeed. I wonder if my stockbroker knows that his job is filling the potential space between individual and society? I'm always telling him that his job is to make me rich.

Perhaps you are interested in "Trauma and the Rorschach." No? How about "Men and Traumatic Life Experience: The Impact of Gender Identity and Socialization on How Males Cope with Psychological Trauma"? I like that one. Guys have been getting kind of left out with the current spate of female victims. It's been a long time since the Vietnam War. (These courses are taught by faculty at the Boston-area Trauma Clinic.)

"Working Women Unhappy About Working"? "Mothers and Adult Daughters Hurting"? "Psychodynamic Psychotherapy with Gay Men and Lesbians"? The list goes on and on and on and on. (Why do these titles sound like shows on *Geraldo*?) It is an enormous business, all done in the name of protecting you, the public, from the dangers of rampant ignorance on the part of your psychotherapist. (Well, there may be *some* profit motive in all of these offerings, but surely money is not the primary goal.)

Learn While You Sleep

Now, the busy psychotherapist may not have time to go to these long workshops and weekends because of a very active caseload, so how can the continuing education requirement for the license be met? That is easy.

"The Institute for the Study of Human Knowledge [as opposed to Alien Knowledge?] has selected books and tapes on Cognitive Therapy, Building Pleasure into Daily Life, Practical Uses of Social Psychology, The Healing Effect of Confiding in Others, Trust and Optimism, Positive Illusions, The Cultural Differences Between Men and Women, The Evolution of Consciousness, Stress Management, and Women's Health." For as little as $8.50 a credit, the overworked psychotherapist can learn all he or she needs to know to keep an up-to-date license just by reading the book, listening to the tape, and sending in a test.

Entrepreneurial Psychotherapy

Many such course tapes are available for laypersons (or is that future patients?) as well as for practitioners. This happy circumstance can be thought of as a mental health community outreach program, I guess.

For example, Dr. Brian Ford of Bellevue, Washington, offers two series of what he calls trance-induction tapes, "Dealing with Life" and "Happy Childhood." As part of his trial testimony in the civil injury case above, he explained the "Happy Childhood" series so: "For instance, if I were to take you through a guided visualization and you were to imagine a scene, a positive scene, say with a parent, and you were to do that in a relaxed, even a hypnotic state, then after you went through that visualization, you would remember it. . . . So, in short you'd remember having had the experience on tape" (*Mateu v. Hagen*, 1993).

Dr. Ford explained this process during his testimony in a recovered memory civil trial, and followed up by saying that if people can be brought to relax and imagine a fantasized past, then they will come to remember that past as part of their own childhood, their "happy childhood."

This trance tape entrepreneur was until October 1996 a licensed psychologist in the state of Washington. That month he lost his license for twenty years for having an affair with a patient. He did not lose it for messing with people's memories with his "Happy Childhood" trance tapes. And why should he have? He is but one of many thousands of such entrepreneurs all over the country peddling their nonsense both inside our courtrooms and out.

Access Your Angel

The trainings and topics, the therapists and techniques covered in this chapter do not represent only the fringe of the mental health profession, or only the most exotic and irresponsible of clinical practitioners. Would that it were so, but it is not. Consider this workshop on "Spirituality, Creativity, and Healing," offered by the Boston Center for Adult Education:

> This workshop will explore the vital link between spirituality and creativity in the healing relationship from an alchemical [seeing illness and wellness as a process of transformation]

> perspective. Through a demonstration of a meditation-based video technique developed by [the teacher], participants will experience the central role that transpersonal vision has in accessing and empowering the client's inner healer. (Catalog, BCAE, 1995)

This workshop is taught by a Ph.D. psychotherapist who teaches in the graduate program in counseling psychology at Leslie College in Cambridge.

Or how about "Grof Holotropic Breathwork," taught by a certified master's degree psychotherapist in Massachusetts?

> "Holotropic Breathwork" is a powerful method of cooperating with the healer that exists within each of us. "Holotropic" is a word derived from Greek and means "moving forward toward wholeness." Using the breath and evocative music, this process allows unproductive patterns and emotions, frozen with past traumatic events, to surface. Focused bodywork may be used as an adjunct to help free the energy. Mandala drawing and group sharing complete the process. ($175.00). (Workshop and Course Catalog, *Interface*, 1995)

What about "Inner Bonding Therapy" or "Healing Your Aloneness: Finding Love and Wholesomeness Through Your Inner Child," each of which is taught by Los Angeles–based therapists? "NeuroLinguistic Programming," taught by a Cambridge, Massachusetts, Ph.D. who will also teach you Ericksonian hypnosis? "The Inner Child Workshop," taught by a Newton, Massachusetts, licensed social worker? No?

Well, then, here is one you can't resist, given how hot and timely the topic: "Past Life Regression Therapy," taught by an R.N., M.Ph. The catalog reads:

> Regression therapy has been increasingly accepted as an approach to helping people break through blocks which have not responded to more conventional therapies. Whether past lives are "real" or not, there is now a body of therapeutic experience which tells us that these regressions are useful for clearing

> out the debris of the past. . . . There will be one induction exercise using the rattle and drum, followed by a guided visualization into metaphysical time. *Please bring a pillow and blanket and wear comfortable clothing*. ($75.00). (*Interface*; italics added)

Did I have to shop around all over the country to find these far-out examples just to scare you? No. This last little batch of offerings is all from one source, an outfit in Cambridge, Massachusetts, called Interface, and the illustrations I have chosen are really quite conservative. I didn't put in the one taught by the lady who has a private practice in animal telepathy, and, believe me, there are a great many such offerings at Interface. But not to worry. Their course catalog is filled with M.D.s. Ph.D.s, M.A.s, R.N.s, Ed.D.s, M.Ed.s, M.S.W.s, and so many other strings of initials that only a truly paranoid student could feel anything but the greatest trust in the competence and authority of the teachers and the worth of the offerings.

You can access your angel through guided visualization and meditation or you can access the intrauterine you. You can relive the suffocation of the womb or fly back into the freedom of a former life. You can float back to age two in the hot tub or float a margin loan into potential investment space. You can create a happy childhood for yourself or for your "significant other." You can learn hypnosis—Ericksonian or otherwise—and never go on a diet again! You can do all these things and more with the help of mass distribution psychotherapy tools. Fortunate you!

People believe this stuff. Life is hard and unfair and frightening. People want to believe, they need to believe, in magic and in the possibility of effortless control over their lives and their miserable fates. This sort of nonsense, taught by lecturers with their perfectly correct but wildly misleading titles of "counselor," "psychologist," "psychiatrist," and "social worker," is not harmless. It is the inevitable, logical, and pernicious extension of clinical psychologists' continuing to grasp the fig leaf of science while engaging in an increasingly blatant appeal to humankind's most primitive and desperate needs.

SO WHY NOT BREATHE THROUGH YOUR GENITALS?

Where's the harm? What's wrong with listening to inspirational lectures and tapes, and reading provocative books, and participating in life-enhancing seminars and workshops? We need all the help we can get to manage our family lives and work lives and personal problems better.

What is wrong is that the psychological industry takes advantage of the public's desperate need for answers to impossible psycholegal questions and claims to be able to satisfy that need. It is a lie.

These snake oil salesmen pretend to a gullible public and to our courts to know things—to have been *trained* in things—they cannot possibly know anything about, and pretend to be able to provide help they cannot possibly promise. Worse, professional organizations stand behind these claims of psychological expertise, not only by permitting advertising but by providing continuing education credit for what is nothing more than complete nonsense. Worse, our state governments license practitioners to make claims of expertise based on this same nonsense.

It *is* crucial that we determine whether someone will kill again or if a child will be harmed in a particular setting, whether someone is guilty of a particular action, when someone is lying. Because these matters are so vital, our courts are *desperate* for certainty and they search for this certainty beyond their own limitations.

In the current system of American jurisprudence, psychologists are asked to make these decisions under the assumption that they—unlike their poor, benighted, nonpsychological brethren—are specially trained and skilled at making these decisions. They are not. They cannot be.

Claims about psychological expertise are being made on and off the witness stand, and psychological "services" are being offered to the public by entrepreneurs who represent themselves as certified and licensed and expertly knowledgeable in matters about which they cannot possibly qualify as true experts because no one on earth could.

Let us be very clear about the true state of the psychologist's art. Psychologists do not know any more about behavior than the average man or woman in the jury box or the judge's robes. Psychologists do not know what causes behavior and they are entirely incapable of pinpointing some hypothetical event in the past that has led to the present state of an individual. They do not know what got done, how it got done, or whodunit. And not only are they unable to predict future behavior any better than the man or woman on the street, they are actually worse at it, blinded as they are by the illusion of their own expertise. Diagnostic categories are not validly established and diagnoses cannot be rendered reliably. Neither can therapy be reliably used to change the behavior of our citizens, juvenile or adult, violent or simply wayward.

Psychologists have no special ability to read into the soul—or mind or psyche—of another human with any more accuracy than the rest of us. Upon finishing graduate or medical school they are not given special soulographs or psychometers that let them plumb the depths of anyone's psychological being. There simply is no mental stethoscope, no matter how much our justice system wishes there were.

Clinicians are not trained to perform the myriad tasks the legal system asks them to perform because no body of knowledge exists to support such training. It is a sorry state of affairs, but it is the only state we've got.

5
Getting Away with Murder

Criminal Diagnostics

> Criminal defendants increasingly claim that their criminal behavior was caused by social toxins that excuse or mitigate their guilt. . . . These claims are not aberrational doctrinal proposals, but rather are sophisticated extensions of existing criminal doctrine commensurate with scientific advancements.
>
> Patricia Falk, "Novel Theories of Criminal Defense Based upon the Toxicity of the Social Environment," 1996

BATTERED WOMAN SYNDROME DEFENSE

> In 1978, a sophisticated insanity defense was used successfully to win the acquittal of a Michigan housewife, Francine Hughes, in the so-called "burning bed" case. The technical rationale for pleading temporary insanity was to make evidence of long-standing abuse admissible in court. The defense attorney, Ayron Greydanus, argued that the battering itself caused Hughes' insanity, not any frailty inherited with gender. (Stark 1995)

The battered woman syndrome defense is invoked increasingly these days in a number of trials for murder across the country in which a woman is charged with killing her man, or ex-man, under conditions that are less than a fair fight. She sets fire to his bed as he lies passed out, or shoots him as he sleeps, and she is charged with murder. In the past, the women in such cases were routinely tried, convicted, and sent off to the slammer, juries being notoriously unsympathetic to the crime of burning people alive as they sleep.

Drawing on fashionable dysfunctional family theory and traditional legal theories of diminished culpability, Arrested Feminist clinicians, along with their attorney cohorts, crafted a novel defense for the women in these cases. According to their reasoning, these battered women had been so abused by their men that they had lost the ability to act rationally, lost the ability to premeditate their actions, lost the ability to foresee the consequences, and lost the ability to control their behavior. The abuse they received at the hands of their men had rendered them utterly impotent, utterly without responsibility for anything they might do, and utterly without responsibility for the killing of their batterers.

Lenore Walker, who almost graced our television sets as a defense witness in O. J. Simpson's criminal murder trial, claims to have successfully employed the BWS defense in over 150 murder trials, though forensic psychologist Charles Patrick Ewing and others have questioned the basis for these claims. Reviewing twenty-six cases in which expert testimony on BWS was admitted, Ewing reports that in seventeen, roughly two out of three, the battered woman defendant was convicted of murder, manslaughter, or reckless homicide (Stark 1995).

In one third of the cases in which the BWS defense was allowed to be presented, the woman was acquitted. The same study found that in 100 percent of the cases in which the evidence was excluded, the women were convicted.

As a consequence of longtime abuse at the hands of their men, the women mounting a battered woman syndrome defense for their crimes claimed that they had been driven mad.

Yes, mad. The most poisonous, dangerous—deranged!—element of the battered woman syndrome defense is not the recognition that the ordinary rules of self-defense do not apply well to situations in which the two participants are of greatly differing physical stature. That would almost make some sense. We do, after all, have a number of laws that seem to rest on the assumption that if two 170-pound men are having a dispute wherein, for example, one fellow says to the other, "I'm going to kill you, you son of a bitch," and lunges forward, and the second guy whams his fist into the first's esophagus and crushes his windpipe, killing him, then it is not murder but self-defense.

Now, for a number of reasons like size and acculturation, this scenario runs into difficulties when we try to apply it to a man and a woman in a dispute. Women's advocates might well have made the claim that the customary male response to repeated insults and threats is unavailable to most women since the probable outcome of attempting to punch a threatening, insulting male is a vicious beating or even death at the hands of the male. Since realistic escape from the home into another life of economic strength and safety is generally an alternative that exists only in the minds of prosecutors, the battered woman in such a situation might well feel that knocking her assailant off as he sleeps or is passed out drunk is her only realistic way out of the situation. Given the number of women who try so hard to escape these men through the legitimate means of separation and restraining orders and who in the end are killed by them, she may well be right.

Is this inequality of strength and combat skill the basis of the battered woman syndrome defense? Of course not. We're dealing with a *mental illness syndrome* here. That a battered woman kills her man as he sleeps is not the sensible act of a person trapped in an impossible situation from which society will not rescue her. Oh, no. It is the crazy act of a mentally disordered woman driven mad by the conduct of her man. Arrested Feminist attorneys and the feminized psychology establishment have to see it that way. To see it as an act of power, of taking control, of actively, willfully killing the enemy, is completely out of keeping with seeing all women as the helpless victims of men. They'd rather see them as crazy than as taking charge as well as they can given realistic constraints. That is nuts.

Let's get the syndrome out of this defense and name it for what it is: women taking the law into their own hands when the law refuses to protect them from their men. Whatever juries might make of that, at least they won't be blinded by the dust of a pseudo-syndrome.

The Societal Family

The modern view that today's dysfunctional family is a microcosm of modern society as a whole is more than a metaphor for today's clinicians, it is a fundamental truth about the roles people play in life and the reasons they play them.

Under this view, the white males who constitute the establishment power structure in the country today are seen as the only members of society who have sufficient power to assume the general burden of accountability. Thus, white men as a group are responsible for the pain felt not only by women and children but by the disadvantaged as well.

Minorities outside the white power structure—principally blacks and Hispanics but also gay people, immigrants, drunks and druggies, the disabled, and . . . well, everyone who somehow qualifies as a member of the great disadvantaged class—are seen as morally equivalent to adult abused children. As such, they are not, cannot, and should not be held responsible for the shape of their lives or for changing that shape by taking any action. Broken in childhood and manipulated by outside forces they cannot resist, they cannot be held accountable for their behavior no matter how heinous the crime or how innocent their victims. This makes it impossible to conceptualize members of the "disadvantaged" as the masters of their own fates, as the captains of their own souls. As adult abused children, they could not be.

This grotesque characterization of the societal family, like the equally grotesque characterization of the nuclear family on which it is based, throws the weight of scientific psychological authority behind traditional liberal characterizations of society's problems and greatly strengthens liberal clout, especially in the legal system.

The characterization of disadvantaged and minority groups as infantilized victims of powerful white males automatically generates a million excuses for every possible minority failure or crime. This instantaneous dispensation from any responsibility for any wrongful act at all extends itself in a drowning wave of compassion even over the faces of the cruelest and most callous of murderers, including, for example, the youths who viciously beat and raped and murdered Kimberley Rae Harbour in Boston, and their New York counterparts who beat and raped and attempted to kill the jogger in Central Park several years ago.

Toxic Shock Syndromes

> Felicia Morgan, a Milwaukee teenager, . . . shot and killed another teenager when the latter refused to surrender posses-

> sion of a leather coat. Morgan used *urban psychosis* to support an insanity defense. Robin Shellow, Morgan's attorney, argued that her client's "traumatic childhood in a violent inner-city home and neighborhood created in her the urban counterpart of the post-traumatic stress disorders that affected some Vietnam veterans.
>
> [Dr.] Charles Ewing asserted that Morgan's condition was brought about by severe physical and mental abuse from her mother. [Dr.] James Garbarino testified about the deleterious effects of being the victim of and/or witness to violence on a daily basis.
>
> Morgan was convicted and sentenced to life in prison for armed homicide, armed robbery, and other charges. [But] the judge ruled that Morgan would be eligible for parole in the minimum time—thirteen years and four months, rather than the sixty years requested by the prosecution. (Falk 1996, p. 738)

> [T]hirty-year-old Turhan Taylor . . . grew up in a violent family in a tough neighborhood in Milwaukee. He had been abused as a child, sexually assaulted as a youth, and gang-raped in prison. During a flashback to the gang-rape, Taylor stabbed a sexual partner to death. In addition to *urban psychosis*, Taylor also claimed that he had rape-trauma syndrome. After the judge ruled that evidence of Taylor's PTSD was admissible at the guilt phase of the trial, the prosecutor reduced the charge and Taylor pleaded guilty to reckless homicide. (Falk 1996, p. 739–40)

Urban psychosis? What is that? Like battered woman syndrome, it is simply a natural extension of our old friend, post traumatic stress disorder. Just as we have women being driven mad by the traumas of rape and battering, so too are inner-city residents driven mad by "urban psychosis"—"the daily reality of violence in our nation's home, neighborhoods, and communities."

Dr. Patricia Falk, an assistant professor of law at Cleveland-Marshall College of Law, also claims that people can be driven nuts by having their minds "poisoned" by "television intoxication"—"the incessant barrage of graphic depictions of violence presented in the media," and by "black rage"—the persistence, if not resurgence, of racism despite the guarantee of legal equality."

I, for one, was happy to discover in the course of reading Professor Falk's review of cases that judges, juries, and courts at every level have been quite unresponsive to the argument that violent perpetrators are not responsible for their acts because they watched violent television, violent movies, or violent pornography.

The defenses of urban psychosis and black rage, however, have fared a little better in the courts, at least in terms of providing evidence of mitigating circumstances leading to a lesser charge or a reduced sentence. There is even a variation of urban psychosis available called urban survival syndrome, in which defendants claim that living in a violent, urban environment induces in them a mind-set of heightened fear and danger that in turn causes them to be violent.

> Prosecutors plan to retry a teen-ager whose lawyers won a mistrial yesterday after arguing that "urban survival syndrome" had forced him to gun down two other teen-agers with whom he had been feuding. . . . [Daimion] Osby's lawyers acknowledged that he had killed the men but said the two had threatened him with a shotgun the week before. The defense strategy centered on the claim that because Osby was raised in a poor, violent neighborhood, he suffered from "urban survival syndrome" and believed he had no alternative but to kill the men. (Compiled from dispatches, *Newsday*, April 21, 1994)

In his second trial, Osby was found guilty of two counts of capital murder on November 10, 1994 (AP, *New York Times*, November 13, 1994).

Perhaps the best known of the cases in which some version of the black rage defense has been invoked is that of Colin Ferguson, the 1994 mass murderer on the Long Island Rail Road who chose exclusively white, Asian, or "Uncle Tom" black victims (defined by Mr. Ferguson). He killed six and wounded nineteen passengers on the commuter train. He was convicted and sentenced to more than two hundred years in prison.

His defense attorney, William Kunstler, the noted liberal-radical lawyer, said:

> Ferguson's rage was a catalyst for violence resulting from a preexisting mental illness, most likely schizophrenia. It was a mental condition no different from the battered-wife syndrome, *post-traumatic stress disorder*, or the child-abuse-accommodation syndrome in that, in conjunction with mental illness, it gave rise to terrible acts of violence. Ferguson, from a wealthy Jamaican family, had attended private school, enjoyed many luxuries, and was never able to adjust to the white racism that he found when he came to this country. He never developed the defense mechanism that American-born blacks are forced to learn. (Falk 1996, p. 752)

This is not science. This is racism. The demand for accountability is not racism; the lack of such a demand for blacks certainly is.

Still, one cannot help but applaud the creative equal opportunity extension of PTSD to these uniquely minority exculpatory complaints.

As Patricia Falk above explains, it was the American Psychiatric Association that gave us, about fifteen years ago, what is today's most flexible and generally applicable mitigating defense, post traumatic stress syndrome.

POSTAL WORKER PTSD MURDER DEFENSE

> I saw flashes, flashes like incoming round hits, like fire crackers, hearing machine guns, I heard machine guns, I heard rifle fire, I heard more explosions and I couldn't move. I was happy because I knew I was going to die. (*State v. Felde*, 1982)

This is testimony from Wayne Felde, a Vietnam veteran accused of killing a police officer in Louisiana in 1982. It is a perfect example of what has become the classic PTSD-made-me-do-it defense—in all of its modern guises—against criminal charges.

Louisiana's first criminal defense based on PTSD, Mr. Felde's defense did not prevail. The jury found him guilty of first-degree murder and he was executed seven years later, in 1989, by the state of Louisiana.

But as Michael Davidson, in a 1988 *William and Mary Law Review* article on the history of PTSD, wrote, "Vietnam veterans have used PTSD successfully as an insanity defense against charges of murder, attempted murder, kidnapping, and drug smuggling. PTSD has also been used to mitigate sentences in convictions for crimes such as drug dealing, manslaughter, assault with intent to commit murder, and even tax fraud" (p. 423).

PTSD provides a compelling defense for both the public and the media because it has such a straightforward appeal to psychocultural mythology disguised as common sense. PTSD became popular during the minor epidemic of postal workers coming to work berserk, toting submachine guns they used to mow down their fellow workers. Because the Postal Service has an affirmative action program for veterans, most of these fellows were Vietnam-era vets. (Not all of them had been to Vietnam, but that's getting picky.)

Now, almost all of us can sympathize with the urge to blow at least some of our fellow workers to kingdom come, but we don't do it. It is not normal to blast away at people no matter how angry you are about the other fellow's promotion. So when someone comes to work spraying a submachine gun all over, we conclude that he is sick indeed.

How might a Vietnam-era vet have gotten sick? Well, from that sick war. For some people, the Vietnam war was sick because so many people did not support the actions of our government or of the men who were sent there to fight and to die. For others, the war was sick because of the apparent absence of clear-cut issues of good and evil.

It is not hard to accept that living through such a hell could poison the mind. It is not hard to believe that the terrible experiences of that war could so sear the mind that the soldier never wholly returns home, and although he may seem to function well, he is never truly okay. Along comes the straw that breaks the camel's back, and he snaps. He feels he is in hell again and he responds as he was trained to respond to hell. He blows enemies away with a gun.

That makes a great deal of intuitive sense in today's America, particularly when the defense is claimed by veterans of a war about which so many Americans feel conflicted. (Recently in Boston, the lawyer for a Mafia hit man who had served in Korea briefly floated the PTSD excuse for his client.)

> In its first five years of use [1980 to 1985], the PTSD defense has helped at least 250 Vietnam veterans get shorter sentences, treatment instead of jail, or acquittals. (Davidson 1988, p. 423)

That statistic should give all of us pause since some experts estimate that as many as 800,000 Vietnam combat veterans suffer from moderate to severe symptoms of PTSD. (Estimates vary from about 15 percent to 70 percent.)

Psychologists come along and validate our psychocultural beliefs about the fragility of personality and its vulnerability to stress, and tell us pseudo-science stories about the almost magical manipulation of memory by trauma. It was psychologists who came up with PTSD; it used to be called combat fatigue, and before that shell shock, and we now have an authoritative, scientific diagnosis to support what seems to us to be only common sense.

Modern feminist clinicians like psychiatrist Judith Herman of Harvard have adopted the notion that rape and combat are pretty much the same thing, so now the noncombatant who has experienced sexual assault, abuse, or battering can also claim to suffer from PTSD. It's an equal opportunity disorder.

For defense attorneys who would like an up-to-date guide on how to use post traumatic stress disorder as a defense at trial, and for prosecutors who would like to blow them out of the water, I strongly recommend the article by Roger Pitman, Landy Sparr, Linda Saunders, and Alex McFarlane, "Legal Issues in PTSD" in the 1996 book *Traumatic Stress*, edited by Bessel van der Kolk and others. It is also quite handy as a guide for using PTSD in disability suits.

DEFENSIVE DIAGNOSTICS, OR HE HAS A DISORDER SO HE'S NOT RESPONSIBLE

For better or worse, the American legal system incorporates the concept of diminished culpability in various forms. Passion, alcohol, insanity, and mental retardation in one guise or another all enter into the equation of personal responsibility for adults. "I was too angry/too drunk/too crazy/too stupid to bear the full weight of responsibility for my actions" are claims with a long tradition of acceptance in our legal system.

There have been a number of formulations of the insanity defense used in this country over the years, with applicability varying according to state law. Courts variously use one of three tests, the M'Naghten Rule, the irresistible impulse test, or some version of the American Law Institute (ALI) Model code definition of insanity.

The venerable M'Naghten Rule requires that at the time of committing the act, the defendant was operating under a mental illness that caused a defect of reason so that the defendant did not know the nature and quality of the act or did not know that what he or she was doing was wrong. Essentially, the defendant did not know right from wrong—the defendant suffered from a cognitive impairment.

The irresistible impulse test requires that as a result of mental disease or defect, the defendant lacked the capacity to *control* his or her actions or conform conduct to law—the defendant suffered from a "volitional" impairment. That is, the defendant may have known the conduct was wrong but could not stop himself or herself from doing it anyway.

The ALI test combines the two. In 1988 twenty-six states used some version of the ALI standard, twenty-two used the M'Naghten rule, and two, Idaho and Montana, had eliminated the defense of not guilty by reason of insanity altogether. Today, Utah too lacks this defense.

There is one final wrinkle in the disordered mind defense department: In some states it is also possible for a defendant to argue that he or she suffers not from insanity but from some mental state that diminishes either guilt or the ability to form the guilty intention to commit a crime.

> David Willard Phipps, Jr., a Gulf War veteran, was convicted of first-degree murder and sentenced to life imprisonment for killing his wife's lover, Michael Presson. Phipps did not deny killing Presson and did not plead insanity. Instead, he claimed that he was unable to formulate the *mens rea* for first-degree murder because he was suffering from depression and post-traumatic stress disorder. (*Tennessee v. Phipps*, 1994)

Judge Julian Guinn of Tennessee apparently thought this claim did not hold water and instructed the jury, "The defendant contends that he was suffering from mental conditions known as post-traumatic stress disorder and major depression at the time of the commission of the criminal offense giving rise to this case. I charge you that post-traumatic stress disorder and major depression are not defenses to a criminal charge." This judge also added that expert testimony is "beset with pitfalls and uncertainties" (*Tennessee v. Phipps*, 1994).

He was reversed on appeal for being unduly wary of expert psychological opinion and for failing to appreciate the other varieties of diminished accountability one could suffer given certain conditions—like our old friend PTSD. Too bad. Judge Guinn was the sanest person in that courtroom.

It is frequently reported that the insanity defense is used less than once in every one hundred criminal cases. Only 4 to 5 percent of these cases result in a verdict of innocent by reason of insanity. *Defense, Myths and Realities*, a report prepared by the National Commission on the Insanity Defense in 1983, stated that the insanity plea was rarely used and that acquittals were very rare. In Virginia, for example, less than 1 percent of the felony cases plead an insanity defense, according to a 1988 *William and Mary Law Review* article, and acquittals numbered no more than fifteen per year.

These statistics might make it seem that insanity defenses are rarely used and are even more rarely successful. Not true. It depends on what you mean by "insanity defense" and what you mean by "success." The statistics are true when we look only at straight cases of NGRI, Not Guilty by Reason of Insanity. When we start adding in cases in which a theory of defense based on some version of diminished mental ability induced the prosecutor to bring a lesser charge as well as cases in which the alleged mental condition reduced the amount of time served, the picture is quite different.

A June 1995 *Minnesota Law Review* article by John Henderson covering diminished capacity as a reason to reduce the sentences of criminals convicted in federal courts found that, in 1989, approximately 1.1 percent of those reductions were for diminished capacity (p. 1475). That is not so many; it is in line with the number usually quoted. In 1992, however, leaving aside reductions through plea bargaining, diminished capacity sentence reductions were almost 8 percent of the total. If the trend has continued—and with the proliferation of new, incapacitating diagnoses spewed out by the APA with its new manual, how could it not?—then the likely number of diminished capacity sentence reductions at the federal level alone by 1998 should be close to 25 percent of the total of reductions for cause in sentence to be served.

This number covers only federal cases in which defendants were already convicted and their sentences were reduced subsequently. It does not include charges or sentence reductions that occurred through plea bargaining.

The overwhelming majority of felony cases—85 to 95 percent—in this country do not come to trial. They are settled through plea bargaining.

Adding in state cases resulting not in acquittals—the defendant is not guilty because the defendant is insane, drunk, blinded by passion, etc.—but in convictions on a *reduced charge*—manslaughter, for example, instead of murder—plus convictions in which a lesser sentence is imposed, then the total number of felony cases in the United States in which some form of psychological defense claiming reduction in capacity to understand the crime or control criminal actions could account for between one third and one half of all felony convictions by 1998.

Why not simply abolish the insanity defense? Well, nothing is ever simple. The evaluation of intention is an intrinsic component of the evaluation of criminal responsibility in the United States, so, even in states that have abolished insanity as a straight defense, evidence of a mental illness or defect can cast doubt on the ability of the accused to have the required culpable state of mind for conviction.

In Montana, abolition of insanity as a substantive defense seems to have merely shifted disposition of cases involving impaired defendants, resulting in greater numbers of accused being diverted, pretrial, into civil commitment for treatment or release following findings that these defendants were incompetent to stand trial.

And in Utah:

> [T]wo years after Utah statutorily abolished the special defense of insanity, the clinical director of forensic psychiatry at Utah State Hospital, Peter Heinbecker, reviewed the state's experience. During the roughly ten years when the ALI standard was

> operative in Utah (1973–1983), only seven defendants were found NGRI [not guilty by reason of insanity]. In the two years following abolition of the special defense, however, another seven defendants were exculpated under the *mens rea* law. In other words, abolition of the more generous standard of exculpation was followed by a five-fold increase in the annual rate of successful mental state defense. (Applebaum 1994, pp. 182–83)

Whether the legal system's acceptance of psychological defenses based on diminished cognitive or volitional capacity is a good thing or bad is a matter of legal philosophy beyond the scope of this book. What's critical here is the role that modern psychology has played in offering its services as a sort of medical absolution, a clinical dispensation from responsibility.

At every point in the long process of bringing criminals to justice in America today, psychological experts have the opportunity to offer a diagnosis of mental disorder to mitigate the awfulness of the offense.

Not Competent to Stand Trial

At the very beginning of a potential court case, before the issue of insanity as a defense even arises, the accused is examined to determine competency to stand trial. Competency generally means that the accused is capable of assisting in his or her own defense. Leona Helmsley's husband, Harry Helmsley, for example, suffered from advanced Alzheimer's disease and was judged not competent to assist in his own defense in the tax avoidance case in which his wife was convicted.

Competency to stand trial is determined by a court-appointed forensic psychologist. In most cases these evaluators work for the state or for a private company contracted to the state to provide forensic services. In Massachusetts, the seven forensic evaluators who work out of Bridgewater State Hospital evaluate about one thousand cases a year. Since Massachusetts has about twice the average state population, a fair estimate of the number of such evaluations is about 27,000 nationally per year, at least in recent years. In Massachusetts, the state-employed evaluators earn an average of $80,000 a year in salary and benefits. (In the spring of 1996 the whole group of seven state evaluators quit briefly in a dispute over salary and workload.)

The essential point of psychological competency evaluation is this: If the defendant does not pass #1, he or she will not get to #2. If the forensic clinician does not determine that the defendant can assist in his or her own defense, then that defendant will not stand trial for the crime of which the defendant is accused.

If the judge chooses to bypass or ignore the recommendations of competency evaluators, the trial verdict is in grave danger of being overturned.

On January 26, 1994, the Massachusetts Supreme Judicial Court found the *absence* of a disabling diagnosis reason to overturn the murder conviction of Alfred J. Hunter, who was charged with shooting his wife on May 9, 1989, then stealing a plane to buzz Boston while firing an assault rifle.

> An inmate who shared a van ride with Hunter from Salem District Court to Bridgewater State hospital testified that Hunter said he was angry with his wife for taking him to court and making him sleep in his car. The same man also said that Hunter told him he was not under the influence of drugs or alcohol at the time of the killing. A second man, who shared a holding cell with Hunter at Salem District Court on May 10, 1989, said Hunter told him he shot his wife once in each breast, once in the head and once in the crotch because she had "cheated on him, and kicked him out of the house." (Nealon, *Boston Globe*, January 27, 1994)

The court ruled that the trial judge erred because he did *not* hold hearings to allow a court psychiatrist to testify that the accused was mentally incompetent when he confessed his crime to his jailhouse cronies.

Why did the Supreme Judicial Court believe the psychiatrist was a better judge of character than the judge himself?

This court's decision incidentally provides a piece of pretty good advice for prospective murderers: During or after the murder, do something so gruesome or so bizarre that you get yourself shipped off to the criminal funny farm for evaluation. This gives you a shot at a diagnosis of some form of diminished responsibility. If you do get convicted despite the best efforts of your psychological experts to slap a mentally ill label on your actions, then the disabling diagnosis can be called into play at the time of sentencing or on appeal. If they don't ship you off for evaluation and you are convicted of your crime, then you've got a shot at an appeal because of their omission.

Richard Rosenthal of Framingham, Massachusetts, who in September 1995 choked his wife, broke both of her arms, beat her to death with a rock, and then cut out her heart and lungs and impaled them on a garden stake, provides an excellent example of this maneuver. His behavior certainly seems crazy, does it not?

Rosenthal was sent to the state hospital after his arrest, but what if he had not been evaluated for competency to stand trial, what if he had been treated like any other accused murderer and sent to jail if he couldn't make bail? Then, like Mr. Hunter, who also killed his wife, Mr. Rosenthal, if convicted, would have had an excellent shot at an appeal based on the lack of a competency examination.

Decisions like that of the Massachusetts Supreme Judicial Court overturning Hunter's conviction on such grounds remove all judgmental discretion from the judge—and, of course, ultimately from the jury—and hand it directly to the professional psychologist, whom the Supreme Judicial Court clearly believes is a reliably superior judge of an individual's competence to stand trial.

Where did the court get that idea?

Why aren't grand juries granted the power to assess competence just as they are granted the power to decide whether to indict an individual for a crime? If they can weigh the evidence of guilt, why are they presumed to be incapable of weighing the evidence for and against competence?

Grand juries are presumed to be incapable of making this difficult evaluation because the psychological establishment has convinced laypersons that they are too ignorant to render valid decisions about the psychological competence of their fellows. The psychology establishment has convinced the lawmakers—if not *all* the judges and prosecutors—that matters psychological are best left in the hands of the professional psychologists. When they are not, a miscarriage of justice has occurred.

Most important, in the spring of 1996, the forensic psychology establishment carried the day with the Supreme Court and convinced the highest court in the land that only the trained psychological professional, and not the poor benighted judge, had the necessary skills, intelligence, and perception to determine the mental ability of the accused to stand trial. If a judge overrules the professionals, an appeals court will overrule the judge.

SUPREME BAMBOOZLING

In 1989, Byron Cooper brutally killed an eighty-six-year-old man in the course of a burglary. An Oklahoma jury found him guilty of first-degree murder and recommended punishment by death. The trial court imposed the death penalty and the Oklahoma Court of Criminal Appeals affirmed the conviction and the sentence.

The case went to the United States Supreme Court. The following is taken from the Supreme Court's summary and judgment in that case.

Mr. Cooper's competence to stand trial was assessed on five different occasions before and during his trial for murder. The first time, a pretrial judge relied on the opinion of a clinical psychologist employed by the state and found the defendant incompetent to stand trial. He committed him to a mental hospital for treatment. After three months in the hospital the defendant was apparently cured of his incompetence and was released from the hospital. Now the trial judge heard testimony from two state-employed psychologists who disagreed with each other about the defendant's ability to participate in his defense. The judge agreed with the psychologist who said the defendant was competent, and ordered Mr. Cooper to stand trial for murder.

One week before the trial was to begin, the lead defense attorney raised the question of competence yet again, explaining to the court that Cooper "was behaving oddly and refusing to communicate with him. Defense counsel opined that it would be a serious matter 'if he's not faking.' " The judge listened but decided again that the defendant was competent.

Then, on the first day of the trial, the defendant's bizarre behavior prompted the court to conduct yet another competency hearing, this time with testimony from several lay witnesses, a third psychologist, and the defendant himself. Bizarre behavior means that the defendant refused to wear street clothes for the trial because they would burn him, communed with a spirit who gave him counsel, feared that his attorney was trying to kill him, and remained throughout much of the hearing crouched in the fetal position, talking to himself.

The psychological expert "concluded that petitioner was presently incompetent and unable to communicate effectively with counsel, but that he could probably achieve competence within six weeks if treated aggressively. While stating that he did not dispute the psychologist's diagnosis, the trial judge ruled against the petitioner," expressing his uncertainty in the following terms:

"Well, I think I've used the expression . . . in the past that normal is like us. Anybody that's not like us is not normal, so I don't think normal is a proper definition that we are to use with incompetence. My shirtsleeve opinion of Mr. Cooper is that he's not normal. Now, to say he's not competent is something else. . . . But you know, all things considered, I suppose it's possible for a client to be in such a predicament that he can't help his defense and still not be incompetent. I suppose that's a possibility, too.

"I think it's going to take smarter people than me to make a decision here. I'm going to say that I don't believe he has carried the burden by clear and convincing evidence of his incompetency and I'm going to say we're going to go to trial."

At the end of the trial, the defense attorney moved again for a renewed analysis of his client's competence, to no avail. (Summarized from *Cooper v. Oklahoma*, No. 95–5207, Supreme Court of the United States, 1996.)

The case went to the U.S. Supreme Court in 1996. What did the Supreme Court justices decide? They sent Mr. Cooper back to the psychologists—to the professional judges of competence and sanity—for yet another competency hearing. The first four must have persuaded the justices of the utility of such a move. They noted, "The Oklahoma Court of Criminal Appeals correctly observed that the 'inexactness and uncertainty' that characterize competency proceedings may make it difficult to determine whether a defendant is incompetent or malingering," but they were not much dismayed by that prospect, having, as they apparently did, considerable faith in the skills of trained psychologists to diagnose not only mental illness but legal insanity and incompetence.

The Court said, "We presume . . . that it is unusual for even the most artful malingerer to feign incompetence successfully for a period of time while under professional care."

Why in heaven's name do they presume that when the evidence

so clearly contradicts it? Faced with the clear inability of Mr. Cooper's numerous licensed, certified, state-employed professional forensic evaluators to agree on the matter, why would the justices send this defendant to yet another? Or back to the same for another evaluation? Are forensic psychological decisions supposed to mirror the four out of seven games for the World Series?

The need to believe in the competence and special skills of the forensic psychologist is evident, the will to believe distressingly obvious, and the lack of any foundation for the belief is equally and far more distressingly clear.

The Supreme Court justices are willing participants in their own bamboozling and in the bamboozling of the American people.

In well over 100 cases since 1844, the Supreme Court has ruled that psychological evaluations are essential to the pursuit of justice. They ruled that they are a critical factor in resolution of questions of competence in 48 cases; insanity in 51 cases (some overlapping with the competence cases); determination of mental and emotional injury, disability, and psychological trauma in 19 cases; deciding questions of custody and fitness in 15 cases; treatment in 42 cases; determining the possibility of rehabilitation of youthful offenders (most of whom had been sentenced to death) in 15 cases; and various other matters psychological.

The need to believe that the determination of competence—and of sanity—can be made scientifically, certainly, absolutely, clearly, that the determination can be and will be made on the basis of some evidence of far greater weight and reliability than the opinions of judges, breathes through every paragraph of the justices' decision.

The Best Defense Is a Good Diagnosis

Once the court-appointed forensic clinician has determined that the accused is competent to stand trial, more psychoexperts are called in by the defense to diagnose the defendant with various disorders and disabilities that diminish his or her personal accountability to the point that criminal guilt is greatly lessened and often even completely dissipated, while other experts are called by the prosecution to rebut these claims.

At trial, Richard Rosenthal, the Massachusetts man who murdered his wife in such a vicious and "bizarre" manner, had several psychiatrists testify for him that he had just about every delusion ever suggested in the casebook for the DSM. Perhaps he read it before meeting with his experts. Might as well cover all the bases. (Actually, since Rosenthal did not cooperate with his competency evaluators—funny concept that, is it not?—and was subsequently convicted of first-degree murder, perhaps his appeal on incompetency grounds will prevail.)

Of course, this whole business of putting on opposing experts is by no means cheap.

> [For Rosenthal's trial, t]he state hired Dr. Park Dietz of Newport Beach, Calif., one of the nation's leading prosecution psychiatrists, reportedly at $350 an hour plus first-class accommodations, food, expenses and airfare.
>
> Prosecutor Martin Murphy would only reveal that Dietz conducted 15 hours of interviews, but didn't say how much time he spent on reports the state never introduced.
>
> The state will also get a bill for at least 160 hours of work by Dr. Alison Fife, a psychiatrist who charges up to $250 hourly.
>
> But they faced a defendant with deep pockets, a high-profile case and the almost unheard-of fact that Rosenthal had cut out his wife's heart and lungs. . . . The defense sunk tens of thousands of dollars—they would not reveal numbers—into Chatham psychiatrist Dr. Marc Whaley, Belmont psychiatrist Dr. Larry Strasburger and Dr. James Butcher, a national expert on a personality test called the Minnesota Multiphasic Personality Inventory. (Talbot, *Boston Herald*, November 8, 1996)

Hey, if you have to ask how much it costs to be found crazy, you can't afford it.

Making Up Their Minds

> SEATTLE. A Montana woman believed to have a rare psychological disorder has been charged with allegedly injecting bacteria into her 4-year-old son, who had to have his gall bladder removed and nearly died, prosecutors said yesterday. Police who arrested Nashelle Wood, 24, at Children's Hospital in Seattle found a needle and syringe contaminated with the potentially fatal E. coli bacteria in her pocket. Prosecutors said they believe

> the mother has Munchausen's Syndrome by Proxy, a rare condition in which a parent exposes a child to medical danger as a way to get attention. (*Orlando Sentinel*, February 15, 1995)

Actually, Munchausen's Syndrome by Proxy is an interesting defense diagnosis because it is usually made by prosecutors, or by physicians bringing the charge to prosecutors. One doctor at Children's Hospital in Seattle, Jacqueline Farwell, has diagnosed four separate cases. It is odd. One would think that such a diagnosis would obviate the possibility of any prosecution. If the parent harmed the child because she was crazy with a "syndrome," then she needs help. If she harmed the child but had no syndrome, then she should be prosecuted. Strange too is the fact that harming the child is not prima facie evidence of illness yet the means of effecting the harm is, so Susan Smith is guilty of murder but Ms. Wood above is guilty of Munchausen's Syndrome. Strange.

How do psychoexperts hired by the defense (or prosecution, of course) determine that the accused is or is not sane enough to be found guilty of the crime of which he or she is accused, or that the responsibility of the accused for the crime is vastly diminished by mental illness? How do evaluators conclude that a defendant was suffering from an incapacitating disorder weeks or months before evaluator and defendant have ever met?

On December 30, 1994, John Salvi, carrying two guns, walked into the PreTerm clinic in Brookline, Massachusetts, and shot the receptionist to death. He returned to the street, got in his car, and then drove down Beacon Street to the Planned Parenthood clinic, where he again shot a young female clerk to death. In the course of committing these two murders, Salvi wounded two other people.

> Park Dietz, a psychiatrist in Newport Beach, California, who as a witness for the prosecution helped convict Jeffrey L. Dahmer, the Milwaukee serial killer, said he believed that the key question for a jury is not whether a defendant is sick but whether he knew what he was doing was wrong.
>
> To reach a verdict, Dr. Dietz suggested, the best evidence for a jury is the defendant's behavior immediately surrounding the crime. If a suspect called 911 after killing someone and said he had just rid the world of demons, he is probably ill,

> Dr. Dietz said. If the killer changed clothes and washed off the blood, he probably knew what he did was wrong. (Butterfield, *New York Times*, March 4, 1996)

Not so, says Dr. Phillip Resnick, testifying for the defense:

> Dr. Resnick testified that Mr. Salvi knew the legal consequences of his actions and tried to prevent his capture. But, Dr. Resnick insisted, Mr. Salvi's delusions governed his mind so completely that he was unable to understand the "moral wrongfulness" of his acts and . . . was legally insane. (Butterfield, *New York Times*, March 4, 1996)

What is the point of asking a highly paid psychological expert whether trying to escape indicates awareness of the need to escape? This accomplishes nothing but the subversion of the legal system by fraudulent claims of psychoexpertise.

What the jury must consider basically is what made Salvi act as he did. Was it a crazy delusion that if true would have made the killing justifiable, so he should be found not guilty by reason of insanity? Was it a belief that although shared by many would still not give a private citizen a license to kill, so Salvi should be found guilty of murder? Or was it some other motive entirely unrelated to the whole issue of abortion, like attention getting or thrill seeking, so again he should be found guilty of murder? These are very hard questions to decide. But there is nothing that a so-called psychological expert can do or say about the state of the defendant's mind that would assist the jury to reach a more just decision. Nothing. These "experts" do not and cannot know these things any better than you or I or the average layperson in the jury box.

The jurors in John Salvi's trial did not buy the defense psychologist's argument that Salvi's guilt was absolved or even diminished by his alleged delusions; they reached the conclusion that he was guilty of first-degree murder. But why were they subjected to the time and money-wasting farce of listening to "experts" testify about matters about which they cannot possibly know anything different from what the jurors know?

Why do the professional organizations like APA tolerate this farce? Why don't they blow them all away for malpractice?

Why do judges allow these hired experts—defense and prosecution—to pour personal opinions into the ears of jurors with those personal opinions rhetorically disguised as expert, scientific opinions when they are no such thing?

Why do lawmakers, judges, and prosecutors tolerate this farce?

We know why the defense does it—because sometimes it works. What is the excuse for the rest of the officers of the court?

Some diagnosticians take only a few minutes to reach a diagnosis, others take numerous sessions with the client. Seldom will the clinician ask other people what's been going on with old Charlie lately, although he certainly must take into account the unfortunate fact that Charlie was arrested for shoving a stranger onto the subway tracks in front of an oncoming train. Occasionally family members and friends come in for consultation. Usually, however, there is very little relationship between behavior corroborated or directly observed by the forensic evaluator and the diagnosis he or she reaches.

Brief Psychotic Disorder

Consider a hypothetical case in which the insanity defense rests on the mental diagnosis of brief psychotic disorder. This defense, which has gone under various names in the different versions of the diagnostic manual, is very useful for those defendants who have no history at all of mental illness to call upon.

Brief psychotic disorder is characterized by any *one*, *only one*, of the following symptoms—delusions, hallucinations, disorganized speech, or grossly disorganized or catatonic behavior—and the symptom has to last *more than one day and not more than a month "with eventual full return to premorbid level of functioning"* (*Diagnostic and Statistical Manual of the American Psychiatric Association*, 1994, p. 302).

First, the evaluator interviews the accused:

"Last Thursday, when I killed her, Doc, I heard voices all day long. Something in my head kept saying she was a devil who would eat my liver if I didn't kill her first. When I woke up Friday in jail the voices were gone. And so was Mary."

And the evidence to back up this claim that the defendant/client suffered from delusions or hallucinations last Thursday? Well, there is none except from the accused's own mouth, but who can dispute it?

Are there objective diagnostic tests to see if the accused is telling the truth? Well, no. Do the psychoexperts actually have any objective basis at all for distinguishing false claims of delusions from true delusionary claims, so to speak? No, of course not. How could they? There is no such thing as a secret delusionary litmus paper given out in graduate school.

The most impressive thing about this particular diagnosis—brief psychotic disorder—however, is the retrospective clairvoyance the evaluator must possess in order to reach it.

After all, this is a twenty-four-hour disorder that would quite naturally—if you will pardon the expression—have come and gone long before the psychoexpert could even have laid eyes on the defendant. How is the clinician supposed to be able to diagnose what the patient's condition was at the time of the crime last week or last month or last year? Apparently courtroom diagnosticians all possess the highly specialized skill of retrospective clairvoyance.

Do clinicians actually do this? Do judges and juries actually listen to expert psychological testimony that defendants suffer from fleeting, in-the-past, incapacitating mental illnesses that, however brief, nevertheless should absolve the accused of guilt for the crime?

Oh, yes.

Eric Smith and Explosiveness Disorder

In the murder trial of Eric Smith, a teenager from western New York who bludgeoned a four-year-old boy to death and violently sodomized him with a stick, the defense, through its psychoexpert, claimed that Eric suffered from intermittent explosive disorder.

> Testimony by a defense psychiatrist portrayed him as an immature 13-year-old at the time of the crime, with a low-average I.Q., and severe problems of self-esteem. . . . In relating the impulses that led him to kill a small boy on a chance encounter, Eric described the moment to the psychiatrist as "a mad switch" that vented anger building within himself and directed it on a child who was "smaller and practically helpless." (Nordheimer, *New York Times*, November 8, 1994)

The good news is that the jury didn't buy the story, but what is this pseudo-witness doing in a courtroom testifying about criminal responsibility?

The psychiatrist concluded from Eric's mad switch story that Eric suffered from an incapacitating explosive disorder—mad switchitis—that washed away the guilt for the murder of an innocent child. Retrospective clairvoyance allows this expert to know with certainty that this disorder was incapacitating Eric at the time of his crime even before the expert had ever met Eric. Apparently this clinician's intuition functions as a time machine to allow him to see into the past. (He could not possibly have believed that the mad switch tale alone was sufficient to make a reliable and accurate diagnosis of a mental illness so serious as to excuse this crime.)

Seemingly it would take tremendous nerve to get up on the witness stand and testify as to the mental condition of a defendant at a time weeks or months before the clinical exam, but there seem to be a good many clinical practitioners with more than enough nerve. Moreover, retrospective diagnostic clairvoyance is not confined just to forensic evaluations in murder cases. It is all over the courts.

Bipolar Embezzler

In a Boston trial in which a prominent cardiologist was accused of embezzling a fair amount of money from both colleagues and hospital, a defense psychoexpert testified confidently as to the cardiologist's state of mind at the time the money went missing:

> Dr. John Maltsberger [testified] that Nadal-Ginard was subject to so-called bipolar mood disorder, which caused mood swings that made him arrogant and energetic at some times and deeply depressed and self-doubting at others. The mood disorder made it impossible for Nadal-Ginard to appreciate whether his actions were criminal, Maltsberger said. (Langner, *Boston Globe*, May 17, 1995)

How would Dr. Maltsberger know what Dr. Nadal-Ginard was thinking the year before? He wouldn't, but I do think it was a bold attempt to defend the indefensible. It didn't fly, but on the grounds of chutzpah alone, it deserves points.

How do I know? The patient told me so.

In a recent case in Arizona, the defendant claimed that his failure to pay income tax resulted from the disorder of pathological gambling. He claimed that one of the associated features of this disorder was "distortions in thinking," which kept him from realistically appraising the extent of his winnings and losses. The federal judge took these claims very seriously, carefully weighing which parts of the mental illness defense met federal criteria for admissibility and which did not, relying very heavily on the particular edition of the DSM in use at the time of the crime to decide which symptoms were legit and which were not. I cannot help but wonder if that judge has any idea at all of the procedures for deciding which symptoms will be included and which excluded from the diagnostic bible. I also cannot withhold my admiration for a defense based truly on nothing but chutzpah. It will be interesting to see if it flies. After all, pathological gambling is a disorder in the current DSM, so the guy is sick, is he not, if he can find an expert to testify that he is. That should not be hard.

What is diagnosis of this order doing in court? What is it doing in our courts every day? Why are psychoexperts of every persuasion welcomed into our courts to make a pitch to judge and jury that somebody should be granted a dispensation from the rules of decent society and absolved from guilt for any little unpleasant action like cheating on income taxes or murdering a spouse because the person was suffering from "organic personality disorder," "pathological gambling disorder," or an "involuntary dependence on alcohol"?

The highly paid professional conducts brief interviews, puts a mental disorder stamp on the defendant's forehead, and responsibility for murder goes poof? The psychoexpert has no basis for making such a diagnosis. He or she has no special ability to see into the client's soul at the present time and certainly lacks the clairvoyance necessary to determine the particulars of the defendant's past history.

Perhaps one of the most astounding examples of the modern clinicians' belief in total clinical clairvoyance—not to mention nonverbal telepathy—appears in cases in which the forensic psychologist is asked to perform a psychological evaluation of an animal to check out the beastie's mental health—its past mental health, that is, at the time of the "crime."

> A large dog will be undergoing court-ordered psychiatric examination after it bit and disfigured a 2-year-old girl.
>
> Justice David B. Saxe of State Supreme Court in Manhattan ordered the exam on Friday to determine whether the dog, a 7-year-old Akita owned by her grandmother, had vicious tendencies before its attack on the toddler, Sarah Engstrand, in her aunt's home in Huntington Bay, L.I., on September 5, 1994.
>
> Guy Gabizon, a lawyer for Wende A. Doniger, Sarah's mother, said that to collect damages in dog bite cases in New York, a plaintiff must show that the dog is "vicious." (*New York Times*, September 29, 1996)

STARING THEM RIGHT IN THE EYES

Conversely, clinicians are quite obviously unable to see what is right before their eyes. Making evaluations of clients after the crimes have been committed, forensic clinicians clairvoyantly gaze into the past through the crystal ball of clinical intuition; for patients right in front of their faces, however, clinicians are too blind to see imminent homicide, suicide, or family abandonment.

Brian Gaboriault, the Fairhaven, Massachusetts, man who stabbed to death his infant son and the boy's mother, had seen his therapist just one or two days before the killings. Presumably the therapist was unaware of any danger to the young man's family or he would have issued a warning to the authorities or to the murdered woman herself.

Sinedu Tadesse, the Harvard junior who stabbed her roommate dozens and dozens of times as she lay sleeping, killing her, and who then hanged herself, had been seeing a therapist at the Harvard Student Services for two years. Again, imminent homicide and suicide seemed to have escaped the therapist's notice.

It is depressingly clear that the patient's behavior—his or her "symptoms"—provide no clue to the therapist of the present state of mind or intentions of the patient. Yet, on the witness stand, hired evaluators claim their observations of clients are reliable indicators of past states of mind and motivations. Our courts buy this foolish claim over and over again.

Malingering or Pretending to Be Nuts

Forensic psychoexperts, whether they work for the court or for the defendant, claim they can determine through their interviews and their tests—and, of course, their much-vaunted clinical intuition—who is or is not competent to stand trial and who is or is not insane. With their supposedly finely honed skills and instruments, they can weed out the sick from the sane, the guilty from the psychologically not-so-guilty, and the fakes from the true sufferers.

Given the alarmingly shaky foundations of their enterprise, it would be logically impossible for them actually to be able to do so. People have said this for years. It falls on deaf ears. So what happens when you actually test it out? Can clinical evaluators even tell the truly sick from those who are faking it? A diagnostic mix-up here and there is only to be expected, but surely the trained professionals can at least pick up on the malingers. Or can they?

The famous 1973 study by David Rosenhan on being sane in insane places is a perfect illustration of the old adage, "There are none so blind as those who will not see." Rosenhan and eight accomplices (all sane) gained admission to psychiatric hospitals in five states on both coasts by complaining that they heard voices. Immediately after admission, all the pseudo-patients stopped faking their auditory hallucinations, responded honestly to staff members' questions about significant life events, and attempted to interact normally in all respects with the staff. All this conspicuous normalcy made no impression whatsoever on the staff. All but one of the "patients" were diagnosed as schizophrenic and not a one was detected as a fake.

In a second experiment, the team alerted hospital staff to the possibility of fake patients showing up, but even a forewarned staff was incompetent at distinguishing the sane from the insane. Staff did indeed judge 10 to 20 percent of the new admissions to be faking, but, alas, none of them were members of the experimental team.

Other than the usual clinical intuition aided by selective amnesia and the confirmatory bias, what other evaluative tools does the forensic diagnostician employ in assessing competence to stand trial or responsibility for criminal acts?

PSYCHOLOGICAL ASSESSMENT INSTRUMENTS

Ordinary clinicians, when not required to explain or justify their conclusions in courtrooms, usually reach their diagnoses using precisely the interview techniques described earlier. But forensic psychologists, or any clinician who is called to the witness stand, speedily resort to another technique to buttress those vulnerable opinions: testing.

Laypersons believe that forensic psychological evaluators have tests to detect any number of mental disorders, dysfunctions, and disabilities, as well as tests to tell who is faking it. And, indeed, courtroom psychologists employ a dizzying array of tests designed to bolster their conclusions and blind the opposition.

The most frequently used personality tests are the MMPI and the Rorschach. As we have already seen, these tests are useless even for arriving at conventional diagnoses of mental illness. What possible utility can they have for determining the competency or sanity of an individual in a criminal case? None whatsoever.

If you ask a forensic evaluator why he or she employs tests of such shoddy validity and ephemeral reliability, the evaluator will tell you that some set of scales or other, some "profile" or "code" correlates in some study somewhere with some aspect of behavior of individuals who have been diagnosed with mental illness. With some nine thousand such correlational studies, that is bound to be true. It is also vacuous nonsense.

There are no valid or reliable psychological tests for determining legal competency to stand trial. There are no psychological tests for determining legal insanity.

Individual evaluators use whatever strikes their fancy and rely on their clinical intuition for interpretation of the results.

There are no special tests, no secret skills, no "expert" clinical method for determining either competence or insanity. There is nothing but the standard diagnostic techniques, and they cannot even do the job for which they were designed.

WE DIDN'T SAY THEY WERE *LEGALLY* INSANE

Putting aside for the moment the issue of validity and reliability, does a particular diagnosis like brief psychotic disorder or PTSD mean that the accused is truly "unable to assist in his own defense" or, at the time of the crime, was "unable to appreciate the wrongfulness of his acts," or "unable to conform his behavior to the law," or any of the various state-by-state formulations of diminished accountability for crime due to some mental impairment? No, in reality it does not, but oftentimes in the courtroom it does.

> A judge ruled today that a man accused of stabbing and beating four nuns, killing two of them, is not criminally responsible because of mental illness.
>
> Justice Donald Alexander of Superior Court committed the man, Mark Bechard, 38, to the custody of state mental health officials indefinitely. He will not face further criminal penalty for attacking the nuns at their Waterville convent in January. Whether he ever goes free depends on his mental condition.
>
> "The facts of this case are this, that Mark Bechard is severely ill, he came into this world biologically cursed," Mr. Bechard's lawyer, Michaela Murphy, said during closing arguments in the nonjury trial.
>
> . . . [The prosecutor, Assistant Attorney General Eric] Wright, said the assault had more to do with Mr. Bechard's history of violence than with his mental illness.
>
> "The truth is this defendant goes off when he doesn't get his way and that's what happened here." (*New York Times*, October 17, 1996)

Put as baldly as possible, having a screw loose does not mean that you cannot choose to do right. Hearing voices does not mean that you cannot choose to disobey their instructions. No mental illness required Joan of Arc to go to war in order to put Charles VII of France on the throne, no matter how compelling she found the apparently divine command to do so.

Consider the case of the young woman in New York who last year slashed a woman's face on the subway. She had a history of mental illness. Was she compelled to slash a stranger's face? She got rid of the knife and waited to be arrested. She knew if she was not holding the knife she would not get hurt, and she knew that with her history she would not be punished for cutting the woman's face. What did she have to lose? Nothing.

A diagnosis of mental illness does not imply anything definite about the level of functioning or degree of impairment of a particular individual in a particular situation.

In fact, the American Psychiatric Association is at pains in its new manual to point out the lack of any relationship.

> In determining whether an individual meets a specified legal standard (e.g., for competence, criminal responsibility, or disability), additional information is usually required beyond that contained in the DSM-IV diagnosis. . . . It is precisely because impairments, abilities, and disabilities vary widely within each diagnostic category that assignment of a particular diagnosis does not imply a specific level of impairment or disability.
>
> Moreover, the fact that an individual's presentation meets the criteria for a DSM-IV diagnosis does not carry any necessary implication regarding the individual's degree of control over the behaviors that may be associated with the disorder. Even when diminished control over one's behavior is a feature of the disorder, having the diagnosis in itself does not demonstrate that a particular individual is [or was] unable to control his or her behavior at a particular time. (*Diagnostic and Statistical Manual of the American Psychiatric Association*, 1994, p. xxiii)

Do all these disclaimers slow down the defensive diagnostician? No, indeed not. Despite lip service to the possibility that a mentally ill individual *might* be able to exert control over his or her actions, the American Psychiatric Association, through the offices of its ever-expanding diagnostic manual, has medicalized not only the concept of diminished accountability but all criminal conduct as well.

The Criminal Mind and the Sick Brain

Mental diagnoses are described by the American Psychiatric Association as a subset of medical diagnoses. That is, mental disorders are supposed to be simply another category of all the physical disorders that plague humankind. The authors of the newest version of the manual actually apologize for using the term "*mental* disorder," explaining that "mental disorder unfortunately implies a distinction between mental disorders and physical disorders" (*Diagnostic and Statistical Manual of the American Psychiatric Association*, 1994, p. xxi).

Now, clearly, the implied biological source of mental disorders is not the foot or even the heart; it's the brain. That means that for each of the almost four hundred different mental disorders recognized by the American Psychiatric Association, the association is claiming that there must be a different kind of organic brain dysfunction.

The unhappy truth, however, is that medicine in fact does *not* have the faintest idea of the biological mechanisms postulated to be the causes of the overwhelming majority of the disorders it has classified in the mental diagnostic manual.

Nevertheless, the APA's assumption of a biologically determined cause for every mental disorder in their nine-hundred-page diagnostic manual has led clinical practitioners in a stunning logical non sequitur to attribute all bad behavior to brain damage, and, indeed, to dismiss the whole idea of personal responsibility for behavior.

Whatever the cause of the mental disorder—abuse, alcohol, trauma, imminent menses, badly wired brain synapses, or degeneration of the brain cells—the perpetrator of the crime is a disabled, sick person who should not be held accountable for actions as he or she would be if well. How can we send victims of pyromania or pathological gambling, for example, to prison for behavior stemming from a condition beyond their control? How can we throw people with serious, medically bona fide mental disorders into prison for conditions and behaviors they can't control?

Because even some members of the psychological community are aware that proliferating diagnoses of mental disorders inevitably proliferate defenses against criminal charges as well, there was considerable controversy surrounding the inclusion of certain diagnostic categories in the last two revisions of the official diagnostic manual. One of the proposed disorders was paraphilic rapism, a condition in which the "sufferer" is said to experience intense sexual arousal while fantasizing about rape. This is a disorder that would lead one, quite naturally, to commit rape. Can you blame the poor guy? He's sick.

Intense political pressure quashed this diagnosis but I think that's unfair. It's right in keeping with the belief that there are no bad people, only sick and injured ones.

The inclusion of PMS, premenstrual syndrome, excited considerable controversy before the DSM-IV was finalized because including it in the manual would both stigmatize hundreds of thousands of women as raving lunatics three days a month and simultaneously provide them with a diminished accountability excuse for crimes committed during these times. Feminist practitioners led the assault against including this diagnostic category in the revised manual, but society as a whole has just as great an interest in the exercise of common sense in defensive diagnosis as do feminist psychologists. (PMS wound up in Appendix B in the new manual under "insufficient information to warrant inclusion," in the hope that further study will clarify the issue.)

LIBERAL INSANITY

Liberals who have swallowed the claims of mental health professionals about everything from the reliability of diagnosis to the effectiveness of treatment find themselves these days in an interesting dilemma.

Occasionally, persons who have been treated for mental illness in the past commit crimes that catch the public's attention. In Massachusetts two years ago, one inmate at a new neighborhood halfway house attacked a staff member while another attacked one of the neighbors. In Maine recently a past patient stabbed to death two elderly nuns in a cloistered convent; in New York City a fifteen-year-old patient was accused lately of shoving a young woman to her death on the subway tracks during a robbery attempt; in Massachusetts a mental patient who murdered his parents was seeking release in the spring of 1996 after two decades of treatment, having been found not guilty of parental murder by reason of insanity.

All cases like this create serious difficulties for the politically correct. After all, if the mentally ill are just like folks with arthritis, then they are no more dangerous to their neighbors than are the arthritic. Yet, at the same time, when the officially designated mentally ill commit horrible crimes, liberals say that it is not the mentally ill persons' fault; it is the fault of their illnesses.

Even the *New York Times* recognizes that that is a no-win characterization, so it has come up with a brilliant way out of the dilemma: Crimes committed by the mentally ill are the fault of the mental health professionals who failed to properly medicate the patient.

Consider the case of Jaheem Grayton, the fifteen-year-old New Yorker accused of killing while stealing. Jaheem had a long history of violence and theft, with incidents including the slashing of a schoolmate and the substantial abuse of drugs and alcohol. Following a suicide threat in the autumn before the robbery killing, Jaheem was committed for a month to a hospital and given medication for his problems along with an outpatient treatment appointment following his release. He didn't make that appointment, or any others, and he stopped taking the medication. Eight weeks later he stood accused once again of violence and theft, this time resulting in the death of his victim.

What does the *Times* write about Jaheem? "Who was most responsible for insuring that Mr. Grayton, a troubled youth under treatment for mental illness, took his prescribed medication—the hospital that treated him for a month and then discharged him, the clinic that was to provide follow-up treatment but did not, or his family?" (*New York Times*, February 29, 1996).

What about Mr. Grayton himself? Even according to liberal logic, Mr. Grayton must have been in his "right mind" and responsible for his own actions while *on* the medications that treated his mental illness, was he not? If so, then he was responsible for the continued taking of his medication. If not, if he was just as irresponsible medicated as unmedicated, then it makes no sense at all to blame either the medications or the medics for his commission of this crime.

Still, this is an interesting point of view and one that takes us even farther down the twisted path hacked out by the conflicting claims that the mentally ill cannot be held responsible for their crimes and the mentally ill are no more likely than the rest of us to commit horrible crimes.

Of course, the conflicting claims are never made at the same time, nor are they made for the same purpose. The innocuousness of the mentally ill generally surfaces during housing controversies. The innocence of the mentally ill, regardless of their particular actions, usually arises as the legal system attempts to attribute responsibility for those actions. Then we get the accountability psychocircus that arouses the wrath of even the most somnolent of the gulled public.

The Laying of Blame

Alan Dershowitz has railed against what he calls the abuse excuse in criminal trials like those of Lorena Bobbitt for mutilation and the Menendez brothers for parental murder, in which defendants claim that due to prior injury by their victims they were unable to control their actions, but Dershowitz has hold of the wrong string in the psycholegal tangle. Abuse excuse claimants seek to put the blame for the injury they have caused onto the shoulders of the one who originally injured them, but it is not necessary to displace the blame. Thanks to the American Psychiatric Association, it is enough to disavow it. "I am mentally ill so I cannot be held responsible for my actions."

All this defense requires are really compelling and persuasive psychoexperts willing to work as hired guns. With the weight of enough credentials behind them and aided by a plausible-sounding story sprinkled with medical jargon and Latin terms, it is pretty hard for the layperson just to dismiss the experts' medically authenticated testimony. After all, these "experts" are certified as such by their professional organizations, by the state, *and* by the courts themselves. Most alarming is the willingness of our higher courts to accept the claims of the forensic experts over the judgments of the trial court judges. It cannot be long before the decisions of juries to refuse insanity pleas will likewise be reversed on appeal because they had not weighed the expert opinion sufficiently.

Experts indeed! Where do these well-paid, fraudulently trained but extensively credentialed, psychological professionals get off representing to the courts and to society as a whole that they can do a better job than you or I, than the average judge or juror, at deciding who is too crazy to stand trial and who is too crazy to bear all the guilt for his crime?

Shouldn't such misrepresentation itself be a crime?

6
Music Therapy for Wife Killers

Rehabbing Convicts

> The proof of our success is in our high referral rates from the courts and the probation officers. And we are very near national accreditation from the Association for the Treatment of Sex Offenders. We do good work here. . . . It's a simple fact. If we weren't successful, we wouldn't be in business.
>
> Shari P. Geller, *Fatal Convictions*, 1996

THE TEMPORARY DIET-PILL CRAZINESS OF OFFICER QUINTILIANO

Former Stratford, Connecticut, police officer Matthew Quintiliano "was in his Stratford Police uniform on May 23, 1975, when he shot and killed his first wife, Mary Ann, with 10 bullets outside Bridgeport Hospital, just days after she filed for divorce. In 1978, he was found innocent after pleading temporary insanity, his defense attorneys successfully arguing that he suffered from amphetamine psychosis from overusing diet pills.

"Quintiliano was held in Fairfield Hills Hospital, a state psychiatric unit in Newtown, for three months, but was released in 1979 and soon after married Sally Coppola Lawlor." On February 16, 1983, one week after Sally had said

> she would file for divorce, he shot and killed her, using a police service revolver that belonged to his son by his first wife. He was released from prison in December 1993. (Weizel, *Boston Globe*, December 10, 1993)

That's pretty impressive. First the psychological experts get him off for murder on the grounds of temporary craziness caused by taking diet pills, then they cure him and judge him fit to reenter society, and marriage, in just three months.

We have already seen how clinical practitioners hired by clever defense attorneys arrive at their exculpatory diagnoses, but the Quintiliano case is a real stunner.

How could anyone come up with a diagnosis of amphetamine psychosis, of diet-pill craziness, and get this wife killer off? It would be easy.

Was Officer Quintiliano cured by his three-month course of psychotherapy in Fairfield Hills Hospital? The answer to that kind of depends on your criteria. Since temporary amphetamine psychosis is, by definition, "temporary," Mr. Quintiliano must have been cured, again by definition, as soon as the "temporary" period passed. Also, since temporary amphetamine psychosis was his official diagnosis, once "cured" of that, there would have been little reason to keep him. So he was out in three months.

Of course, *your* criteria for judging a wife killer "cured" may be somewhat different. In fact, a not-so-unreasonable person might expect that Mr. Quintiliano would be required to stay in the hospital until his doctors could pretty much guarantee to society—or at least to future brides—that Mr. Quintiliano would not kill anyone else in the future. By that criterion, he obviously was not cured.

Now, his doctors might argue that they never tried to cure the wife killer of wife-killer disorder because he had no such diagnosis. But let us say that Quintiliano had actually been sent off to get his proclivity for killing women who no longer want him cured. Could psychotherapy have fixed up that little problem for him?

This is an extremely important question because every day our courts are sending men off to treatment for having stalked, attacked, beaten, raped, and killed women—often the women in their lives. Twenty-seven states now authorize courts to order domestic abusers into psychological treatment. Over the last twenty years the number of batterers arrested has increased by 70 percent, according to a report by Janell Schmidt and Lawrence Sherman in the *American Behavioral Scientist* in 1993, but still, most batterers, even when arrested, do not serve time in prison. We seem to have an unspoken assumption that men who kill strangers are bad, but men who kill female friends, lovers, and wives are just mad.

And as madmen, as men suffering from mental disorders, surely they can be helped by psychotherapy. Right?

WHY THERAPY SHOULD WORK

Does psychotherapy work? Well, sure. Of course it does, at least for the average noncriminal types who freely choose it. It *must* work.

Why must it work? Look at the general conditions under which your average slightly messed-up person chooses to enter therapy. Now, what is going to happen to that person? What will happen to you?

When you go into therapy, one of three things can happen: you get better; you get worse; there's no change. Let us suppose that by chance alone, all other things being equal, each of these outcomes will happen about one third of the time. Thus, therapy has to work about a third of the time by chance alone.

What can change these odds? Several factors, actually. First of all, there's the simple effect of expectation on what happens. You expect to get better. After all, you followed Ann Landers's oft-repeated advice to get counseling, and Ann wouldn't mislead you, would she? Of course you expect to get better as a result of the counseling. Also, you are highly motivated to get better. You've been thinking about it for two years and now you've decided you've had all you can take. You are going to get therapy and you are going to get better.

Besides, you are paying $100 per session. Now, unless you really have several screws loose, you are not going to be paying that kind of money expecting to get ripped off. You are only a little bit nuts, not that nuts. Additionally, your insurance company paid for the first $500 in therapy and it certainly wouldn't do that if therapy was not a tried-and-true method of making people better, would it? After all, insurance companies don't pay for experimental procedures or ineffective methods like astrology readings or peach pit treatments. They pay for the real thing.

In addition, unless your therapist is a complete fraud, he or she also expects you to get better. Why else would anyone spend forty hours a week listening to people talk about how distant their fathers were and how cold their mothers? Therapists have to believe that what they are doing is worthwhile and will help their patients get better.

So by how much do all these additional points improve the chance odds of getting better? Let's give a 5 percent increase in the probability that you will get better for each of these factors. Your expectation of getting better adds 5 percent to the chance probability of 33 percent, your powerful motivation adds another 5 percent, your payment of significant dollars adds another 5 percent, the insurance company's confidence adds another 5 percent, and your therapist's expectations add in still another 5 percent. That get us up to a 58 percent chance that you will get better as a result of having gone into therapy.

What else might change the odds? Well, you are now spending several hours a week on yourself, not on your family or your job. You are thinking about yourself and clearly finding the experience sufficiently valuable that you take time to do it. That's a big change from your prior neglect of self. Also, for the first time in your life since childhood, someone else is taking time to devote serious attention to you and your problems and feelings. Clearly, your problems and feelings must be interesting and important or why would that person sit there hour after hour listening to them so intently? Moreover, this person frequently acts as if he or she genuinely likes you. It has been a long time since you met someone new who seems so pleased to see you each time you meet. Also, this person is a person of authority with graduate or medical degrees and a license from the state to do whatever he or she is doing.

All of this is pretty remarkable. Not only are you valuing yourself for the first time, but so is someone else. That ought to add 10 percent to your chances of getting better. Feeling liked, cared about, and wanted, as well as important, is another big plus, worth another 5 percent. And being valued and liked by a person of considerable authority and importance is worth another 5 percent. Where are we now? At about a 78 percent chance that you, the patient, will get better as a result of having gone into therapy, regardless of what that therapy is. So far, we haven't even considered what goes on in all those therapy sessions. It doesn't matter; you should get better anyway for all these other reasons.

So it is at least possible that clinical practitioners can help people who want to feel better or understand more about their lives feel better and understand more even if it is for a number of reasons that have very little to do with formal training and knowledge.

But I say this once again because it is critical: The fact that an individual can be helped tells us *nothing* about the validity of the psychological theories of the helper. The actual causal events producing his or her behavior are unknowable.

Perhaps familiarity with the treatment used by the faculty of the famous Boston Trauma Clinic to treat PTSD will plant the necessary seed of doubt in even the most gullible past or prospective patient. This procedure, by the way, is held by *consensus* of all the faculty to be absolutely the most effective in treating PTSD, according to Dr. Bessel van der Kolk, on staff at the clinic, in a colloquium given at Boston University in October 1996.

To cure PTSD, the therapist has the patient concentrate on the past traumatic event—this only works if he or she can remember it, of course—while staring at the doctor's fingers as the doctor wags them slowly back and forth, back and forth, in front of the patient's eyes. The patient follows the wagging with his or her eyes. Dr. van der Kolk suggested that each session last ninety minutes and that after only three sessions, the patient would be cured! Now, isn't that amazing? This therapy technique is called EMDR, for Eye Movement Desensitization and Reprocessing. (I can think of another name for it.)

It certainly goes to show that understanding how the mind works has nothing whatsoever to do with "curing" modern "mental disorders." I wonder if EMDR would work as well if the psychiatrists of the Trauma Clinic wagged gourds and rattles in front of the patients' eyes. Hard to imagine why not.

The lack of connection between the effectiveness of a therapy technique and the validity of the therapist's psychological theories will not be evident to happy patients, or even to most judges, because of the almost universal vulnerability to the witch doctor fallacy. We all know or have heard of people who claim to have benefited from psychotherapy, and you and the person you know—and the person the judge knows or the judge—both attribute the benefits to the knowledge and skills of the therapist. It is almost impossible not to fall prey to the witch doctor fallacy, although the people at the Trauma Clinic seem to be doing their best to help us.

Nevertheless, we should add in the effects of the fallacy to the overall effectiveness of psychotherapy for a full estimate of efficacy independent of therapy itself. If we throw in another 2 percent for the effect of this fallacy, just to round things up, about 80 percent of the people who go into therapy ought to get better no matter what kind of "therapy" they choose.

Real Life and Therapy

There is another reason that you should get better in the course of therapy that also has nothing whatsoever to do with what goes on in your sessions with your psychotherapist. What most people seek help for in therapy are real-life problems—problems with spouses, children, or jobs. These quite ordinary real-life problems are not diseases of the individual like breast cancer just because clinical practitioners, in their zeal to medicalize everything, label them so. So psychotherapy also works because the diseases it purports to treat are not actually diseases; they are just the vicissitudes of ordinary life.

Unhappiness is a problem; it is not a disease. Low self-esteem also is not a disease. Eating too much is not a disease, and neither is eating too little. And, despite a huge lobby to the contrary, drinking too much alcohol is not a disease either. As we have seen, the psychological establishment has defined virtually all less-than-desirable behaviors, from hatred of first grade to serial rape, as psychological diseases, and represents itself as uniquely able to provide the necessary "therapies" for them.

In the normal course of events, with or without psychotherapy, most real-life problems resolve themselves one way or another. These mundane problems are "treatable" because most life situations change over time, solving old problems and creating new ones, and when the situation does not change, people get used to it. Yes, people do adapt to the commonly occurring miseries of ordinary life and even to the most extraordinary situations. To live is to adapt. It is the fundamental definition of a living system. Psychotherapists have defined human beings as unadapted to the human environment, and as unadaptable without their help. That's an offensive and utterly unsubstantiated assertion.

Horrible Life Experiences and Therapy

Even horrible life experiences are just that, horrible experiences. They are not precipitating conditions for insanity. But life is full of dreadful experiences. Our babies die from leukemia, our teenagers get crushed to death on telephone poles, our spouses die or leave us. Our mothers drink, our fathers beat us, and our kids deal drugs. We lose our jobs and are betrayed by friends. We break our backs at twenty, get breast cancer at thirty-six, and lose a finger to a rotary saw at forty-five. We go blind and inexorably deaf. Our houses burn down, or are swept away in floods or by the sea. We get robbed, we get mugged, we get shot at.

Are we all, then, crazy? Do we all need psychotherapy to make it through life? What kind of idyllic life must people possess to make it through without going crazy? No sickness, no death, no hunger, no loss? What sort of witless 1950s Norman Rockwell romanticism informs this distorted view of life?

Life is a complex series of highly varied events to be dealt with; it is not a condition to be cured by psychotherapy.

Life situations that make people unhappy change, and then people feel better. Many miserable situations do not change much for the better, but people get used to them; they adapt. And people themselves, like situations, change over time. Most people who are depressed or anxious will, with time, be less depressed and anxious. With more time, they will be depressed or anxious again. Stasis for living beings is inconceivable. When we have been hurt, we heal. With time, we change. It takes time to feel better, but it happens, and it happens without the offices of any therapist.

Given all these powerful factors pushing people who enter therapy to feel better, how could it fail to work almost every time?

THE FAILURES OF THERAPY

That is a good question and it has to be asked because the failure rate of psychotherapy is astonishingly high. In fact, for a long time, since the middle 1950s, research studies have shown *no effect at all* of therapy for your average patient. Some people got better; some didn't. People were as likely to get better with the simple passage of time as under the guidance of a therapist.

It is amazing that the business of therapy blossomed and grew at such a rapid rate in the last few decades despite the lack of any evidence of treatment effectiveness, but, of course, people are reluctant to admit they have been had, and the propaganda that therapy works has been extensive and powerful.

In their 1992 *Consumer's Guide to Psychotherapy*, Jack Engler, Ph.D., and Daniel Goleman, Ph.D., write that despite all those years of evidence to the contrary, a modern "meta-analysis" supposedly shows that psychotherapy *does* work after all. Really?

What does this meta-analysis supposedly show? It shows that if you combine the results of the hundreds of studies on whether therapy works, ignoring completely what the different patients suffered from, what kinds of therapy they had, and what kinds of measures were used to indicate that the therapy worked, then, overall, there is indeed some evidence of a net positive effect of psychotherapy.

That is like saying if you gathered up every single study of whether physical medicine worked regardless of disease, doctor, or treatment, you might find that, overall, medical treatment had *some* effect on helping people get better.

Well, that's just dandy, isn't it? What is the public supposed to conclude from that? Because some medical treatments had some effect on some diseases sometimes, all medical treatments for each and every disease are effective? We should believe that physicians can fix anything, and our insurance companies should pay for any and all treatments for each and every disease?

Newspapers these days are full of demands that all medical providers—insurance companies, HMOs, and such—be required to pay for psychotherapeutic treatments exactly as they would pay for treatments for the flu or breast cancer, despite the shocking lack of evidence that psychotherapy does anyone any good at all, except the psychotherapist who is getting paid.

It seems extremely unlikely that any medical professional other than a psychiatrist would have the chutzpah to demand payment for services so clearly *not* rendered, but psychotherapists and their lobbyists cite the "meta-analysis" repeatedly in their demands for more money from all of us.

Clinical psychologist and researcher Neil Jacobson, in a recent (1995) issue of a family therapy journal, presents another telling and disturbing fact. He points out that in those studies that supposedly *do* show an effect of therapy, the effect is solely statistical, with very little of what he calls clinical meaning. To illustrate his point, he gives the case of a weight-loss technique that produces a statistically significant weight loss of 10 pounds on the average for each patient, but, alas, since the average patient in the study weighed 300 pounds, this statistically significant weight loss of only 3.3 percent for the average patient was not *clinically* significant for the morbidly obese. The 300-pound, morbidly obese subjects were still morbidly obese at 270 pounds. Psychotherapy is supposed to make a *real* difference to patients, not just a minor statistical effect, or it is extremely misleading to patients and the public at large to publish it.

Further, he notes that the claims of effectiveness when looked at carefully are really quite small. In one extensive multimillion-dollar study of depression treatments, comparing psychotherapy with drug therapy, the percentage of patients who stopped being depressed and stayed that way for a year and a half ranged from 19 to 32 percent for the drug and psychotherapy groups, and was 20 percent for what is called the placebo group. The placebo group patients talked about hockey or gardening with the therapists instead of anything specifically designed to improve their mental health.

Jacobson's study showed two things: First, talking about hockey is just as effective in curing depression as talking about your mean mother who didn't want you; and, second, *70 to 80 percent of the patients in the study stayed depressed* whether they talked about hockey, badmouthed their mothers, or took an antidepressant drug.

He reports similar small effects in a series of studies on conduct disorders in adolescents, marriage counseling for couples, and anxiety disorders:

> We have found the recovered patient [one who shows few or no signs or symptoms of the initial complaint and believes himself or herself to be "cured"] to be the exception rather

> than the rule for every type of disorder examined and every type of therapy we have looked at—psychodynamic, behavioral, cognitive and family therapy. When one considers even more intractable problems, such as addictive behaviors, schizophrenia and personality disorders, the clinical significance data are even more bleak. The only exception we have found . . . to these modest recovery rates is the cognitive behavioral treatment of panic disorder. (Jacobson 1995, p. 44)

For almost every mental problem studied, psychotherapy makes about 20 to 25 percent of adults feel better, but so does placebo pseudo-therapy—talking about sports or gardening—so therapy as therapy can't really be said to work at all for adults, and for children there is no evidence that it works even as well as talking about sports.

The real reason that psychotherapy doesn't work even as well as one might expect from placebo effects alone is that it is *not* generally designed to do so. That seems unlikely only as long as you don't look too closely at what actually happens in the course of therapy, as long as you don't look at what has *always* gone on.

How Therapy Is Not Designed to Change Behavior

In Freud's time, all psychological problems came from sex—too much or too little, excessive masturbation, coitus interruptus, incest real or imagined, and unfulfilled erotic fantasies. Today, all our problems come from low self-esteem engendered by an inadequate home life. To cure his patients' conditions, Freud developed the "talking cure." Patients talked about supposedly illuminating dreams and revealed themselves further through free association and Freudian slips. In various forms, this is still the dominant approach today.

> MEADVILLE, PA (AP). An Amish man who beat his wife to death and cut out her intestines was convicted of a lesser charge of involuntary manslaughter Saturday. Edward Gingerich, who was charged with murder, admitted to killing his wife, Katie, on March 18, 1993, in Rockdale Township, about 100 miles north of Pittsburgh. He beat her, kicked her in the head with heavy work boots and then used a kitchen knife to remove her organs, according to trial testimony. Gingerich's

> lawyer said his client thought he was possessed by the devil because he had headaches, and that he was too mentally ill to know what he was doing. The jury found Gingerich "guilty but mentally ill" of manslaughter. A judge will decide whether to send Gingerich to a mental hospital or to prison for up to four years. (*Napa Valley Register*, March 27, 1994)

How would a therapist go about curing Mr. Gingerich, and how would one know when success was in hand? Deciding if and when therapy has "worked" depends on what one means by "worked."

From the outcome point of view, therapeutic techniques fall into four broad categories that can be usefully distinguished as insight seeking, emotional validation—both modern implementations of Freudian psychodynamic theory—behavior modification, and plain foolishness.

Insight Seekers

Let us say your therapist is an insight specialist. What is he or she after? Insights, of course, but what's an insight and who is supposed to have them, you or your therapist?

An insight occurs when you suddenly realize that your mother didn't really want any more babies after Harry, your much older brother, was born, that she resented having to work full-time until she was almost sixty years old, and never having any money to spend on herself, or any time for herself and her husband.

Why should the sudden realization that your mother wished you had never been born make a difference in your life? No reason. There is zero evidence that therapeutic "insights" have any effect on the patient's life at all. Why would they? You grew up the way you grew up; you live the life that you live. Suddenly seeing your mother through a different lens won't change any of that. Insight theory is nothing more than romanticized wishful thinking. Having an insight about your mother's feelings from thirty years ago is not the same as discovering that your spouse is having an affair today. The latter is an "insight" that might well have a significant effect on the course of your life.

By the way, where is the evidence that any particular "insight" is correct? How do you know that your mother really didn't want any more babies after Harry was born? Why do clinicians give such weight to these so-called insights, to their own interpretations of the patient's revelations?

Simple. Because they make sense. Ah, the lure of the coherent narrative.

Given a cultural backdrop of pervasive Freudianism, it only takes acceptance of a few basic assumptions for the patient to accept the therapist's story as true, to accept the insights as valid: To wit: The mother-child relationship defines all love relationships in the future, and if mother was hostile but in denial she constantly gave the poor child mixed messages about love and acceptance, which resulted in an emotional insecurity that makes the adult child a demanding and conflicted lover today, with an unhappy marriage entirely due to the mother's initial ambivalence.

Is that sad story really the only possible narrative to account for the emotional ups and downs of the patient's life? Of course not, but apparently only an overly critical person would object that there are probably any number of relationships, experiences, attitudes, expectations, and patterns of behavior that go into determining the quality of a marriage or parenthood; that no one has the ability to re-create the complexity of the mother's many feelings and the way they changed over time and expressed themselves in innumerable actions and omissions; and that it is quite possible to write dozens of stories to fit the few known "facts" of the case.

Any story that "makes sense" to therapist and client is considered not only good enough, but *necessarily true*.

Dr. Lenore Terr gives a fascinating and highly disturbing account of the process of Eileen Franklin discovering "true" insights about her father, George:

> A few months after she remembered Susan Nason's murder, Eileen began to see herself around the age of seven or eight being raped by a black man with a green-tipped Afro haircut. . . . *After telling this story to [the prosecutor's] investigators*, Eileen realized that her mental representation of the rapist had come from a Jimi Hendrix poster on the rapist's wall. . . . [Soon] the man who actually raped her came to mind. It was her own godfather. His white face gradually imposed itself

> onto the memory. This man . . . had arranged with George to rape George's daughter. It was a sick gift from a father to a friend.
>
> *I felt satisfied that we understood* how Eileen's mental shift from her black Jimi Hendrix rapist to her white godfather had occurred. (Terr 1994, pp. 41–42; italics added)

It is nice that Dr. Terr felt satisfied by Eileen's creative turn, but didn't she think it a little odd that Eileen changed her story only after the prosecutor's investigators expressed doubt about it?

Every therapist has encountered any number of "insights" that are all too soon replaced by newer ones. Why are they allowed to testify otherwise in court? Therapists know that so-called insights can be both wrong and dangerously misleading. They know that memories can be false. But they need to hold on to belief in the validity of insights to make sense of the whole therapeutic process in which they are engaged.

They also need to believe in insight if therapy is ever to be terminated, since illuminating insights are supposed to provide the key that leads to psychodynamic resolution and the end of distressing symptoms. (Freud, oddly, both disclaimed the process yet followed the practice.) That some people remain years in therapy with the same therapist might lead one to believe that there is a certain deficiency in insight theory or else a certain insight deficiency in the particular relationship, but it's not necessarily so.

More likely, these long-term clients, like Woody Allen, have therapists who are into emotional support rather than insights.

Emotional Validation and Esteem

Emotional validation is huggy therapy; it is supposed to build up the patient's self-esteem, and make him or her less anxious or depressed or whatever.

Huggy therapists say things like "I hear you saying that it hurts your feelings when your daughter says she hates you and you are a bad mother" and "How does it make you feel to have spent ten years at a job you despise?"

Huggy therapists put you in touch with your feelings and validates them once you are in touch. In plain English, that means you express feelings in therapy that you didn't express much before and the therapist tells you it is okay to feel the way you feel.

So what's wrong with talking with a warm and sympathetic listener about your problems? Nothing at all. It's a perfectly sensible thing to do. This support service is a necessary social function that used to be provided by our wise old grandmothers, our experienced Uncle George, or the family minister—people who had seen a great deal of life and had given it a great deal of careful thought. In today's highly mobile and less traditionally religious society, it is quite appropriate that these services be provided by "professionals"—people whose job it is to listen, to give warm support, to provide perspective on problems, to help people feel better.

But what effect is this so-called emotional validation supposed to have on your life? The therapist, after all, is just a paid, professional emotion validator. How is his or her validation supposed to transfer into your real life outside the therapist's office? Your daughter still hates you and your boss still thinks you're a slacker. Who cares if your therapist is sympathetic? Not your daughter or your boss, that's for sure. There's no evidence that warmth from a therapist changes the patient's life for the better.

Why would it? Huggy therapists have promulgated the utterly unsubstantiated notion that talking about your feelings, "unbottling the rage" or "letting the anger out," will effect real change in a person's life. The idea seems to be that encouraging adults to throw tantrums will make them better people. That approach is about as effective with grown-ups as it is with kids. It springs from nothing other than the psychocultural belief that restraint and responsibility are bad, the free expressiveness of the innocent and primitive child is good. At least wise Uncle George and the family minister insisted on imposing some sense of perspective when they were being emotionally supportive. The current psychotherapeutic enshrining of emotional expression does no such thing, and flies in the face of common sense about behavior and well-being. Feeling good in the therapist's office is nice, but what does it have to do with feeling good about the management of life's normal checks, opportunities, and challenges? Nothing.

Emotional validation therapy stands on the same insubstantial ground of wishful thinking as insight therapy. Insight therapy and emotional validation cannot work because they are not really designed around any other goal than simply talking to the patient and making up stories with the patient—and, all too often, the therapist—as the star. They are certainly not designed to change the behavior of the patient that is contributing to his or her unhappiness.

For all that talking can be a pleasant, if expensive, way to pass the time, what is important is what you do, how you change your life to make it better, how you change the way you live your life to make you feel better. Changes in how you feel about your daughter or your boss come from actually making changes in the way you interact with those people; they do not come from talking about the daughter or the boss in the therapist's office.

Behavior Modification

For clinical practitioners to claim that therapy works, they should be able to show that not only do their patients feel better, they *act* better too. They lose weight, drink spring water instead of wine, make more time to spend with their children, perform small acts of kindness to please their spouses, double their productivity at work, and begin to trust the boss and co-workers. Dysfunctional, unhappy-making behaviors should decrease, and functional, happy-making ones increase. Do they? No, in general, they don't.

For dysfunctional behaviors to change, both therapist and patient must focus on changing them. Most therapists never dream of directly attempting to change dysfunctional behavior, but there are some therapists, the ugly stepchildren of the therapy world, for whom behavioral change is the sole goal of therapy. These behaviorists, as they call themselves reasonably enough, can be fairly effective, especially with some behaviors that are highly undesirable to the patient, for example, phobias. No one wants to be scared witless by harmless situations. Patients with phobias are usually highly motivated to get rid of the distressing behavior, and inch by inch they change the way they act and react in the phobic situation.

Behavior modification essentially involves making a new behavior more desirable for the client than the old behavior. For instance, you can train a puppy to hold its bladder until it gets outside, but the training requires that the master turn bladder evacuation inside the house into an unpleasant experience while simultaneously making evacuation outside pleasant.

This same procedure was undertaken in the film *A Clockwork Orange*. The patient was a young man who got his kicks terrorizing and raping women. His government therapists modified this behavior by making any actions or reactions in that direction extremely unpleasant, while rewarding their opposites. It worked well enough, in the film, but it required that the government agents—therapists—control the whole world of the patient.

Behavior therapy can change behavior; there is no question about that at all. But there is also little question that its effectiveness is a function of the amount of control over the situation the therapist has. When behaviorists train animals, the usual approach is to starve the animals down to 80 percent of normal body weight so that they will work for food rewards. A hungry animal will work quite hard to get food; a satiated animal will do nothing at all. It is just not feasible to starve down the entire behavioral therapy client population to 80 percent of their normal body weight.

Viewed strictly in terms of behavioral change for the betterment of the individual and for society, the outcome picture for modern psychotherapy is rather bleak. Insight therapy and emotional validation therapy can't change behavior because they are not designed to do so. Behavioral modification, which is so designed, cannot change behavior because the controls on the individual necessary to effect change are not consistent with the ideals of our modern society. That leaves only the last category of therapy techniques—plain foolishness.

Plain Foolishness

This testimony and cross-examination, from a 1993 civil trial for past psychic injury, provides a flawless example of this approach.

Attorney: Can you help me understand some of the terms that you use in describing some of your therapy work? What are Bio-energetics?

Therapist: Bio-energetics is a form of therapy that deals directly with breaking down "Body Armor" through doing various physical activities.

Attorney: And what kind of physical activities do you employ in your therapy group or individual therapy?

Therapist: It's primarily in Group Therapy and Anger Work in which a person might use a tennis racquet to hit pillows. They might use a Rage Restraint in which people restrain a person so that they're safe and able to use the full force of their body to release energy.

Attorney: How do you use, if you use, Psychodrama in your therapy?

Therapist: Through reenacting different life experiences that people have. Either to re-create, to reenact, the same experience so that people can get in touch with their feelings about that. Or, sometimes to reenact it in a way so that they have the experience of a different outcome.

Attorney: Do you do Trance Work?

Therapist: Yes. Through either a Visualization or Guided Imagery. Usually if I'm doing Trance Work it's around people developing a relaxation or Guided Imagery in terms of constructing their own inner place of solitude or—primarily, I use it for relaxation.

Attorney: Can you give me an example of Guided Imagery?

Therapist: Um-hmm, sure. There's one that's rather famous about allowing yourself to relax and to create a pink bubble or balloon for you to climb into, and to experience the sensation of floating. Be able to experience that as a relaxation. In particular teach people how to use that so that if they're in a stressful situation they can use that to help themselves relax. (*Mateu v. Hagen*, 1993)

This is just a small sample of the modern techniques used by countless therapists to help their clients regain their mental health, just a taste of the many "treatments" paid for by our various insurance plans.

What's wrong with them? What is wrong with bio-energetics, with breaking down body armor, anger work, hitting pillows with tennis racquets, and rage restraints, with using the full force of the body to release energy, with psychodrama, corrective parenting techniques, age regression, trance work, visualization, guided imagery, and pink bubbles?

Is there any evidence at all—objective, scientific, impersonal, disinterested evidence—that falling into trances, fantasizing about pink bubbles, and beating pillows with tennis racquets while screaming out hatred improves mental health or quality of life, or changes behavior? There is not.

Pushing this foolishness onto the gullible public as respected, valid, effective therapeutic techniques destroys the ability of the whole society even to begin to ask whether psychotherapy does work or whether it ever could. In the face of clear unreason on the part of the therapist, where does that leave the question of reasonable evaluation?

The testimony above was given *on the witness stand*, as the therapist was explaining supposedly scientifically sound and reliable techniques for accessing the hidden psyches of her patients. Why, in the name of sanity, do the judges sit there and listen politely to such stuff? When this is the so-called therapy that leads a patient to make a legal claim for compensation for psychological injury—and it so often is—how can that claim be anything but suspect? When this is the so-called therapy that is offered our judicial system by the suppliers of rehabilitative services for convicted criminals, how can the public be anything but outraged?

Given this as state-of-the-art, court-ordered, taxpayer-paid, rehabilitative psychotherapy in America today, society would be better off tying wife beaters, sex offenders, and substance abusers to trees with gourds shaken in their faces. At least the trees and gourds wouldn't cost the country so much.

Plain foolishness cannot work with patients because it is just that, plain foolishness.

REHABBING CRIMINALS

So can psychotherapy work for the average slightly messed-up person who chooses to enter therapy for help with his or her problems? Sadly, the answer is usually not. One cannot then help but wonder just how well it works to "fix" the criminally insane.

All over the country, those judged not guilty of their crimes by reason of some definition of mental mess-up are sent to hospitals where they receive therapy for wife beating or disemboweling, child molesting and other assorted allegedly mentally caused behavior problems. When they are better, they are released back into the general populace.

There is an even larger number—actually, a vast number—of criminals who are sentenced to some form of psychological treatment or are forced into rehabilitation therapy as a condition either of avoiding prosecution or of parole.

That is a lot of clients. Rehabbing criminals is a *very* big business. We—the public, that is—pay for it. Does it work?

Why Therapy Can't Change Criminal Behavior

How could it?

If psychotherapy works no better than talking about hockey with the average, unjailed population of the mentally distressed, how could it possibly be thought to be more effective with the jailed population of matricides, drunks, druggies, sex offenders, and wife and child murderers? (Well, certainly therapy works for matricides. Nobody does that twice.) How could it be said to help unwilling wife beaters coerced into "treatment" as a condition of probation or parole?

What is the goal of sentencing criminals to therapy? It should be behavior change, right? What else? Criminals behave in ways that seriously inconvenience the rest of the members of society. We want them to stop. American society and our legal system want to use psychotherapy treatment programs to rehabilitate criminals, both adults and "troubled youth." We want to change their behavior and make them less inconvenient, more productive members of society.

But can rehabilitative psychotherapy accomplish this? No. We've already seen that insight and emotional validation therapy are unable to produce behavior change in anyone. They have nothing to do with changing behaviors. How about beating on pillows with tennis racquets or fantasizing about pink balloons? Will that cure the rapist, the child molester, or the car thief? Get real, as the kids say. Okay.

What about behavior therapy? We ordinary people want to change the behavior of criminals without the expense of keeping them in prison. Can we do it with behavior therapy? No, not unless we could control their environment as thoroughly as that of a laboratory animal. This degree of control would evaporate when we released them.

> On February 23, 1988, Jesse Timmendequas concluded a six-year prison term for molesting and trying to strangle a 7-year-old girl. He walked out of the Adult Diagnostic and Treatment Center in Avenel, [New Jersey,] the state's thera-

> peutic prison for sex offenders, a free man, unsupervised and anonymous.
>
> Last week, the 33-year-old laborer—a reluctant participant in therapy at Avenel . . . was charged in the rape and strangulation murder of another 7-year-old, Megan Kanka, his neighbor in Hamilton Township. (Patterson, *Star-Ledger* [Newark], August 7, 1994)

Some advocates for criminals argue that the incarcerated or the potentially incarcerated have a higher motivation to change than their unjailed counterparts, but there is no evidence that that is true. That many of them certainly have a strong motivation to get out of jail is not quite the same thing. But it makes no difference in any case.

It must not be forgotten too that part of the modern therapist agenda is the view that criminals are *victims*, that it is their family and society that are to blame for their crimes, not the criminals themselves. Since it is quite likely that the criminal agrees with this view, what progress should society expect to follow from the happy meeting of the therapist and criminal minds? A real change in attitude?

In 1978, Michael Kelley was found not guilty by reason of insanity of the rape and murder of two young women in Massachusetts. He was sent to Bridgewater State Hospital—the state hospital for the criminally insane featured in the 1960s Fred Wiseman documentary film *Titicut Follies*, which was banned in Massachusetts for more than twenty years after its release. In 1993, forensic clinicians who evaluated Kelley determined that he had recovered from his mental illness and was no longer a danger to others. Kelley was released into the general prison population and four months later was paroled. A little more than one month after his release into the community, not quite six months after his doctors judged him cured, Kelley lured two young women, under the pretense of conducting job interviews, to an isolated location where he raped and killed them. Soon arrested, he was sent to Bridgewater yet again for another psychiatric evaluation. Eventually Kelley pleaded guilty to these crimes and was sentenced to spend the rest of his life in prison.

> A psychologist who helped run the state's Treatment Center for the Sexually Dangerous at Bridgewater said last night he

> was "shocked and saddened" to hear that two of the institution's former inmates, whose release he recommended in evaluations he made as a private practitioner after leaving the center, have again been charged with committing violent crimes.
>
> "It's a horrible situation, of course," said Theoharis Seghorn. "It's certainly a painful experience for any professional who conducts an evaluation of an individual who is released and goes out and commits another crime."
>
> Seghorn was referring to Michael Kelley and Ralph O. Houghton, who are among 28 inmates released from the Bridgewater center since 1990, many over the objections of the state Department of Mental Health.
>
> Six of the inmates have been charged with crimes since their release. Only Kelley, charged with two murders, and Houghton, charged with raping a retarded man, are accused of violent or sexual offenses. (Benning, *Boston Globe*, June 21, 1992)

Charges against Houghton were later dropped for insufficient evidence.

The people of the Commonwealth of Massachusetts trusted the forensic clinicians who testified that Mr. Kelley was mentally ill. They trusted the clinicians who treated Mr. Kelley's illness. Lastly, and most foolishly, they trusted the clinical psychologists who declared Mr. Kelley rehabilitated and ready to return to society.

> Seghorn was head of clinical psychology at the Bridgewater treatment center and was administrative assistant there for nearly 10 years before leaving to set up private practice in 1986. Seghorn said yesterday that professionals like himself are hired to conduct independent evaluations and are paid a standard fee for their time.
>
> Plymouth District Attorney William O'Malley yesterday questioned whether Seghorn should have testified on behalf of two inmates he had overseen. . . . O'Malley questioned Seghorn's "expertise" in predicting whether inmates such as Kelley . . . are "cured."
>
> "The two cases in question are both cases where he formed

> an opinion where they were termed not sexually dangerous," O'Malley said. "I wonder how 'expert' that is. Certainly the safety of the community shouldn't depend on such predictions." (Benning, *Boston Globe*, June 21, 1992)

Nearly every state in the union today provides psychological treatment programs for sex offenders, both violent and nonviolent, and for men who beat up their domestic partners and their children, sometimes with sexual violence added in and sometimes not. These treatment programs are generally paid for by the unwitting, taxpaying public.

> The overwhelming majority of apprehended sex offenders are not incarcerated or institutionalized at all. For those who are convicted, probation with mandated treatment (and perhaps some jail time) is the most common disposition. In response to the increasing demand for sex offender treatment, there has been a proliferation of both public and private outpatient programs. (Furby, Weinrott, and Blackshaw 1989, pp. 3–4)

How well do all these proliferating programs work, Michael Kelley aside?

Effectiveness of Sex Offender Treatment Programs

> At [New Jersey's] sex offender prison, 70 to 80 percent of the inmates are pedophiles; their average stay is between five and six years. . . . At Avenel, a team of 16 therapists treats inmates. Their presence drives the average maintenance cost per inmate up to $31,000 a year compared to about $25,000 at other state prisons. A staff member explains, "Every Avenel inmate gets a basic treatment plan upon admission. . . . Some people think that individual therapy might be more effective, but group therapy is the preferred method of treatment. . . . We also have ancillary groups that teach victim empathy, anger management, and relapse prevention."
>
> Today, Avenel officials do not have recent recidivism studies to support their program. "We don't really have a

standard recidivism study. Resources just don't permit us to do what we'd really like to do." (Patterson, *Star-Ledger* [Newark], August 7, 1994)

Does anyone know how well the various states' efforts to teach their sex offenders victim empathy, anger management, and relapse prevention work?

The classic study of the effectiveness of sex offender treatment programs is that conducted by Lisa Furby, Mark Weinrott, and Lyn Blackshaw, published in 1989 in *Psychological Bulletin*. The authors collected and reviewed the results of forty-two studies of male sex offenders who had been convicted of a sex crime under the prevailing law or who had admitted to a treatment center that they engaged in criminal sexual behavior. They included only men for whom the recidivism data was on record in the criminal justice system, and for whom follow-up data were available.

These forty-two studies covered a wide variety of crimes, and various lengths of follow-up periods, and any number of "treatment" techniques, with recidivism rates varying wildly from 4 to 50 percent for untreated offenders and from about 4 to 60 percent for treated offenders. What did the authors find when they pooled and combed all those data?

Nothing. Right. Nothing.

"We can at least say with confidence that there is no evidence that treatment effectively reduces sex offense recidivism" (Furby, Blackshaw, and Weinrott 1989, p. 25).

Well, that should have been the end of that, right? That was back in 1989. It was not the end. Treatment programs proliferated still more. There is just too much money involved, too many careers, livelihoods, and reputations to just shut down the whole scam. Sex offender therapy *must* be shown to work.

So yet another analysis of their effectiveness was undertaken. This one was by Gordon Nagayama Hall, and it was published in 1995 in the *Journal of Consulting and Clinical Psychology*. What did Professor Hall discover? Looking just at more recent studies, twelve of them from 1988 to 1994, with a range of participants from 16 in the smallest study to 299 in the largest, Hall found that 27 percent of untreated sex offenders committed additional offenses compared with only 19 percent of the offenders who had received treatment. That 8 percent improvement supposedly due to treatment is an overall average. Four of the twelve studies—that is, one third—showed results in the opposite direction. That is, untreated offenders were *less* likely to commit new offenses than treated offenders. Hmmm.

Also, when one looks a bit more closely at what constitutes "treatment," the picture takes a slight shift. Ninety-nine of the "treated" sex offenders were *castrated*. Only three of those guys reoffended. If the castrated men are removed from the "treated" group, then the difference in recidivism rates shrinks: It is 27 percent for untreated offenders and 22 percent for psychologically treated ones.

That is only a 5 percent difference overall. Moreover, the types of treatment programs and the types of crimes committed by both treated and untreated groups are so varied that it is impossible to generalize these findings to anything.

Given this enormous variability, it is also dishonest to present a 5 percent treatment effect as so robust as to warrant millions of dollars spent in ever more proliferating programs. Furby, Weinrott, and Blackshaw sounded the warning call. It is past time it was heeded, and useless treatment programs abandoned for the entrepreneurial scams they are.

According to Nathaniel Pallone, a Rutgers University professor and expert on the rehabilitation of criminal sexual offenders:

> We know what works, but certain constraints have been placed on states by the Supreme Court. The most effective means is surgical castration. The second is aversive behavior therapy. The third is "bioimpedence," or chemical castration. So, I think the world would be a safer place if you, as a sex offender, went every week to your parole officer, and every two weeks to your doctor for an injection. It wouldn't make you a good boy, but there would not be another victim. (Quoted in Patterson, *Star-Ledger* [Newark], August 7, 1994)

A reasonable person looking only at available data might conclude that psychotherapeutic treatment programs for sex offenders are a waste of taxpayers' dollars, but such a view is by no means universally held. Turning a blind eye to the facts, willing victims of the psychologists' lobby continue to call for ever more—daring, innovative, promising—treatment approaches.

The quote that opened this chapter is by a character in a work of fiction—the director of a for-profit sex offender clinic in the novel *Fatal Convictions*—but there could be no more realistic an expression of the true facts about the "proven" effectiveness of sex offender treatment programs in our country today.

How do we know it works? Because we say it does.

An editorial in the *Boston Globe* on June 26, 1992, following the tragic murder of the two young women by Michael Kelley after he had been "cured" at Bridgewater, opined:

> Kelley's release was a terrible mistake, but it would be equally wrong to impose harsh punishments on sexually violent criminals without offering them treatment. With improved treatment programs, state government has a much better chance of preventing such crimes and protecting its residents once these offenders leave prison.

Improved treatment programs? This is not wishful thinking; it is willful blindness.

In another editorial written four years later, after the vicious knife-point rape of an eleven-year-old boy by a repeat offender, the *Globe* wrote, "Far too many crimes are committed by ex-convicts released from prison after too little time and too little treatment. When convicted rapists rape again, the criminal justice system, along with the actual perpetrators, is guilty" (May 25, 1996).

Too little treatment? And they never learn.

Effectiveness of Domestic Violence Treatment Programs

How well does court-ordered, taxpayer-paid psychotherapy work with wife beaters?

The 1993 Survey on Women's Health, commissioned by the Commonwealth Fund and conducted by Louis Harris and Associates, estimated that 1.1 million women had been kicked, bitten, or hit with a fist or some other object and 2.9 million women had been pushed, grabbed, shoved, or slapped in that year alone. Now, the overwhelming majority of these instances do not result in arrests. Even in states like Connecticut, where arrest is mandated once police are called in, 80 percent of the domestic violence cases involve a plea of nolo contendere or are dismissed in court. It is many of these no-contest boys who wind up in the ever-growing number of treatment programs for wife batterers, for perpetrators of what is always, these days, called domestic assault, no matter where or with whom the man and woman involved live.

We have a staggeringly large number of treatment programs designed to help the domestic abuser get over his problems—experts estimate that there are some fifteen hundred such programs in place now around the country—so that the people he abuses can get over theirs. How well do they work?

In September 1995, Officer Curtis Wilson from Barnstable County on Cape Cod shot and killed his wife and then himself with his service revolver. Officer Wilson had been arrested previously for threatening to kill his wife and had been suspended from the force. After he and his wife reconciled, Wilson entered a psychological treatment program for batterers. And the police returned his gun to him.

> Brockton police declined to comment yesterday. Brockton Mayor Winthrop Farwell Jr. said Curtis Wilson had been forced to surrender his service weapon in 1993 after he handcuffed his wife and put a loaded gun to her head. Farwell, who spoke with reporters on Saturday, said that Curtis Wilson, who began active duty in 1986, completed individual and group counseling and received a nine-month suspension and an administrative job before returning to active duty. (O'Brien, *Boston Globe*, September 25, 1995)

Apparently the batterers' treatment program didn't work very well for Officer Wilson.

In an angry column for *Boston Globe*, Eileen McNamara wrote:

> What is harder to comprehend is the combination of arrogance and ignorance that prompted two mental health professionals to stake a woman's life on their assurances that Brockton patrolman Curtis Wilson was no longer dangerous.

> He was not exactly a guy who had demonstrated an impulse toward rehabilitation. He beat and threatened Cheryl Wilson for years, handcuffing her and knocking her unconscious after putting his gun to her head during one attack in 1993.
>
> For all the benefits of heightened public sensitivity toward domestic violence, that very attention has spawned a cottage industry of therapists who think they know how to cure men who terrorize the women they claim to love.
>
> An admirable goal, that. But where is the science on which it's based? Where is the empirical research; where are the outcome studies? Is domestic abuse a psychiatric disorder? A behavioral problem? A neurological glitch? Is it different from street violence? Is it about anger? Or about power? Both?
>
> The truth is that we don't know very much about why men beat and kill women. We don't know how to make them stop. And we have not spent the time or the money to find out. (McNamara, *Boston Globe*, September 30, 1995)

Our ignorance about such matters does not, however, affect our confidence in the batterers' treatment programs. No, indeed. Just a short time after Curtis Wilson killed his wife and himself, the *Boston Globe* reported that the same town mayor had hired yet another woman beater as a cop. After the uproar, the new recruit was sent off to the local domestic violence treatment center—Emerge—for evaluation.

Mayor Winthrop Farwell said, "We need an evaluation and review of his past relationship—what went wrong and why did it go wrong. It will do two things: assure the public that we do take domestic violence seriously in Brockton and especially seriously when we're talking about a police officer" (Anand, *Boston Globe*, October 8, 1995).

Nothing like faith.

How well do such domestic violence programs work in general? (Leaving aside the case of the violence control counselor in Hawaii who became enraged and beat one of his clients to death.) Well, there the picture is much murkier than it is in evaluating the effectiveness of sex offender treatment.

Emerge, the principal court-ordered treatment program for batterers in Massachusetts, and the longest running in the country—it has been in service since 1977, "the first program for abusive men in the nation"—does not keep statistics on whether the program works. Or, if it keeps them, it does not provide them to interested inquirers. Most programs queried about their rates of success either cite confidentiality or a lack of resources to explain their inability to provide statistics on success and failure.

John Keegan was one of two Massachusetts men who allegedly raped a woman, Kristen Crowley, whom they happened to encounter one night, June 2, 1996, in a convenience store after a long evening of drinking in a nearby strip club. After allegedly raping her, Keegan and his buddy, Timothy Dykens, allegedly smashed her head in with a thirty-pound rock, killing her. Keegan, just the previous year, as a condition of probation for attacking his girlfriend, had been sent to a domestic violence treatment program at the Gavin House in South Boston. Apparently he flunked. Like Emerge, the Gavin House provides no statistics on the effectiveness of its treatment programs for men who threaten and beat up women.

Where we do have statistics, the picture is not encouraging. Research shows that there is no reliable effect of treatment programs on incidence of men's violence toward women.

Melanie Shepard, in a 1992 study, found that 40 percent of one hundred men aged nineteen to fifty-eight were identified as recidivists after treatment because they were either convicted of domestic assault, the subjects of an order for protection, or police suspects for domestic assault.

According to Richard Tolman and Larry Bennett (1990), men who batter drop out prematurely from treatment programs at very high rates; the average is 40 percent dropouts. For men who *do* complete programs, follow-up statistics over periods of from six months to one year show recidivism rates, according to the men's reports or police reports, from a low of 15 percent to a high of 47 percent. Is that good? Well, again according to self-report of the men, an average of 37 percent of men who do *not* complete programs also abuse their women again. It doesn't seem like much of a difference.

Also, we can't measure "success" of batterer therapy only by the absence of a re-arrest or by the reports of the batterers themselves.

They are quite likely to say, "Oh, yeah, great program. Helped me a lot." With these measures there cannot be any way of knowing whether the men actually stop beating the women in their lives any more than one could tell if sex offenders who have not been arrested have actually stopped committing criminal sexual acts.

According to Evan Stark in a 1995 article, "Most domestic violence offenders have a long history of assaultive behavior (against their partners at a minimum) and are unrepentant" (p. 979). Underreporting has got to be the rule unless one believes that every sex offense and every violent act against a woman results in an arrest. And no one believes that. No one believes that any more than 10 percent of such acts ever reach the attention of the police.

When the women victims themselves are asked about the results of treatment programs, the results are quite different from what we get with men's self-reports and re-arrest statistics. A 1989 study showed that after a careful test of a twenty-four-week program, 23 percent of the men who completed the program were not violent toward their partners versus 22 percent of the noncompleters. No difference. Thirty-six percent of the completers made violent threats toward their partners versus 30 percent of the noncompleters. Worse. And 26 percent of the completers were directly violent (shoved, bit, slapped, etc.) versus 27 percent of the noncompleters. Again, no difference. Lastly, 15 percent of the men who completed the program were severely violent (burned, punched unconscious, threatened with weapon, etc.) in the first six months after program completion versus 22 percent of men who did not complete the program. Great.

In short, there was no effect of the treatment program in the most carefully run of all the empirical studies. The bottom line is that simple arrest is just as effective as treatment, especially for men who are employed, and neither may be effective at all unless you keep the perpetrator locked up. Treatment programs teach batterers to be more careful about getting arrested again. Period.

As Zvi Eisikovits and Jeffrey Edleson put it in their 1989 review, "Several major problems appear in research on all levels of intervention. First, most of the studies . . . have been conducted by the very people who have designed the intervention and thus should be regarded as self-evaluations at best" (p. 407).

These are classic double-sighted studies. We already know that when we ask therapists if therapy works, they usually say yes.

The absence of evidence that domestic violence treatment programs work has not slowed down the willingness of courts to sentence such offenders to treatment, however. This is doubly ironic when you consider that a significant number of the men sentenced to psychological treatment for their criminal acts are both physically and sexually violent toward women.

PREDICTING DANGEROUSNESS

Michael Kelley, who was treated and released at Bridgewater in Massachusetts, suffered from both of these disabling conditions. For him the combination problem was obviously intractable, given the startling speed with which he repeated his appalling crimes as soon as he was released from the hospital. How could Kelley's doctors have failed to know that he was still dangerous? It is their job, is it not?

> Forensic experts frequently appraise the potential for violent behavior. Their opinions may influence decisions involving criminal sentencing or involuntary commitment. Studies on the prediction of violence are consistent: clinicians are wrong at least twice as often as they are correct. (Faust and Ziskin 1988, p. 241)

Will this man be violent in the future, Doctor X? Is he dangerous?

Absolutely not. He has been in the hospital setting for five years without any trouble. He has met and interacted with numerous people in different roles and has not displayed any acting out behavior. Note how he shyly looks away when confronted by others. He is a fine candidate for release.

What do you think, Doctor Y? Is he dangerous?

As a snake. He has bided his time in the hospital for five years, watching and waiting for just this opportunity. A clever and manipulative fellow, he can make almost anyone believe that he is a changed man, a peaceful man. See how he slyly drops his eyes when you look at him. Throw away the key.

Ridiculous? It is not nearly as ridiculous as what actually happens when psychiatrists and clinical psychologists are asked to predict which hospital patients will be violent in community settings after release. They are worse than chance. *Worse than chance!* They are wrong two thirds of the time! How can that be?

John Monahan, in his 1981 book *Predicting Violent Behavior*, reviewed and summarized all the available research on the ability of psychiatrists and psychologists to predict violent behavior. One of the first was a large study by Kozol et al. (1972) of 592 male offenders at the Massachusetts Center for the Diagnosis and Treatment of Dangerous Persons (Bridgewater). Most of the men had committed violent sex crimes. Over the first "five-year follow-up period following release, 8 percent of the 386 men predicted not to be dangerous became recidivists by committing a serious assaultive act, and 34.7 percent of the 49 predicted to be dangerous committed such an act during the ten-year period studied" (Monahan 1981, pp. 72–73).

That 8 percent means that only 31 men out of 386 committed another violent sex crime after being judged no longer violent or dangerous by the professional state-employed forensic evaluators. That sounds pretty good unless you are one of the victims of these violent predators. How safe would you feel crossing the street if you knew that eight out of one hundred times you would be hit by a truck?

As Monahan points out, 65 percent of the men identified as dangerous did *not*, in fact, commit a dangerous act, at least in the ten years they were followed. That means the forensic evaluators were *wrong in two out of every three predictions* of discovered violence. (Again, no one knows how many acts of undiscovered violence were committed.)

A 1977 study run at the Patuxent Institution in Maryland showed that 31 percent of the inmates recommended for release committed another violent act in the three years following release, compared with 41 percent of the men who were judged to be still violent. That means these forensic evaluators were wrong some two thirds of the time for violent offenders judged to be either dangerous or not dangerous.

These data are not isolated findings. They have been replicated in very large studies in New York and Pennsylvania. In a review article published in the *American Journal of Psychiatry* in 1984, Monahan concluded that the bottom line was, "Clinical predictions of violent behavior among institutionalized mentally disordered people are accurate at best about one-third of the time" (p. 11).

Terrence Campbell, in a 1994 article in the *Michigan Bar Journal*, writes, "The accuracy with which clinical judgment predicts future events is often little better than random chance. The accumulated research literature indicates that errors in predicting dangerousness range from 54% to 94%, averaging about 85%" (1994b, p. 68).

Why not just flip pennies or draw cards? Why not put on a blindfold and choose without being able to identify the patients? It could hardly hurt an accuracy rate that hovers at less than one out of three times correct.

In 1995 the city of Boston paid out $1 million in a wrongful death settlement to the widow of an elderly man who suffered a fatal heart attack during a police drug raid mistakenly targeted at his apartment rather than at the neighbors upstairs. Shouldn't the families of victims of state-certified-mentally-healthy-ex-criminals likewise be empowered to sue for wrongful death at the hands of a negligent state? The family of one of Kelley's victims is reportedly suing the Commonwealth of Massachusetts.

Sylvia McFarland of Tacoma, Washington, is also trying to make the state accountable. Ms. McFarland's "teen-age daughter [allegedly] was stabbed 56 times by a man psychiatrists had called a sexual psychopath who was likely to harm women if he was free. Now, McFarland has filed a wrongful death lawsuit accusing state correction officials of gross negligence in releasing Johnny Robert Eggers, failing to supervise him and then failing to warn the community." The state is claiming that the parole board is covered by judicial immunity (*Seattle Post Intelligencer*, August 9, 1996).

There is no psychological cure for the desire to beat up women, to rape and murder them. The very idea that psychotherapy today could even pretend to such an ability is ludicrous. Yet liberal news editorials call endlessly for ever more "treatment" for these offenders. This shows either extraordinary faith or willful blindness.

It is not just potential victims of crazed killers who are hurt by the fraudulent presumption that forensic psychologists can predict dangerousness accurately. It is also the "dangerous" criminals themselves. People convicted of violent crimes are sentenced to death when psychological professionals tell the jury and the judge that the defendant is a continuing danger to the community.

In the 1983 case of *Barefoot v. Estelle*, the Supreme Court of the

United States ruled on the habeas corpus petition of Thomas Barefoot challenging the reliability of psychiatric predictions of dangerousness.

The Court turned him down and let his death penalty stand.

Justice Harry Blackmun, writing for the dissenting minority, provided the following evaluation of the psychiatric testimony at the trial court level.

> Last, the prosecution called Drs. Holbrook and Grigson, whose testimony extended over more than half the hearing. Neither had examined Barefoot. . . . Dr. Holbrook . . . informed the jury that it was "within [his] capacity as a doctor of psychiatry to predict the future dangerousness of an individual within a reasonable medical certainty," and that he could give "an expert medical opinion that would be within reasonable psychiatric certainty as to whether or not that individual would be dangerous to the degree that there would be a probability that that person would commit criminal acts of violence in the future that would constitute a continuing threat to society."
>
> Doctor Grigson . . . testified that with enough information he would be able to "give a medical opinion within reasonable psychiatric certainty as to the psychological or psychiatric makeup of an individual," and that this skill was "particular to the field of psychiatry and not to the average layman."
>
> . . . Finally, Dr. Grigson testified that . . . there was a "*one hundred percent and absolute*" *chance* that Barefoot would commit future acts of criminal violence that would constitute a continuing threat to society.
>
> The defense counsel questioned the psychiatrists about studies showing wildly unreliable predictions of dangerousness by psychiatrists. Dr. Holbrook said that he disagreed with their conclusions. Dr. Grigson said he was not familiar with most of these studies, and anyway their conclusions were accepted by only a "small minority group" of psychiatrists, not by the American Psychiatric Association.

Because of the testimony of these two overconfident psychiatrists, Thomas Barefoot was sentenced to death.

In this case, the APA filed an amicus curiae brief informing the Supreme Court that the unreliability of psychiatric predictions of long-term future dangerousness was an established fact within the profession, that two out of three predictions of violence made by psychiatrists are wrong—usually in the overprediction direction, and that a layperson with access to relevant statistics can do at least as well as a psychiatrist and possibly better, and that the most that can be said about any individual is that a history of past violence increases the probability that future violence will occur.

The majority of the Court was not impressed by these facts, stating essentially, Hey, the APA didn't say they were wrong *all* of the time, only *most* of the time.

Nor was the Court concerned that the psychiatrists presented their conclusions about Barefoot—sight unseen—to the jury as *medical science*. Justice Blackmun was outraged and wrote:

> Scientific evidence impresses lay jurors. They tend to assume it is more accurate and objective than lay testimony. A juror who thinks of scientific evidence visualizes instruments capable of amazingly precise measurement, of findings arrived at by dispassionate scientific tests. In short, in the mind of the typical lay juror, a scientific witness has a special aura of credibility.
>
> One can only wonder how juries are to separate valid from invalid expert opinions when the "experts" themselves are so obviously unable to do so. . . . There can be no question that psychiatric predictions of future violence will have an undue effect on the ultimate verdict.
>
> Even judges tend to accept psychiatrists' recommendations about a defendant's dangerousness with little regard for cross-examination or other testimony.

Thomas Barefoot may not have been a very nice man. There are certainly a good many people who would argue as well that he deserved to die. But no one, absolutely no one, should be misled into believing that the decision about whether a man should live or die should be based on the "scientific" opinion of mental health professionals about his future dangerousness. Such testimony is an out-and-out fraud and should not be allowed in our courts.

BUSINESS OF HELPING PEOPLE

It is possible that at least some of the innumerable psychological professionals involved in providing rehabilitative therapy and predicting dangerousness in the criminal justice system—and quoted in every news organ across the land—are simply ignorant about their ineffectiveness and inaccuracies. Perhaps they are simply unaware of the research that shows they are so bad at what they claim to be able to do. I don't think so, at least not entirely. I think that you will hear vague citations of meta-analysis studies, assertions that the researchers doing the studies don't know what to measure, or vague claims that new research is showing some effect of some treatment programs, and, of course, that their own clinical experience shows otherwise. Forensic clinicians don't think that such research applies to them, only to other, less competent, practitioners.

Again, don't forget too that we are talking about the livelihood of tens of thousands of mental health professionals.

What would happen if psychology admitted that despite all the rhetoric and millions of dollars expended on the development of treatment programs, the profession is unable to help sex offenders, wife batterers, or any other criminals change their behaviors?

There would be a lot of people out of work. With so much at stake, it is too much to expect the truth.

It is also true that psychologists are afraid to tell the truth about the uselessness of psychotherapy because they fear that someone out there might commit suicide who would somehow have been helped by therapy if only he or she had not been told it was a waste of time. In the mistaken belief that however ineffective therapy may be, at least it doesn't hurt anybody, the field of psychology keeps silent about its ineffectiveness even in crucial legal applications like court-ordered sex offender and domestic violence programs.

Remember too that scientific evidence about therapeutic efficacy does not really constitute evidence in the eyes of most clinical practitioners. Most clinicians feel that science is unable to match the clinical intuitions of the experienced practitioner, and most of them believe that what they spend their lives doing is not entirely futile. Therapists, most of them, believe in therapy.

John Monahan, addressing other professional clinicians, wrote, "We should decline to launder for the legal system the social and demographic factors that anticipate future crime and decline to let judges fob off on us the moral balancing of competing claims for the offender's freedom and the predicted victims' safety. . . . [The] buck should stop at the judge's bench, not at the witness box" (1984, p. 14).

What the rest of us have to do is take Professor Monahan's words to heart and implement them without waiting for professional psychologists to shoot themselves in the economic foot. They are not about to do that.

The outraged public must do it for them.

7 Construction of the Psychological Child

The Child and the Law

> I looked at the kids for a moment. They were not something new. They were something very old, without family, or culture; prehistoric, deracinated, vicious, with no more sense of another's pain than a snake would have when it swallowed a rat. I'd seen atavistic kids like this before: homegrown black kids so brutalized by life that they had no feelings except anger. It was what made them so hard. They weren't even bad. Good and bad were meaningless to them.
>
> Robert B. Parker, *Walking Shadow*, 1994

JUVENILES, JUSTICE, AND PSYCHOLOGICAL KNOWLEDGE ABOUT CHILDREN

On October 13, 1994, in a crime that shocked the country because of its callousness and the youth of the perpetrators, two boys—one ten and the other eleven—dangled a five-year-old boy, Eric Morse, for five minutes off the roof of a fourteen-story building in Chicago before dropping him to his death. The older boys tortured and killed the younger one because he would not steal candy for them.

What is the appropriate course of action for society to take with respect to such children?

Long before modern clinical psychology entered the picture, the American legal system distinguished between children and adults in assessing responsibility for criminal acts. When children are accused of crimes it is thought necessary to assess their maturational competence to stand trial and to determine the appropriate legal consequences of the crimes for children of different maturational levels.

It is generally believed that children below a certain age do not have either the necessary thought processes or the knowledge to appreciate their criminal actions, and that children under a particular age can have their criminal behavioral tendencies eradicated by psychological treatment. The assumption is that most children, unlike most adults, can be rehabilitated; they can be taught to be better people, to return to society as full, productive, noncriminal citizens.

For children, the legal issue of the possibility of psychological rehabilitation arises not only in the context of sentence, but also in the initial determination of competence to stand trial. Under common law, a child under the age of seven is conclusively presumed incapable of knowing the wrongfulness of crimes. From ages seven to fourteen, there is a presumption of incapacity that can be rebutted by clear proof that the child appreciated the quality and nature of the acts. Again under common law, a child over the age of fourteen is treated as an adult. Common law has, until rather lately, applied in most states, subject to statutory age changes from state to state. In most cases juvenile defendants under the age of eighteen are processed under juvenile delinquency statutes that are set up to implement the rehabilitation of the juvenile. Juvenile court, however, can waive jurisdiction, and authorize the trial of a child under eighteen as an adult.

If a forensic evaluator thinks that a young offender can be rehabilitated by psychological treatment, then the child is tried not as an adult but as a juvenile. This often means, depending on the state, that he or she will be out of custody at age twenty-one after serving time in a youth facility, which is essentially a locked hospital.

Where this determination is not a matter of statute, courts turn to psychologists to judge whether a particular child understands his or her crime—if that child is competent—and/or if that child can be rehabilitated by psychological counseling.

Can psychologists tell the court whether the ten- and eleven-year-old boys from Chicago who deliberately dropped the five-year-old child to his death from the roof of a fourteen-story apartment house are capable of understanding that their action was wrong?

According to Don Terry, in a story in the *New York Times* of January 30, 1996, the younger killer had an IQ of 60 and the older one 76. Mr. Terry, in reporting these scores on the front page of his paper, is apparently suggesting that the boys were either too stupid or too immature mentally to understand the nature of their crime. Is that really what intelligence test scores of 60 and 76 reveal about these children? Or about anyone else with such scores?

MATURATIONAL COMPETENCE

How do psychologists tell if a child has the necessary competence to understand the nature of his or her criminal actions? How do psychologists determine, for example, whether a six-year-old child who attempted to kill a newborn baby actually understands the concept of the permanence of death? Do psychologists have any special knowledge unavailable to courts and the public on the mental abilities and general knowledge of children of different ages? Yes, they do, but not as much as they say they do.

Intelligence Tests

When forensic psychologists are asked to evaluate the maturational competence of a child defendant, they often give the child an IQ test. IQ tests do perform fairly well at predicting academic performance in school. Since these tests are at bottom general knowledge tests—with age norms—the psychologist is simply determining whether the child has more or less general knowledge than other kids of the same age. And of the same racial background. Different ethnic groups have different IQ norms for how well children of different ages perform, on the average, on the tests, so any such evaluation must be interpreted relative to the child's own ethnic group.

Does giving the ten- and eleven-year-old children from Chicago such standardized intelligence tests tell the courts anything about whether they are capable of appreciating the wrongfulness of their act?

No. It does not. It showed that both boys perform on the IQ test at a significantly lower level than their age and race peers, but it tells us nothing about their understanding of their crime.

To make that judgment, any psychological professional would have to do what any nonpsychologist would have to do—talk to the boys extensively, in their own idiom and age-appropriate language; talk to their teachers; and then wing it.

It is hard to imagine what people expect in this line from psychological tests. Do they expect a test of whether the boys knew that holding a child off a roof fourteen stories up and then dropping him would kill him? They knew that. Even the terrorized five-year-old knew that as he screamed and struggled. Whether it was wrong to do such a thing? They knew that. They did not invite the little boy's mother along. Whether they had the emotional maturity to control their actions? What does that mean? Murdering a child at the age of ten is not the same thing as throwing a tantrum at two, although I am sure some child psychologists can be found to say that it is.

A California case in April 1996 involved a violent act by a six-year-old boy that provoked analysis seemingly from half the clinicians in the country. The boy pulled a four-week-old baby from his crib and beat him nearly to death with his fists and a stick. The baby now suffers severe brain damage. The prosecutor, Harold Jewett of Contra Costa County's juvenile division, was quoted in the *New York Times* that April as saying, "The minor knew what he did was wrong, and he did it anyway" and should thus carry responsibility for his crime" (Goldberg, *New York Times*, April 26, 1996).

The young assailant was initially charged with attempted murder, but the charges were first reduced and then the prosecution was suspended after three psychiatrists evaluated the boy. They diagnosed him with various cognitive disabilities, including attention deficit disorder, that would make it impossible for him to contribute to his own defense or understand the trial proceedings. He has been "sentenced" to live in a group home under strict supervision and with intensive counseling from a psychiatrist and child specialists.

These same psychologists will no doubt tell you that even in cases in which a child was mature enough to understand his or her action and its consequences, and controlled enough to perform that action deliberately, the child can still be turned around if only the child receives enough psychological counseling.

RUINED LIVES AND REHABILITATION

So what do psychologists do when they are asked to make a determination of amenability to rehabilitation in the case of a child? They do the same thing the rest of us would do. They look at the child's family history and make a prediction informed by demographics. For example, children of intact families have a statistically lower prevalence of criminal conduct than do children of single-parent families, so a child from an intact home gets points toward higher probability of rehabilitation.

They also look at a child's past conduct as a predictor of probable future conduct, because everyone knows that what one has done before is the best predictor of what one will do in the future (e.g., he got good grades for the last six years, so it is likely that he will get good grades in the next six years). Nothing is a perfect predictor, but these factoids are how we—all of us, psychologists included—make our best bets.

Psychologists, like the rest of us, also look at the nature of the particular crime the child committed, and the more horrific the crime, the more pessimistic they feel, the more so as the child's age increases. This assessment is rather problematic—as are all pretrial evaluations that weigh the significance of the crime—because the child before trial has not yet been convicted of any crime, yet the nature of the crime and the criminal intent strongly affect the psychological evaluation.

The 200-Pound Child and the Neighbor Lady

Edward O'Brien is the fifteen-year-old in Massachusetts accused of murdering a neighbor by stabbing her some ninety-six times. His court-ordered psychological evaluator, Dr. Richard Barnum, no joke intended, described O'Brien as an undeveloped teenager (he meant emotionally, since the accused was six feet four inches tall and weighed well over 200 pounds) who was a good candidate for rehabilitation.

This conclusion was based on O'Brien's school history—extremely poor—on anecdotes from teachers and family friends, and on the doctor's interviews with the boy, who refused to discuss the crime with this psychological evaluator.

A teacher and a coach said he was a nice boy. So what? Every kid in the country accused of a hideous crime seems to have innumerable neighbors who say things like "He seemed like such a nice boy," "He was always so nice to my Stevie," and "He was just about to turn his life around by graduating from high school and getting a good job." Right.

What do foolish anecdotes have to do with whether Edward O'Brien will be a danger to the public or whether he will respond to psychotherapeutic treatment? Nothing. Will he stab another neighbor to death? Or, next time, a stranger? Just going with the odds, the answer is no. Most murderers kill only once, so if O'Brien is like most, he's finished with murder. But most murders make somewhat more sense than this vicious, relentless slaughter of a helpless woman by this six-foot-four-inch, 200-pound teenager. Who can understand that? Most ordinary people shake their heads at something like that and say, "There must be something goofy going on in his head."

That's what Dr. Barnum said too. He actually hedged his bet on the question of future dangerousness. The newspaper article describing Barnum's testimony says, "The report states that if it is proved O'Brien had a 'consuming preoccupation' with [the victim] that led to a vicious attack, it's reasonable to conclude that 'this sort of preoccupation might be expected to recur' " (O'Brien, *Boston Globe*, December 29, 1995). That means if something goofy in his head led to the attack, then it's reasonable to conclude that something goofy might happen again. Brilliant.

Presumption of innocence aside, what special professional expertise allowed the doctor to reach this careful conclusion? What special knowledge did he possess that you and I do not have? How many psychological studies do you think there are of adolescents who stab their neighbors some ninety times?

There are none, of course. This is the kind of crime that just does not happen very often, thank God. Anyone, you or I or the court's psychologist or highly paid defense experts, would be relying on exactly the same level and amount of information and intuition in concluding whether this young killer could be straightened out and set on the right path. Your guess is as good as mine. Your guess is as good as that of the official psychological evaluator.

We have already seen that psychological evaluators cannot predict who will do what in the future, not even who will be violent and who will not, so whom do these well-paid professional evaluators of a youth's amenability to rehabilitation think they are kidding?

Two of the doctors at O'Brien's pretrial hearing testified that whether Edward provided investigators with clear, accurate, and consistent accounts of his actions should be taken as an indicator of his probable responsiveness to psychotherapy. Their thinking apparently is that it is easier to turn a truthful boy from the path of multiple murder than a lying defensive one.

This isn't science. It is a farce. Child clinicians do not make their evaluations and recommendations based on sound psychological science. They make them out of the liberal philosophy that views both children and criminals as victims of their families and of society, and the child criminal doubly so.

Court-ordered psychological evaluations of children generally find that nearly all of the child criminals are not sufficiently mature to stand trial as adults, and, second, and not surprisingly, that nearly all of these children are amenable to psychological treatment as well. (Whenever psychologists are asked whether psychological counseling is a good and needful thing, they say yes. Naturally.) With such a cultural philosophy, what else would they find?

Psychologists cannot make "expert" determinations of whether a child can be rehabilitated, of whether a child will be responsive to psychotherapy, any more than they can make "expert" judgments about children's capacity to understand the crimes of which they are accused. If society feels that such determinations are necessary and useful to its ends, then laypeople must bite the bullet and make those determinations themselves without the spurious assistance of pseudo-expertise.

The Ineffectiveness of Psychotherapy with Children

The ten- and eleven-year-old boys in Chicago who dropped the five-year-old boy off the roof to his death because he would not steal for them were sentenced to juvenile detention until the age of twenty-one.

With their attorneys and advocates insisting on intensive psychological counseling for the boys instead of punishment, the Department of Corrections officials assured everyone that psychiatric treatment will be available to these "troubled" children, and the judge in the case demanded that she receive a detailed treatment plan within two months.

Why? What is the point?

Psychotherapeutic treatment cannot ameliorate even the quite mundane problems of ordinary children who seek help on their own or because of their schools or parents. What possible chance does it have to "cure" a disregard for life so callous that it resulted in the murder of a small and helpless younger child?

It sounds good to say, "Oh, my gracious, those kids need help. We have got to get them some help. Get them into counseling." But it is all romanticized, politicized nonsense. There is no therapy that cures juvenile murder disorder. For children there is no evidence that therapy works even as well as talking about sports.

In a 1992 review of child therapy both in clinical trials and in professional settings, John Weisz, Bahr Weiss, and colleagues found that in naturalistic therapy settings, *child psychotherapy has not been shown to have any effect at all* either from the point of view of simple statistical significance or actual clinical effects on the mental health of children. That means that we actually have *no* evidence, not even weak evidence, that child therapy, recommended by every advice columnist in America and required by our judges and courts across the land, works at all.

"What Works" in Juvenile Treatment Programs

> Krys Lloyd is an art and poetry therapist at a Department of Youth Services secure treatment facility in Westborough, [Massachusetts,] a home for violent adolescent offenders. She teaches young rapists to glimpse their own frightened souls in the heart of a rhymed stanza. She gives tough, seemingly impenetrable gang members permission to paint their own fears. No one judges. No one accuses. But everyone learns. (Smith, *Boston Globe*, May 24, 1996)

There are dozens—thousands—of treatment programs for juvenile offenders. Anyone involved in the juvenile justice system, when asked about the effectiveness of these programs, will tell you that, sure, some of them are not very effective, but that is not true of *all* of them. Just recently, in October 1994, the Department of Justice published a big report, a guide to "what works." How could they do that if there is no evidence that rehab programs for young criminals work? Good question.

Anyone who seeks objective information on the effectiveness of all those compassionate, taxpayer-funded, child rehabilitation programs would do well to contact the Department of Justice to request a copy of that report, *What Works: Promising Interventions in Juvenile Justice*.

The naive might believe that a report on juvenile offender treatment programs entitled *What Works* might actually be an evaluative study of the outcomes in terms of recidivism, future schooling, and later employment of the youths served by these rehabilitation programs. It is not.

No objective or statistical evaluative analysis whatsoever went into the report. As the principal investigator, Imogene Montgomery, put it:

> Limited in our efforts to conduct an extensive evaluation of each program, we designed a research methodology that first identified essential components of effective programs. . . . We then asked 3,000 experienced judges, court administrators, and chief probation officers to nominate and rate programs they had recently used. We then sent surveys to the administrators of the nominated programs. The results of our efforts comprises *What Works*, a program directory that contains 425 nationally nominated programs. (Montgomery, Torbet, Malloy, Adamcik, Toner, and Andrews 1994, p. ix)

It is clear that it is not just clinical psychologists who don't understand science.

What is the likelihood that program administrators who received a survey from the Office of Juvenile Justice and Delinquency Prevention asking them to evaluate the programs that provide them with a living would send back the questionnaire saying their programs were a waste of time and taxpayers' money? Zero.

Program administrators, when asked to evaluate their own programs, repeatedly reported that the programs were working quite well for an important number of troubled youths. They communicated these findings to the Department of Justice, which put them in its report on *What Works* in the kid rehab business.

Many program administrators failed to provide the Justice Department with the requested information on costs, but calculating from the data that were made available, for programs based on psychological counseling (individual, group, or family counseling) of the offenders, the average stay is about ten months, and the average cost per day is about $115 per child. That works out to about $34,000 per child to rehabilitate the child through psychological counseling. This despite the fact that psychotherapy has never been shown to work with children.

Thirty-four thousand dollars per child across ten months times the thousands and thousands of youths remanded to these programs is far too much money to throw away through this hall-of-mirrors exercise in intellectual dishonesty.

Judges believe in the value of these programs because they sentence children to them, and no judges in their right mind would do that if they had not been given reason to believe in their value by the people who administer and evaluate them.

Probation officers likewise rely on the psychological professionals who make their livings in the youth rehabilitation business. And those psychological professionals will be the last to disparage either the effectiveness of the treatment programs or their own skill at evaluating and effecting the rehabilitation of youth offenders.

We continue to believe that this kind of treatment works, and our related desire to treat children as less responsible for their actions than adults leads to other problems as well.

THE MYTH OF COURTROOM TRAUMA

Todays news reports are filled with accounts of trials where the judge has befriended the young accuser, dropped judicial ropes in favor of less formal raiment, and allowed the child to testify with his or her psychotherapist seated up on the witness stand, holding hands with the alleged victim.

The particulars of any individual case aside, are setups like these fair trials? In a fair trial, the prosecutors would be trying to prove to the judge and the jury that the child was injured or kidnapped or whatever and that the defendant was the perpetrator. The court itself, and the judge of that court, is not supposed to take a position on guilt or innocence until the evidence is heard.

But what is happening in cases involving children accusing adults of terrible things? Why are psychotherapists seated up on the witness stand holding hands with the testifying children? Because child psychologists—who must know—say they should.

The child psychologists on whom the courts rely have numerous ideas for helping supposedly fragile children navigate the legal system. Several of the proposals are designed to spare children the supposed trauma of testifying in court face-to-face with the people they have accused. One proposal is that children should be allowed to testify on video, another that children should testify in the judge's chambers, or behind some kind of screen, or via closed-circuit television. It is frequently suggested that children not be called to testify at all, or if called to testify that they not be subject to cross-examination. In the flurry of proposals to protect children from alleged testimonial trauma, the memory of the child testimony in the Salem witch trials seems to have been lost to the mists of time.

In the interests of further protecting children from courtroom trauma, some judges have invented other novel trial procedures. In the Massachusetts trial of Fells Acre day care worker Gerald Amirault, Judge Elizabeth Dolan removed her judicial robes during the trial and, in her street clothes, sat down next to the children who were seated in front of the jury box flanked by their parents, who served as a screen between the children and the defendant.

The idea behind all these protective procedures is the underlying psychological assumption that children will be severely traumatized by open court testimony and cross-examination, that confronting the accused face-to-face, and being challenged by a defense attorney, will subject the child to a trauma as great if not greater than that of the original experience.

Research and Reality

How do psychological experts know that testifying in court traumatizes children? They don't; they just think it does. Their clinical intuition tells them so. Is there good, solid research to support the belief that testifying in court damages children psychologically? No.

Is there good, solid research to support the belief that testifying in court is worse for a ten-year-old than for a twenty-year-old? Is worse for a child than for an elder? That a ten-year-old child recounting molestation will be more "damaged" than a twenty-year-old woman recounting rape, more damaged than the frightened eighty-year-old terrorized and beaten in a home invasion? No, no, and no.

Let's be clear about this. Testifying in court about something horrible that somebody terrible did to you is a lousy, rotten experience. It is extremely likely that it will make your heart race and your blood pound and the sweat pour off you. You may well have horrible nightmares. You will drag your feet into the courtroom, avoid the eyes of the defendant, and feel diminished and cheapened by the tactics of the defense attorney. This is true whatever your age. There's no way around it.

It is perfectly reasonable that parents and prosecutors and courts—even psychologists—want to spare children the unpleasant experience of testifying in court. But in their quest to spare the children, they have further sabotaged the entire trial process.

Traumatizing Our Justice System

Protecting a child from the supposed trauma of confronting and accusing an alleged perpetrator in court presupposes the guilt of the accused; protecting the child from the defendant presumes that the defendant is guilty of the crimes before the trial is heard. The whole trial is a sham.

Are psychotherapists seated next to witnesses supposed to be invisible to juries? Are jurors supposed to be unaware of their supposedly protective role? Are they supposed to disregard as irrelevant to guilt or innocence the supportive behavior of parents and judge? Is there a standard bench instruction to that effect? "The jury will disregard all of the extraordinary measures taken to protect this innocent child from that dangerous and guilty defendant"? Of course not.

An assessment of the guilt of the defendant is the reason for the trial, but the whole arrangement tells the jury that the defendant cannot be innocent. It tells the jury that the defendant hurt the child before and is likely to hurt the child all over again in the courtroom. Are jurors presented with such biased trial procedures even capable of considering the idea that the accusations may have come not from a basis in fact but from overzealous prosecutors or even from the supportive psychotherapist—an increasingly common occurrence these days? How could they be when the judge has made it clear that he or she believes that the truthful child must be protected from traumatic contact with the guilty defendant?

What does this do to the right of the defendant to a fair trial, to the presumption of innocence, and to the assumed impartiality of the judge? It completely obviates them. The trial is biased, the defendant is presumed to be guilty before the prosecution has even begun to make its case, and the judge has already reached a judgment before the trial even opens. All of this because psychologists convinced the courts on the basis of nothing more than myth that children are permanently damaged psychologically by testifying against accused abusers in court.

There is no reason to believe that appearing in court as a victim, a witness, or a subject of dispute will traumatize a child. There is considerable reason to believe that the extraordinary measure undertaken to protect children from this hypothetical trauma has severely traumatized our justice system. The myth of courtroom trauma for children does not exist on its own. It derives directly from the broader clinical myth, the myth of the fragile child.

MYTH OF THE FRAGILE CHILD

The myth of the fragile child derives from the core clinical belief that individuals are created, essentially, by the forces acting upon them—principally parents, but also the larger society—and that the process of formation is fraught with peril for the child. Almost anything can and does go wrong. The smallest mistake on the part of the caretaker forever damns the child in some indefinable way. Clinicians hold that the fate of the child lies in the hands of the caretaker, but the grip of the parental hand on the child's collar of fate is about as sure as a grasp on water.

The overwhelming majority of clinical psychologists believe this myth to be true in the absence of any evidence that it is so, and, indeed, even in the face of evidence that the opposite is true. Research shows over and over again the resiliency and adaptability of children even in the face of horrific—if all too common—experiences like war, mutilation, starvation, loss of family, destruction of the home, and so on.

Even brain functioning in young children is quite adaptable. Children quite often recover from brain injuries that leave their elders impaired for life. We don't get less vulnerable to mental injury with increasing age, we get much more so. Resilience is a characteristic of youth.

So why do the child clinicians have such a different view of the vulnerability of children to psychological injury? Part of the answer may be that the children clinicians see every day are children who have been noticeably hurt by something in their lives, children who for one reason or another are having trouble functioning well at home or in school or in the larger community. A steady diet of hurt children might well make one feel that all children are fragile creatures who are easily hurt.

How did psychological experts get courts and lawmakers to believe the myth of the fragile child? That was easy. Judges, prosecutors, attorneys, juries, and parents—we all live in the same culture, and because we do, we all buy into these same psychocultural myths. We all buy into the belief that "children"—*legally* defined—are not responsible for their commission of criminal acts however vicious or violent, that legal children are indefinitely malleable and can easily be rehabilitated by the trained psychological professional, that "children" can and will be irreparably traumatized in court—that even testifying can shatter the glass of their psychological being, and that all children at bottom are essentially as fragile as glass.

We believe these myths, and the ramifications for our justice system have been extensive.

The worst myth that has been perpetuated through the unremitting offices of the professional psychologist is that not only are forensic evaluators—in their various guises of social worker, child psychologist, and psychiatrist—specially trained to unerringly detect what is good or bad for the minds of children, but that they have as well the power to read those minds, to peer into the souls of children, and to see their certain pasts and their likely futures.

Preying on the understandable fears of parents and concerns of justifiably concerned social policy makers, professional child evaluators have been not only greatly but uniquely empowered by our legislatures to "advise" our courts—with an iron hand—on the determination of any and all facts relating to children as victim or as witness.

MYTH OF THE WHOLE TRUTH AND NOTHING BUT THE TRUTH

This extraordinary empowerment of the self-styled child expert has had several serious consequences for our justice system. Police, prosecutors, and judges are left with very little choice but to accept the word of these experts about the psychological nature and functioning of any and all children, both generally and individually. Thus, we have Larry Hardoon, a lead prosecutor in one of the Massachusetts Fells Acre day care abuse cases, on national television, making the unaccountable claim that children do not, cannot, and will not make false allegations about anything even faintly sexual or, indeed, about any very important matters.

Why did he say that? Because the state-certified child psychology experts told him it was so. He wasn't making it up. He was relying on experts.

Are the experts right? Do children make false claims about vitally important matters? Can they? Will they?

Of course they will and they can and they do.

Believe the Child Experts

Consider some of the claims children made in a few of the more prominent day care abuse cases that came to trial over the last dozen years. Children in the McMartin Preschool case in California, under the tutelage of social worker Kee MacFarlane of Children's Institute International, accused various members of the McMartin-Buckey family who worked at the school of killing animals; killing babies; molesting children in hot air balloons, on distant farms, in cemeteries, and in tunnels under the school. Some of the nonexistent tunnels supposedly led to cemeteries. In the Little Rascals day care case in Edenton, North Carolina, children accused center workers of throwing children into shark-infested waters, taking them on trips to outer space, and worshipping the devil. In the Massachusetts Fells Acres case, pediatric nurse Susan Kelley reported on "disclosures" from the children that they were attacked by a robot, forced to eat frogs, and were molested by clowns, lobsters, and sharp pointed sticks.

Prosecutors took these cases to court because they were told by child professionals that the allegations of the children were trustworthy. They were told that the children's statements had been systematically and reliably validated and their behavior carefully analyzed by the clinical intuitions of these selfsame experts who carefully interrogated the children using special psychological techniques known only to the trade.

Everyone who is involved even peripherally with cases involving allegations by children must read the 1995 book *Jeopardy in the Courtroom: A Scientific Analysis of Children's Testimony* by Stephen Ceci of Cornell and Maggie Bruck of McGill University. The authors do a painstaking job of reviewing all relevant research on the subject of children's testimony, including their own new research, and describe clearly the types of conditions and techniques that can lead children to make false accusations. Their position is objective and their tone nonpartisan, but their research findings are undeniable. It would seem impossible for any clinician having once read their research to again make the statement that children do not make false claims about a whole range of matters, including important matters like sex and death.

The June 1995 issue of the journal *Psychology, Public Policy and the Law* also contains more than a dozen not-to-be-missed articles on the suggestibility of child witnesses. These two offerings, plus a host of other related publications, leave no one any excuse for repeating the mythological nonsense that children are incapable of making any statements that are anything short of the truth, the whole truth, and nothing but the truth.

It is very strange. All parents know that children will make up stories about anything, yet when it comes to flamboyant ritual abuse allegations, parental awareness of reality is blanked by a red curtain of fear and anger and horror.

It is quite easy to understand why parents depend on the expert opinions of child psychologists to help them judge what did or did not happen to their children, just as it is quite easy to see why prosecutors, police, and judges rely on the word of these experts. It is even easy to understand why the media welcome flamboyant allegations involving youngsters—it sells. But why do so many *clinicians* believe absolutely in the unfailing veracity of children? And believe me, they do.

(It should go without saying—but in today's highly charged climate it does not—that there are countless children whose accusations of abuse are completely, tragically true, and unknown numbers of children who do not speak up because they do not know what to say, or they don't know who will help, or they do not think that they will be believed. It should also go without saying that belief in hot air balloon and cemetery tunnel molestation is prima facie evidence of a serious problem in an *adult's* mind.

Why did the psychoexperts who interviewed the children in these cases believe so many utterly outlandish and physically impossible allegations? Their wholehearted acceptance of the children's claims is entirely different from the metaphorical belief accorded by clinicians to their unhappy *adult* clients who claim—with no physical evidence whatsoever—that as teenagers they were repeatedly raped and forced to bear infants used as sacrifices in Satanic abuse rituals, that their brothers had testicles surgically removed for ritual use, that they regularly disinter and hack up corpses from graveyards, and so on. Adults who make such claims may be experiencing a "personal, subjective reality not shared by others," clinicians say, but the equally outlandish claims of the children are as real as real gets.

Clinicians believe the claims of children because they believe that children *cannot* lie about vitally important matters like sex or death or mutilation. Moreover, they believe that they cannot be led to make false allegations about such crucial matters either.

Is that true? Can children be led to make false claims about something as intensely personal as, for example, an injury to the self? Sure they can.

> In a . . . series of studies, Dr. Ceci and Dr. Bruck and their colleagues asked several classrooms of preschoolers to remember things they really had experienced, such as an accident requiring a doctor's visit and stitches. They were also told to think of events that had never happened, like getting a hand caught in a mousetrap and having the trap removed at the hospital.
>
> Once a week an interviewer asked children individually

> about both events. When a child said that an imaginary scenario like the mousetrap accident had happened to her, she was asked about details, such as what she was wearing when she went to the hospital and who went with her. . . . [B]y the seventh week, about half were claiming they'd been hurt by mousetraps. Not only that, but some of the stories were as detailed, coherent, and emotional as true recollections.
>
> These experiments show that suggestive questioning about events that never happened can contaminate young children's memories with fantasies. In the real world beyond the psychology lab, Doctors [Stephen] Ceci and Maggie Bruck suspect that the same thing happened to children in the day care scandals.
>
> In [another] one of their experiments several preschoolers got a routine checkup from a doctor who avoided touching their genital areas. All the children were then asked to show how they'd been examined by the doctor, and they were given dolls with sexual parts to help them explain. In response, many said they had been touched sexually. Some hit the dolls' penises, vaginas, and anuses, or stuck spoons into the orifices; they said the doctor had done the same to them. When challenged, one continued to vehemently insist that the doctor had touched her abusively. Playing with the anatomically detailed doll had apparently altered her memory. (Nathan, *Redbook*, April 1996, p. 14)

In another study they call "Misled Preschoolers," Ceci and his colleagues looked at the effects of both negative stereotyping and suggestive questioning on children's reports of events. They found that three- to four-year-old children were quite accurate in reporting what did and did not happen during a particular event at their preschool—the visit of a strange adult named Sam Stone—when completely neutral techniques were used by adults to query the children.

But when the young ones were subjected to both repeated, negative, stereotyping and to suggestive questioning, *72 percent of the three- to four-year-olds reported that they had seen "Sam Stone" commit clumsy acts he did not in fact commit.*

When challenged, most, but by no means all, of the children in these groups backed off from the false allegations (*Children Today*, Ceci and de Bruyn, 1993).

Getting a hand caught in a mousetrap, being abused by a pediatrician, seeing a strange adult damage a book and a toy—these are claims not that dissimilar from those being made by children in their testimony in our courts every day.

These researchers explain that although there are no reliable figures on the number of children who end up participating in family court or criminal justice proceedings, an extrapolation from some recent New York State data to the entire nation suggests that this number could be in the vicinity of 100,000.

> If one adds to this 100,000 figure the large number of nonabuse cases that result in children participating in court proceedings [e.g., as witnesses to domestic violence, road accidents, playground injuries], then their participation in the legal system rises considerably. Thus, it has become common to see young children providing testimony in a range of cases, from custody disputes to felonious murders. (Ceci and de Bruyn 1993, p. 5)

It is very important that we understand the limits of children's testimony, particularly their vulnerabilities when they are subjected to adults with an agenda.

Human Lie Detectors

Are clinicians human lie detectors? Do clinicians believe the claims of children because they have a special capacity to tell when children are telling the truth and when they are not? My undergraduates say that experienced clinicians would know if children were lying. Are they right?

To find out just how good clinicians are at detecting the truth, Ceci and his colleagues showed the "Sam Stone" story videotapes of children, fabricating or telling the truth about various things, to more than one thousand psychological experts, and asked them to pick out which was which. How did they do? Was there an impressive display of unerring human lie detection, making any future machine obsolete before it even sees the light of day? Au contraire.

Ceci and de Bruyn explain:

> Some researchers have opined that the presence of perceptual details is indicative of true memories, as opposed to confabulated reports. In this study, however, perceptual details were no assurance that the report was accurate. In fact, it was surprising to see the number of false perceptual details children in the stereotype and suggestion condition provided to embellish the non-events [e.g., claiming that Sam Stone took the teddy bear into a bathroom and soaked it in hot water before smearing it with a crayon].
>
> So strikingly believable were their reports that we presented videotapes of these interviews to researchers and clinicians who work in the area of children's testimonial competence to see if they could discriminate erroneous reports from accurate ones.
>
> We did this at two recent conferences [the American Psychology-Law Society Biennial Meeting, San Diego, March 15, 1992; and a NATO Advanced Study Institute, Italy, May 19, 1992]. The results were the same at both conferences: The majority of the audience got it wrong—very wrong.
>
> The audience was shown the videotapes of the children giving free narratives during the final interview. They were instructed to watch the tapes carefully and decide which of the children was the most accurate, next most accurate, etc., and to rate their confidence in the accuracy of each of the child's statements. They were not told whether the children saw Sam Stone do things, but were asked to decide for themselves which of the things that were alleged by the children actually transpired during Sam Stone's visit. Since so many of the children claimed that Sam ripped the book and/or soiled the bear, most of the audience assumed that these events must have transpired, otherwise they found it hard to imagine how so many children could make the same incorrect claim.
>
> *Experts who do research on children's testimonial competence, provide therapy to children suspected of having been abused, and conduct law enforcement interviews of child victims, all failed to detect which children were accurate and which were not, despite*

> *being confident in their opinions.* The children's reports would fool anyone who thinks that it is easy to detect a young child's false report, contrary to claims from some quarters. The reason is that, unlike the typical study in which a child is presented a single erroneous suggestion, these children received persistent and intense suggestions that built on a prior set of expectations (i.e., stereotype).
>
> We believe that this ingredient is more similar to what transpires in some actual cases; it is common for child witnesses to be interviewed many times prior to being given a formal, videotaped interview with anatomical dolls, or to testifying in court. This is the first research to examine over long periods of time the effect of persistent, erroneous suggestions that are consonant with children's expectations.
>
> Thus, the procedures we employed occur, albeit in altered form, in actual therapy sessions and law enforcement/CPS [child protection services] interviews. We patterned our experimental manipulations after materials that we have collected over the past decade from court transcripts and therapeutic interviews. (Ceci and de Bruyn 1993, pp. 5–6; italics added)

The experienced psychological experts were worse than chance at detecting when the children were lying. *Worse than chance!* How could anyone be worse than chance? Only by believing that children tell the truth, no matter what they say.

Belief may be the default value that makes our society function, but it is a serious roadblock in the pursuit of scientific impartiality, not to mention a little short on reality testing. Our parents lie to us, our children lie to us. Our teachers lie and our students lie, and so do our patients. We believe them all. Most of us are reluctant to admit we can be suckered, but we know in our heart of hearts that it is so. Clinicians believe in their heart of hearts that it is *not* so, that no one can sucker the trained psychotherapist. They are wrong.

What do clinicians do when they are confronted by a child's allegations so bizarre that no clinician—except perhaps the space invader specialist from Harvard—and no parent who was not also completely delusional, could possibly believe them to be true? To the rest of us, patently false allegations would suggest that the child was not telling the truth, the whole truth, and nothing but it. Not to the clinician.

Psychological Trauma Tales

Psychologists rush in to explain that fantastic, unbelievable stories are the way children deal with trauma. Their psychological trauma tales are as inventive and as insubstantial as those of the imaginative children. They strongly resemble in their ad hoc logic the creative inventions of defense experts called upon to defend the indefensible—like the Larchmont murder of the two innocent, helpless strangers.

Clinicians offer scenarios like these: The child will invent a clown or a robot to distance himself from the immediacy of the traumatic event. The child will embed his or her terror within the context of a less frightening, more familiar fantasy like a trip to outer space or Halloween-inspired cemetery stories. Floating in a hot air balloon is just a metaphor for dissociation. For a child, penetration with knives and sticks is just a psychological metaphor. And so on, and so on.

Is there any evidence that these creative fictions of the clinician are true? None at all. But the lack of evidence is not noticed by the clinician. The surface plausibility, given cultural psychological assumptions, makes for a good and convincing story. Nothing more is needed.

How can any court let a clinician sit up on the witness stand, spin these yarns, and claim to be able to read children's minds infallibly?

"Penises Are Gwoss"

The right mind-set can create criminally damaging evidence from the most innocuous of children's conversation.

"Penises are gwoss."

That was out of the mouth of the five-year-old daughter of friends. Now where might that have come from? There are four males in her house, so there are several possibilities. Maybe I prompted it. I brought home so-called anatomically correct dolls to see how she would react to them. She immediately said, "That's a boy and that's a girl." "How do you know?" I asked. She reached down and grabbed the male organ and said, "Because he has a penis. Boys have penises." "How do you know?" "Because my daddy has a penis. I've seen my daddy's." Was that true? And is the sight of a penis sufficient to prompt the comment that penises are gross?

Several days before the comment was made, both the little girl and I had been subjected to an eye-level view of my dog's penis. Remy—the dog—had been sitting at the top of the stairs on which the child and I sat, partway down, putting on our boots before going outside. The dog sat, utterly unconcerned, quite unaware, as his penis moved rhythmically in and out of its sheath as he breathed. One might say that it was kind of gross.

Was it the dog that prompted my neighbor child's remark? Or the absurdly appended Raggedy Andy dolls? Who knows? Maybe other children in her preschool told her penises are gross. Maybe her eight-year-old sister told her. Maybe "gross" was her word of the week. Who can say? Not you. Not I. Not any "child psychologist."

However, put this little conversation in the mind of child psychologists with agendas—financial, emotional, or political—and you have real trouble. They can take such utterly innocuous stuff and destroy families, reputations, and lives.

Parents and prosecutors have little choice but to believe that the professional child expert knows what he or she is doing, that the expert must indeed have trustworthy instruments and highly trained skills for determining reliable statements and evidence of crimes witnessed and suffered by children. They do not.

Some of these professionals delude themselves into thinking that they have a special gift for the task they have undertaken. Since so many clinicians believe absolutely in their infallible powers of clinical intuition, they must believe as well in their intuitions about children. Some of them too must deliberately stifle the doubts about their infallibility that must inevitably crop up even in the most credulous and self-deluded mind. Sometimes too it seems that if people greatly fear a particular outcome—like letting a child abuser go free—they will do anything to stop it.

Sometimes my students say, "Well, something must have happened there, so they must be guilty of something even if it is not sex in cemeteries or hot air balloons." Andrew Vachss, an attorney in New York who represents children, wrote in the November 3, 1996, issue of *Parade* that getting convicted is no big deal for an innocent adult because the conviction can always be reversed. He did not himself volunteer to spend ten years in prison for the cause, but he had no objections to others doing so as an acceptable level of damage collateral to successful prosecutions of the truly guilty.

Seeking a greater good than justice is following a dangerous path.

And a Little Child Shall Be Led

Stephen Ceci and Maggie Bruck's research shows clearly that many of the questioning techniques of parents, psychologists, and professional investigators can lead directly if not inevitably to false accusations. In their book, they demonstrate that the beliefs and biases of interviewers can strongly influence both the behavior of the interviewers and the eventual statements of the children and that repeated questions can cause a child to change what has been said (e.g., Why is this man still asking the same question? I guess my answer must be wrong). They show too that describing a suspect in stereotypically negative terms (clumsy Sam Stone) or claiming that other children made allegations can increase the instance of abuse claims, that the status or authority of the person doing the interviewing might bias the content of what the child says.

Lastly, but very importantly since it is a common technique used by clinical psychologists to "refresh" memory, the instruction to children to think hard about or visualize an alleged event can bring that event to life in the child's mind whether it actually occurred or not.

Ceci and Bruck believe that even quite young children can offer valuable and reliable testimony if they are very carefully questioned by adults who are both well informed of the dangers involved in interviewing children and conscientious about avoiding them.

It seems undeniable that their work makes it clear that videotaping the procedures of investigative professionals is essential both to protect the child—being involved in a criminal investigation is no picnic for a child—and to avoid miscarriages of justice when children's allegations are the basis of prosecution.

Moreover, it is a frightening fact that interrogations of children can result not only in mistaken charges against adults but even in having children confess to crimes they did not commit. In Boston, at the end of 1996, a fire destroyed an empty factory and spread to the adjoining neighborhood, leaving one hundred people temporarily homeless. A nine-year-old boy was charged with arson on the basis of his "confession" following police interrogation.

> According to police, the 9-year-old approached officers at the fire Tuesday night and told them he had seen three men carrying gasoline into the mill.
>
> When he was taken to police headquarters for questioning, he allegedly made "incriminating statements," and was charged with one count of second-degree arson in Providence Family court.
>
> But last night, [police] said that the investigation into the cause of the blaze had produced a witness who led police to two 14-year-olds. (Lyons, *Boston Globe*, October 27, 1996)

Most professional child evaluators do not think that videotaping interrogation procedures is necessary to guard against the intrusion of the evaluator's agenda into the child's story. Why would they? They have their clinical intuitions to guide their procedures in the pursuit of truth. After all, they very seldom tape their therapy sessions either.

TRAGIC RELIANCE ON PSEUDO-EXPERTS

American society is taking needed and long overdue steps to safeguard children both by opening our eyes to the reality of child abuse and by institutionalizing steps to prevent it. The reliability and veracity of children as eyewitnesses to crimes both against themselves and against others is also getting a long overdue reevaluation.

Where we have gone tragically astray both in our efforts to protect our children and in our efforts to engage them more fully as effective witnesses in the criminal justice system is in trusting self-styled experts—with their supposedly infallible intuitions—to take over the responsibility of eliciting statements from children and of "clinically" validating them for truth and falsehood in all particulars.

In court, these child psychologists offer as corroboration of children's testimony their professional endorsement of the claims, based on nothing more than the unquestionable validity of their intuitions. It is the psychologists who make unsubstantiated assertions about the vulnerability of children, the innocence of children, their veracity, and their invulnerability to suggestion or coercion. It is the psychologists who are responsible for the suspension of rationality by our law enforcement agencies in cases involving children as victims or witnesses. It is the psychologists who have told law enforcement, prosecutors, and courts, who have told our entire judicial system, "Trust us. We know what we are talking about when it comes to the minds of children and you do not."

They do not know what they are talking about.

Nevertheless, bombarded by an endless barrage of statements and theories about the psychological nature of children, made with absolute certainty and backed with every kind of professional seal of approval, parents, teachers, and the entire family court system have had little choice but to hand the affairs of this fragile, complex creature—the Psychological Child—over to the tender ministrations of its creator—the child mental health professional. Sometimes it seems that we not only tolerate the promulgation of this mythology as science but beg for it and institutionalize it at every possible opportunity. (Are attorneys all married to psychologists?)

When we admit into our courts as experts those whose main claim to professional expertise is their admittedly anti-scientific intuition guided by a psychopolitical mythology with intellectual foundations akin to tea leaf reading, the concept of expert opinion becomes a farce indeed.

> Child advocates and sexual abuse specialists said yesterday that a 10-year-old [New Hampshire boy] who commits such acts [as the rape of children] may be reacting to overexposure to pornography and adult sexual acts or the early onset of puberty. (Ferdinand, *Boston Globe*, August 23, 1996)

The early onset of puberty? For heaven's sake!

> They added that most young perpetrators are reliving childhood trauma. "Kids don't learn these things unless they have been perpetrated upon them," said Frances Belcher, executive director of the New Hampshire Children's Trust Fund. (Ferdinand, *Boston Globe*, August 23, 1996)

Interesting, is it not, then, that most abused children are female, but most abusers are male? A farce indeed.

Turning to clinical psychologists to make judgment calls that society deems necessary about children's understanding of crimes and the likelihood of rehabilitation does nothing but obscure the extreme difficulty of making those judgments; it does not make the judgments easier, more valid, or more reliable. It just makes them more comfortable for those who hand them off. We are all more comfortable if we can believe that these tough decisions are made on the basis of something other than personal opinion. They are not. We've just substituted the clinicians' personal beliefs for our own.

In Andrew Vachss's *Parade* article, "If We Really Want to Protect the Children," he suggests that we hand over *all* the fact finding about matters of child abuse to specially trained—and presumably infallible—child evaluation experts to an even greater extent than we do now.

> We need an objective "one-stop shop" system to avoid the confusion that results from subjecting a child to a series of interviews. All cases would be referred to a multidisciplinary resource center which has no vested interest in the outcome and which has the sole job of finding the facts. No party to the case—be it prosecution, defense, a parent in a custody battle or otherwise—would be permitted to control the investigation. A full and complete record should be made available to all once it is finished.

God help us. Vachss has a touching faith in the neutral stance and extraordinary fact-finding skills of forensic psychologists, although he shows no respect at all for the rights and responsibilities of parents. He thinks that growing the professional child protection industry to a size and power even greater than now will somehow not only further the cause of justice in America but protect our children from harm. He could not be more wrong. We have done enough damage by abdicating our responsibilities as fact finders in these terribly difficult matters—designating fatally flawed and inadequate pseudo-specialists to do the job for us. Magnifying the error is sure as heck not going to erase it.

Miscarriages of justice *do* matter, both to individuals and to society.

In our fervor to save the children, we are simply damning our society from another direction. Unexamined mythology, unwarranted prejudice, and unanalyzed opinion of clinical psychology are burrowing like termites into the foundations of the justice system of our country, and they will topple it if left unchecked.

8
In the Best Interests of the Child

Parental Rights and Psychoexperts

> In considering psychological factors affecting the best interests of the child, the psychologist focuses on the parenting capacity of the prospective custodians in conjunction with the psychological and developmental needs of each involved child.
>
> American Psychological Association Guidelines for Child Custody Evaluations in Divorce Proceedings, *American Psychologist*, 1994

CUSTODY WARS AND THE EXPERT WITNESS

In a 1990 custody case in New York State the mother lost custody of her five-year-old son after a psychiatrist, hired by the father, told the judge that the mother incessantly demeaned the father, even in front of the child.

> The mother's expert witness, also a psychiatrist, recommended that the parties be given joint custody. Although he alternately suggested that the mother be granted sole custody, he conceded that if such an award were made and the mother continued her barrage of negative comments about the father in the child's presence, the child could become extremely disturbed. He further conceded that if the mother were awarded custody, she might interfere with the father's visitation of the child. (*Gage v. Gage*, 1990)

What is going on here? Nothing special. It is par for the course in modern custody fights. Every year, more than a million children under the age of eighteen are affected by family dissolution. It is extremely hard to determine the total number of these cases in which child custody is disputed because many cases—even those involving court-appointed or parent-hired expert child evaluators—do not go to trial. Nationally, it is certainly well into the hundreds of thousands.

Psychological professionals are hired by the warring mother and father or appointed by the court—often both—to evaluate the worth of both claims and claimants, absolutely and relatively. In a national sample of judges who hear custody cases that come to trial after the failure of bargaining between the divorcing spouses, 25 percent of the judges said that the testimony or report of a mental health professional is presented as evidence in a majority of contested custody cases in their courts.

Since there are usually two experts hired, one per parent, and quite often another appointed by the court, sometimes as a guardian *ad litem*, the costs of all this psychological expertise mount up pretty quickly. Let us assume that those one million children of divorce are the products of 500,000 divorces a year, and assume further that custody is disputed in about one quarter of those divorces, some 125,000 a year, and that psychoexperts are used in about one quarter of those contested cases (31,250 divorces). With three experts per divorce, each charging about $200 an hour and spending about five hours each per case to interview the parties and write up the report, then we get a dollar figure of $3,000 for psychoexperts in each case. We arrive at a total national cost of using psychological experts in custody disputes of around $93.75 million annually. That is not a bad piece of change if you are in the expert business, although it probably seems rather appalling if you are one of the divorcing spouses.

The results of psychoexperts' contributions to resolution of custody disputes are often quite a shock to the parties involved. Many previously unaware people are brought to a stunned realization of the awesome power accorded the professional psychological decision maker in our legal system. Accustomed not only to making their own decisions about what is in the best interests of their children, but to the respect society accords parents faced with those daily decisions as well, parents in disputed custody proceedings are often affronted and outraged to find themselves the target of a stranger's evaluation for parental fitness. Bewildered and incredulous, they find that statements they make about their children, about their own lives, and about the lives of their ex-spouses will be weighed by a professional psychological evaluator frequently held by the courts to have a special lock on the truth.

In a transfer of custody case that would remove a girl from the home of her mother with whom she had always lived to the home of her father one thousand miles away from the mother, the Wisconsin Court of Appeals considered testimony from a psychologist who had not actually even met with the mother or the child, but testified that, hypothetically speaking:

> anxieties would normally be expected on the part of the child who has maintained a close association with the noncustodial parent on being suddenly deprived of that association. . . . According to Dr. [Linda] Marinaccio, if contact is not maintained with the noncustodial parent, the child often tries to form a new family and may substitute a stepparent, pretending that the noncustodial parent does not exist. (*Pamperin v. Pamperin*, 1983)

The family court took custody away from the mother, who lived with her new husband in Tennessee, and gave it to the father, who lived with his new wife in Wisconsin, the site of the original family home.

The mother appealed, contending that the psychologist's opinions were nothing but responses to hypothetical questions and did not take into account the actual persons involved. Moreover, she said that an expert's answers to hypothetical questions provided an insufficient basis to change custody.

As the court of appeals put it so succinctly, "We disagree."

The appeals court ruled that the trial judge was quite right to give custody to the father since the mother had shirked her duty of having her parental fitness weighed by a professional psychologist. They also had no objection to the psychologist offering "hypothetical" opinions about the mother she had never met. After all, they seemed to say, whose fault was it that they had not met?

Judges use psychological testimony and reports in custody cases much as the King of England used the Archbishop of Canterbury back in the old days when even the king sometimes thought the archbishop had the ear of heaven.

Sometimes parents conspire unwittingly in the unwarranted empowerment of the psychologists.

> In March 1991, the father commenced this proceeding for sole custody. . . . After a hearing which took place on various dates over a period of at least five months, and which primarily involved the testimony of a psychologist who had been treating [the daughter] for almost a year [a four-year-old child!], the parties stipulated that they would be bound by the report and recommendations of a mutually agreed-upon, court-appointed therapist. The therapist conducted extensive interviews with the parties, their spouses, and [their daughter], and ultimately recommended that the father should have primary custody of the child. The Family Court subsequently issued an order awarding primary custody to the father.
>
> On appeal, the mother contends that the Family Court improperly delegated its custody decision to the court-appointed expert. (*Hennelly v. Viger*, 1992)

The appeals court agreed that the lower court could not "abdicate its duty to determine custody by relying solely on the report of a court-appointed expert," and sent the case back down to get a fuller explanation of the grounds for the custody decision.

That decision by the appeals court to ask for more information might suggest that at least the higher courts are cautious about the usurpation of judicial power by the psychoexperts, but this prudent weighing of psychological testimony is by no means a uniform happening.

In *Lobo v. Muttee*, a 1993 case in New York, the state appeals court acknowledged that it "would be seriously remiss if we allowed a custody determination [to grant sole custody to the mother] to stand without . . . complete forensic evaluations of the parties and the child. . . ."

In *Johnson v. Johnson* from 1994, the same court slapped down the decision of a family court to award custody of two daughters to the father, in part because the lower court ignored "a thorough and carefully reasoned 22-page report, [by] the [court-appointed] psychologist conclud[ing] that the mother would be a more fit custodian for the younger daughter [because the] mother allowed the daughter to freely express and develop her emotional and intellectual capacities, whereas the father was more didactic and demanded compliance, even if indirectly."

It was quite clear that in the opinion of the appeals court, it is the *psychologist*, not the trial judge, who is the best judge of each "parent's ability to provide for the child's emotional and intellectual needs" (*Johnson v. Johnson*, 1994).

In the decision of *Young v. Young*, the New York Appeals Court was positively indignant when the lower court ignored the opinion of the psychoexpert. It wrote:

> It is evident that the court completely disregarded Dr. Reubins' recommendation; and, without any discernible reason or basis in the record to support such a determination, its conclusion is nothing short of arbitrary. . . . Dr. Reubins performed the only complete evaluation of the parties and children as the court-appointed forensic expert. His opinion was strong, firm, competent, weighty, *and unbiased.* (*Young v. Young*, 1995; italics added)

Today, the courts seem not only to accept psychological expert testimony on complex family issues but to demand it to effect what they see as reasonable resolution to problems with no single correct solution. Today, a psychological professional—even one who has never met you or the children who are the subject of the dispute—may in fact hold the fate of children's residence and familial well-being in his or her hands.

In actual fact, of course, it is the king—the judge—who ultimately empowers the archbishop. And a scattershot review of custody cases at the appeals level reveals an interesting pattern of endorsement and rejection of forensic psychology by the courts. It seems as if the court embraces the opinion of psychological experts when that opinion bolsters its own criterion du jour and rejects it when it does not.

But the buck does not stop with the initial trial judge. In our legal system the king must bend the knee to a still higher king—another judge or set of judges with different criteria—in a chain of authoritative review that in family law cases usually stops at the state appeals level. Since one of the measures of judicial competence is the number of times the judge gets reversed on appeal, it is no surprise that judges do their best to make sure their decisions have a sound and substantial basis. It is in seeking such a basis that they allow psychoexperts to overrun their courts with the madness of their pseudo-expertise.

Aware of the large and growing number of psychologists taking on the role of critical adviser to courts in custody cases, the American Psychological Association has issued to its members a set of guidelines outlining the duties and responsibilities of the ideal custody evaluator.

Knowledge, Skills, and Abilities Required to Be the Better Parent

In as bold and upfront a manner as can be, the APA tells its members that their primary duty—in the best interests of the child—is to evaluate each parents' "capacity for parenting," including an assessment of all the "knowledge" the person has to be a good parent, all the parenting "skills" he or she has, and all the parenting "abilities" each parent has to do the parent job.

That seems to me to be a rather daunting job. What, exactly, is the requisite list of "knowledge" one must have to be a good parent? Does knowledge mean knowing how to cook and do the laundry? Or is it about knowing how to play softball, or hopscotch? Is it knowing how to do algebra or search the Internet for source material for term papers?

What are these parenting "skills" that the psychological evaluator is looking for? Is it the skill of changing diapers or teaching potty training? Is it the skill of inducing the child to do homework? To share with siblings and friends? To patiently finish a task? Does the better parent play a mean game of soccer or squash?

How does one distinguish all this knowledge and all these skills from the parenting "abilities" one also must possess to pass the evaluator's muster? What abilities? The patience of a saint? The ability to shape the young through behavior modification? The freedom from work to coach the soccer team? The financial resources to pay for college?

Whose list is this? Who could make—who would presume to make—a definitive list of necessary or even desirable parenting knowledge, skills, and abilities? For one family, it is crucial that the parent have a strong sense of religious faith and practice to hand down to the children. For others, it a strong sense of ethnic identity. For others, an active political conscience and the willingness to work for change in the world. For some parents, a life without a significant portion devoted to sports and physical fitness seems a life only half lived. For others, a life not strongly intertwined with matters intellectual is similarly a life half lived. One family believes that a child should learn a trade and get on with life right out of high school. Another believes that every child who is to have a decent chance must spend four years at a college or university.

Try asking half a dozen friends—both with and without children—to list the top ten things every boy or girl should know how to do by age eighteen. Ask them to list the ten most important aspects of life. How much agreement do you think you will get? It depends on how randomly you sample, of course, but achieving consensus would be a miracle.

It should be absolutely clear to everyone that whatever the claims of highly paid professionals with impressive credentials and fancy-sounding titles, there is not, there cannot be, and there never will be any sound scientific research on the specific types of knowledge, skills, and abilities that one must have to be the psychologically "superior" parent, to be the parent who should have custody of the children of a marriage.

Remember, we do not ask the psychologist to tell us which parent knows that children must be taught to wash between their toes. We are asking him or her for a *psychological* evaluation. If we want evaluations of old-fashioned, hands-on, child care skills, we should ask our grandmothers.

Superior Values of the Better Parent

The American Psychological Association also instructs custody evaluators to assess the relative merits of the *values* of the disputing parents.

Evaluating relative parenting abilities was hard enough, but how are the child "experts" going to go about determining who has the better *values*? How does this business of identifying the parent with the "superior" values actually work out in practice? Jay Ziskin, in *Coping with Psychiatric and Psychological Testimony*, describes a case of an application for a change of custody of a child from the mother to the father after the father's recent remarriage.

> Biases may arise out of identification with or shared value systems with one litigant as contrasted to another litigant. In this case, there appeared to be shared value systems between the psychologist and the father, as indicated by the fact that both have earned Ph.D.'s, both are very much achievement oriented, as indicated by their accomplishments, and as indicated by the similarity of their choices as to areas of residence (Eastern, metropolitan) in contrast to the mother's choice of area of residence (Western, small city). (Ziskin 1995, pp. 624–25)

Biases about superior values may also arise out of the psychologist's personal views of motorcycle riding, of hiring a babysitter while a parent attends school, of drinking beer while watching television, of parents' working for twelve hours a day—or of not working outside the home at all—or what he or she feels about the importance of traditional values in terms of roles, morals, sexual behavior, education, and religion.

It is no step at all to turn those personal value judgments into professional opinions to support the case of a parent making claims along these lines:

> Plaintiff claims that his son . . . is suffering emotionally from lack of supervision, guidance and attention from his mother, which has fostered a feeling of lost love and affection. . . . [H]is former wife's work load and professional responsibilities . . . dictate that she be away from [the child] for unconscionably long periods of time, thereby prohibiting her from taking an active parenting role. [I *do* have the time, however, as does my new wife . . .]. (*David W. v. Julia W.*, Supreme Court of New York, 1990)

Of course, these appeals do not always prevail. This one did not. But the wife here was a psychiatrist and shot back with two of her own experts.

When hired psychological experts pretend that their evaluation of respective parental values is a scientific endeavor rather than a strictly personal echoing of their own values hierarchy, they will see every aspect of the custody evaluation through lenses ground by that delusion. Having decided which parent they most respect or admire, they then find evidence everywhere to support that bias and distort every piece of the report to make the preferred parent look better to the judge.

In a critique on one expert witness's testimony in a change of custody case, Jay Ziskin, in *Coping with Psychiatric and Psychological Testimony*, wrote:

> Several features of the psychologist's report point to bias in favor of the father. . . . Throughout the report when using the proper names of the litigants, the psychologist refers to the father as "Mr." but refers to the mother by her first name, indicating a considerable difference in the status he accorded to each. . . . He saw the father first . . . but then saw the father a second time before seeing the mother at all, thus obtaining a great deal of negative information about the mother before ever having seen her. He spent a total of five hours with the father and less than two hours with the mother . . . while his report shows considerable information concerning business successes accomplished by the father, there is nothing in his report or notes to indicate that he obtained similar information concerning the lesser, but still considerable, business successes of the mother. (Ziskin 1995, pp. 624–25)

There is more in this vein, a number of seemingly small things. Taken individually they mean little, together they weigh the report overwhelmingly in favor of the father.

This evaluator was top-of-the-line, a diplomate of the American Board of Professional Psychology and the American Board of Forensic Psychology in addition to having an impressive array of other credentials.

Wittmann, in a 1985 article on child custody determinations written for the *Journal of Psychiatry and the Law*, wrote, "Mental health professionals . . . are often questioned regarding matters about which there is little consensus within our disciplines. Our field is famous for supporting conclusions during testimony simply on the basis of 'accumulated clinical experience,' a phrase which may mean nothing more than accumulated personal bias" (p. 77).

Where there is no solid foundation for an expert's opinion for the determination of custody and visitation, it is inevitable that bias fills the void. One must, after all, write something on the evaluation for which one is being so handsomely paid.

Blind Justice

With regard to the neutrality of the evaluator, the custody guidelines for the American Psychological Association state, "The psychologist should be impartial regardless of whether he or she is retained by the court or by a party to the proceedings."

Well, that is a good thought, but let us think it through a moment. Let us say that as a practicing clinical psychologist, I make a significant portion of my income hiring myself out to do child and family evaluations in disputed custody suits. Let us say further that I have the idealism of a first-year graduate student and so I maintain an absolutely rigid and translucent neutrality as I perform my evaluations for my first clients. Let us say further that by chance alone I find the client who hired me to be the superior parent in exactly half the cases, and in half, alas, he or she is judged by me to be inferior. Let us say, lastly, that my colleague testifying for the other sides invariably finds that there is sufficient reason to believe that the parents who hired him have the superior claim, evidenced, apparently, by their vastly superior intellect and good judgment in hiring said colleague.

After half the attorneys who hired me lose their cases because of my highly judgmental and prejudicial reports and testimony, whom do you think will be hired for the next disputed custody case? Me? The loose cannon who can be counted on to shoot his own client in the foot half the time? Or the other psychologist, who smoothly makes a compelling and plausible argument that the client who hired him is the superior parent for any number of reasons related to knowledge, skills, abilities, values, and mental health, as that highly skilled psychological professional has perceived them?

I think I am going to have to go into another line of work pretty quickly if I want to continue to be able to feed the cat and make the car payments.

Identifying the Crazy Parent

The APA also suggests that it can be quite important to determine whether one of the parents is crazy, but that not too much weight should be placed on this component of the evaluation.

"Psychopathology may be relevant to such an assessment [in custody evaluations], insofar as it has impact on the child or the ability to parent, but it is not the primary focus."

That is too bad. About the only thing psychologists claim to learn how to do in graduate school is diagnose people, and that is supposed to be hardly relevant at all to the custody evaluations. Oh, well. That doesn't keep mental health assessments from figuring largely in many divorce actions whatever the APA guidelines may say.

> The mental health of a mother is always a consideration in custody battles—even when it was never a consideration in the marriage or in any other aspect of her life. A woman faces a nightmare in the judicial system when mental health experts, who are actually hired by the father or are biased and acting as surrogates for the father, go on a mission to destroy the woman's character before the judge. (Winner 1996, p. 61)

In her book *Mothers on Trial*, Phyllis Chesler wrote that in child custody disputes "Fathers' lawyers always routinely and falsely accused mothers of 'sexual promiscuity' or 'mental illness' " (p. 199). Certainly a number of courts are quite responsive to such charges whether they come from the court-appointed experts or from experts hired by the father.

New York's appeals court, in *Landau v. Landau*, accepted the opinions of two court psychoexperts that the mother was too crazy to have custody or even overnight or extended visitation.

> After performing comprehensive evaluations of the parties, a court-appointed psychiatrist and a court-appointed psychologist both concluded that the father was the more appropriate custodial parent. The mother was found to suffer from, among other things, severe depression, persecutorial [*sic*] delusions, extreme emotional lability [openness to change], exceedingly poor judgment, and distortion of reality, all of which impaired her parenting skills. (*Landau v. Landau*, 1995)

The court also required the mother to undergo psychotherapy as a condition of any expanded or overnight visitation. "Absent therapeutic intervention, further visitation would not be in the child's best interest." Perhaps the court felt that losing her child would make the mother feel even more depressed and persecuted. (What, exactly, is a therapist supposed to do about that?) It is to be hoped that her therapist turned out to be someone other than the court-appointed evaluator who found her so lacking in the first place. Then she could at least be taught how to get through a psychological evaluation without a diagnosis of mental illness.

Is it really that easy to diagnose someone with a mental disease? Well, sure. With 374 diagnoses to choose from, the psychologist has considerable latitude in finding a diagnosis that fits some behavior of the parent who did not hire him or of the parent with whom she is not simpatico. (It is important to remember that even the best of the evaluators are not saints.) It is easy because, as we have seen, there is little or no relation between actual symptoms or behaviors and most of the diagnoses available to the evaluator, and, for many, many diagnoses the set and range of possible "symptoms" that will fit the necessary criteria are enormously flexible.

Why do wrangling spouses attack each other with psychoexperts? Because it works.

It is all very well for liberals to say that the mentally ill are just like you and me and should not be discriminated against, but if it comes down to it in court, no judge is going to grant custody of a minor child to a crazy person over a sane one just to make some politically correct point. It would be irresponsible. And certainly not in the best interests of the child, right?

Why do courts tolerate attack psychologists in custody suits? Because invoking the opinions of "experts" both diffuses the responsibility of deciding the impossible and buffers the judge from reversal on appeal. In addition, judges either buy into the validity of the testimony of the experts they so freely appoint, or use them at will to accomplish their ends. In what must be one of the most quoted of New York custody cases, *Nir v. Nir* from 1991, the appellate division of the state trial court wrote:

> This vigorously contested custody dispute was the subject of 13 days of trial testimony which included detailed and extensive testimony from several mental health professionals consulted by the parties both prior to and after the commencement of the instant action, as well as from a psychiatrist who conducted the court-ordered forensic evaluation of the parties and their child.
>
> Although the court-appointed psychiatrist found the wife to be the most "critically attuned parent to the needs" of the child, the expert testimony also revealed that she suffered from a personality disorder characterized by paranoid features. [It is interesting that so many women in divorce proceedings are found to be suffering from paranoia. Just because you're paranoid doesn't mean they're not out to get you.]
>
> While we are mindful that the Supreme Court also expressed concern over the husband's lack of "hands on" parenting experience, when this deficiency is balanced against the evidence concerning the wife's psychological disorder, and her pattern of distorting the truth, it cannot be gainsaid that the Supreme Court's decision [to grant sole custody to the father] is supported by a sound and substantial basis in the record. (*Nir v. Nir*, 1991)

That most psychological diagnoses of these hired and appointed experts are fictions that exist only in the minds of the people who make their livings coming up with them cuts no ice with the court.

CUSTODY WARS AND THE ISSUE OF ABUSE

In the *Landau* case, the New York appeals court found in the psychologist's report still further evidence of the mother's unfitness for the custodial role in addition to her diagnosed depression and "persecutorial" delusions. She accused the father of abusing his children.

Reporting Abuse

The court wrote that the mother's "unfounded allegations that the father had sexually abused the child, and physically abused her, are further evidence of her unfitness to act as the custodial parent." They cited *Nir v. Nir* for this part of their opinion (*Landau v. Landau*, 1995).

The issue of physical and sexual abuse is a legal snakepit for both accused and accuser and, unbelievably, even for those who make no such allegations at all. If the mother *does* make a claim that the father abused either her or the children, and the court does *not* find those allegations to be substantiated, then the allegations per se are taken as evidence that she is an unfit parent. Accusations of abuse that cannot be soundly corroborated can function quite easily as prima facie evidence of mental illness, making the mother an unfit parent by virtue of her "delusions" and her "unreasonable" bias toward the father of the children.

In *Young v. Young*, the appeals court wrote:

> Although the father had, during the early stages of the divorce action, stipulated to the mother having custody of the children, he moved . . . for a change of custody to him, with the mother to be given only supervised visitation, based upon what he claimed to be the mother's "bizarre and dangerous behavior" which was "calculated to destroy the children's relationship with [him]."
>
> We now turn to the underlying basis for [the psychiatrist's] recommendations for a change of custody; namely, the mother's constant interference with the father's visitation with the children. While the mother's interference took on many forms . . . its most pernicious form was the numerous false allegations of sexual abuse made by the mother against the father. . . .
>
> As Dr. Reubins indicated in his report, "She sees only before her the obligation to protect her children from her fear with no appreciation that the totality of allegations she has raised have been unfounded.
>
> "These repeated uncorroborated and unfounded allegations of sexual abuse brought by the mother against the father cast serious doubt upon her fitness to be the custodial

> parent." . . . The mother's conduct in this instant case was so egregious as to warrant a change of custody to the father. (*Young v. Young*, 1995)

Many courts and many judges understandably have little tolerance for false accusations of abuse, but the complexity of unsubstantiated abuse claims put parents in an intolerable dilemma. It is simply impossible to substantiate many cases of abuse, particularly where the abuse has left no clear physical sign, but that does not mean that abuse has not occurred. What is a concerned parent supposed to do when he or she is faced with the problem of suspected abuse that lacks physical corroboration?

Very few parents will take the route followed by Elizabeth Morgan, who sent her daughter to her grandparents in New Zealand while she herself went to jail for two years for refusing to concede that her daughter was in no danger from her father.

Making unsubstantiated allegations could lead to the loss of the suspicious parent's custody as well as visitation, but that cannot mean that it is reasonable to simply ignore abuse because it cannot easily be corroborated. Moreover, it is illegal to do so.

Failing to Protect Your Child

If the mother *fails* to bring an abusing husband or father to the attention of the authorities, then she is equally liable to lose custody of her children for failing to provide them with a safe environment. If the mother was herself abused by the man in question, then the courts may decide that she is an unfit parent for her failure to protect the children.

According to a review by Elizabeth Schneider:

> [T]hirty-five of the forty-eight states criminalizing child abuse include *omissions* as well as *commissions* in their definitions of the statutory offense, and eight states expressly define the crime of failure to protect.
>
> Most of the statutes frame the crime in terms of criminal child endangerment. . . . [I]n Maine, endangering the welfare of a child includes knowingly endangering "the child's health, safety or mental welfare by violating a duty of care or protection," and in Montana, a person may be found guilty of child

> endangerment for "violating a duty of care, protection or support." (Schneider 1992, p. 537; italics added)

Failure-to-protect laws, well-meaning though they may be, exacerbate the already complex issue of abuse allegations surfacing during custody disputes, putting parents between a rock and a hard place. Failure to act to stop suspected abuse puts the child at risk. But failure to substantiate charges of abuse leaves the parent at risk not only of losing custody but also of termination of all parental rights or even of going to jail.

It is precisely this impossible situation that throws already highly stressed and vulnerable parents to the mercy of self-styled psychoexperts who will either validate the charges or come to a determination that they are "unsubstantiated."

How do they validate charges of abuse that leaves no physical evidence? Through their clinical intuition, of course, applied to the "behavioral evidence." Judges go for this.

In a 1994 case decision, a judge in a family court of New York wrote, "It must be noted that behavioral evidence, albeit not tangible, is no less real than physical evidence. It is subject to the same criteria for admission as physical evidence" (*Eli v. Eli*, 1993).

Of course, this is only true if the "behavioral evidence" is evaluated by a certified psychological analyst of some kind like, say, a social worker.

> In the instant proceeding, the Family Court held . . . that the validation testimony of a social worker, Yael Layish, constituted sufficient corroboration of the aforenoted allegations of abuse. We agree with this ruling and disagree with our dissenting colleague's view that Ms. Layish was incompetent to serve as a validator. On the contrary, the credentials and competence of Ms. Layish are amply established in this record. (*Erika K. v. Steven K.*, 1991)

Many courts and many judges, as well as many parents, apparently believe that these behavioral analysts—these experts in child psychology—can indeed perform this impossible task with secret tools known only to the trade.

What secret tools? Well, first off, in addition to the ever-available clinical intuition, we've got those popular "anatomically correct" dolls—a stunning misnomer if ever there was one unless you think a Raggedy Ann–style doll with grotesquely caricatured genitals is anatomically correct.

In *Swift v. Swift*, the judges noted that at the family court level the judge had been treated to the "expert testimony of a certified social worker with the Broom County Family and Children's Society corroborating the child's hearsay statements by 'validation evidence,' i.e. a determination by means of various interview techniques, including the use of anatomically correct dolls" (*Swift v. Swift*, 1991).

Ms. Layish, the amply credentialed social worker in the *Erika K. v. Steven K.* case, likewise employed dolls with penises and vaginas in her validation evaluation. "In support of her conclusion that abuse had taken place, Ms. Layish relied heavily upon the children's demonstrations with the anatomically correct dolls. . . . [T]he children had been previously exposed to these dolls on at least two occasions."

Using the dolls, this social worker determined that a four-year-old child with an intact hymen had nevertheless been subjected to repeated acts of penile-vaginal intercourse. It is precisely this sort of incomprehensible "finding" that has led organizations like the American Academy of Child and Adolescent Psychiatry and the American Psychological Association to strongly counsel restraint in the use of such dolls and the interpretation of a child's play with these "toys."

Why don't they come straight out and tell people not to be damn fools? I have said it before, and I will say it again, there are no reliable, valid, mental or "behavioral" tests for suspected child abuse worth a damn. It is a shame. It makes the assessment of much suspected abuse pretty much impossible. But wishing that the situation was different does not change it. Pretending that it is different is a tragic farce.

The New York family court judge in the *K. v. K.* case, who was a big believer in "behavioral evidence," was a bit skeptical himself about some of the "tools" used by "validators" to judge abuse allegations. He dumped on the use of anatomically correct dolls, noting that "interpretation of doll play, even when made by experts . . . is of questionable value. Indeed, the State of California does not permit such evidence at all."

This judge wasn't very enthusiastic about the use of toy bears to evaluate abuse allegations either. "Ms. [Barbara] Pilcher, [a certified social worker], who has a psychoanalytical orientation, gave considerable weight to symbolism and the child's play with certain dolls, including a bear with a long nose, which nose she saw as a phallic symbol."

It is heartening that at least some of this foolishness meets with the occasional judicial rebuff. Sadly, though, even the most skeptical judge can be snowed by a pseudo-science blizzard. Consider the following from the judge's remarks in the *Eli v. Eli* case described above: "Of the three witnesses who gave expert testimony on sexual abuse issues, Dr. [April] Kuchuk had the most formal education, the most knowledge of the literature. . . . Her opinions in this case were based on experimental data in the sexual abuse area, of which she appeared to have encyclopedic knowledge. . . . [It is] Dr. Kuchuk's opinion that this child does not present classic signs of sexually abused children her age. . . . "

Unfortunately for the validity of this expert's opinion, *there are no experimental data supporting the existence of "classic signs" of abuse for children of different ages, or, indeed, for children in general*. That lack makes such "scientifically" couched opinions a shocking fraud, for parents, children, and courts alike. According to the authors of a major review of current research, "No one symptom characterized a majority of sexually abused children. Some symptoms were specific to certain ages, and approximately one-third of victims has no symptoms" (Kendall-Tackett, Williams, and Finkelhor 1993, p. 164). Whatever this expert may have told the court, she could not have been relying on scientifically reliable data to support her opinion.

We are better off with bear's noses and rag doll penises than we are with unwarranted assertions of scientific expertise where none exists. After all, just about anyone—outside of the truly devout Freudian—will find the phallic nose symbolism laughable, but who can laugh off claims of scientific proof? Perhaps these experts even believe their own claims.

HE WHO PAYS THE PIPER CALLS THE TUNE

How long does a psychological custody evaluation take? A review of New York State custody cases from 1990 through 1996 showed that some psychological evaluators saw the children and/or the parents for as much as fifty hours; some never saw the subjects of their evaluations at all. Typically, the evaluative process last two or three hours. Then the expert has to write up the reports.

Courts seem to give more weight to the opinions of the evaluators who conducted the more extensive interviews. In one case, *Young v. Young*, cited above, the supreme court (the trial court) of New York weighed the competing evaluations of two psychiatrists so:

> In this case, after having spent *approximately 56 hours* meeting with and evaluating the parties and the children, Dr. Marc Reubins, the court-appointed psychiatrist, was of the opinion that it was "not in the best interest of the children to remain living in the house with their mother. . . ."
>
> [T]he opinion of the mother's expert, a Dr. Green . . . was concededly flawed. Dr. Green himself, who had interviewed the mother and children *for only a few hours* over a two-week period in February 1994, admitted that his qualification to make a custody recommendation was limited since he had not seen both parents and he had not seen the children interact in the presence of both parents. *Under these circumstances, little or no weight should have been accorded to his recommendation that custody be awarded to the mother.*

It clearly behooves the wary parent in a custody fight to make sure that his or her expert spends at least as many hours with any and all family members in all possible situations as the spouse's expert and the court-appointed one, if there is such.

This could get a little expensive. Costs do vary enormously from expert to expert and from place to place, of course (Manhattan, for example, is a very expensive place to have a disputed custody case), but if we figure a low of about $50 per hour and a high of $200, then hiring a well-credentialed expert of one's own for fifty-six hours would cost some $2,800 to $11,200. It seems a bit unfair since, clearly, the richer parent has a significant advantage here.

What Is in That Expensive Evaluation?

It is not clear, however, that the judges evince nearly as much interest in what, precisely, goes into the body of the evaluation—whether the psychoexpert simply chatted with parent and child, or whether he or she administered tests to buttress the subsequent opinion submitted to the court—as opposed to the time it took and the final recommendation.

What *is* in the report? The fruits of clinical intuition, of course, about which parent has the better values or which one is a little loony. What else would there be? Well, many evaluators do use a number of tests. There is the same problem with that as there is with any use of psychological tests to plumb the depths of the soul. They don't work. They can't work. (Psychological tests of reading ability and such things, by the way, are not too bad. It is when we get into soul-plumbing that the reach of testing far exceeds its grasp.)

Think about it. What would be the point of using the Minnesota Multiphasic Personality Inventory, for example? Is the evaluator going to match the child's little response profile code with one of the parents? Or decide which parent profile code correlates with more attractive parent-type attributes? That is absurd. How will the child's or the parents' responses on a personality test help determine the relative superiority of the parental knowledge, skills, abilities, and values of the mother and father? They won't. There are no tests to perform such a function.

Tests allegedly useful for determining which parent should have custody of a child are not worth a hill of beans—the very idea of such a test or battery of tests is absurd, so why do psychologists use them? Well, why not? They take time, cost money, beef up the report, and add a nice, if spurious, aura of authoritative substance to it. Besides, test results reassure our courts that something valid is taking place when an expert is hired.

Because of this assumption of test validity, it is crucial that any parent in one of these awful cases make sure that his or her attorney is armed with weapons powerful enough to bring down the missiles of tests that can be rained on the unwary parent—or attorney.

There are three such guns available, easily found in the reference section of most university libraries and good town libraries. The first is the massive *Tests in Print*, a regularly updated bibliographic encyclopedia of information on every published and commercially available test—*some three thousand*—in the areas of psychology and achievement. The second big gun is the book concisely entitled *Tests*, from Pro-Ed in Texas, that also lists the thousands of the most frequently used tests in psychology, along with those in business and education.

Pro-Ed also publishes the critical volume for administering the coup de grâce to a test-heavy expert on the opposing side—a separate volume called *Test Critiques* that covers the *administration, interpretation, and practical applications of the tests, along with information on their reliability and validity plus opinions of experts about their usefulness and limitations.* Practical applications for this book in the courtroom abound.

Don't leave home with out these three. At least not if you are going to court.

SOLOMON'S SWORD

The APA has not taken a stand on whether forensic clinicians should present their scientifically empty opinions in custody cases to the court as the substantiated and definitive recommendations of an expert, saying, "[T]he profession has not reached consensus about whether psychologists ought to make recommendations about the final custody determination to the courts."

In actual practice, whenever a forensic clinician makes a recommendation about custody to the court, he or she is telling the judge who is the better parent for the child or who will be the "best match" for each child's needs.

Not all the practitioners who do custody evaluations are comfortable wielding Solomon's sword so boldly. Some are comfortable making recommendations only if they strongly feel that one parent is unfit, but not when both parents seem adequate. When confronted with a situation in which the two parents are equally fit, from a psychological assessment standpoint, to be custodial parents, then some psychologists state that it is not possible for the psychologist to have a *professional* opinion about which parent should have custody. These clinicians argue quite rightly that the evaluator's *personal* opinion should be irrelevant.

Custody evaluators on both sides of the recommendation issue would likely claim that it makes no difference whether they choose to decide between the parents because the court is free to disagree based on different information or on different weights of information.

Well, that is not so obvious.

In a recent Massachusetts custody case that reached national prominence, an appeals court threw out the custody determination made by probate and family court judge James Lawton that allowed each of two twelve-year-old twins to live with the parent of her choice. The judge in making that decision relied in large part on the wishes of the two girls. The appeals court felt that the judge *did not give enough weight to professional recommendations* that separating the twins would harm them emotionally. According to the *Boston Globe*, "The appeals court judge, Roderick Ireland, writing for the three-judge panel, said, '[A]ll of the evidence from a guardian *ad litem*, a school guidance counselor and a therapist for [one of the twins] clearly showed that the children needed each other to shield themselves from the turmoil that led to their parents' divorce and subsequent custody battle' " (Ellement, *Boston Globe*, July 19, 1996).

Maybe the girls themselves knew what they "needed" and maybe they did not. But it is as sure as the rising sun that those professional evaluators did not *know*. They had personal opinions about twins and the needs of children and the trauma of divorce, and they applied those general opinions to these individuals as if they were written in the stone of a thousand psychological studies. They are no such thing. That the supposedly objective recommendations offered to the court by forensic evaluators are no more than personal opinions arrived at through clinical intuition and the inevitable biases of the evaluator and then couched in a barrage of jargon and professional rhetoric does not mean that courts are free to disregard those opinions at will.

Weight given psychological testimony varies from judge to judge, from court to court, but whatever its true substantive value, it clearly behooves the parent who wishes to prevail in a custody suit to avail himself or herself of the most highly credentialed expert possible. And, as we have seen, one with plenty of time to spend on the evaluation.

By the way, it should be possible to further enhance your hired expert's credibility with the judge by matching him or her as closely as possible to the personal characteristics of the judge—gilding the portrait, of course, with those impressive credentials, thus combining the appeal of a peer with the weight of an authority—sort of like a judicial golfing buddy who looks like Marcus Welby.

There is another crucial issue here. Who is going to make all these custody decisions if professional child and family experts are not? Eliminating all those experts throws the business onto the shoulders of the parents to make the best claims they can, and onto the judges to call them as he or she sees them. That would be a better system than the one we have at present, at least in that the parent with more money would no longer be able simply to outspend the poorer in the parade of experts.

It would, however, leave parents stuck, without any hope of counterbalancing opinion, in the coil of the judge's own prejudices and biases. That is bad, but if we left it to the judges alone without any bolstering expert opinions, we would force them to lay bare their own prejudices for all to see. Perhaps that would force the law to become more explicit about what does and does not count in the parental superiority sweepstakes, but it is no wonder that judges do not want to find themselves all alone behind that eight ball.

It must be said too that in many cases of trying to determine what is in the best interests of the child, the judges—our judges, our courts—are simply desperate for advice on how to make right decisions because the very lives of children are at stake.

THE DEATH OF A CHILD

> The body of Michelle Walton was found on the second-floor landing of the Morton Street home of Anita and Charles Johnson, her foster parents, on Oct. 6, 1994. The Johnsons claimed the child was accidentally injured when 10 pieces of sheetrock collapsed on her. But Cambridge District Judge Arthur Sherman, who conducted a closed-door inquest last summer, has concluded [Michelle] was murdered. Sherman also found that [Michelle] was repeatedly sexually abused during her two-year stay in the Johnson home. Sherman's findings were unsealed yesterday. (Ellement and Grunwald, *Boston Globe*, October 11, 1995)

Michelle had been taken from her own home, where she had been neglected and mistreated, and placed in the care of a foster family. In their care, she died under the Sheetrock. The foster family said the child's death was accidental. The coroner said he could not determine the cause of death because the wounds on her body were so many and so varied. Whatever the cause—whoever the cause—a little girl is dead because neither her family nor her guardians were capable of taking the necessary actions to keep her alive. Her foster parents, the Johnsons, were never charged in this case. Neither was anyone else.

On November 27, 1995, in New York City, another little girl, Elisa Izquierdo, six years old, was found beaten to death by her mother. Everyone—teachers and neighbors—had noticed the child was limping and bruised and, eventually, no longer attending school. Five times child protective services personnel had been called in to help this child, to save her from what was indisputable abuse. Three times the department returned the child to her mother, deciding that it was in the best interests of the child to keep her in her home with the mother who was step by step killing her until at last she lay dead at the feet of the clinical social workers who had held her very life in their hands.

The fates of these two innocents are not that unusual. Some three hundred children each year in our country are killed by their parents or foster parents. Countless more are beaten, starved, exploited, and drugged in scenarios so ugly they could come, seemingly, only from the pen of the most sadistic of sensationalist writers.

THE BEST OF INTENTIONS

The problem of child abuse is not new, nor is our society's awareness of the desperate need of these children to be saved from the awful ministrations of their lawful caretakers. It was in response to their need that Congress passed the Child Abuse Prevention and Treatment Act in 1974, mandating that all adults in positions of responsibility with respect to a child are required to report to the proper authorities any known or suspected child abuse. No more could teachers, doctors, and nurses say that, yes, they knew there was a problem in that family, but it was really none of their business to do anything about it. For too long, out of a traditional, if somewhat myopic, respect for the privacy of the family and the rights of parents to rear and discipline their own children, state and federal government agencies had been most reluctant to venture behind the closed doors of familial privacy even in cases in which the hurts of a child were impossible to ignore.

CAPTA, as the act is known, was a laudable and responsible attempt both to stop the carnage and to make clear that society did not accept the principle that parents have an unlimited right to abuse their children any way they wish, whatever their stated reason or excuse. The National Center on Child Abuse and Neglect collects and publishes national statistics on child abuse. According to the testimony of Senator Dan Coats before a Capitol Hill hearing, in 1963 there were 150,000 reported cases of abuse, in 1993 there were 2,898,000. Two thirds of these abuse and neglect allegations are unsubstantiated or determined to be unfounded, but that still leaves nearly a million children with documented abuse in a single year.

> Mental health professionals may be involved at all stages of legal inquiry in cases of child maltreatment. . . . If an evaluation is sought, it will probably be under a statute requiring a finding of harm as an element of abuse or neglect. In such a case, the clinician will usually be asked to determine whether a "mental injury" has resulted from maltreatment of the child. Thus, the evaluation will be focused on the child's mental status and, if significant disturbance is present, whether it was caused by trauma. (Melton, Petrila, Poythress, and Slobogin 1987, p. 320)

Revised in 1984, CAPTA today requires that any adult—whether in a position of responsibility with respect to the child or not—is required to report to child care authorities within thirty-six hours any known or suspected child abuse—physical, sexual, or emotional—and those authorities in turn are required to investigate the suspicion and, if it is confirmed, take steps to guarantee the safety of the child and to report the suspected abuse to the police.

Further—this is a critical provision of the law—any adult reporting such known or suspected abuse is *utterly and absolutely immune* to any sort of charge or prosecution, criminal or civil, for having reported the abuse to the authorities. This step was taken so that concerned observers who were justifiably suspicious but not certain that abuse had taken place would not be intimidated by the fear of civil lawsuits to make their suspicions known to authorities who could protect the child who might be in danger.

That the need for a law such as CAPTA was great is undeniable. That the intentions of the lawmakers who drafted and passed the legislation were honorable also seems undeniable. But like so many well-intentioned attempts to heal society's hurts by legislating them out of existence, the law produced vast and unexpected ramifications and, in many cases, has caused as much hurt to as many children as the situation it was designed to correct.

THE ROAD TO HELL

In 1995, a veteran testified at a Senate subcommittee hearing on child protection:

> I am a retired chief petty officer in the United States Navy. I proudly gave twenty years of my life and my family's life to defend a way of life that I believed in and I repeatedly swore an oath to support and defend the Constitution of the United States, a document that I understood ensured the rights of the individual against the kind of institutional abuses, in the name of my government, that my family has endured.
>
> On May 9, 1989, my eight-year-old daughter was discovered to have been viciously sexually assaulted. This was discovered during a medical examination at a health care facility that my wife and I had taken Alicia to after she complained of pain. . . . Alicia informed the doctor and police detectives that someone had taken her out of her brother's window and had put her in a green car, drove to a secluded area and had hurt her, threatening to kill her if she cried out. Alicia gave a very detailed description of this individual. . . .
>
> Alicia was placed with a therapist [Kathleen Goodfriend] who immediately expressed her conviction that I was to blame and that Alicia was obviously covering up for me. [She convinced the court] that the only way to ensure Alicia's safety was to severely restrict her family's access to her as much as possible. . . .
>
> By early June of 1989, Joshua [my six-year-old son] had been added to the list of my victims by the social worker on

the case by submitting a charge to the court that "Joshua had been sexually molested and that he was in danger of being molested again." Joshua was never interviewed or examined by anyone.

In July of 1989, my wife and I were taken to trial on charges of sexual abuse and failure to protect for both Joshua and Alicia. . . . They told us a plea bargain had been offered. . . . My wife and I could plead no contest to a charge of neglect and after complying with several conditions. . . . Alicia would be returned home. They never intended to return Alicia to us. They blackmailed us into submitting a plea of no contest by promising to return our daughter. We did, and they then told us that Alicia's therapist had told the court that if they returned Alicia to us, I would kill her. Alicia was not returned, but the plea bargain stood. We lost our day in court. . . .

My wife went for 11½ months without seeing my daughter. I went from October 1989 till October 31, 1991 without any contact.

I was required to attend and "successfully" complete the following: 1. Individual therapy, twice a week, the object of which was for me to admit my guilt; 2. Group therapy in what was called a denier's group, with other men who had the misfortune to have been "accused" and found "guilty" of molesting [their] children. . . . The only acceptable graduation from this therapy is for you to admit your guilt; 3. Therapy with my wife in concert with other families who have been accused of similar crimes, twice a week. Again, the only acceptable conclusion to this group is to admit your guilt.

We discovered early in 1990 that the therapist and the foster mother had been telling Alicia that the only way she could come home was to tell them that I was the one who had hurt her. Alicia had complained to the social worker and asked for help, but her pleas fell on deaf ears. After 13 months of isolation and intimidation, in June of 1990, they succeeded in getting Alicia to say, "Daddy did it." . . .

I was at work at the air anti-submarine warfare headquarters on the 13th of December 1990 when they came for me. I was handcuffed and led away. . . . At the court hearing in February of 1991 I remember the anger and frustration of having to sit in the court room, the absolute insanity of sitting there listening to my daughter tell a completely fabricated story of her assault. . . . This was the first time in 1½ years that I had seen my daughter or heard her voice.

When it became known to the juvenile authorities that DNA evidence was soon likely to clear me of the awful charges, they moved quickly. In August of 1991, we were summoned to juvenile court where the social worker, the therapist and the county counsel tried to have Alicia adopted away. . . . The blood sample reports . . . proved that it was not Alicia's biological father who had assaulted her and that whoever had assaulted her was sterile. . . . The county counsel then said that . . . it was immaterial to them who had actually perpetrated the rape. Alicia was being adopted out solely because we had pled no contest to a charge of neglect back in November of 1989.

With the intervention of the San Diego County Grand Jury . . . and the public support generated by a series of newspaper articles written by Jim Okerblom and John Wilkerson, Alicia was returned home. . . .

The price of this kidnapping into the compassionate world of child abuse prevention is difficult to calculate. My wife tried to commit suicide and was hospitalized for 9 months in a locked psychiatric ward. My children are afraid of policemen and others in authority. They have learned to fear those whom they should most be able to trust. . . . My son lost all of his friends and was told by their parents that he could not play with their children because his father raped his sister. Joshua was 6-years-old at the time. My parents spent their entire life savings trying to keep me out of jail. We spent 2½ years not knowing from one day to the next what they were going to take away next, just knowing and dreading the inevitable fact that more was coming. . . .

Above all, and, by God, most of all, I lost 2½ years of my daughter's life and my family's life, that we nor she will ever get back, and nothing that is ever said or done will ever make

> up for that. (Testimony of James B. Wade to the Senate Committee on Labor and Human Resources, Subcommittee on Children and Families, Hearing on Child Protection, May 25, 1995)

How could this happen? How could this innocent child be ripped from the bosom of her family, torn away from a security she must have needed desperately after the terrible injury done her by the rapist? How could an innocent man find himself accused and, indeed, to all intents and purposes, convicted of such a hideous crime against his own flesh and blood on the basis of nothing but the clinical intuition of the social worker assigned to protect his child?

"We Had to Destroy the Village to Save It"

How could what happened to the Wades happen?

> A 3-month-old girl suffocated in Spokane in February 1995 when her mother fell asleep with her on the couch and then rolled on top of her. "I guess I picked a bad night to get drunk," the mother reportedly told a friend. The crib was filled with debris and soiled diapers. (Wilson, *Seattle Times*, August 4, 1996)

It happened because of parents like this, because adults like this do such terrible harm to children that no state that is not itself corrupt can sit idly by and let such atrocities occur in the sacred name of parental rights. A decent society is responsible for the welfare of the future generation. Individuals cannot simply say of another's children, "They are not my problem."

Nor can society simply wait until the child is killed or permanently damaged to take action. CAPTA was deliberately designed to *prevent* the destruction of innocent children, not simply to jail their out-of-control parents after the damage was done. With prevention as a goal, it is neither necessary nor even desirable to wait until harm has been confirmed, until the perpetrator has been positively and certainly identified, to remove the child from harm's way. "It is better to be safe than sorry" is the motto of CAPTA, but, of course, the definition of what will be a sorry state is rather narrowly defined. What

CAPTA does to families is rather reminiscent of General William Westmoreland's famous—or infamous—remark about an incident in Vietnam: "We had to destroy the village to save it."

Prevention as the ultimate goal requires that everyone involved act not solely on the basis of knowledge but on the basis of suspicion alone.

Open Season on Powerless Families

Suspicion, under the law, is interpreted so broadly that even adults in a position to know better are required to take the flimsiest of allegations seriously. For example, if one member of a couple in the course of family counseling during divorce proceedings—an activity usually putatively undertaken to help keep people calm and ease the pain of family breakup—accuses the other of having been too harsh several years previously in disciplining the children, their family counselor is required by law to report the alleged long-past abuse to the child welfare services for immediate investigation.

Whatever the consequences for family counseling practice—and it does not bode well—the most immediate result of such reporting laws is a vast increase in the number of child abuse investigators required to check out all those reports. Just consider. The number of adults in real or nominal positions of responsibility for children—and thus required by law to report anything suspicious—is vast indeed. Most children have two or three teachers of one type or another, a school principal and nurse or guidance counselor, a family physician or therapist or counselor or some kind, priests or ministers, scout leaders, camp counselors, and day care workers, to name just a few of the more obvious adults who come into contact with children while in some position of authority over them. Each and every one of these people is required by law to report any suspicion of abuse of whatever kind immediately after they suspect it, even if the suspicion is based on nothing more than a spiteful and unsubstantiated allegation made by another adult.

Nearly three million reports of known or suspected abuse are received by state child welfare agencies each year. Each and every one of these three million must be investigated promptly, and not by insensitive cops or untrained citizens. Oh, no. Proper investigation requires the clinical sensitivity of the trained professional.

Wow! An indefinitely expanding, virtually unlimited, full employment bill for child welfare workers. What a boon for the industry. And industry it is. In response to the growing demand for trained professionals in child welfare and family psychological functioning to investigate these three million abuse allegations a year, child welfare bureaucracies have swelled their ranks until they burst their buildings at their seams overflowing into the space and budgets of all other state agencies.

It is open season on helpless families and the number of hunting licenses out there is truly astronomical.

The Rape of Parental Rights

How could this happen? It was inevitable, given the way the law was written.

The law took parental rights away from parents and effectively vested those rights in paid professionals who claim that their knowledge and their training makes them better parents than parents themselves, and better judges of the best interest of the child than parents, police, or the courts. Before their awesome authority—and their vast armamentarium of claimed knowledge—all the amateurs in the child welfare business must fall silent and bow the knee. The legislators bought their claim of unequaled expertise; the police and the courts have no choice but to buy it as well.

That the scientific basis of their claimed superior knowledge is as insubstantial as smoke hardly gives the paid child professionals pause. Why should it?

The mental health professionals who serve as forensic evaluators in child maltreatment cases have no way at all to determine whether a particular individual harmed a child or even whether a particular child was harmed on the basis of psychological or behavioral rather than physical evidence. There is no clear pattern of behavior exhibited by all battered and abused children. And there is no clear pattern of behavior to identify adults who harm children, despite pseudo-scientific efforts going so far as to create a "syndrome" supposedly typifying batterers.

> The review of the literature indicates that the scientific basis for the battering-parent syndrome is very weak. . . . Psycho-

> dynamic researchers have not succeeded in identifying a consistent pattern of traits common among abusers. Gelles found that at least two or more authorities agreed on only 4 of 19 traits reported in the literature. . . . When [this evidence] is used in combination with medical evidence as to the cause of physical injuries, it is likely to be highly prejudicial and misleading. (Melton, Petrila, Poythress, and Slobogin 1987, p. 315)

Quoting a 1972 review in *Psychological Bulletin* of battering parent studies by Spinetta and Rigler, the authors continue, "While the authors generally agree that there is a defect in the abusing parent's personality that allows aggressive impulses to be expressed too freely, disagreement comes in describing the source of the aggressive impulses" (Melton, Petrila, Poythress, and Slobogin 1987, p. 315).

There is a defect in parents who beat up their children that allows them to beat up their children? That is so vacuous it is hard not to laugh.

> A mental health professional may also be asked to give an opinion as to whether a child has been abused. However, it is hard to imagine careful psychological testimony that would be very helpful to the fact finder. Although child maltreatment is certainly not benign in its psychological effects, the behavioral signs are not distinguishable from those seen in other clinical populations. (Melton, Petrila, Poythress, and Slobogin 1987, p. 321)

Linda Meyer Williams, who, along with her colleagues, conducted the oft-quoted emergency room "amnesia" study (discussed in chapter 9), was also the co-author of another very interesting study published in 1993 in the *Psychological Bulletin* and noted briefly earlier. She and her colleagues reviewed some forty-five separate studies of child victims of sexual abuse in which all the children were eighteen years of age or younger. They were attempting to determine whether the child (eighteen is very old for such a study!) who has been abused is in any way distinguishable, at least to the eye of a trained expert, from a child who has not been abused. They found that no particular symptom or cluster of symptoms or syndrome differentiated abused from unabused children, and that about one third of the abused children showed no symptoms at all (Kendall-Tackett, Williams, and Finkelhor, 1993).

These studies make it very difficult for any expert—whatever the impressive list of credentials—to claim that he or she can infallibly detect either an abuser or a victim of abuse.

Then what are these so-called professionals doing in court expressing their utterly unfounded opinions one way or the other about these matters? They have no knowledge, but they do have the power.

The law was written to place the power in the professional's hands; the entire legal system set up to deal with abuse of children is predicated on there being child professionals—psychologists of one type or another—on whom the rest of us can rely to determine the best interests of the child. Someone has to fill the bill and there are about 100,000 diplomas out there claiming that right to do so.

These people are supposedly trained, and they are certainly well paid, to tell the rest of us what is wrong with a particular child, if anything, who did it, and what should be done for the child. We want them to make these judgments. We beg them. The law demands it of them. Of course we get what we ask for.

Carol Lamb Hopkins was the deputy foreman of the San Diego County grand jury that reviewed the country's juvenile dependency system in 1995. She was also a member of the San Diego district attorney's ad hoc Committee on Child Abuse. In her testimony to the Senate subcommittee's hearings on children and families on May 25, 1995, she said:

> I could share anecdotal stories about the destruction of families, the insensitivity of social workers, the collusion of juvenile court judges, which might well cause you to decide that the damage done to children and families in the name of child protection far outweighs the good. . . .
>
> It is time to bring common sense to our justice system and to recognize that the protection of children is almost always synonymous with the protection of families. We cannot

> allow the protection of family to be the rhetorical claim of any one political agenda or segment of the system. I strongly believe the protection of the family is essential to the protection of our society and essential to the survival of a healthy democracy.

Abuse of Immunity

Both willful blindness and fairy tales have served as the basis for breaking up families, removing children from their homes, and placing them in foster homes where they are quite likely to be abused; and they have resulted in numerous criminal charges being brought against adults targeted by the tales.

Why aren't those professional validators a little worried about making allegations so bizarre that it would seem that no one in his or her right mind could possibly take them literally? If they are not worried about harming others, shouldn't they be a little worried about getting sued for irresponsibility? Well, no.

In an unsurprising extension of the immunity granted to those who report suspected child abuse, the courts have ruled that immunity also shields the activities of the authorities—the child care professionals—who are called in to investigate those reports. It is this extension of immunity that allows doctors and nurses, social workers and psychologists who induce children to make bizarre allegations to do so without any fear of retribution.

One might think that at least in cases in which the defendants were found not guilty that someone, somehow, would be held responsible for dragging both the helpless children and the innocent accused into court, but it is not so, not even when the allegations are of so extreme and nonsensical a character that if uttered by any but the certified child care professionals, they would land the utterers in a safe environment for evaluation themselves.

The abuse evaluator is immune as well from the charge of having irresponsibly violated all sense of ethics, decency, and even common sense.

> Ray Buckey and his mother, Peggy McMartin Buckey, were found not guilty Thursday of molesting children at the family-run McMartin Pre-School in Manhattan Beach, a ver-

> dict which brought to a close the longest and costliest criminal trial in history. An eight-man, four-woman jury—10 of the members parents themselves—acquitted the Buckeys of 52 counts of molestation after deliberating for nine weeks over evidence that had been presented over the course of more than two years.
>
> The acquittals concluded the longest criminal trial in history, a case that stemmed from a 2½-year-old's report to his mother six years ago that he had been sodomized at his school by a "Mr. Ray." The case ultimately cost taxpayers more than $15 million, altered scores of lives and careers, and provided a national focal point for the issue of child abuse. (Timnick and McGraw, *Los Angeles Times*, January 19, 1990)

When the McMartins of the famous day care abuse case were finally vindicated, they sued Kee MacFarlane, the child psychological specialist who interviewed the children, as well as the corporate entity for which she worked. The California court ruled that they could not sue Ms. MacFarlane—or Children's Institute International—for her role in the raising of bizarre allegations like hot air balloon molestation and tunneling trips to graveyards to dig up graves and hack up corpses because she was just doing her job under the shield of immunity. Immunity applied because her investigations arose directly out of the initial reports of abuse (*McMartin v. Children's Institute International, California*, 1989).

Extraordinary. If the initial cause is just, then any evil in its service is justified?

In the case of Wade, the naval officer above, the situation turned out a bit better in the end. In part this was because a very interesting series of events had been taking place during the family's ordeal but unknown to the Wades. It happened that a convicted sex offender was being tried for abducting and molesting children in the very neighborhood where the Wades lived with their daughter who was raped. The so-called therapist and abuse specialist never told these poor parents, although both professionals were aware of it all along.

When the facts came out, the Wade family sued their daughter's "therapist," Kathleen Goodfriend. The California Court of Appeal found that for the family therapist Kathleen Goodfriend, her supposedly "therapeutic" activities extending over a two-and-a-half-year period after the initial report of the abuse "had nothing to do with the child abuse identified and reported at the outset by the hospital. [The] alleged coercion of Alicia continued over the next two and one-half years—long after any 'emergency' had passed, after Alicia was out of harm's way, and after the authorities were actively involved, investigating and prosecuting.

"To hold such conduct protected is to immunize virtually anyone coming in contact with an abused child. We do not believe such an interpretation is warranted by the reporting statute" (*James W. et al. v. Superior Court of San Diego Co., Kathleen Goodfriend et al.*, 1993).

Following this decision, the Wade lawsuit was settled, for a total of $3.7 million. The county paid about $750,000 for its share of the damages.

In most cases the injured family is without recourse. "I was just doing my job." Doing it badly doesn't seem to have a negative impact on the pocketbook either. Kee MacFarlane, despite the overwhelming rejection of the bizarre allegations of nursery school children undertaking grave robbing and corpse mutilation that appeared over the course of her interviews with the children, still works as a clinical child psychologist and commands hefty fees as a speaker on her experiences.

None of this should come as a surprise to anyone. Abuse of immunity is inevitable. Where there is no accountability, there is no responsibility. It is as simple as that.

IT IS A TOUGH JOB

The abuses and excesses of so many child welfare specialists should not be allowed to obscure the indisputable fact that there are many decent, caring, hardworking professionals who do their absolute best with huge caseloads to help the children as well as they can be helped with the psychological tools available. It would be cruel and ungrateful and stupid to say otherwise.

The problem for them and for us is that the psychological tools just do not exist for them to do their jobs, and no one can or is willing to admit that. It is just too difficult to deal with the awful reality that in the three million annual cases of alleged abuse, our already overworked police forces would be called on to investigate and make determinations essentially without any evidence at all of where, with whom, and by whom abuse has occurred. Who can blame the police and the prosecutors' offices—along with our courts—for wanting the assistance of professionals who know what they are doing?

It is just too bad that there are none available.

Both in custody cases involving allegations of grave risk to children in the home, and in cases arising where parents cannot agree on custody for reasons both profoundly serious and dismayingly foolish, our judges—our whole family legal system—desperately seeks guidance about where to find and where to place the best interests of the children involved. Agencies, parents, and judges alike turn to psychological professionals to help them find the truth or make their case.

Our common desperation seems to have produced the common delusion that experts actually exist who really can determine with the unerring instinct of a homing pigeon exactly where the best interests of a child lie, where a child should live, whether and how a child has been hurt, how a child should be protected, who will be the superior parent, and who is unfit to be a parent at all, who should have the right and the duty to care for a child, who should see the child only under restricted conditions, and who should be kept away from the child altogether.

Acceptance of their expertise has led us to trust professionals to make these decisions for the family court system. That means ultimately that we also grant them the power to make these decisions for our own families. The abstract need of society to protect its children becomes inevitably the rape of the rights of the real parents of individual children. Once again, the institutionalization of society's desire to "do good" results in terrible harm for those in the path of the do-gooders.

The marriage of law and psychology has reached the heights of disproportionate power for the psychologists not just in family courts but in all legal disputes in which a psychological matter is at issue. Judges buy the validity of the expertise of the confident psychological practitioner and no doubt welcome the opportunity to make their own decisions on some foundation other than personal opinion and bias.

It is this understandable desire that has led to the recent explosion in our courts of cases alleging mental and emotional—psychic—injury, all requiring the expert testimony of the psychological witness.

9
Remembrance of Things Past

Psychic Injuries from Long Ago

> It is important to stress that, in considering the admissibility of repressed memory evidence, it is not the role of the court to rule on the credibility of this individual plaintiff's memories, but rather on the validity of the theory itself. For the foregoing reasons, the Court hereby denies the Defendant's Motion in Limine to Exclude Repressed Memory Evidence. For the law to reject a diagnostic category generally accepted by those who practice the art and science of psychiatry would be folly. Rules of law are not petrified in the past but flow with the current of expanding knowledge.
>
> Edward F. Harrington, United States District Judge,
> District of Massachusetts, *Shahzade v. Gregory*, May 8, 1996

THE JUDGE AND THE EXPERT WITNESS

In the spring of 1996, in Massachusetts, an elderly woman brought suit against her equally elderly male cousin from California for wrongs he allegedly had done her nearly half a century before.

Ann Shahzade, sixty-eight, claimed that from the time she was twelve years old until she was seventeen, her cousin George, five years older than she, had subjected her on a number of occasions to nonconsensual sexual touching.

Ann claimed also that she had been so traumatized by these events that she repressed all memory of them despite frequent contacts with her cousin over the years, with frequent loans from George to Ann. In 1991, during a course of psychotherapy when, coincidentally, her cousin refused to lend her an additional $30,000, Ann said she regained her memories of the numerous incidents of fondling of fifty years ago; she subsequently sued her cousin for damages.

Her cousin, George, objected to Ann's suit, arguing that the touching was consensual and, moreover, that suing fifty years after the alleged tort vastly exceeded the statue of limitations for a personal injury suit. Further, George claimed that Ann's failure to bring suit earlier could not possibly be due to traumatic repression with memory loss because no such thing existed in science.

U.S. District Judge Edward Harrington, of the First Circuit, heard George's objection and issued a ruling in May 1996, declaring that, at least for the First Circuit, repression of memory due to trauma—along with its long-delayed recovery years after the traumatic events—had been firmly established in science. Thus, Ann's civil suit could go forward, fifty years old or not.

In reaching his decision, Judge Harrington relied strongly on the testimony of Dr. Bessel van der Kolk, the psychiatrist from Harvard University Medical School whose work on trauma and memory was briefly described earlier. Dr. van der Kolk told the judge that repression was a scientific fact. Judge Harrington wrote that an expert witness claiming that a theory is scientific "must testify as to whether that theory can be, or has been, tested or corroborated, and, if so, by whom and under what circumstances, whether this theory has been proven out . . . whether the theory of repressed memory is widely accepted in the field of psychology. Dr. van der Kolk's testimony satisfies these fundamental factors" (*Shahzade v. Gregory*, 1996).

In an interesting application of modern technology, when the judge made his ruling accepting that the psychological evidence was truly scientific, the Harvard psychiatrist and trauma specialist had the ruling broadcast all over the Internet. The broadcast was no doubt in the interests of science rather than for the purpose of personal advertising.

"Scientific" Evidence Cited by the Expert

> Yesterday, the expert witness, Dr. Bessel van der Kolk, testified that the phenomenon of repressed memories among

> trauma victims, especially those suffering childhood sexual abuse, is widely accepted by scientists and doctors. (Rakowsky, *Boston Globe*, April 10, 1996)

In support of his assertions, Dr. van der Kolk told the judge that he relied on a study by Judith Herman, who teaches in the Department of Psychiatry at the Harvard Medical School, and Emily Schatzow, who is Dr. Herman's colleague at the Women's Mental Health Collective in Massachusetts, on incest victims who were said to "recover" their lost memories through group therapy.

Dr. van der Kolk swore to the judge that with this study Dr. Herman and Dr. Schatzow have provided the world with unshakable proof that traumatic repression of the memories of childhood sexual abuse is common. The judge believed him.

As Judge Harrington explains:

> One such study, which Dr. van der Kolk referred to as the Herman and Schatzow study, looked at victims of sexual abuse and found that only approximately one-third of the victims remembered all the details of the abuse. Another one-third of the victims had a partial memory of the abuse, while the final one-third of the victims remembered nothing relating to the abuse. Dr. van der Kolk stated that these figures represent "the sort of figures that every study comes in with, regardless of what the methodology is. . . . " (*Shahzade v. Gregory*, 1996)

Let's look at this study "proving" traumatic repression and recovery of memory.

The Miracle of Amnesia

> In group, Doris initially reported almost complete amnesia for her childhood. She spoke little until the sixth session, when she began to moan, whimper, and wring her hands. In a childlike voice she cried, "The door is opening! The door is opening!" She was instructed to tell her memories to go away and not to come back until she was ready to have them.

> This she did, first in a whisper, and then in a loud voice. Her anxiety then subsided to bearable levels.
>
> In the three weeks following this session, Doris was flooded with memories which included being raped by her father and being forced to service a group of her father's friends while he watched. The sexual abuse began at about the age of six and continued until the age of twelve, when she was impregnated by her father and taken to an underground abortionist. (Herman and Schatzow 1987, p. 9)

It should be noted here that "Doris" is not a real patient. She is just a made-up case used by Drs. Herman and Schatzow to illustrate the findings of their "study." Clinicians often do this, the burden of finding authentic illustrative cases apparently being too heavy.

For the real women who were part of the incest survivors therapy group run by these two therapists, 26 percent of the patients had no memories of sex abuse *at all*. Yet the therapists write that the women who can't remember being abused at all suffered the abuse at a younger average age (4.9 years versus 10.6 years) than the ones who did remember. How can they possibly know the age when the abuse supposedly occurred if the women don't remember anything about the abuse at all?

What are these women doing in an incest survivors group in the first place if they can't remember any incest? Ah, but after a while they can.

> Participation in group proved to be a powerful stimulus for recovery of memory in patients with severe amnesia. During group therapy, more than a quarter of the women experienced eruption into consciousness of memories that had been entirely repressed. (Herman and Schatzow 1987, p. 8)

Are their memories true accounts of what actually happened to these women as children? Well, who is to say that they are not? They seem true to the patient. They were accepted as true by the therapists. Why should the patients in such a circumstance doubt the authenticity of either their memories or the supposed process of "losing" and "recovering" them?

Since the majority of their patients—64 percent—"discovered" some new memories of child abuse in therapy, Herman and Schatzow classified the majority of their patients as having "some degree of amnesia" due, of course, to traumatic repression.

Amnesia due to repression?

Is this proof of repression—proof that the trauma of incest forced those memories out of the reach of consciousness? It is no such thing.

They are actually reporting only that many women who have no memories of incest—who nevertheless join an incest survivors therapy group on the recommendation of their therapists—do, in time, claim to have memories of incest.

This study is proof of nothing. We can have proof of repression and recovery of memory only if we have no other explanation for the absence of memory before the women joined the group and then the presence of memory some time after they had joined it.

Are there no other possible explanations? Sure there are.

What might be possible reasons for the failure to remember? Perhaps some of these women chose not to think about what happened to them; many victims of sexual abuse may choose to turn their minds from the unpleasant memories. Perhaps some of the women were so young at the time of the abuse that clear memories will forever be impossible for them.

And, perhaps, for some of the women who have no memory of abuse, the abuse just did not actually happen.

Can the researchers rule out the possibility that the memories were simply created by the patients and by the therapists who believed that patients in an incest therapy group should have memories of incest, who believed that in time they would have them—and have them they did? No.

Unless Herman and Schatzow can rule out all of these confounding factors, they cannot possibly conclude that amnesia due to traumatic repression is the only explanation for the lack of memory. Because these researchers chose essentially to control nothing in their "study," they can conclude, essentially, nothing.

Imagine, for example, that you find that money is missing from your purse that had been sitting on the kitchen counter next to the refrigerator where your son and a neighbor kid had been standing. You cannot jump to the conclusion that the neighbor boy took the money from your wallet without first ruling out all other possibilities. That is not just good science; it is simple common sense.

How could Dr. van der Kolk tell Judge Harrington that this hopelessly confounded example of junk science constituted scientific proof for repression of memories of trauma? It seems impossible that anyone could do so.

Maybe judges should be required to read the psychoexpert's source material themselves instead of relying on some expert to summarize it for them. A lot gets lost in the translation.

Trauma in the ER

Dr. van der Kolk also told the judge that repression was scientifically proved in a study by the sociologist Linda Williams on women's reporting memories for child abuse incidents that occurred seventeen years earlier.

As Judge Harrington explains:

> A study conducted by Linda Meyer Williams, which Dr. van der Kolk referred to as "the best study on all of this," further validates the theory of repressed memories. As a graduate student in psychology at the University of Pennsylvania from 1973 to 1975, Ms. Williams did her doctoral dissertation on sexually abused children who had been treated at the Philadelphia Children's Hospital. She conducted extensive interviews with young women who had been sexually abused, and her dissertation detailed the experiences which they had undergone.
>
> Seventeen years later, as a research psychologist, Ms. Williams reinterviewed patients who had been the subject of her dissertation to see what impact the earlier sexual abuse had on their later life. She was able to locate about half of her original subjects, and after reinterviewing them, she found that thirty-eight percent of her patients no longer remembered the abuse.

(Ms. Williams is actually Dr. Williams and has a Ph.D. in sociology, not psychology.)

Note that Dr. van der Kolk told the judge that the Williams study was the *best ever done* on the repression of traumatic memory. Let us look at the best study ever done.

In a 1992 issue of *The Advisor*, a newsletter for an organization of professional child abuse experts, Linda Williams, a member of the organization's board, reported the results of interviews she and colleagues conducted with women seventeen years after they had been brought as young children to the emergency room of a city hospital for suspected sexual abuse.

Williams claimed that, "38% of the women were amnestic [*sic*] for the abuse or chose not to report the abuse to our interviewers 17 years later." Leaping to generalize her findings, she concludes, "These preliminary findings suggest that amnesia for sexual abuse in a community sample is not an uncommon event."

Amnesia? For unfathomable reasons, psychological amnesia is almost as popular with clinicians who specialize in sex abuse as it is with Hollywood writers. Williams is saying exactly what Herman and Schatzow said—that the trauma of the abuse was so great that the children probably repressed their memories of it.

Did Linda Williams really find that over a third of women who were abused as children had "amnesia" for the abuse seventeen years later? No, she didn't. She discovered that 38 percent either did not remember the incident *or* did not choose to tell her researchers about it. Dr. Williams never even asked the women directly whether they remembered the abuse. She did not hand them the hospital report and say, "See this? Now remember?" She has no idea what would have happened had she done so.

Is this proof of amnesia—proof that the trauma of childhood abuse forced those memories out of the reach of consciousness? As above, it is no such thing.

Williams's study, like that of Herman and Schatzow, is proof of nothing. Williams can argue that she has scientific proof of repression if and only if there is no other explanation for what happened with these women.

Are there no other possible reasons than amnesia to explain why 38 percent of the interviewed women failed to report an incident of child abuse from seventeen years before? Sure there are.

Her youngest subject was ten months old at the time of the

reported abuse. Ten months old! Just how much does anyone remember about being ten months old? Or one year? Or two? Or even three or four?

Also, for many of the children, the reported abuse consisted only of "touching and fondling." What's a child supposed to think about inappropriate touching and fondling? It is likely that such actions were uninterpretable and nontraumatic for the younger children.

It's important to consider too that there was no physical trauma in 34 percent of the cases, and in 38 percent no physical force was reported. For molestation that leaves no physical evidence, with young children one often has only the word of the mother or other caretaker that the abuse actually occurred. Maybe nothing happened. Maybe the mother was overly conscientious. Maybe she was angry at someone. Who knows?

In addition, the women in this study were from inner-city families who used the hospital emergency room as their primary health care provider, so there is nothing that would make a visit to the ER stand out for these children. Did Williams test to see how many of the other visits to the ER in the course of their childhood these women remembered? Did she find out what percentage of visits they forgot? And what kind of incidents they forgot? She did not. She didn't test how well or how much nonmolested adults remember about their trips for medical care as children either. She has no idea what kinds of injuries or sicknesses get forgotten over seventeen years.

There is nothing at all remarkable about the failure of 38 percent of Williams's subjects to relate an incident of reported sex abuse from seventeen years prior to the interviews. It would be completely unbelievable if 100 percent of them had remembered the incidents.

When something does *not* happen in a study, when women do *not* describe to interviewers a particular incident of reported abuse, the researcher *cannot* conclude that there is only one possible reason—amnesia!—for the absent finding. There are any number of possible reasons a particular finding does not show up in a particular study.

This study, along with that of Herman and Schatzow, belongs in the dustbin of junk science, not in supposedly authoritative legal briefs handed to our legislators and judges.

This study actually had nothing to do with repression at all. There were so many other reasons for the women's failure to report that single incident of abuse, no researcher could claim, with any degree of honesty, that repression was the sole possible reason, or even the most likely. It was no such thing.

Perhaps expert witnesses do not swear "to tell the truth, the *whole* truth, and nothing but the truth," but they should be required to do so if they do not. Dr. van der Kolk apparently forgot to tell the judge some additional crucial facts about Dr. Williams's study.

To quote from the 1979 book *The Aftermath of Rape*, written by Linda Meyer Williams with her colleagues Thomas McCahill and Arthur Fischman, the book that reported the original data:

> "Finally, *child victims [under twelve] of rape [broadly, statutorily defined] exhibit the fewest short-term [one year] adjustment problems. In many cases, the nature of the event [or events] is merely confusing*. Whereas the event is disturbing to the victim, it is perhaps no more disturbing than so many other aspects of a child's life. In the first year following the rape, the victim's family may deliberately maintain an "everything-is-normal" posture. These efforts, combined with the child's natural tendencies to forget and to replace bad feelings with good feelings, usually result in the appearance of few adjustment problems. . . . The changes that did appear were often difficult to attribute to the rape, as they may have reflected normal developmental growth and change. (Williams, McCahill, and Fischman 1979, pp. 44–45)

Why would Linda Meyer Williams have expected the "well-adjusted children" with their "natural tendencies to forget" to report a "merely confusing" event from seventeen years in the past to her interviewers in the 1990s?

Why would Dr. van der Kolk have neglected to share the earlier data on the lack of trauma in the child rape victims with the judge before whom he is testifying about trauma and memory? It is extremely hard to understand.

Dr. van der Kolk presented the Williams study to Judge Harrington as "the best" there is to prove "scientifically" the existence of repression. He was right about that. It is the best there is, and the best is really, really bad.

Most bewildering in the shabby display of pseudo-evidence for the existence of repression paraded before the judge in *Shahzade v. Gregory* is the research conducted by the number one expert-for-the-plaintiff himself, Dr. Bessel van der Kolk. Dr. van der Kolk testified that he conducts research on trauma using what he thinks of as advanced, sophisticated, neuropsychological techniques.

Dr. van der Kolk asserts that we have a special video trauma memory that works according to different rules than ordinary memory. He claims that while ordinary memories of such events as, for example, your first day at college, will indeed be distorted, decomposed, selectively highlighted, and badly contaminated both by what transpired before and what occurred afterward, memories of traumatic events are etched indelibly and unalterably into the very synapses of the brain.

Is there any evidence that special video trauma memory is a fact? No. But Dr. van der Kolk claims to find that when patients are asked to remember horrifying events in their lives like the death of a child in a car accident, their PET scans look different than they do when the patients are asked to think about getting up, brushing their teeth, and going to work. A PET scan is a picture representing the amount of brain activity in different colors. Dr. van der Kolk hooks up volunteers to the PET scanner—the machine that measures brain activity and makes the picture—and asks them to remember something terrible. He takes a "picture." Then he asks them to think about brushing their teeth. He takes another picture. The pictures look different.

What can one conclude from that? Nothing.

How do the PET scans look when the patients think about an event that was unpleasant but not horrific, like having your car stolen? Who knows? How about a highly emotional event like a wedding day or an episode of adultery? Do they look more like traumas or teeth brushing? Nobody knows. What do the scans look like when the patients are asked to fantasize a horrifying event instead of remember one? Nobody knows.

It wouldn't make any difference if we did have answers to all these questions. Whether PET scans vary when subjects think or fantasize about various types of events cannot prove that anyone has a trauma engram etched in his or her brain. How could it? And there is no logical connection between distinctive PET scans and Dr. van der Kolk's favorite pseudo-phenomenon, flashbacks. There is no necessary connection between distinctive PET scans and indelible memories.

For example, let us say that my PET scans always look different when I fantasize than they do when I remember real events. Would that necessarily mean that my memories of real events were exact and accurate? Of course not. There are innumerable reasons why the two classes of scans might differ.

Researchers who jump on "the special indelible character of trauma memory" bandwagon as the only possible explanation are simply bamboozling the public. This bamboozling is especially intimidating when it is sprinkled with a hefty dose of neuropsychology jargon. What is the poor layperson supposed to say? "I don't buy that PET scan stuff!" Of course not. Who would be so bold? That's why we have experts to explain these matters to the lay public. Nevertheless, fancy terms and expensive technology aside, no one ever has shown that memories of trauma have special etched-in-the-brain characteristics. Dr. van der Kolk's research certainly shows no such thing and he had no business telling the judge that it did.

Dr. van der Kolk was testifying about this research to prove that repression of memory due to trauma is a scientific fact. He seems to have forgotten for the purposes of his research the paradox that if his subjects are able to focus their minds on the memory of a "traumatic" event, then, by definition, that event was not repressed out of memory due to the trauma or they couldn't have been thinking of it during the experiment.

Of course, even if Dr. van der Kolk had avoided this crippling difficulty, his PET scan experiments cannot be said to have even the vestiges of control.

Who Needs Good Science?

Is there any scientific evidence that repression, in the sense that "researchers" like Herman and Schatzow, Williams, and van der Kolk mean it, actually exists? What they mean by repression is, "Something terrible happened to me and it was so awful that I *cannot* remember it, try as I will, and my failure to remember is not because I was too frightened to pay attention to what was happening, and not because I was hit on the head, but only because my mind is trying to protect me from the pain of the awful memory."

People like this story. It has an inherent plausibility—at least to the ear of psychologized Americans. It makes sense. Well, not to me. Psychologically, I'm from Missouri. Show me. Where's the sound, scientific—carefully controlled and unconfounded by floating variables and researcher bias—proof that repression exists? There is none.

David Holmes, in a recent comprehensive review of all of the evidence on repression, found that:

> despite over sixty years [it is over seventy years now] of research involving numerous approaches by many thoughtful and clever investigators, at the present time *there is no controlled laboratory evidence supporting the concept of repression.* It is interesting to note that even most of the proponents of repression agree with that conclusion. However, they attempt to salvage the concept of repression by derogating the laboratory research, arguing that it is contrived, artificial, sterile, and irrelevant to the "dynamic processes" that occur in the "real world." (Holmes 1990, p. 96)

Our George Franklin murder trial expert, Dr. Lenore Terr, takes exactly this tack. Dr. Terr, in describing her trial testimony in *Unchained Memories*, wrote:

> I explained why clinical studies of people who have undergone traumatic events are the best way we currently have to understand how these events are perceived, stored, and recollected. It was important that the courtroom "finders of fact" see that there are great differences between the mistakes that a group of kidnapped children will make, or that a raped little girl will make, and the mistakes a college student in a psych lab, for instance, will make after watching a movie of a simulated automobile accident. (Terr 1994, p. 51)

Dr. Terr packed a lot into that piece of testimony. She was saying that having a horrible experience is different from having an experience that is not horrible. That is undeniably true on some level if not all levels. She is saying also that adults are different from children. Also manifestly true in many but not in all respects.

Most important, she is saying that her interpretations and intuitions, and those of other clinicians, are a far better source of reliable and valid information about memory and trauma than are scientific studies of memory that do not involve actual trauma.

Now, that is a self-aggrandizing claim with no substantive scientific support whatsoever. That clinicians think they are great judges of how the mind works does not make them great judges of how the mind works. It just makes them clinicians.

In an outpouring of pride in the infallibility of her clinical intuition, Dr. Terr writes, "Psychological experiments on university students do not duplicate in any way the clinician's observation" (1994, p. 51).

That is actually a strange and rather pathetic statement. A reasonable person might expect that at least some of the clinician's observations ought to be scientifically verifiable. If a clinician's observations cannot be duplicated *in any way* by scientific psychological experiments—whatever the age or educational status of the subjects—then something is seriously wrong with the clinician's observations. It is hard to imagine why anyone in the medical professions would take such obvious pride in being beyond the touch of science.

Despite the disdain frequently expressed by clinicians for the inferior research efforts of their lesser scientific counterparts, we nevertheless have clinicians and trauma specialists like Williams, Herman, Schatzow, and van der Kolk all claiming that their scientific efforts to prove the existence of traumatic, "amnestic" repression have been wildly successful and downright definitive.

They should be joking, but they are not. Their work should be assigned in classes on research design to illustrate "What is wrong with this study?" It certainly should not be presented in court as science to a judge trying to make an honest and informed decision about the scientific status of some psychological concept.

It is especially frightening to realize that the professional organizations on which both the courts and the public rely are utterly unwilling to rein in these pseudo-experts when they testify. In fact, in *Shahzade v. Gregory*, the plaintiff even offered as supporting evidence a statement of the American Psychiatric Association that said, "Children and adolescents who have been abused cope with trauma by using a variety of coping mechanisms. In some instances these coping mechanisms result in a lack of conscious awareness of the abuse for varying periods of time. Conscious thoughts and feelings stemming from the abuse may emerge at a later date."

The judge was so impressed by that statement that he wrote in his decision, "The American Psychiatric Association, which is the major professional association for psychiatrists in America, recognizes the theory of repressed memories and believes it is very common among people who have experienced severe trauma."

The American Psychiatric Association should be ashamed of itself for writing a statement on the aftereffects of abuse that is so vague and so open in its terminology that any practitioner with an agenda can wiggle a pet theory into its framework. Do some people "cope" with the memory of an awful event by not thinking about it? Sure. Well, call that repression. Do some people simply forget with time and go on with their lives? Sure. Well, call that repression too. Why not?

Well, why not is pretty darn clear. Judges and legislators all over the country are not going to rewrite the law on the statute of limitations for either criminal or civil actions based on the "scientific discovery" that people sometimes avoid thinking about awful events in the past and sometimes they forget about them. They *are* rewriting the law because the APA has told them that what is responsible for the absence of conscious memory of terrible events is nothing ordinary but rather the mysterious mental process of repression, whose existence has been so clearly demonstrated by the clinical techniques of Sigmund Freud and his modern descendants. Shame on them.

The American Psychiatric Association knows perfectly well that whatever the private ideological beliefs of its members about the unconscious repression of the memory of psychological trauma, there is no scientific evidence supporting the factual existence of this hypothetical mental phenomenon. It is grossly unethical for the APA or any of its members to mislead the legal community into thinking otherwise. Because they would like repression to be a fact does not make it so.

PSYCHIC INJURIES LOST AND FOUND

We have frequently been called a litigious society; Maureen Dowd has lately called us a therapeutic society: The courtroom spawn of a marriage of these two is a dizzying image indeed. Thanks to liberal latitude in interpreting discrimination and injury under the Civil Rights Act, various Employment Discrimination Acts, the Americans with Disabilities Act, and the Child Abuse and Prevention Act, there are not nearly enough clinical practitioners to ferret out all the mental and emotional injuries committed in every imaginable public or regulated domain.

The newest (1994) *Diagnostic and Statistical Manual of Mental Disorders* provides the civil litigant with literally hundreds of possible disorders, each neatly laid out with the necessary symptoms. It is hard to imagine that anyone could live in today's society and not be diagnosed with at least one of these many disorders. After all, they include such exotic stuff as smoking cigarettes, having lousy sex, feeling rotten about your life or trapped in your job or marriage, and hating your body because you think you are too fat or too ugly. Anybody out there with low self-esteem?

If you are not Pollyanna-happy—and complain loudly about the fact that you are not—the odds are great that a psychoexpert can and will diagnose a mental problem for you.

Once society has accepted that the hundreds of ways people can be unhappy can all be labeled as specific mental disorders, then the diagnosis of those states of unhappiness, those disorders, becomes the special province of mental disorder experts. Using diagnostic criteria of the American Psychiatric Association, public health officials have determined that over 10 percent of working Americans suffer from alcohol disabilities. That doesn't just mean that they drink too much. Oh, no. It means they have a mental problem that makes them drink too much. The layperson has signed away the ability to say, "Oh, hell. If she drank less and spent more time thinking about somebody besides herself, she'd be okay." This insensitive lay analysis not only recommends a change in behavior as a cure for unhappy-making activity, it also places the blame for the situation on the sufferer. A strict no-no in the psychopolitics of modern America.

A layperson may look at the behaviors that characterize, for example, adjustment disorder, and say, "Oh, baloney. Disorder, smorder. She's just having trouble breaking up with her boyfriend." But what does our typical layperson know? Has he had any clinical experience with patients suffering from adjustment disorder? No.

He's had a lot of experience with people breaking up with their boyfriends and girlfriends, but commonsense experience no longer counts in the courtroom.

Today we have psychological experts to characterize life's events and their aftermaths in terms of disorders and treatment. This wholesale pathologizing of every possible response to the less-than-perfect aspects of life has been a real boon to tort attorneys and their plaintiffs.

In all civil tort (injury, discrimination, disability) cases—he did me wrong and I demand compensation—it is necessary for the plaintiff to show some damage or injury to claim compensation for said damage or injury. You can't go into court and say, "He ran me over with his car and I feel just perfect both physically and mentally, but I want a million dollars anyway."

Now, determining physical injury is by no means a simple task in every instance—just consider the wrangling over breast implants and secondhand smoke—but it's an absolute breeze compared to demonstrating psychological injury. I can see that your hand is badly burned, for example, but how am I supposed to know if you really suffer from depression? You say you do, but, after all, you are suing for a million bucks in damages, so you have to claim you are suffering from something, and I can see your hands look fine.

Diagnoses of mental disorders play a crucial role in establishing injury in cases in which no injury is evident to the casual observer.

Let us say that your falling off the ladder produced no clearly broken bones or other specific physical hurt. To recover damage for injury, you must establish the presence of some injury. If no damage is noticeably present, it behooves both patient and psychoexpert to unearth some. A diagnosis of mental or emotional disorder does the trick quite well.

It is noteworthy too, not to say terrifying, that a great many of the psychoexperts leaping onto the witness stand, hired to testify in civil trials in which thousands, often millions, in damages are demanded in compensation for psychic injury, are willing not only to diagnose the claimant but to identify for judge and jury the actual cause of the disorder—whodunit—even when that cause lay in the distant past, decades before the hired gun ever met his or her employer.

Of course, we have had claims of psychological injury for a number of years, but the exponential growth in such claims over the last twenty-five years has been astounding.

This is matched by the corresponding growth of graduate and professional education in the various branches of psychology over those years. The total number of Ph.D.s in clinical psychology granted in the United States from 1920 to 1974 was 8,687. In the twenty years since, there have been some 23,000 clinical Ph.D.s awarded. Today, there are some 75,000 clinically trained psychologists in the United States. This exponential growth has been accompanied by a like expansion in the number of master's-level clinical social workers, especially since they achieved the goal of licensing in the early 1980s, as well as holders of master's degrees in the different varieties of counseling. Psychiatry alone has suffered something of a drop-off in popularity over the last two decades, although with nearly 40,000 psychiatrists and close to 1,000 registered psychoanalysts, their ranks can hardly be called thin.

All these highly qualified people need jobs.

Mental and emotional injuries provide almost limitless vistas of employment for the psychologically trained. It should come as no surprise that job opportunities and skilled workers arise hand in hand, especially in a line of work where the worker defines the job.

THE PSYCHOLOGISTS AND THE STATUTE OF LIMITATIONS

Nevertheless, what psychological expert testimony about repression and recovery of memory has done in the arena of civil redress for mental and emotional injury knows no precedent. Lenore Terr's testimony in 1990 in the twenty-years-late George Franklin trial for the murder of the child Susan Nason provided an entree for expert psychological testimony on the alleged phenomenon of repressed memory in civil cases.

In both the number of cases it has inspired and in the changes of law it prompted, the Franklin case has had unprecedented "psychological" impact on the American civil justice system. That is surprising, in a way, and ironic, because the Franklin case was, of course, a criminal trial, not a civil action, and the absolute length of the delay on Eileen's part in bringing forth her allegations against her father was not the central issue, since there is no statute of limitations for murder in California.

Nevertheless, expert testimony on the status of repressed memory in the Franklin trial triggered an explosion of psycho-pseudo-science in the witness box and opened the floodgates to a new kind of civil case for hurts from decades past, and a new kind of delayed discovery law. In 1993 the California Court of Appeal ruled that Lenore Terr's testimony on trauma and repression was a useful thing to have had in the courtroom "to disabuse the jury of the identified misconception that a child witness to murder would not be able to forget the event only to recall it accurately twenty years later."

This opinion lays out clear acceptance of the psychoexpert's claim that as far as memory, forgetting, and the effects of terrible experiences go, the ordinary citizen is an ignorant boob. This court accepted the psychoexpert's claim that laypersons suffer from "misconceptions" about these matters and require "disabusing" through the good offices of the knowledgeable psychological professional who can infallibly ferret out the deepest buried secrets and the most elusive and complex mental processes.

Given what seems to therapists and patients to be the overwhelming intuitive evidence that traumatic repression exists and operates in just the way they have observed with their patients, many clinical practitioners supported a change in the statute of limitations for prosecuting past crimes and for bringing civil suits based on past injuries.

The move to extend the tolling of the statute of limitations indefinitely puts a great many people in a very dangerous situation. The legal system is supposed to protect the right of the defendant to mount a reasonable defense. That means if you are accused of a crime or accused of injuring someone, you must have the right to be tried in a time frame in which it is possible to obtain evidence and witnesses.

You also have the right to expect that the evidence brought forward will be something other than the highly dubious and utterly unscientific claims of personally invested "experts" in psychological "phenomena" that have absolutely no scientific basis in fact. You have this right as a defendant, and the people—judge, jury, and society as a whole—have a right to expect that defendants and plaintiffs will be found guilty or innocent or injured or competent or whatever on some basis other than the will-o'-the-wisp that is a clinician's personal opinion based on clinical practice.

However, due process notwithstanding, in response to the testimony of such experts, legislatures in some two dozen states across the country have changed their laws because they were told, and they believed, that there is reliable, generally accepted, *scientific* evidence for the operation of involuntary, unconscious repression. Clinicians presented as a scientific certainty a phenomenon whose existence is to date wholly unsubstantiated.

It is also likely that the people in the state legislatures are scared to death to vote against it. In my state, Massachusetts, the measure passed without debate. The issue is tied very closely to the problem of child sexual abuse and no legislators in their right mind want to be seen voting in favor of child molesters.

Proponents of the change wanted the law applied to recovered repressed memory to mirror that applied to the "discovery" of damage in, for example, surgical cases in which the forgotten sponge only makes its ill effects felt long after the statute of limitations for surgical malpractice has passed. If you buy the clinicians' belief system, that's a perfectly reasonable position. If you want sound, scientific evidence to support a change in the law, then it's real crazy.

The crucial difference between genuine discovery cases—"My god, he left the sponge in there!"—and recovered memory of trauma cases is that in the former there is no doubt that the sponge is indeed present in the claimant's body because the poor old claimant had to hire another surgeon to remove the disgusting thing. There is no question about the identity of the physician who left it there (although given the surgical masks and the anesthesia there may be room for doubt, but the surgeon's name is on the bill, isn't it?), and there is no doubt that had the patient been aware of the mislaid sponge within the time period specified by the statute of limitations, he would have sued to recover damages. Unless he was a very saintly and understanding patient.

But with so-called recovered memory cases, there is often no objective or even supporting evidence that the alleged trauma occurred, no evidence of the identity of the alleged perpetrator, and no evidence whatsoever that the plaintiff was unaware of the traumatic event—or "countless" events—causing the alleged damage during the period specified by the statute of limitations.

The widespread changes in the statutes of limitations due to legislators' acceptance of the scientific validity of repression and recovered memory have been a fabulous boon to litigators. Before the courts accepted this interesting story as proven science, plaintiffs could bring suit only for psychic wrongs done them within a few years of the injury. Now the grave is the limit. As long as the accused still breathes, suit can be brought for wrongs done more than half a century ago. The only evidence required is the claims of the plaintiff and the clinical intuition of the hired psychoexpert gun.

By the middle of 1996, nearly seven hundred lawsuits involving claims of repressed memory were at the trial level. Nearly two hundred had reached appeals courts.

For the whole clinical psychological profession in whatever guise, the increase in power and prestige in the civil litigation arena has been dizzying. Just think of it. Judges genuflecting before your sagacious testimony, and changing the law to fit your word. Legislatures galvanized into rewriting out-of-date statutes of limitations so that citizens wronged by their fellows decades in the past can nevertheless seek retribution as long as they were injured badly enough to lose their memories in the interim. It is a compelling picture of a powerful profession flexing its muscles as never before.

The clinician has, almost by definition, cornered this market. Because diagnosing psychological injury supposedly requires skills born of years of training, it is clear that only the trained psychological professional can do the job. No wonder the social workers clamored so for licensed clinical status.

It is also no wonder that the last couple of decades have seen an exponential growth in the number of psychoexperts testifying in litigation of every description involving claims of psychological injury from past abuse, present harassment, and any conceivable form of discrimination The job opportunities are inexhaustible.

SO MANY DIAGNOSES, SO MANY CLAIMS

In a civil trial like that of *Shahzade v. Gregory*, a psychological expert is hired by the plaintiff to mount the witness stand and give forth testimony both about psychological science in general terms—like the experimental basis of repression, for example—and also about the specifics of the particular case before the court at the moment.

For example, in the *Shahzade v. Gregory* case, Ann Shahzade claimed to suffer from an eating disorder, sleeping problems, and problems with her relationships. (Hmmm. Who doesn't?)

So, in testifying before Judge Harrington on the supposedly scientific foundation for repressed memory, Ann's Harvard expert did not confine himself only to generalities. Oh, no. He also diagnosed the plaintiff as suffering from our old friend, post traumatic stress disorder.

Consider that the major symptom of PTSD is horrible, intrusive memories of the traumatic event invading your thoughts and your dreams—those flashbacks that defense experts for Vietnam vets find so convenient. That is kind of hard to claim when you claim at the same time that you were entirely unable to remember the trauma at all for fifty years, isn't it? Of course, another little symptom you may have is the inability to recall an important aspect of the trauma. Maybe the clinician turned that symptom into the inability to remember anything at all even of years and years of horrible experiences. A second symptom cluster for PTSD has to do with avoiding thoughts of the trauma and people associated with it, but if you claim not to remember the trauma at all that whole bunch of possible symptoms is blown away. In this case, Ann certainly did not avoid her cousin; she regularly borrowed money from him over the years. The third category of symptoms you have to display—at least one—has to do with irritability and trouble falling or staying asleep. About ninety million Americans exhibit those symptoms, so the prospective plaintiff is pretty safe there.

What this means in actuality is that there are no symptoms reliably indicative of PTSD. The only important factor in reaching this diagnosis is the claim of the patients or plaintiffs that something horrible happened to them and it made them feel terrible. No psychiatrist, psychologist, counselor, or social worker can evaluate that claim any better than you or I. What is there to evaluate? Only whether the person is lying, and it is impossible for anyone to tell that.

Dr. Gerald Rosen, writing in the *Bulletin of the American Academy of Psychiatry and the Law* in 1996, observed that there is nothing new in the notion that some people feign illness for financial gain. He pointed out, however, that the establishment of post traumatic stress disorder as a distinct psychiatric condition has brought with it the expression of renewed concerns because the symptoms of PTSD are subjective, well-publicized, and easy to simulate.

> Recent findings demonstrate that attorneys can play an active role in furthering the presentation of false PTSD claims. Rosen (1995) reported on 20 survivors of a major marine disaster who all filed personal injury claims and presented with the hallmark symptoms of post traumatic stress disorder. The resulting and extraordinarily high incidence rate for diagnosed PTSD among these litigating survivors was explained, in part, by reports of attorney coaching and symptom sharing. Thus, several survivors disclosed that counsel had advised them that they didn't need to work and it might be worth their while to see a doctor every week. Two other survivors reported after settling their cases that attorneys had explained to crew members how people with PTSD had sleep problems, nightmares, and fears. This information was allegedly shared with others in the group. (Rosen 1996, p. 267)

A number of experts have expressed concern that attorneys might coach their clients in the furtherance of a claim, simply running down the list of PTSD symptoms in the DSM. Lees-Haley (1986) considered this potential for abuse and concluded: "If mental disorders were listed on the New York Exchange, PTSD would be a growth stock worth watching."

If you wish to sue, it is 100 percent guaranteed that a hired gun can be found to give you a diagnosis. With symptoms as vague and contradictory as those of dozens of the so-called mental disorders—with PTSD probably taking the prize—how can the expert miss?

Psychological Breast Lumps

Remember, in a psychological injury trial, a trial in which the plaintiff is claiming that he or she was mentally or emotionally injured by someone else, there is, by definition, no apparent physical evidence. We have only the word of the claimant, who says, "I am badly injured, he injured me, and I want compensation." The claimant is backed, of course, by the testimony of the hired expert psychological witness. (Of course, one may, and many people do, sue for both physical *and* psychological injury.)

In the example below, the supervising therapist hired by the plaintiff in a 1993 Seattle civil trial explains how he arrived at the diagnosis of post traumatic stress disorder that served as the basis of the alleged damage in the lawsuit for vast compensation—$3.4 million.

Attorney: What were the factors that you saw in your clinical experience in working with [the plaintiff] that led you to come to diagnosing her eventually as having Post-Traumatic Stress Disorder?

Therapist: Okay. The fact that what had appeared to be anxiety and depression, some Dissociation, that I initially saw as Adjustment, was more chronic. Secondly, that there had emerged in her therapy clear memories of very traumatic abuse and coercion of her, which is consistent with PTSD diagnosis. Thirdly, there was a disruption to her self image, her esteem of that image. And disruptions in her personal relationships, historically, and currently at that time.

So, for those reasons, among others, it seemed an obvious diagnosis to make. (*Matteu v. Hagen*, 1993)

Was the diagnosis of post traumatic stress disorder caused by childhood trauma reached because of the symptoms exhibited by the patient and carefully observed by the seasoned practitioner? Oh, no, not at all. Because the patient in the course of therapy claimed to recover memories of trauma, the therapist simply diagnosed PTSD on the basis of alleged trauma alone. The diagnosis was made entirely independently of any symptoms. (It is for this reason that PTSD—and its associated symptoms—cannot be used in any correlational studies of trauma victims. If the patient had a trauma, then the patient has PTSD; if the patient has PTSD, then, by definition, the patient had a trauma.)

The list of signs and behaviors that the naive might consider necessary for the diagnosis are nothing next to the claim of historical trauma by the patient. If you can claim a trauma, then you can claim a post trauma mental problem.

Shouldn't there have been at least a psychological lump in the patient's metaphorical breast to justify the diagnosis? Apparently not. This clinician began to "spot" symptoms *after* he reached his diagnosis, not *before*.

What does a psychological breast lump look or feel like? How does the trained clinician spot an authentic psychological symptom?

Let me give you a distressingly clear example of the extremely tenuous relationship between "symptoms" spotted by the sharp clinician hired to come up with a litigatable diagnosis and what the patient actually says in session with the clinician. It is also a beautiful example of the creative clinical intellect at work, utterly unfettered by any constraints of reality.

The plaintiff claimed to suffer from PTSD caused by the childhood trauma of abuse suffered two decades prior to the trial. Remember that a frequent symptom of PTSD is that the traumatic event is persistently reexperienced.

This is actual courtroom testimony illustrating what the patient said that led her therapist to believe that she "persistently reexperienced the trauma" that allegedly caused her PTSD.

Therapist: In [the plaintiff's] case, she continued to choose men in relationships in which there was often sexual deviancy [oral sex]. When she got close in the relationship, she would have difficulty in being sexual. She seemed to have difficulty in making appropriate and healthy choices for herself regarding relationships. So that, in essence, with each relationship, it was a form of sexual abuse that she kept creating.

What I saw in [her] is that each time she got into a relationship it was inappropriate and in many ways it was abusive. That would be re-experiencing the original event. I don't believe that she deliberately, consciously, went out and picked someone that was going to be abusive towards her or would ask her to perform sexual acts that she wasn't comfortable with. But, I believe, that's what kept happening again and again.

Attorney: I see. Anything else?

Therapist: No. (*Matteu v. Hagen*, 1993)

Got that? Any woman who has had a number of unsatisfactory relationships with men is a victim of post traumatic stress disorder. Any sharp clinician could tell you that those lousy relationships are just the poor woman's way of reenacting the abusive relationship from her girlhood. Of course, this will be true even if the woman remembers nothing at all about the past abuse. The unconscious does not lie, does it? And what could lousy relationships be but a reflection of abuse in the past?

What we've got here is evidence for the presence of a symptom—reexperiencing the original event through nightmares, incessant thoughts, or flashbacks—so flimsy I would not have believed it if I had not heard it in court. Bricks out of straw indeed. Yet this trained professional testified that she spotted this symptom—rotten relationships with men—and determined her diagnosis in one impressive leap of illogic. Who can say she is wrong? Only another highly trained professional.

Corroboration

Only another expert can testify that your expert is wrong, and what can he or she say? That you are *not* sick? You cannot prove that a person is *not* sick; you cannot prove the nonexistence of something. Maybe the second expert is just not as sensitive as the first. Who can say? A third expert? There are no objective criteria for most mental diagnoses.

The psychiatric association did not develop its diagnostic categories or the associated symptom lists through any procedure remotely resembling standard scientific practice, and individual practitioners do not arrive at their specific diagnoses for particular patients through any scientific procedure either.

The actual basis for the clinician's diagnosis is what it always was, from Freud to the present, diagnostic manual or no manual: what the patient says about what he or she feels, thinks, and does; and the clinician's interpretation of what the patient says.

James McDonald and Francine Kulick have edited a book called *Mental and Emotional Injuries in Employment Litigation*—a handbook for expert psychological witnesses to use in preparing cases for psychological damage. This handy guide to prospering in court points out, with no sense of irony whatsoever, that:

> In psychiatry and clinical psychology, more than in any other medical discipline, a patient's subjective reporting may be a significant and confounding problem in the diagnostic process. . . . Without clarification, and taken at face value, a patient or litigant who claims to be "severely depressed" may be misunderstood as suffering from a clinically significant depression when the person is simply sad or angry. (1994)

Well, they've got that right.

The clinician relies on what the patient says—filtered, of course, through the focusing lens of the clinician's intuition, and corroboration of the product of this happy union is neither wanted nor needed. Well, actually, corroboration is badly needed, but the legal profession has been conned into believing that it is not.

In a chapter on torts, or civil wrongs, in his book *Everybody's Guide to the Law*, the late nationally famous attorney Melvin Belli writes:

> An early fear of the law was that psychological injuries could be easily faked. Because there were no sure means of verifying these injuries, the danger was that many sham claims would be successful. Today psychological and emotional injuries and other mental disorders can be diagnosed with a good deal of certainty, so the chances that a fraudulent claim for emotional distress will succeed are no greater than for any other type of injury. (Belli and Wilkinson 1986, p. 302)

Mr. Belli was badly led astray there, and so, all too often, are the rest of us. The gullible public is led to believe that clinicians testifying in civil cases truly reach their diagnostic conclusions after carefully gathering corroborating information for what the patient tells them, but, of course, in most instances, corroboration would be impossible. Who can corroborate whether someone sleeps well, has nightmares, feels anxious, or can't remember something?

In some cases, however, clinicians simply spurn the concept of corroboration as irrelevant to the process of healing. They also spurn reality testing as irrelevant to the process of criminal and civil trials, which is truly bewildering.

Dr. Lenore Terr, the star witness for the prosecution in the George Franklin murder trial, displays the classic breezy attitude toward corroborating evidence for a patient's claim. (Her entire acquaintance with Eileen Franklin before her father's trial extended for the whole of four hours.)

> Eileen told me that she became withdrawn at school after Susan Nason disappeared. She began pulling out the hair on one side of her head, creating a big, bleeding bald spot near

> the crown. *Most likely*, young Eileen unconsciously set out to duplicate the horrible wound she had seen on Susan Nason's head. This behavioral re-enactment provided internal confirmation for me of the truth of Eileen's memory. (1994, pp. 35–36; italics added)

It is beyond belief that a court was hoodwinked into believing that this nonsensical psychobabble represents in any way objective evidence or reliable proof that Eileen pulled out her hair to match up with Susan Nason's head wound.

That courtroom diagnosticians ignore even the wispiest constraints of reality in reaching their diagnoses is truly frightening.

Lenore Terr, like all clinicians, trusts her clinical intuition absolutely and is blithely indifferent to the operation of the confirmatory bias in the construction of an interpretative narrative to put on the witness stand. She was testifying in a murder case, a criminal trial, which makes this arrogance and indifference to science particularly difficult to swallow.

Faking It

In the *Shahzade v. Gregory* trial, Bessel van der Kolk told the judge that "there is no scientific basis to believe that Shahzade or other victims could fake such memories and fool psychiatric tests" (Rakowsky, *Boston Globe*, April 10, 1996).

What on earth can Dr. van der Kolk have meant by that?

Did he mean that patients can't fool doctors about whether claimed memories are real? Not true. Patients themselves can even be fooled.

Jean Piaget, the famous Swiss child psychologist, gives us an oft-quoted example of exactly this phenomenon. He relates that a vivid childhood memory of his was of an attempted kidnapping he suffered as a small child in the care of a nanny who saved him from the danger. Years afterward, in a fit of remorse, the nanny confessed to Piaget's parents that she had made up the whole story to cover some indiscretion of hers. Yet, for the young "kidnap" victim, the memory was as clear and as detailed as any memory of an actual event. Of course, the story was probably vividly related by the maid, and no doubt recounted a number of times by family members, so it was a clear story in young Piaget's mind. How was he to know it was not true?

No one can tell the difference between a true memory and a mistaken one. There are no reliable differences in accuracy, in the number of details, or even in the confidence a person feels in the memory.

(For very readable books that deal directly with this issue as it applies to real-life situations, the reader is directed to any of several recent offerings by Elizabeth Loftus and her colleagues.)

Did Dr. van der Kolk mean that a patient couldn't fool a test for traumatic repression? Not true. There are no psychological tests for such things. What test could there possibly be? Unless someone pops up and says, "Wait a minute! She told me all about it in 1972," there is no possible way to gainsay the claim of a traumatic inability to remember. What secret psychological tests could Dr. van der Kolk have had in mind?

Is he claiming that no well person could fake responses to psychological tests well enough to fool a clinician into thinking he or she was sick? Not true. P. Lees-Haley and R. S. Dunn in 1994 found that college freshmen in the first quarter of an introductory psychology course were quite capable of picking out the appropriate symptoms for different diagnoses. Ninety-seven percent of these untrained youngsters picked out the "right" symptoms for depression, 97 percent for generalized anxiety disorder, and 86 percent for PTSD (Lees-Haley and Dunn 1994, pp. 252–56).

Moreover, a famous study by David Faust, Kathleen Hart, and Thomas Guilmette showed that the situation was just as bad even for the accurate detection of brain damage in children.

> Children were instructed to "fake bad" on comprehensive neuropsychological testing but were given minimal guidance on how to proceed. Of the 42 clinical neuropsychologists who reviewed cases, 93% diagnosed abnormality [in normal children!], 87% of these 93% attributed the results to cortical dysfunction, and no clinician detected malingering. The results are consistent with other studies that have examined the capacity of adolescents and adults to fake believable deficits on neuropsychological testing. (Faust, Hart, and Guilmette 1988, p. 578)

There is half a century of research showing that it is not only possible but quite easy to fake and fool both psychiatric tests and the psychiatrists who give them. There is also a decade of research showing that people can be fooled even by their own mistaken memories.

Is Dr. van der Kolk claiming that in an evaluation interview no client could fool a trained clinical psychiatrist into thinking she suffered from PTSD when she did not? That's a joke, right? To get a diagnosis of PTSD, all you have to do is tell your doctor that you have nightmares about some awful event in your past, or, alternatively, that you remember nothing at all about some awful event, and that you are cranky and have trouble sleeping. Bingo! PTSD.

Dr. van der Kolk must have been fooling the judge, or maybe he was just putting him on.

It is exactly this extraordinary flexibility in claiming and interpreting symptoms that makes customized diagnoses not only possible but inevitable. The good attorney Belli could not have been more wrong.

The system is foolproof. Opportunities for litigation for psychic injury—for mental and emotional distress—are wide open. Add in the unprecedented expansion of time to bring suit afforded the allegedly injured plaintiff by state and federal acceptance of repressed memory as an excuse to throw reasonable statutes of limitation out the window, and the opportunities become virtually limitless.

Any underemployed clinicians or attorneys would do well to hotfoot it to the nearest bookstore and purchase a copy of the DSM-IV as well as the handy how-to-sue book edited by McDonald and Kulick. The latter is an excellent source for information on laws that provide avenues for recovery of damages due to psychological injury and for frequently claimed injuries along with their diagnostic criteria.

WHAT DOES IT COST TO BRING A CIVIL SUIT?

The situation is made worse by the way the current legal system pays for itself. Most civil suits like *Shahzade v. Gregory* are brought under a contingency arrangement. So suing is itself a little bit expensive, but mostly for the attorney, not for the plaintiff. The attorney usually foots the bill for all those expensive expert witnesses at several hundred dollars an hour for court time plus preparation, travel, and lodging. Sometimes the plaintiff and the plaintiff's attorney will split these costs. In all cases, these matters are subject to negotiation.

If the plaintiff loses, then he or she must usually pay only court costs, which essentially amount to fees for photocopying documents and such.

This is nothing compared with what it will cost the defendant to fight the suit.

Yes, these suits for compensation for past injury do have defendants. After all, somebody has to foot the bill for your injury, and why should it be you?

RETROSPECTIVE CLAIRVOYANCE, OR I KNOW WHO CAUSED THE INJURY

In civil cases in which the plaintiff is seeking compensation for injury, the plaintiff must show not only some hurt or injury, but *who or what is the cause* of that injury.

That means that any plaintiff in a civil injury tort trial must hire a clinician who not only will diagnose the client with something psychologically injurious warranting compensation—preferably lots of it—but also will imprint a psychological kiss of authority on the pointing finger when the client claims to know who caused the injury.

Where is the evidence that the person accused is guilty of causing the injury? Enter the expert witness. When Dr. van der Kolk diagnosed Ann Shahzade with PTSD, he also testified that the disorder was brought on by the sexual traumas she suffered in adolescence at the hands of her teenage cousin fifty years before (Rakowsky, *Boston Globe*, April 10, 1996).

Now, that is a diagnostic feat! How did the expert know that? How would a clinician go about diagnosing a sixty-eight-year-old woman as suffering from PTSD brought on by a series of incidents *more than fifty years in her past*? No one could know that. It makes no difference.

Hired diagnosticians cheerfully mount the stand and tell court after court not only that this person is suffering from PTSD, or anxiety disorders, or dysthymic disorder, but also that it is obvious to the diagnostician who or what caused the mental or emotional injury and when it happened. They have to do that if the plaintiff who hired them is going to win the case.

For example, if you are going to sue your employer claiming that job-related stress or sexual harassment from your supervisor caused you grievous, incapacitating, expensive-to-treat psychological injury, then clearly you must show that your alleged problems do indeed stem from the job situation itself and not from some other cause like preexisting lifelong depression or the sad fact that your spouse has left you for a younger model.

So your expensive psychological expert witness must not only claim to discern for the mystified public the psychological injury invisible to the ordinary person in the jury box or to the judge—but clear in the mind's eye of the trained clinician—but must also unabashedly identify the cause and perpetrator of the injury no matter how distant in the past the source may lie.

Now, how could your recently hired, never-been-to-your-place-of-employment expert possibly know that your anxiety, sleeplessness, stress, or depression was due to sexual harassment by your supervisor last year and to no other cause? He cannot, unless you tell him.

If clinicians can't even diagnose disorders reliably, how are they supposed to be able to peer into the past and pick out the cause of this or that problem?

Let's look at the *Shahzade v. Gregory* case again. Let us, just for the sake of argument, grant for the moment that the plaintiff in *Shahzade v. Gregory* does indeed suffer from an eating disorder, sleeping problems, and problems with her relationships. Let us even grant that she herself feels quite confident about her memories of sexual abuse.

What has any of that to do with her clinician's ability to tag that remembered abuse as the source of her present problems? Nothing at all. Absolutely nothing at all. Can any clinical diagnostician really claim with confidence that nothing in the intervening fifty years of this person's life might not equally well be responsible for whatever unhappiness or distress she may exhibit? Of course not. It is logistically impossible to rule out the innumerable stresses and strains of fifty years of living with all the attendant heartbreak, frustrations, and disappointments. It is also impossible to claim with any confidence that it is not these disappointments and difficulties with life that disturb the sleep or the disposition of the claimant.

There is no test for causes, no secret trick taught only in graduate and medical schools for peering into the history of a human being and pinpointing the cause of any behavior, disorder, good or bad habit, preference, or style. There is no evidence that people who are extremely neat were aggressively toilet trained or that those who cling too tightly to their loved ones were weaned too abruptly. Those are just interpretations that seem more or less plausible, depending on the depth of one's Freudian acculturation. The source material for the interpretations is what it always is, the stories the patient tells the clinician.

There is no symptom or set of symptoms displayed by an adult woman that are invariably caused by sexual harassment on the job. There is no set of symptoms that are linked invariably to long-past childhood sexual abuse. The "symptoms" shown by the overwhelming majority of female claimants in such cases—problems with food and men—are so common among women in our society that they cannot possibly be tied to any particular childhood event, traumatic or otherwise. It would be absurd to try.

This is especially important to remember given the recent rash of cases involving such allegations of abuse in both the near and the distant past.

It is crucial that the public know that clinical practitioners have no special ability to evaluate these claims.

THE SEARCH FOR JUSTICE

There are, no doubt, any number of people who were hurt in their childhood by adults. There are also, no doubt, any number of people who are not living, in the present, the lives they wish to live. Perhaps there are causal connections between these things, and perhaps there are not.

What we as a society have done to right these past wrongs, to render justice where there was none, and to compensate the injured is to accept wholesale an elaborate tissue of lies that we think allows us to trace the psychological connections from one time to another, and the causal psychological relations between an earlier event and a later condition.

We can do no such thing. The fanciest psychological expert in the world cannot do that. Psychology herself as a field cannot do that.

In our pursuit of justice, we have gone completely astray from the pursuit of truth.

10

Four Hundred Ways to Avoid Responsibility

Disordered, Disabled, Dispensed

> There is probably never a physical injury without some measurable psychic trauma. . . . The past 30 years . . . have seen the exploitation of this truism in worker's compensation and personal injury litigation . . . resulting in a staggering number of physically fit, mentally competent individuals forever being relieved of responsibility for earning a living—on psychiatric grounds.
>
> Barton J. Blinder, *Abuse of Psychiatric Disability Determination*, 1979

TRADITIONAL FARCE RENEWED

Psychological farce on the part of both claimant and clinician is hardly unique to injury claims made under recent recovered memory legislation. Oh, no. The first intense flowering of this poisonous blossom took place in the fertile soil of what might be called traditional torts. Recall that by 1989 damages paid out to compensate people for the "loss of the full enjoyment of life" approached $14 million. Loss of "mental health," according to Jury Verdict Research, Inc., had reached one hundred times that amount by the 1990s.

> Teen-age airplane passenger Jarret Halker says he screamed in panic, banged on windows and punched seats after waking up

> on a commuter jet—semi-dark, empty and far from the terminal at Logan Airport last summer. . . . Halker . . . and his mother . . . are suing the company and its contract commuter carrier for $21 million over trauma the [thirteen-year-old] boy says he suffered as a result of the July 15 flight. (*Boston Globe*, July 31, 1995)

> Two residents of a Bronx condominium complex filed suit yesterday, charging they were injured when their newly installed toilets exploded. . . . One of them, 10-year-old Philip Garner, suffered "psychological injuries" when his toilet blew up November 20, said [attorney] O'Dwyer, who is seeking $2 million for the boy and $100,000 for his parents. (Mangan, *Daily News*, December 29, 1995)

> A schoolboy was forced to wear a woman's wig, bra and skirt as punishment for talking in class while his teacher looked on and laughed, according to a $22.5 million lawsuit. [The] punishment left seventh-grader Caleb Guerrier with psychological damage and other personal injuries, the lawsuit charges. (*Legal Intelligencer*, New York, May 25, 1995)

> This is my favorite:

> A student who accidentally shot a classmate during a law-enforcement class now is suing the community college, Aurora police, and others for $1 million, claiming their alleged "reckless conduct" caused her emotional distress and mental injury. (Robey, *Denver Post*, August 18, 1994)

The tremendous growth of psychological injury compensation cases in standard torts led inevitably to a similar pattern of growth wherever the ground proved fertile. And nowhere in the American legal terrain has the ground proved more fertile or opportunities more plentiful than in the area of evolving social welfare law.

Consider race discrimination. Congress outlawed it in 1964 and the American Psychiatric Association has since pathologized it—not for the racist, quite yet, but certainly for the victim.

> The Massachusetts Commission Against Discrimination yesterday ordered the town of Freetown to pay $250,000 to a black police sergeant for emotional distress he underwent after he was passed up for promotion almost nine years ago. The award is the largest ever ordered by the commission for emotional distress in a racial discrimination case. The officer, Detective Sgt. Alan L. Alves, who is of Cape Verdean ancestry, also was awarded $13,500 in back pay. (Hunger, *Boston Globe*, June 21, 1996)

So, over a nine-year period, the failure to be granted the promotion cost him $1,500 a year before taxes in salary, but it also "cost" him almost $28,000 a year in emotional distress? There seem to be no reasonable limits to calculating the incalculable.

Exactly the same pattern of payment occurs in sexual harassment and discrimination suits. The actual tangible damages—however wrongly inflicted—are often slight, but the alleged intangible damages like emotional and mental injuries are judged to be great indeed.

Still, however great the field of operation afforded the psychological injury evaluator by standard civil rights law touching on race and sex discrimination, nothing exceeds the expansion of opportunities created by the Americans with Disabilities Act. It cannot be denied that for the attorney and the clinical psychologist with active imaginations the growth of case possibilities in both scope and size of award has been, even by traditional tort standards, truly phenomenal.

ANTI-DISCRIMINATION LAW AND DISPENSATION FOR THE DISABLED

The Americans with Disabilities Act was signed into law by President George Bush in the summer of 1990. It represented both an expansion and an updating of the federal Rehabilitation Act of 1973 and of Title VII of the federal Civil Rights Act of 1964.

The intent of the law—if not its particulars and ramifications—was clear: Congress wished to end employment discrimination against the handicapped based not on genuine inability of workers to do the job but on negative attitudes of employers, and to open access for the handicapped in the arenas of public accommodations and telecommunications. It seemed clear to Congress, and to many others in society, that many impediments to both job success and freedom of movement of the handicapped resulted not from their disability but from an unwillingness of both employers and various levels of government to consider their abilities as well as their disabilities, or to accommodate those disabilities to increase both job productivity and public access.

In short, the handicapped were being ripped off by municipal and state governments unwilling to spend money to accommodate the needs of disabled taxpayers and citizens, and by employers unwilling in the face of their prejudice to make even the most trifling of accommodations to workers with special needs for job performance. Surely all of society would benefit—monetarily as well as morally—if the obstacles to productive employment and civil services were removed from the paths of the handicapped.

Accordingly, the Americans with Disabilities Act—ADA—was written to prohibit discrimination in the realm of employment against persons who are disabled by a physical or mental handicap but who are nevertheless qualified to do the job with or without reasonable accommodation to their disability.

According to ADA, a person is judged to be "disabled" within the requirements of the law if he or she has a current physical or *mental impairment* that substantially limits one or more of the individual's major life activities, has a record of having such impairment, or is regarded as having such an impairment. Major life activities are all the normal things that people without impairment can do easily like walking, seeing, hearing, breathing, learning, and working. (The last two are rather tricky.) According to ADA, *a mental impairment is a mental or psychological disorder like mental retardation, organic brain disorders, emotional or mental illnesses, and specific learning disabilities* (Americans with Disabilities Act of 1990, Pub. L. No. 101–336, 104 Stat. 327, codified at Sec. 42 U.S.C. 12101–12213, Supp. III 1991).

Employers are liable to charges of discrimination if they refuse to hire an otherwise qualified individual to do a job because of a disability, or if they refuse to undertake reasonable accommodations to a disability in the workplace that would permit the disabled individual to engage in productive work.

The intent of the law was rational, perhaps even rather noble, but like all social welfare legislation requiring assessment of mental state, its implementation was another do-gooders' Pandora's box.

It is true that in the past, the handicapped undeniably suffered from blanket discrimination that took no account of the actual nature of the handicap or what efforts, societal and individual, would be required to overcome it. That America as a society has chosen to make fuller use of the talents and abilities of more of its citizens and provide those citizens with access to more of the fruits of modern society is a good and sensible thing.

Abuse of all of these well-intentioned efforts, like abuse of the disability system, also makes perfect sense in that it is inevitable. If there is an opportunity to make a buck the easy way—without working for it—then certainly there will be those who will take advantage of that opportunity.

Let us say that a secretary goes into therapy and realizes that she really wants to end her ten-year marriage, becomes miserable and depressed, starts missing a lot of work, and is inefficient even when she does show up. She is fired, and sues under the ADA. How do you reasonably accommodate someone who is so depressed that she is always thinking about her problems at work? Is her depression enough to be qualified as a disability? What about a salesman who claims that he suffers from agoraphobia? Must he be taken out of the field and given a cold-call desk job? What about an engineer who suffers from so much generalized anxiety that she is incapable of submitting a finished design? The guy who suffers from delusions of grandeur and can't work on a team? Do all of these difficulties at work qualify as legally protected mental disabilities?

"Accommodate the disabled so that they can do the job" became "Accommodate the job to those who are essentially unwilling to do it." Engage in disruptive and abusive behavior during company meetings? That would get any healthy person fired. Claim that such behavior is due to a disabling mental disorder and you get $900,000. Yell obscenities at students, colleagues, clients, or customers? Grab and grope them? Get a diagnosis or get fired.

If you can get a diagnosis of mental illness attached to the foul language or sexual assault, then you are in line for a big payoff. Psychological injury has a huge multiplier effect on compensation both in cases in which the claim of discrimination is just and in cases in which it is not. Consider traditional discrimination cases in which, for example, a black person unjustly passed over for promotion might have been awarded the promotion and the back pay that would have been due. Today, in addition, that person receives compensation of ten or twenty times the back wages because, according to the testimony of a mental injury diagnostician, the injured party *also* claims to be suffering from grievous mental or emotional distress caused by the discrimination.

Even an innocent employer is helpless to combat the claim that the allegedly injured party was emotionally damaged, but an employer actually guilty of disability or racial or other discrimination is pretty much dead in the water. Such an employer has to get attorneys and psychological experts to argue that prejudice and discriminatory salary and promotion practices—however unjust—do not harm people psychologically at all, or, if they do, it is not that bad, certainly not bad enough to be worth many times the wages due. That argument, however true it may be, does not have a chance in hell of prevailing in today's climate where a damaged psyche is held to be a greater loss than a missing arm.

What started out as an idea for reasonable accommodation to end mindless discrimination has become mindless accommodation to irrational and irresponsible behavior. The legal implementation of Congress's intention to make full use of the capabilities of all citizens became at the same time a golden opportunity for mental health providers to use their inventive powers to their full capacities.

This is not exactly a big surprise when you look at the psychological evaluators' track record with older, traditional social welfare programs.

THE POSTER GIRL OF THE ANTI-WELFARE MOVEMENT

Clarabel Rivera Ventura is the poster girl of the anti-welfare movement. Ms. Rivera is the twenty-seven-year-old Massachusetts mother of seven who was charged with scalding the hands of her four-year-old child and then failing to get him any medical treatment. She fled the country for some weeks but eventually returned to stand trial on charges of child abuse and neglect.

Ms. Ventura had sixteen siblings, one of whom is dead, and two of whom live in Puerto Rico. None of the others, residing in the

United States, works. The siblings on Aid to Families with Dependent Children are no surprise. The surprise is the five brothers and sisters who are *unable* to work because of "medical" disabilities.

> "It's happened different ways. It is complicated. Most of the boys are disabled and two of the girls are disabled. There's been a lot of problems," said [Clarabel's sister] Maribel. "You have to talk to each one." Explaining why she receives $470.00 a month in Social Security Disability Income (SSDI), Maribel said: "I have anxiety attacks. They come when I'm never expecting it." . . . Juan, who is a father of five children and divorced from his wife, was asked why he doesn't work. "I have a nervous condition. I fill out the medical reports and everything for disability. There is no way I could work," he said, explaining that he receives $302 a month in Emergency Aid to the Elderly, Disabled and Children, a form of state and federally financed disability pay. On another day last week, Juan was asked again why he didn't work. He showed a reporter his hands, which were shaking, and said, "Look at this. I'm having an attack right now." He called a doctor and told him that he had to see him immediately and soon left the house. Asked the same question, Benjamin said, "I have the bad nerves. I have a lot of problems." (Sennot, *Boston Globe*, February 20, 1994)

Considerable attention was focused on this family because, collectively, they cost the welfare system some $1 million a year, but little attention was paid to the grand scam of a welfare system that supports all fourteen nonworking sibling adults in a single family, plus their mother and all of their children, through cash grants, food stamps, subsidized housing, and miscellaneous other benefits. What resourceful people they must be!

The beneficiaries of such governmental support for the nonworking do come, of course, from many walks of life and suffer from a number of different ailments, but it is true that perhaps no case study better illustrates the potential for abuse of the support system by mental health practitioners, who experience no check whatsoever on their license to find a mental disability in nearly every member of the Rivera family.

THE SOCIAL SAFETY NET FOR THE OCCUPATIONALLY INCAPACITATED

For some sixty years the U.S. government, with the help of the country's psychological establishment, has provided base-level financial support to those of its citizens who, like the Ventura siblings, are unable to work due to mental incapacitation. (Likewise for physical incapacitation, of course.)

The two principal federal programs under the Social Security Administration (SSA) providing financial support to those judged mentally incapable of work are Social Security Disability Insurance (SSDI) and Supplemental Security Income (SSI). These are the very programs that so benefit the nonworking members of the Ventura family. In the jargon of the trade, "occupational incompetency"—no kidding, that is what they call it—is the affliction of beneficiaries of these programs. In regular parlance, recipients suffer from a mental disorder (or physical, of course) that renders them essentially incapable of working. It is not that they do not wish to work, mind you. They are mentally incapable of it. (And not just on Monday morning.)

The requirements and benefits of the two programs are much the same; the main difference between them is that recipients of SSDI must have at least some history of work in their lives before they fell victim to their incapacitating mental illnesses.

Who certifies the prospective welfare recipient as mentally incompetent, occupationally speaking? The professional mental health evaluator, of course.

Technically, the true legal authority for determining the recipients of disability benefits resides, of course, in various levels of the Health and Human Services Administration, but in practice the real authority is in the hands of the psychological evaluator who checks off qualifying signs and symptoms, writes the report, and signs the form. It is the classic de facto/de jure distinction. The law says one thing but the real situation determines another.

In fact, Melton, Petrila, Poythress, and Slobogin's 1987 highly regarded handbook for psychologists and lawyers on performing mental health evaluations for the courts notes, "*A mental status examination is a prerequisite to a determination of a psychiatric disability*. Although the exact parameters of this requirement are not clear, the Social Security Administration has observed that the *absence* of such an examination is the most common error in cases reversed on review." Also, "*The clinical examination and report are critical to determinations of disability under the Social Security regulations; indeed, without appropriate clinical evidence, the determination cannot be made*" (p. 266).

Demonstrating Occupational Incompetency

Actually, not all judges genuflect automatically and completely at the command of the professional mental health evaluator, but enough of them do to make the handwriting on the wall alarming indeed.

Consider the case of Jerry Dalton, who pursued his claims of disability over sixteen years, up to and including suing the secretary of Health and Human Services. Mr. Dalton fought long and hard to remain legally disabled, switching from early claims of disabling physical injuries sustained in a fall from a ladder to later claims of mental injuries and defects of unknown origin.

How did Mr. Dalton's vocational psychologist determine that Mr. Dalton was mentally unable to work anymore?

> Dalton underwent a psychological evaluation. [The social worker] administered a series of tests [Wechslar Adult Intelligence Scale, Bender Visual Motor Gestalt Test, Wide Range Achievement Reading Test, Mental Status Evaluation, Rorschach Inkblot Test, and the Clinical Interview] and concluded that he was of [low] average intelligence and had a passive-dependent personality disorder. . . .

What does that mean? Low average IQ means that this guy was not a rocket scientist, as they say. It certainly does not mean that he was incapable of working. If it did, half the current labor force would be on the dole. A passive-dependent personality disorder means that the patient lies around doing nothing—a condition that could no doubt be pretty easily induced by the absence of work in the claimant's life for so long (*Dalton v. Secretary of Health and Human Services*, 1990).

> At the request of Dalton's attorney, another psychological evaluation was conducted by Dr. David Goldsmith, a clinical psychologist . . . [who] concluded that "with his education level, medical history, employment record, and psychological

> status . . . he would be very unlikely to succeed at gainful employment." Dr. Goldsmith also concluded that Dalton would not be a suitable candidate for vocational rehabilitation. (*Dalton v. Secretary of Health and Human Services*, 1990)

What has Dr. Goldsmith added to our assessment? Well, he is essentially saying that in addition to being lazy and none-too-bright, the claimant is also short of educational and job skills, and his present habit of unemployment will be hard to break.

Well, the court of appeals was insensitive to the psychologists' sad case and, after sixteen years of living without working, Mr. Dalton lost his disability payments. One of the appeals court judges, however, strongly dissented from the majority's opinion. He thought Mr. Dalton's psychoexperts had made a convincing claim that all thought of work was beyond Mr. Dalton.

> I respectfully dissent from the majority opinion because I take a different view of Dalton's intellectual capabilities and psychological impairment . . . the results clearly show that Dalton's intelligence is significantly below average. . . . The vocational expert testified that a passive-dependent personality disorder of the severity noted in the evaluations . . . would prevent Dalton from [performing any jobs existing]. . . . The vocational expert was an experienced, licensed psychologist. Therefore, he was perfectly competent to testify as to the effect of Dalton's passive-dependent personality disorder on his ability to work. (District Judge Cohn, dissenting, *Dalton v. Secretary of Health and Human Services*, 1990)

In the determination that a person is occupationally incompetent by virtue of mental illness, it is not enough for the psychological evaluator simply to come up with one of the nearly innumerable allowable diagnoses. The psychologist must also conclude that the effects of the mental disorder are such as to render the claimant so disabled that he is incapable of work—any kind of work—and is thus eligible for compensation by the government.

Judging that an individual is pretty much broadly occupationally incompetent—occupationally challenged—requires that the psychological evaluator assess such matters as a person's ability to understand, carry out, and remember simple instructions; the exercise of judgment; the ability to respond appropriately to supervision, co-workers, and the usual work conditions; and the ability to deal with changes in a routine work setting.

Let us say that like Clarabel Rivera Ventura's siblings, you have a bad case of the nerves that you claim prevents you from working. When you go to the psychologist with this claim, it is a simple matter for him or her to reach a diagnosis of an anxiety disorder once you explain that you are very nervous, your hands shake, you can't sleep, you are startled by the least little thing, and so on. And it is a simple matter to test your ability to follow simple instructions. The evaluator could just give you a number of instructions and see how well you carry them out. You could get a score from 1 to 10, say. Is your judgment any good? Well, the evaluator could ask you a series of questions about "What is the thing to do if . . ." They've been doing this with intelligence tests for decades so if they stick to a standard set of questions, it is even possible to see how you stack up next to other people of your age and background.

But how is the evaluator supposed to judge how well you get on at work? The evaluator has never seen you at work. How is he or she supposed to determine how well you respond to your supervisors, co-workers, and your usual work conditions, or how you deal with changes in routine at work? By relying on what you say, of course. The evaluator could give you questions from various little checklists that psychologists have devised to tell how a worker functions at work, but checklists are really nothing more than ways of neatly organizing what the client tells the evaluator.

The best that the evaluator could do would be to request copies of your employment records, if you consent, and if they exist, and if your past employer is willing to provide them. Or the evaluator could ask you to talk about how badly you do at work. It is not at all likely that you are going to tell the evaluator how well you do. In fact, why bring up employment records at all if you can apply for SSI rather than SSDI?

And what is the evaluator supposed to do about judging your functionality in a work environment if you have never worked at all? If you have never even tried working, how do you know you cannot do it, and how does the evaluator know that you cannot? It is ridiculous.

For those persons who are severely disabled, it takes no special skills to judge that work would be difficult or impossible for them. For the rest who are claiming that their nerves are too shattered or their intelligence too low or their personalities too passive for them to go to work, the evaluation is just a scam.

How did a job performance evaluation ever come to fall within the special province of the trained psychological professional? What special skills could a psychologist possibly be said to possess that would allow him or her to come up with an assessment of a claimants' work ability any more accurate than the information the claimant provides?

There are no such special psychological skills. And professional vocational psychologists are not especially good at it either.

The Seattle Times reported recently that in Tacoma, Washington, a man named Narith Por Kong was charged with coaching over fifty people how to fake mental illness to obtain public assistance benefits.

> An undercover informant using the code name "Kosal Chan" recorded conversations in which Kong repeatedly urged the Cambodian refugee to lie about his mental health, authorities said. The informant told Kong he was in good health and working at a Chinese restaurant, but Kong advised him to fabricate a story about having severe headaches and nightmares resulting from abuse under the Pol Pot regime, according to court documents. Kong came under federal scrutiny when a state claims worker noted that assistance applicants helped by him had markedly similar symptoms of mental distress. "He basically taught people to lie," Assistant U.S. Attorney Stephen Schroeder said. (Tizon, *Seattle Times*, March 18, 1994)

Well, now, that's a scandal indeed. How could it happen? Aren't those trained clinicians supposed to have the critical capacity to distinguish the truly disordered from the frauds? They are supposed to have it, but they do not. Their track record here is as bad as it has proven to be elsewhere.

Medicalizing Normal Responses

Psychological evaluators may lack special skills to assess the true character and authenticity of supposedly occupationally incapacitating mental dysfunctions, but they do have a hidden agenda. And that agenda includes the mandate to increase the number of diagnosable mentally disabling conditions, which in turn increases the number of billable hours for the mental health practitioner.

Consider the issue of granting workers' compensation for work-related phobias, like fear of flying, fear of strangers, and fear of heights that interfere with the continuance of work in past surroundings or conditions. Fears are not mental injuries. The mental health provider's role in all this, as it so often is, is to turn the ordinary and understandable responses and adaptations of individuals to unfortunate life events into mental disorders.

After all, many of us are mentally incapable of doing construction work forty stories in the air or mining two hundred feet below the surface of the earth. We would go screaming buggy from terror. But these little afflictions, phobias though they be, are not enough to qualify us as disabled for pretty much all work. They could be judged as disabling, however, in a classic workers' compensation case, with the added twist of phobia following upon a job trauma. Clinicians turn fears into phobias and phobias into disabilities.

In *Bailey v. American General Insurance Company*, a 1985 Louisiana case, the court allowed compensation for a claimant who, after watching his partner fall to his death from a scaffold eight stories above the ground, could not resume working on high scaffolds. Why does that reaction to the tragedy make Bailey a mentally ill person? Many of us are afraid to go that high without ever having seen anyone fall even ten feet. Do we all have occupationally incapacitating agoraphobia?

What about the *Guillot v. Sentry Insurance Company*, another 1985 Louisiana case, in which compensation was allowed for a claims adjuster who suffered a nervous breakdown upon being unexpectedly informed that he was fired? Does just any disorder in the DSM qualify as a "nervous breakdown," or must one be hospitalized to make a creditable claim? John J. Nicholson, from Massachusetts, where the state workers' compensation and disability services hit the scandal pages every other year, was granted workers' compensation after claiming that he was disabled by stress when his boss berated him (Sciacca, *Boston Herald*, May 2, 1996).

These may be work-related reactions, but they are not mental illnesses.

One of the most controversial of the worker's compensation cases was that of a sixty-three-year-old white female employee who was mugged by a black male while making a work delivery in another part of town. Thrown to the ground, she broke a vertebra and was left in a state of shock.

> She has nightmares in which she relives the attack, and being near black males causes her to experience panic attacks. The attacks bring on sweating, panic and a rapid heartbeat. She is undergoing psychiatric treatment and has been diagnosed as having post-traumatic stress disorder and simple phobia. . . . Allegedly, her phobia prevented her from working without a guarantee that she would not come in contact with black males. Florida awarded her workers' compensation benefits for a work-related disability, and the award was affirmed per curiam by the Florida Court of Appeals. (Casey 1994, p. 381)

It is easy to characterize such reactions as mental illness. Remember that one of the possible symptoms of the ever flexible post traumatic stress disorder is avoidance of situations similar to the traumatic events, is it not? Well, it takes no great stretch to see an unwillingness to return to the work situation as a reasonable form of avoidance.

Of course, the medicalizing of normal reactions is just part and parcel of what Kirk and Kutchins, in their book *The Selling of DSM* (1992), have called the psychology establishment's commitment to medicalizing all of life. In so doing, they turn rational behaviors into illnesses.

Guerrilla Theater of the Absurd

With years of practice in the criminal domains of competency and insanity, mental health practitioners in civil suits involving disability, discrimination, and compensation have rushed in not only with bushels of diagnoses, making it impossible for the pitiable claimant to hold a job, but with exculpatory diagnoses accounting for any and all kinds of lousy job performance. "It is not his fault, Your Honor; he was too manic to treat his co-workers politely; she was too phobic to make her sales calls; she was too stressed to come in on time; he was suffering from Tourette's when he cussed out the IRS."

What any rational person would regard as simply flat-out unacceptable behavior on the job or even on the school campus has become a "medical mental disorder" thanks to the psychological establishment's vast lobbying efforts to persuade the general public of the equivalence of physical and mental "dysfunctions."

Just as criminals are not responsible for their criminal behavior if they can persuade a forensic clinician—or hire one—to say that they suffer from a condition that somehow diminishes their capacity to bear the responsibility for their actions, so too are the "mentally disabled" relieved by the label of their disability of having to conform to the demands of civilized society on the job.

This perversion of common sense in the name of mental diagnosis does a great and tragic harm to those who are truly mentally handicapped—like the severely retarded—but who are quite capable of performing their jobs well with some accommodation to their disability. Like all scams, it creates an outrage in its victims that all too often spills over onto innocent bystanders. The abuse of mental diagnoses and the proliferation of absurd demands on employers made in the name of wiping out discrimination against the mentally disabled will make cynics and skeptics not only of the business establishment but of all of us who read of such absurdities in the news.

According to a July 16, 1995, report in the *San Diego Union-Tribune* by Brian Doherty of *Reason* magazine, the Coca-Cola Company was found liable for over $7 million in front and back pay and compensatory and punitive damages for firing a man who was under treatment for alcoholism—a DSM mental disorder. The $6 million in punitive damages granted by the jury far exceeded the legal limit of $300,000, but under the law juries cannot be informed of this limit.

The town of Mallard, Iowa, banned yard fires because a resident claimed that she was hypersensitive to smoke. She claimed that without the ban she would be segregated from the rest of the community because of her disability.

Reasonable accommodation has developed into politically correct theater of the absurd. We see today decisions based on mental "medical" disabilities that truly defy all reason. Once you have the label of the legally disabled affixed to your forehead, you receive not only a number of benefits from the different offices of government but a number of special protections. Behavior that would never be tolerated in a "normal" person is protected behavior for the disabled individual.

Golden Opportunities for Psychological Evaluators

So how did Congress and its well-meaning minions go about determining what qualifies as a mental disability requiring reasonable accommodation in places of employment and public access? How did it determine what mental disabilities are so great that persons afflicted with them literally cannot work, that they suffer from "occupational incompetence"? How did Congress determine who would qualify as having one of these disabling mental conditions?

Really, in the only logical way possible. It relied on American mental health experts to tell it what constitutes and what defines mental illnesses. The only other alternatives were to rely on the World Health Organization's catalog of disorders, and that was not politically feasible, or to draw up a catalog itself, and that was not feasible at all. Congress did what any sensible Congress would do. It turned to our resident psychological experts. After all, what are experts for?

In turn, the members of the mental health establishment did the only thing they really could do. They handed the bureaucrats a list of disorders from the latest state-of-the-art diagnostic manual of the American Psychiatric Association. It should come as no surprise that the submitted listing of disorders was as long as possible, including rafts of organic disorders, schizophrenic, paranoid, and other psychotic disorders, mood disorders (affective), mental retardation, anxiety disorders, psychosomatic disorders (somatoform), personality disorders, and, those old favorites, substance addiction disorders (drunks and some druggies).

It is quite daunting to think what the list of acceptable disabling mental disorders will look like in 2010. It will no doubt make the Manhattan telephone directory look small if the past rate of diagnostic proliferation continues apace.

Republican unrest led Congress to amend the law in the spring of 1996 so that those "disabled" by alcohol and or drug abuse will no longer be eligible for cash benefits, subsidized health care, or the "treatment" undergone by about one third of the toxically disabled. However, according to the *Boston Globe*:

> Experts say that because most addicts have other mental or physical impairments, a majority are likely to requalify for SSI. A report by the General Accounting Office estimates that up to 80% of those cut off the federal rolls will requalify because of some other disability. But unlike today those addicts will not be required to seek treatment because their benefit claims will be based on another cause. (Vaillancourt, *Boston Globe*, September 27, 1996)

This last fact is regarded by the *Globe* as the bad news. Before the end of 1996, over half of the previously substance impaired had requalified on other grounds. Advocates for the mentally ill were actively seeking out the remainder to help them requalify as well.

We have let clinicians tell us that they and they alone are capable of assessing the mental functioning of an individual—based on their keen analytic abilities and finely honed intuitions—so it is quite reasonable that they should also be in the position of telling the rest of society who needs special consideration due to disorders in that mental functioning.

To make matters worse, the clinicians' determinations of occupational incompetence generally are not challenged. Jerry Dalton's luck ran out in court but he really pushed it by shifting grounds for disability claims repeatedly over the years. Disability specialists rarely go to court. Why should they? Who can dispute their assessments? Only another state-certified, qualified psychoexpert. They do their work out of bureaucratic offices. Signing papers, filling out forms, substantiating claims with the stroke of a pen, diagnosing disabilities for money for welfare clients, insurance claims, workers' compensation cases, and discrimination suits.

Medicalizing Bad Behavior

The American psychological establishment, hand in hand with Congress through civil rights legislation, Social Security laws, and the Americans with Disabilities Act, has medicalized bad behavior and absolved the bearer of the disability label of all responsibility for the bad behavior.

In our society, mental disability is dispensation. In attempting to level the playing field we've reconstructed the whole surface over a bed of quicksand. The psychologizing of American life in part through the wholesale proliferation and consequent ubiquitous diagnosing of mental "medical" disabilities has played a very large role in this.

Recently, a woman in a Washington State discrimination case was awarded $900,000 after she was fired from a job she had held for less than a year. Her employer, a radio station, claimed that she was aggressive and abrasive and insisted on dominating sales meetings. She claimed that her disruptive behavior resulted from a manic-depressive disorder about which she had informed her employer two months before she was fired. The court ruled that her firing constituted unlawful discrimination against a mentally disabled person (Houston, *Seattle Post Intelligencer*, August 22, 1995).

One of my favorite discrimination cases involves a Boston woman, about to be fired from her job for incompetence and repeated absences from work, who claimed that the stress of going to work had itself made it impossible for her to do her job. Through her mental health expert, she argued that firing her for failure to perform did not take into account that her job failure was stress-induced, and, indeed, that the firing itself had added to her stress. Her expert said her disability made her eligible for six weeks' leave with full pay. Her employer, no doubt to avoid the expense of litigation, capitulated to her demands and gave her the paid vacation before firing her. That is pure blackmail. After all, straight firing would have provided even more relief from the job-induced stress, wouldn't it?

Doesn't this sound like a claim so silly that any judge would throw it out just on the face of it?

However, the front runner in the "my bad behavior is not my fault I'm mentally ill" sweepstakes is probably the university professor from Boston, fired for a long record of sexually harassing colleagues and students, who sued the university for insensitivity to the psychological disorder that made him accost women—against his will, of course—whenever an unfortunate female happened to be, for example, riding on the same elevator as our sufferer. He claimed that he suffered from a depression that diminished his capacity to function, and that the medication he took for the depression diminished his capacity to keep his hands off female students and colleagues. You'd expect a large Eastern university to be more sensitive to his pain, now wouldn't you? It wasn't, and I hate to believe this guy ever had a chance of prevailing in court, but there was nothing wrong with the complainant's logic given the court's acceptance of limitless mental disabilities as sources of discrimination suits.

Remember that the American Psychiatric Association almost put the "uncontrollable" desire to rape in the last DSM as a mental disorder. Perhaps it will make it into the next edition.

In fact, U.S. Judge Magistrate Zachary Karol, in dismissing the professor's lawsuit in the summer of 1996, did not reject the disability claim itself but rather the applicability of the anti-discrimination law to the particular case.

> [Professor] Motzkin is incapable, with or without accommodation, of performing the essential functions of his job [teaching]. . . . Whether or not Motzkin did the things he is accused of doing, there is no place in a university community for someone who is as incapable of controlling his impulses as Motzkin insists he is. (Campagne, *Massachusetts Lawyers Weekly*, June 24, 1996)

The judge did not respond with "Hogwash!" to the claim that the professor just could not keep his hands to himself because of a mental disorder. Oh, no. He just ruled that the disorder made the professor incapable of teaching female students or of working with female colleagues. So he was fired for cause and there was no unlawful discrimination. There is nothing to stop another similar sufferer of lack of sexual control to claim that he is a great teacher despite his inability to keep his hands off his students. Which behavior is not his fault; he suffers from a mental disability.

Once I had a student who told me at the beginning of the term that she had a disability that caused her to fall rather frequently into short epileptic episodes during which she would lose touch with the classroom. She didn't ask me to stop lecturing while she spaced out; she asked me if she could tape the lectures to listen to later. Sure. It seemed like a reasonable request. Another time, I had another student warn me that her Tourette's syndrome could cause her to disrupt a seminar with foul language if she felt stressed by the comments of others in the class. Tourette's syndrome, according to the DSM, is a tic disorder that starts in childhood and results in the afflicted being unable to control various movements and vocalizations, including, in some 10 percent of the cases, the uncontrollable "tic" of uttering obscenities. That's called coprolalia.

Recently, in Massachusetts, a student with Tourette's filed a discrimination suit against a graduate school of social work that would not accept her to study for a master's degree. The school claimed that it did not discriminate, that the decision was made on other grounds, but I find myself truly bewildered by the concept of a social worker with coprolalia. Even accepting the highly unlikely proposition that a brain disorder compels persons to scream obscenities against their will, what kind of sense does it make to have some social worker with uncontrollable foul language working with abused children, say, or with battered women? In pursuit of nondiscrimination against the legally defined mentally disabled, we subject the truly beaten to further assault. That is nuts.

There is a homeless woman who frequents Newbury Street in Boston—a tourist and shopping mecca of Irish import and stone gargoyle stores—screaming "piece of shit!" and "fucking bitch" to random passersby, while smiling slyly and delightedly. Another apparent case of Tourette's syndrome.

What all of these cases have in common is the claim of a mental disorder taken as a license to behave badly. All of these claimants acknowledge that their behavior makes them highly undesirable as employees, teachers, or students, but they accept no personal responsibility for that behavior or for controlling it. Backed by the American Psychiatric Association's bible of some four hundred disabling diagnoses and empowered by the sweeping scope of the Americans with Disabilities Act, scores of the employably challenged are filing lawsuits and claims with commissions against discrimination, seeking redress from unwilling and unwitting employers.

As George Will wrote in an April 1996 column:

> Compassionate government has recently rained new rights and entitlements so rapidly that you may have missed this

> beauty; you have a right to be colossally obnoxious on the job.
>
> If you are just slightly offensive, your right will not kick in. But if you are seriously insufferable to colleagues at work, you have a right not to be fired, and you are entitled to have your employer make reasonable accommodation to your "disability." That is how the Americans with Disabilities Act of 1990 is being construed. (Will, *Boston Globe*, April 5, 1996)

A society conditioned by the modern psychological view that the individual is an impotent pawn of society cannot turn a cold back on its mental unfortunates or a snubbing shoulder to its socially accepted archaeologists of all things psychological. Trapped in a pervasive psychocultural mythology, we can hardly put out a hand to stop the flow of claims of psychological unfairness that will clog our courts and harm the innocent immeasurably before the powers-that-be call a halt to this collective craziness. Compassion must be the most blinding of sentiments. Or perhaps pity, bolstered as it is with the rock of superiority.

Substance-induced disorders—and there are a lot of those in the DSM—are a nice case in point. The DSM classifies drunks as mentally ill, and Washington bureaucrats accepted this classification as legally disabled, so drinkers who have beaten their brains in with alcohol qualify for protection from discrimination as well as a number of benefits like public housing assistance. It happens that impoverished elderly people also qualify for public housing assistance. Thus we have feeble old folks living, terrified, side by side with "disabled" drunks.

Where were Congress's collective wits when it passed that chunk of legislation? "Oh, well, all those disadvantaged people who need the government's help are pretty much the same." Is that what they thought? Who in Washington decided that "mentally disabled by chronic alcohol abuse" meant the same thing as "good neighbor"? The road to hell is surely paved with the good intentions of legislators and bureaucrats who sure as hell do not live in the public housing at the end of the road. Is suffering from discrimination really a greater horror than living in terror for your life? Does the government really have a greater interest in outlawing discrimination against drunks than in preventing the terrorization of the elderly?

Dismantling these bizarre housing juxtapositions with the passage of new legislation that "reenables" the previously disabled drunks and druggies should prove interesting in the coming year.

The psychopolitical impediments to leaving any disorders out from under the protective umbrella of anti-discrimination law must have been quite formidable. Nevertheless, it is an interesting side observation that the anti-discrimination law passed by a Republican Congress does indeed exclude some of the more socially offensive disorders like heroin addiction and compulsive arson while the much older workers' compensation legislation does not.

Which ones did the bigots exclude? They left out the sexual disorders of transvestitism, transsexualism, pedophilia, exhibitionism, voyeurism, gender identity not due to physical impairment, and other sexual behavior disorders. Spoilsports. They also excluded from ADA's protection those so-called mentally ill individuals who suffer from compulsive gambling, kleptomania, and pyromania. That means that the employer does not have to hire, retain, or reasonably accommodate workers who feel irresistible compulsions to steal from the till or burn the plant down. That must be a comfort. Employers are also not required to hire or retain druggies. Great.

FULL EMPLOYMENT FOR MENTAL HEALTH PROFESSIONALS

Determining justly and reasonably and reliably who is truly too mentally incapacitated to work may be an impossible job. Certainly it is impossible to make such a determination with the scientific rigor pretended to by the mental health professionals who have cornered the market on the enterprise. There is no ophthalmoscope for the mind, but requiring trained mental health providers, psychiatrists, psychologists, and social workers—on the explicitly stated assumption that they and no others know how—to determine, scientifically, medically, reliably, who truly suffers from "occupational incompetency" perpetuates a society-crazing farce.

"He is just too anxious too work" says the doctor. "How do you know?" asks the judge. "He told me so." Adding in all the checklists and report forms in the world won't change the essential "diagnostic" situation.

Nevertheless, the experts in this field claim that a plaintiff's case will be more convincing if it is supported by an expert witness's exposition of the plaintiff's clinically diagnosed mental disorder. The experts say that such an analysis can help the plaintiff establish both the existence and severity of emotional distress as well as the connection between that distress and the defendant's conduct that all allegedly caused or exacerbated the condition. (After McDonald and Kulick 1994).

As with all things flowing from the marriage of the legal and the psychological, psychological disabilities law in all its present manifestations creates yet further full-employment bills for mental health practitioners. Society buys their authority just as it buys the psychocultural mythology underlying the psychologizing and medicalizing of all of life. One cannot help but suspect that a wildly disproportionate number of legislators in this country must be lawyers married to psychologists.

Whatever the legal distinction between mental *disability* as defined by the Congress and mental *disorder* as defined by the DSM, when it comes down to deciding who has mental disorders that are actually disabling, the only authority we've really got in this country is the authority we have all conspired to grant to the American psychological establishment through its categorizations and definition of disorders in the *Diagnostic and Statistical Manual*, and its determination of who has those disorders and what they mean by clinical practitioners of every stripe. That this hand-off of de facto power is nothing more than a cash cow for mental health practitioners is never acknowledged.

Some people wish to eliminate altogether any ability of Congress to limit disability and discrimination claims, and to hand over all the power to professional mental health providers in law as well as in fact.

Recently John M. Casey, in the *Puget Sound Law Review*, suggested what most people would consider a perfectly logical course of action to deal with the question of exactly what mental disorders should be considered covered by the reach of the Americans with Disabilities Act.

> First, the EEOC [the people who enforce the ADA] could pass administrative rules to settle the question of which standards to use in determining whether an individual is mentally impaired.

> Rather than the courts relying on the DSM . . . in some cases and not in others, the EEOC should study the problem and then decide whether conditions listed in the DSM . . . will be accepted wholesale, or whether the agency will specify the particular conditions protected by the ADA. *Even if the EEOC were to do nothing more than mandate that all disorders specified in the DSM . . . [except those already excluded by the ADA] fit the definition of mental impairment under the Act, it would greatly improve the present state of the law.* (Casey 1994, p. 415)

No, it would not greatly improve the present state of the law. Mr. Casey was worried that under the present haphazard implementation of the law regarding protected mental disabilities, some behavioral and anxiety disorders like phobias might not be comprehensively protected, but his worry was badly misplaced. As was his faith in the American psychological establishment.

There is grave danger in accepting the premise that only self-interested mental health professionals can judge what mental behavior is a protected disability. Common sense goes out the window in the face of self-interest, as well as the almost limitless temptations provided by the money available to those in evaluative practice and by the sheer power that comes from knowing you are the only game in town.

Professionals with actual reality checks on their claims are confined to narrow vertical markets for their services. Psychological professionals, with virtually no checks on the validity and reliability of their claimed expertise, have an almost limitless reach into the recesses of all our lives.

Let's not hand them any more power over the conduct of our lives in the workplace.

DISPENSATION FROM EVERYTHING FOR EVERYONE

The modern psychologizing of America has led us to blame the system—family, background, neighborhood, schools, workplace, etc.—for every instance of failure in every realm. Psychologized Americans do believe that individuals often fail to perform appropriately or adequately, but they believe that they do so for reasons beyond their control. Even the able-bodied, able-minded worker is seen through this lens as somehow not truly responsible for failures on the job.

The professionally compassionate clinician would no doubt claim that this practice does no harm. Wrong. It is damn expensive. It steals from the innocent. It makes a mockery not only of true disability but of sincere and valid attempts to combat the waste of discrimination.

In the spring of 1996, the *Boston Herald* ran an article reporting on the results of disputed firings of Boston city workers who had been loafing and otherwise performing below par at work (Sciacca, *Boston Herald*, May 2, 1996). The arbitrator found for the workers, explaining that it was not one worker's fault that he was always late; it was his supervisor's for not nagging him to wear a watch. The arbitrator also accepted the claim of one fellow who had been sleeping in his car during work hours that he was listening to a stress management tape in order to deal more effectively with on-the-job stress. Quite.

Given such a response to the not-disabled-at-all except in terms of their work ethic, it should come as no surprise that the people who are seen as playing with less than a full deck are essentially seen as playing with no deck at all. The mass of excuses that fly out to excuse the inexcusable behavior of the nonhandicapped are magnified beyond measure for the mentally disabled because the rest of us are so unsure of our ground.

It is not socially acceptable—not politically correct—to challenge claims of mental illness. This poses a much greater danger to our society than the simple threat that society will run out of patience with a system built to engender scams. Mental health providers who fly in the face of common sense, making fools of practical people by claiming skills they do not have, medicalizing bad behavior, and medicalizing normal reactions, gut the spirit of all types of disabilities law and twist the spirit of the average citizen from accommodation to outrage. There is a serious danger that people who are made fools of will pull the plug on a support system that, if sensibly construed and implemented, would be a good thing.

A MODEST PROPOSAL

That society wants to compensate hardworking people who get so badly hurt that they can work no more is good and sensible. That a civilized society recognizes that some of its members need a helping hand from their fellow citizens to get by also is a good and sensible thing. Reasonable efforts by government and the well-intentioned to stamp out mindless and unproductive discrimination, to compensate workers so disabled on the job that they can work no more, and to help those to whom life dealt such a bad hand that they cannot work at all make perfect sense. Anything else would be a shocking waste of human resources and represents a serious disrespect for the value and dignity of work.

But abuses of the disability compensation system and discrimination legislation are inevitable. Historical and current abuses of physical claims are notorious. That abuse of psychological claims would follow was inevitable. This was particularly so since these disabilities are invisible to the ordinary layperson's eye. Such abuse does not necessitate a call to end a social welfare system that compensates honest citizens for their lost or absent ability to work, although certainly it warrants a call for constant vigilance against fraud. And the principal source of fraud in the psychological disability realm is the psychological evaluator.

Let us save everyone a lot of time and money and let the disability claimant bypass the professional evaluator. Make the checklists and report forms as available to the general public as IRS tax forms. Let the claimant fill them out on his or her own—just like tax forms—or with a private, commercial mental health equivalent of H&R Block. Hand them in to the appropriate office just as they are handed in now, and let the SSA decision makers reach their decisions just as they do now. Heck. Put them on line and have them scored by computer and e-mailed to the relevant judge. It would save so much time and money and would drop the level of scam artistry at least a little.

Follow the same course for discrimination claims. Let the individual with a disability who claims that he or she can and will work but reasonable accommodation was not made show the jury directly the evidence for the justice of the claim. Let the claimant show the jury directly the job skills under dispute and what would be required for him or her to do the job. Let a jury of ordinary people decide what is reasonable and what is not.

Retain the safety net but take psychological farce and fake professionalism out of it.

Reliance on maternal government, like reliance on the maternal employer, leads to the elimination of independence from possible life scenarios for the majority of people. Ambition, action, education, and work—the entire arena of personal responsibility for one's life—become irrelevant to the evaluation of the worth of an individual's life, and irrelevant to the conduct of one's life.

The disavowal of personal responsibility is not widely accepted in the workplace, run as it is by powerful white males, but as soon as an employer-employee dispute involving responsibility gets into arbitration or before a commission on discrimination permeated with the truth-according-to-psychology, the picture shifts dramatically.

As a society, we have lost our faith in the dignity, worth, and power of the individual; we have lost our faith in America as a society of empowered individuals. This loss of faith derives directly from clinical psychology's modern view of the pathological American family, a view that is directly, perfectly mirrored in the structure and dynamics of the larger society.

Because we have lost our faith in the individual's power to act and make decisions responsibly, we have lost faith in ourselves. We must rely on experts to explain to us the complexities, possibilities, and limitations of human behavior.

Of course, our reliance on experts has been ably aided and abetted by sales pitches—indeed, downright propaganda—about the inability of the ordinary citizen to make any sort of judgment for which a professional psychologist might possibly make a claim to get paid.

Psychological Solomons to fill the decision void are everywhere for hire.

11
Rest for the Wary

Deciding Without Experts

> These people who deal in psychology and psychiatry really are doctors of the soul. The way the root of that word comes is from the Greek "suka"; it means soul. And we're going to be looking at people's souls, in particular the plaintiff's soul and her memories in this case as we proceed.
>
> Jim Brown, attorney for the plaintiff, opening statement, *Mateu v. Hagen*, Seattle, June 6, 1993

THE FREEING OF GEORGE FRANKLIN

On April 4, 1996, Judge Lowell Jensen of the United States District Court for the Northern District of California granted George Franklin's petition for a writ of habeas corpus, overturning Franklin's first-degree murder conviction on the grounds that his constitutional rights had been violated by the prosecutors' conduct in portraying George's silence when asked by his daughter if he was guilty as proof of guilt, and by their withholding from the jury the evidence that all the details of Eileen's testimony had been readily available in the popular press.

Franklin remained in prison on $1 million bail until July 2, 1996, when the prosecutor determined that her only witness, Eileen, was unreliable, and declined to retry the case.

> Franklin beamed as deputies escorted him into the Redwood City courtroom. In clipped tones, lead prosecutor Elaine

> Tipton told Superior Court Judge Margaret Kemp, "We move to dismiss the charges without prosecution."
>
> "No objection," said [defense attorney Douglas] Horngrad.
>
> "The motion is granted," Kemp said, ending one of the Bay Area's most controversial cases ever.
>
> Speaking outside the courtroom, defense attorneys assailed the use of Eileen Franklin's recovered memory as the basis for Franklin's prosecution. In the future, said [Dennis] Riordan, prosecutors will be more skeptical of witnesses with recovered memories who recall events of 20 years past "better than I remember what I had for breakfast two hours ago."
>
> Ironically, it was a purported recovered memory that finally unraveled the case. After her father was sentenced to life in prison in 1990, Eileen Franklin told investigators that she clearly remembered two more murders her father committed, including the January 7, 1976, slaying of 18-year-old Veronica Cascio of Pacifica, where Eileen said she helped dispose of the body. (Wildermuth, *San Francisco Chronicle*, July 4, 1996)

> Franklin-Lipsker identified a picture of the teen-ager, whose body was found on a Pacifica golf course. She told prosecutors that she remembered witnessing her godfather, Stan Smith, rape Cascio and seeing her father murder her.
>
> But Franklin's defense attorneys uncovered evidence in May that Franklin was at a union meeting at the time of the murder. DNA tests of semen found on Cascio proved that neither Franklin nor Smith could have raped Cascio.
>
> The final blow to the prosecution came with Janice Franklin's [Eileen's sister] testimony about [both Eileen and Janice] being hypnotized before testifying against [their] father. In California, testimony influenced by hypnotic suggestions is inadmissible. (Mary Curtius, *Los Angeles Times*, July 3, 1996)

George Franklin spent over six years in prison because prosecutors and jurors bought a psychofantasy as science. They believed a storytelling psychoexpert was telling scientific truth. It is sad but true, however, that the science fiction basis of the prosecution's case was not the grounds for overturning the conviction. The federal appeals court did not touch upon the issue of whether Dr. Lenore Terr's multiple-trauma fictions misrepresented the state of scientific knowledge in the field of psychology.

Did they?

ADMISSIBILITY OF EXPERT TESTIMONY AND CLINICAL REASONING

Do psychoexperts in our legal system meet the criteria required by law to act as expert witnesses? The answer to this question has a number of ramifications. Just consider this one. In fairness, shouldn't the indigent be supplied with expert psychologists just as they are supplied with attorneys so that they can mount successful psychological defenses? It may be only a short time before all defendants, indigent and not, will demand the same level of psychological defense as they do legal defense, and who can deny them once the courts have determined the indispensability of psychological testimony?

States vary, of course, in their case law and rules of evidence for determining the admissibility of expert testimony, but many states rely on one or some combination of three criteria: the Frye Rule, the 1993 U.S. Supreme Court decision in *Daubert v. Merrell Dow Pharmaceuticals*, or Rule 702 of the Federal Rules of Evidence.

The Frye Rule holds that scientific evidence is admissible only upon a showing that the scientific principle involved must be sufficiently established to have gained general acceptance in the particular field in which it belongs.

The *Daubert* decision of the Supreme Court demanded more of expert testimony, holding that the scientific validity of the principles and methodology that underlie a proposed submission is an absolutely essential criterion for the admission of testimony that is purportedly expert.

More loosely, Rule 702 of the Federal Rules of Evidence, adopted by many states as their own principle governing expert witnesses, reads, "If scientific, technical, or other specialized knowledge will assist the trier of fact to understand the evidence or to determine a fact in issue, a witness qualified as an expert by knowledge, skill, experience, training or education, may testify thereto in the form of an opinion or otherwise."

Does the supposedly "expert" testimony of clinical psychological professionals today meet any or all of the current criteria for admissibility of expert testimony?

General Acceptance in the Field

The most frightening criterion is the Frye requirement that the experts' opinions must simply have gained *general acceptance in the field* to be admissible in court. In psychology, assessing whether something has gained general acceptance depends a great deal on whom you ask. If 95 percent of the *clinical* experts believe something, then do we say that whatever it is that they believe has gained general acceptance in the field of psychology as a whole? Of course not. What about all the experimentalists?

It is very hard to think of anything that rises to the level of general acceptance across the broad spectrum of psychology, clinical and experimental. Even if it were possible to identify such a belief, far more important than breadth of acceptance is *why* a particular belief is generally held to be true.

What if the foundation of the clinicians' belief is strictly personal, manifestly unobjective, and clearly nonscientific? Then, whatever the level of general acceptance, that belief does not belong in courtrooms masquerading as expert scientific testimony.

For example, what if all of the United States were intensely Catholic and every psychoexpert were deeply pious? Then each and every expert on the witness stand would believe in the power of prayer and the action of grace. That still would not make grace and prayer appropriate subjects for expert testimony. Likewise, general acceptance of clinical beliefs by clinicians does not make those beliefs any more appropriate.

When courts use the Frye standard for admission of expert testimony, it should be made clear whether the belief in question is itself scientific or an article of faith. Can it be tested or is it impossible to refute it by any means?

The *Daubert* decision addresses exactly these questions.

Scientific Validity of Theory and Methodology

In 1993, in *Daubert v. Merrell Dow Pharmaceuticals*, the U.S. Supreme Court held that:

> Faced with a proffer of expert scientific testimony, then, the trial judge must determine at the outset . . . whether the expert is proposing to testify to scientific knowledge that will assist the trier of fact to understand or determine a fact in issue. This entails a preliminary assessment of whether the reasoning or methodology underlying the testimony is scientifically valid and of whether that reasoning or methodology properly can be applied to the facts in issue.
>
> Ordinarily, a key question to be answered in determining whether a theory or techniques is scientific knowledge that will assist the trier of fact will be whether it can be [and has been] tested. " 'Scientific methodology today is based on generating hypotheses and testing them to see if they can be falsified; indeed, this methodology is what distinguishes science from other fields of human inquiry.' 'The statements constituting a scientific explanation must be capable of empirical test.' 'The criterion of the scientific status of a theory is its falsifiability, or refutability, or testability.' "

That the fictional "facts" and endlessly inventive "theories" of clinical psychology are no more science than the artful constructs of astrology has been the subject matter of this whole book. It should go without saying that a field in which it is not possible to falsify even the smallest of predictions should not be permitted to exhibit even the smallest of pretensions to the mantle of science. It seems like overkill to pound in once again that intuition is not a scientific instrument and creativity—however admirable in many endeavors—is not the essential hallmark of scientific thinking.

Specialized Knowledge

Okay. So clinical beliefs are not generally held to be true by experimental psychologists as well as by clinicians, and, as we have seen chapter by chapter throughout this book, they are certainly not the products of scientific endeavor. But perhaps they satisfy the admission criteria for expert testimony of the Federal Rules of Evidence. Rule 702, adopted by many states as their own standard, says that if *scientific*, *technical*, or *other specialized knowledge* will assist the judge or the jury to understand the evidence or to determine a fact in issue, then a witness who qualifies as an expert by virtue of his or her *knowledge*, *skill*, *experience*, *training*, or *education* may testify as such.

Perhaps clinical claims about the workings of the mind, so utterly devoid of scientific character, might somehow qualify as technical or specialized knowledge. What is technical knowledge? That's knowledge about how much gas a balloon can take before it blows up, or how much stress an aircraft component can bear before it breaks off. Technical knowledge has to do with how the world works and how it goes wrong.

The only technical knowledge remotely relevant to clinical psychology would be knowledge of how the mind works, how it is formed, and how it changes. We have already established that no one knows how the mind works, however widespread the witch doctor fallacy may be. Any clinician who claims on the witness stand to know how the mind works should be hospitalized for dangerous delusions of grandeur.

But what about *specialized* knowledge? That's a wonderfully vague term. Surely specialized knowledge must be available to the clinician. Indeed it is. A Freudian scholar, for example, might have detailed and specialized knowledge of all phases of the development of Freud's theory, much as a Catholic scholar would have detailed and specialized knowledge about all the essential doctrines of the Catholic faith. If the exposition of the specifics of one of those doctrines was somehow relevant to the deliberations of a court, then surely it would be appropriate to have the scholar testify about what does and does not make up the doctrines. Similarly, if Freud's writings were in dispute in a case, then Freudian experts would be called into court to clarify matters of historical accuracy, for example, for the court.

The use of a specialized knowledge of clinical psychology in this sense is perfectly appropriate. But our Freudian or other scholar, however learned he may be about the claims made by various thinkers and writers at different times about how the mind works, does not himself know how the mind works for human kind in general or for any individual in particular. He has only a scholarly knowledge of the claims of other thinkers. That knowledge can be interesting and useful, but it is not relevant to the determination of any of the pressing psychological issues before our courts like competency, insanity, rehabilitation, custody, fitness, or future dangerousness. How could it be?

Throw Them Out of Court!

The articles of faith offered as testimony by clinical psychologists in courtroom after courtroom—and in the legislative chambers across the country—do not even come close to meeting the current criteria for admissibility as expert testimony demanded by our courts.

The criteria for admissibility of experts will change; they will be amended and added to and displaced by criteria devolving from new law, new cases, new decisions. Will the claims of the clinicians meet these new criteria? Never.

Not unless clinical psychology abandons its fundamental methodology of creative writing and its complete acceptance of acts of faith for arriving at the truth. Not until clinical psychology accepts the limitations intrinsic to the discipline and recasts itself as a real science. Not unless or until the court chooses to abolish all distinctions among types of testimony.

When the law welcomes the astrologer into the courtroom as possessing the same status as the astronomer, when the court listens to the priest with the same critical judgment it applies to the testimony of the physicist, then and only then will the testimony of clinical psychologists about the formation and functioning of the human mind in general or in a particular individual make sense as expert testimony. When the concept of expertise is itself debased to nothing more than personal opinion, then the clinicians should take the stand along with the rest of the opinionated. Why not?

Until then, throw them out of the courts.

Throw them out of our legislatures too.

HOW CAN YOU PROTECT YOURSELF FROM PSYCHOEXPERT HIRED GUNS?

The California Court of Appeals' reversal of George Franklin's conviction is a ray of hope piercing the veil of obfuscating psychobabble presently shrouding our justice system, as are the refusals of various judges around the country to accept recovered memory psychononsense as science.

But the psychologizing of the American legal system is not a trend that is going to be reversed easily. The degree of acceptance of the moral and legal authority of the forensic psychological clinician to decide matters of guilt, innocence, rehabilitation, mental disability and injury, custody, and fitness as a parent, is pervasive and adamantly held.

The most that the individual citizen can do when attacked by a psychoexpert is to hire one of his own and to arm both hired gun and attorney with a copy of Jay Ziskin's three-volume tome *Coping with Psychiatric and Psychological Testimony*.

Ziskin's book provides up-to-date—1995—evidence to attack any psychoexpert's credentials, theories, and the evidentiary bases of the expert's claims. It gives the attorney and the client step-by-step guidance on challenging psychological experts' scientific status, principles, interview procedures, and clinical evaluations, results and conclusions of all the main varieties of psychological tests, the validity of clinical training and experience, the relevance and utility of credentials and qualifications, and the ever-invoked clinical intuition.

Since Dr. Ziskin is an attorney as well as a psychologist, the book also provides guidance on cross-examination in criminal cases, personal injury cases, and child custody cases, with examples of tactics, depositions, and motions. The second volume of his work teaches attorneys and clients how to challenge testimony in some of the specific hot psychological topics and areas of vulnerability running through our courts today—child custody, eyewitness testimony, sexual abuse, post traumatic stress disorder, and diagnoses and prognoses of various mental disorders, along with guidance on the detection of malingering and the reliability of judgments like the assessment of dangerousness.

No attorney facing a forensic psychological clinician can afford not to have this bible of information attacking the scientific status of psychological testimony, now in its fifth printing. Forensic clinicians are afraid of Ziskin. They speak on the Internet of having been "ziskinized" in court when they are challenged on the witness stand by an attorney armed with the knowledge tools Ziskin provides.

Psychocultural Complicity

Certainly blame for the misrepresentation of clinical psychology as a scientific field that uses scientific methods to arrive at scientific results lies at the door of the clinicians themselves. They have their agendas—missionary, political, and financial—that lead them if not inevitably then compellingly to lay claim to a quality of expertise far beyond their ken.

But clinicians are not alone in enacting this farce. The general public likewise deserves a share of the blame for the interweaving of the tenets and tactics of modern clinical psychology into the very fabric of our justice system. Although a people with a proud tradition of respect for the reasoning and reasonableness of the "common man," we have declared ourselves impotent to enact our traditional legal system roles, and have embraced the theories and practices of a gaggle of highly paid experts. Why? Has human behavior suddenly become so complex that only trained experts can understand, explain, and judge it? Why has society been so reluctant to acknowledge the inherent failings of so-called psychological science, and why have we been so eager to welcome its practitioners into our courtrooms?

Part of the reason is that all of us, as a society, buy into psychoexperts' authority, we buy the accreditation of psychiatry at medical schools as if it were on the same standing as any other medical specialty, and we buy psychological research as if it possessed the same standing as any other scientific research.

The mental health propagandists have done their work and the public believes.

Our need to believe in psychological expertise arises largely from our vulnerability to the witch doctor fallacy and our need to believe in the effectiveness of psychological expertise in our personal lives. If we didn't believe in modern psychotherapy we'd be thrown back for advice and help on our priests, rabbis, ministers, and grandmothers—a distressingly premodern situation indeed.

Society's need to believe in psychological expertise is fueled further by the demands of our democratic legal system. We desperately need the knowledge we attribute to psychology. If we didn't accept psychological expertise as scientific, we'd be in the untenable position of asking Miss Marple to testify in court and give us the benefit of her brilliant intuitions.

Our psychoexperts relieve both Miss Marple and the ordinary citizen of the awesome responsibilities imposed on us by our legal system. It is hard to be faced with deciding who is guilty, innocent, competent, dangerous, fit, injured, or liable. Who wants to make decisions with such horrendous consequences for the lives of individuals when certainty is impossible? We can hand it off to the psychoexperts who claim to have knowledge and expertise to make these horrible decisions on a much sounder basis than is available to the ordinary citizen. We can be comfortable while the psychoexperts do the work. Not only do they relieve each and every one of us of the burden of responsibility for the conduct of our own lives, they relieve us as well of the burden of exercising judgment in the courtroom.

Like the judge stuck with judging Byron Cooper's competence to stand trial, we are looking for someone "smarter" than we are to make these decisions. Too bad there isn't anyone.

More important than the great need we have to believe in psychological expertise to relieve us of both personal and legal burdens is the undeniable fact that many, many modern Americans also share the psychocultural beliefs of our clinicians about the formation and functioning of personality, about guilt and innocence, responsibility and accountability. Like the cat chasing its tail, the psychocultural beliefs of the society reinforce the influence of the clinicians, who in turn give us new creative fictions about the roles and responsibilities of individuals.

Justice's New Clothes

America is a country that prides itself on democratic decision making, on a belief in the intelligence and decency of the common people and their ability to conduct affairs of such great import as the creation of laws, their enforcement, and the judgment of violations of those laws.

Ordinary people serve in our state legislatures. Ordinary people become police officers and attorneys. Ordinary people give evidence and serve as jurors in trials. Even our judges in most cases are subject to the will of the people either because they are obliged to accept the decisions of juries or because they must stand for election.

Today tradition is no longer enough. America has undergone a zeitgeist shift, a fundamental change in our most basic values. Americans want a justice system now that is fair in terms that make sense in light of what we believe *today* to be true about individuals and the causes of their behavior. Moreover, ordinary people, as well as honorable members of the legal profession, desperately seek an authoritative basis for making cruel, wrenching, difficult, even impossible decisions about guilt and innocence, responsibility, competence, and dangerousness, about who shall be confined or punished, about who shall be helped and who shall be free.

We do not seek the ancient but harsh options of Solomon the stern father ("Cut the child in half!"), but rather the forgiving understanding of a kindly modern mother ("Those bad companions led you astray, poor baby"). We say, who are we to judge another individual's conduct? We only want to understand it. Modern Americans exhibit little concern for the consequences of an action, but considerable concern for its cause. No matter how heinous the crime, with the dead still uncounted and the wounded still bleeding, we ask, "Why did he do that?" We apparently believe that if we understand the motive, then the chaos created by crime is stilled, order is restored, and our lives remain under control. Because understanding brings us these blessings, to understand is to forgive, to understand all is to forgive all.

Our forgiveness is further compelled by our modern concept of motives. We no longer believe in evil; we scarcely acknowledge the existence of sin. We accept that individuals do harm, but we believe that they do so for reasons beyond their control. This modern, widespread denial of personal responsibility for conduct—what the radio talk show hosts call "victimism"—is both a product of psychology's infiltration of the American legal system and a fundamental cause of it.

Modern psychology—and its psychotherapeutic offspring—is wed to a systemic, liberal view of accountability. The central premise of American clinical psychology is that the individual at birth is an infinitely malleable lump of clay that can be, and is, shaped into any form at all by the hands of parents and family; that form is then fired into its durable personality and character structure by the immediate and larger society. (Not to push the metaphor too hard, but it also follows that the forces of society can break these fragile vessels.) If the child turns out badly, it's the parents' or society's fault.

The psychologizing of America is part and parcel of the liberalizing of America over the last thirty years. It is no step at all to go from blaming parents to blaming the system—background, neighborhood, income, class, sex, race, political and economic inequities—for every instance of failure in every realm. Psychologists, like liberals, blame the system for everything. (Of course, conservatives blame the liberals.)

The truth is that each and every one of us, liberal and conservative—as individuals; as citizens; as voters; as jurors, judges, and lawmakers—has contributed to a comprehensive undermining of the American legal system through the institutionalization in our justice system of the assumptions, principles, and prejudices of current American psychological practice.

We have allowed the tenets of psychology to be written into our law and its practitioners to be sworn as the ultimate experts on all issues in which law touches on questions of human responsibility for behavior because a coherent system of law cannot exist without a moral foundation. American intellectuals and legal experts of all stripes have discarded the religious foundations of their antecedents and have embraced in their place twentieth-century psychology's view of humankind and the moral condition. Stripped of any explicit religious trappings, psychology masquerades as an impartial, scientific foundation for the understanding of human behavior. As such it is welcome in our courtrooms and legislative chambers where frankly religious systems of belief are not.

The Modern Moral Script

Thanks to the persuasive influence of clinical psychology on modern American intellectual life, many, if not most, of the intellectual elite in this country embrace the basic tenets of Freudian theory, however disguised rhetorically in contemporary jargon. The beliefs are as firmly ingrained as those of our traditional religions, and as hard to question.

There are some obvious similarities between modern psychology's view of the human condition and the traditional Judeo-Christian religious view, and some not so obvious. The Tree of Knowledge of Good and Evil in the Garden of Eden is replaced by sex in all its dramatically staged complexity, the snake is repressed into the deepest part of the self, and the apple-eating woman part is picked up by the bad mother who first seduces the hapless child, then punishes him for her own transgressions. Traveling through the psychosexual stages leaves indelible marks on the psyche much like the stain of original sin, or sins. Trouble-free drive satisfaction might be likened to a return to the Garden of Eden, and redemption via the action of a Supreme Being has been transformed into awakening under the wise guidance of the psychotherapist.

The ideas of free will and moral choice have vanished from the landscape. There is no way that a helpless child can be held responsible for what happens to him or her. In the post-Freudian world, by the time a child can make moral choices, by the time a child has a conscience or Superego, most of the damage that can be done to the psyche has already been incurred. Babies are morally neutral, fragile vessels, shaped and cracked and broken by forces completely beyond their control. Present-day psychologists, with no intellectual consistency but insistent vigor, extend the period of extreme fragility way past the Oedipal years, well into adolescence. In this system, sin and guilt are impossible in youth and illogical in adulthood.

Innocence is not simply lost; it is destroyed by cruel parents and bad environments. Drunken and abusive parents can brutalize a child, gangs can lead young people astray, and poverty creates its own deplorable set of values. It is bad parents and an unjust society that cause the innocent child to turn into a criminal. If we understand the cause, then we understand the crime. Whodunit has become an exercise in psychoanalysis.

An interesting inconsistency in modern psychodynamic theory is the assertion that however shaped, cracked, or broken, the mind of the child is infinitely malleable. In the proper hands, the crack can be filled, the shape can be re-cast, the disordered youth can be completely rehabilitated. Belief in rehabilitation is necessarily accompanied by a belief in the effectiveness of therapy. After all, it is through therapy that the initial damage to the psyche is identified, inappropriately fixated ideas are de-energized, and symptoms are dissipated. If lying, stealing, destroying, hurting, and killing are seen as symptomatic expressions of psychological disorders, then they too should respond to therapeutic treatment. So should wife beating, child molesting, public cursing, drug abuse, chronic drunkenness, and any one of the other socially offensive mental disorders. Given such a view, sentencing offenders to therapy is perfectly reasonable.

Variations in modern psychological theory are endless, evolving, and increasingly ad hoc, but the overwhelming majority of what the conservative media call "the intellectual elite," as well as the psychological clinical practitioners in America, in and out of our courtrooms and legislative chambers, embrace at least some of these tenets in some form or other.

What is true of American intellectuals is also true of a great many ordinary Americans educated in our rigidly secular institutions of higher learning. While requiring no course in ethics or the great religions of the world, we do require a great many of our students in both high school and college to take a general course in psychology before graduating into the world as educated persons. Since this has been going on for decades, it was inevitable that many of the tenets of psychology—particularly those addressing the causes of behavior—should have become part of the fabric of American moral life, of core cultural beliefs.

You'd be hard put to find an American who wasn't, at least a little bit, "psychologized," even if he or she denies it vehemently.

Read the sentences below. Do any of them sound familiar? Have you ever heard your hairdresser or your bartender or your classmate say anything similar? How about your teachers? Or novelists? Or movies? Or musicals? Recognize any of these themes?

> *"The mind has to protect itself by repressing the memories of terrible traumas."*
>
> *"There are lots of troubled people like the woman in* The Three Faces of Eve.*"*
>
> *"Homophobic guys are just repressed gays reacting against what they really are."*
>
> *"Psychotherapy can put you in touch with your real unconscious feelings."*
>
> *"Truth serums can reveal ideas and feelings you didn't even know you had."*
>
> *"Hypnosis lets the real you out from under wraps. I'd never let anybody do it to me."*

Just as most Americans are brought up in a society that accepts the Judeo-Christian ethic—and metaphysics—as the fundamental terrain on which we build the edifices of our legal and social structures, so too do we grow up in a society that has taken the psychodynamic script for the drama of life and the nature of man—and, certainly, woman and child—as its psychosocial starting point.

We accept the validity of the psychodynamic script because we feel it makes sense of our lives. We want to understand what makes people behave as they do, and we want to lay blame for everything that goes wrong somewhere outside the individual. We are looking for a moral compass that is intellectually satisfying and scientifically valid.

DYSFUNCTIONAL FAMILY PSYCHOLOGY IN THE COURTS

Modern clinical psychology gives us what we want and need to reach moral decisions in both personal and public domains; it helps us, we believe, to better make laws and administer justice. The disavowal of personal responsibility intrinsic to dysfunctional family theory finds an apparently surprising but really quite natural home in the intricacies of traditional American legal reasoning.

Motivation is a central component in American moral reasoning. We have long accepted the ideas of provocation and mitigating circumstances. It's understandable to steal bread when you are hungry; it's not understandable to steal Porsches. It's okay to shoot the guy if you find him in bed with your wife; it's not okay to shoot the butcher because you didn't like the cut of meat. The consideration of motivation, of intention, and of state-of-mind are essential to evaluation of guilt in the American legal process.

Today, thanks to the "enlightenment" from modern clinical psychology, we go much, much farther down that path. Many educated Americans, along with their attorneys and lawmakers and judges, have bought—lock, stock, and barrel—the modern psychopolitical assumption that, due to dysfunctional families and a dysfunctional society, the individual is simply not responsible for his or her own behavior.

This has led us directly to the currently fashionable battered woman syndrome defense against murder and assault charges, the epidemic of child abuse allegations of every type reaching even into decades past—once you are injured, you stay injured until you work it out in therapy or in therapeutic courtroom actions—and the apparently infinite number and variety of excuses for behavior on the part of the disabled and the disadvantaged that would put anyone else completely beyond the pale.

We accept the psychological experts in the courtroom because they echo our populist beliefs. They put the scientific seal of authenticity on generally held views about the nature of children and human development, about the causes of behavior and personal and societal responsibility. We hear what we expect to hear and we accept it as truth.

It is clear that each and every one of us has contributed to the takeover of the American legal and judicial system by psychology. Grateful patients, hubristic practitioners, unwilling jurors, conscientious attorneys, up-to-date judges, and concerned legislators have all participated in an unwitting conspiracy to hand over our formerly democratic legal system to a handful of necessarily self-interested hired guns. That our motives—and theirs—were sometimes the best hardly improves the situation.

There are no innocent bystanders. We have all been willing witnesses to the marriage of psychology and the law, we have all been willfully blind to the dreadful offspring they have spawned.

And their offspring are everywhere.

The system is a nightmare of misrepresentation and injustice, of fantasy and distortion. It must change.

DECIDING WITHOUT EXPERTS

Society has created its own monster here. Asking people, demanding of people, that they do what they cannot do forces them to believe that they can. Demanding that psychology give us answers it does not have inevitably forces it to cut loose from the short bonds of science and to fly into the freer realms of art. In the face of our demands the experts also blind themselves. They become what we have demanded that they be. Now it is time we demand that they stop.

If psychologists won't step down from the witness stand voluntarily, the courts must throw them off forthwith. True science itself suffers from so many limitations that the public does well to listen with skepticism when it enters our courtrooms and legislative chambers. Pseudo-science, fraudulent science, should be shown the door without a hearing and sent back to wherever its proper domain may be. The pervasive acceptance of clinical psychology's claims by our justice system must be undone piece by piece and step by step if we are to save our sanity.

We could start by having each "expert," court-employed or defendant-hired, attach exact probabilities to judgments of diagnosis, competence, and responsibility, then force the expert to show scientifically why those judgments are more likely to be correct than judgments of laypersons. Do not permit one single use of so-called clinical intuition to buttress flimsy, unsubstantiated testimony. If this is supposed to be science, then restrict it to science.

That should go a long way toward getting Miss Marple off the witness stand.

The courts are not helpless. They can throw the experts off the payroll and off the witness stand. They can fire the forensic evaluators who work for the state. They can give the determination of competence over to grand juries and let trial juries decide on their own how much responsibility an accused individual should bear for a crime.

In our system, ordinary people should serve as finders of fact, ordinary people should reach decisions about what the laws of the land should be and who is guilty or innocent of breaking them, who has done wrong and to whom, who should be punished and who should pay, and how.

Ordinary people must take back these duties and rights from the hired guns; we must wrest the legal system back from the psychoexperts. Americans must reclaim their rights as citizens and resume the burdens imposed on them by our legal system.

It should be the people through their judges and juries who decide the degree, if any, of diminished responsibility, mental injury, or disability in both criminal and civil cases. It should be up to the people to judge the evidence for claims for all varieties of mental functioning and malfunctioning.

In criminal cases, let the defendant prove directly to the court his or her inability to form or execute a plan, or to appreciate the consequences of an action, or to control actions or whatever the particular law in the case requires without the farcical testimony of putatively clairvoyant clinicians.

In Massachusetts, Governor Weld enraged the liberal press when he pushed for the elimination of the "not guilty by reason of insanity" verdict and its replacement with the verdict "guilty but insane." The later would entail treatment in a mental hospital followed by imprisonment. Referring to the infamous San Francisco junk food insanity defense, the governor said in the spring of 1996,

"If they eat good Twinkies instead of bad Twinkies and they wake up sane some morning, then they go to prison instead of going back out on the street" (*Boston Globe*, March 9, 1996).

What is the point? Why send them to a hospital at all? If convicts are diabetics, we would not send them to a hospital for treatment of their diabetes. They would be imprisoned along with all their fellow nondiabetic convicts and given daily mediation for their diabetic condition. Why should the so-called mentally ill be treated any differently? There is no treatment for the "criminally insane" but drugs, and drugs they can get anywhere. It is a fiction that mental hospitals provide effective treatment above and beyond that provided by the drugs. A mental hospital supplies nothing effective but employment for the staff. Anti-psychotic drugs can be administered just as easily and far more cheaply in prisons than in mental hospitals, and there will be no discernible difference whatsoever in the cure rate.

We must stop pretending that psychology can do what it clearly cannot.

In civil trials, let the plaintiffs demonstrate the injury and its cause directly to the judge and jury without any intervening testimony about the unknowable truth of their claims by psychoexpert witnesses. Let welfare applicants demonstrate their inability to work without the misbegotten advocacy of clinical experts.

Insurance companies and managed health care organizations have to put a stop to reimbursement for crazy diagnoses and ineffective treatments, while patients, and parents and families of patients, must bring suit for malpractice. Prosecutors should look into bringing charges for fraud. If psychologists won't police themselves, society must do it for them.

Any change in the direction of recapturing power for the people would be swimming against a vast tide.

Psychological practitioners have powerful professional and financial reasons for claiming that both diagnosis and rehabilitative treatment are valid, reliable, and scientifically based. Insurance companies and health care administrators have sound administrative and record-keeping reasons for desiring clearly defined and numerically coded diagnostic categories. Various individuals and institutions have understandable humanitarian interests in providing equal access and a social safety net for those for whom the playing field will never be level. Judges and jurors truly *need* expert opinion on the mental functioning—and malfunctioning—of individuals who enter into the legal system.

All these needs and desires are understandable, they are all more than rational, but they cannot be met by the sham of today's level of expertise in diagnosis any more than a baby's nutritional needs can be met by a pacifier.

Judges and juries, the people alone, must decide questions of insanity, competence, rehabilitation, custody, injury, and disability without the help of psychological experts and their fraudulent skills. A democratic society imposes exactly these burdens on the average man and woman and on our judges and legislators. It is time that we give up our attempts to hand off the weight onto the shoulders of professional decision makers. It is past time that we throw out the whores and take back our courts.

BIBLIOGRAPHY

BOOKS, PROFESSIONAL ARTICLES, AND CATALOGS

Adams, David. 1991. "Empathy and Entitlement: A Comparison of Battering and Nonbattering Husbands." Ph.D. diss., Northeastern University, Boston.

Adams, David. 1992. "Historical Timeline of Medical and Psychological Responses to Battered Women." Unpublished, Emerge Treatment Program, Cambridge, Mass.

Akre, L. M. 1992. "628 Struggling with Indeterminacy: A Call for Interdisciplinary Collaboration in Redefining the 'Best Interest of the Child' Standard." *Marquette Law Review*.

Allport, Judith, Laura Brown, Stephan Ceci, Christie Courtois, Elizabeth Loftus, and Peter Ornstein. 1996. *Final Report: Working Group on Investigation of Memories of Childhood Abuse*. Washington, D.C.: American Psychiatric Association.

Anastasi, Anne. 1970. *Psychological Testing*. 3rd edition. London: Collier-Macmillan.

Angell, Marcia. 1996. "Shattuck Lecture: Evaluating the Health Risks of Breast Implants: The Interplay of Medical Science, the Law, and Public Opinion." *New England Journal of Medicine* 334, no. 23 (June 6).

"Appendix to Appellants Brief: The Effects of Segregation and the Consequences of Desegregation: A Social Science Statement." 1953. *Minnesota Law Review* 39: 235.

Applebaum, Paul. 1994. *Almost a Revolution: Mental Health Law and the Limits of Change*. New York: Oxford University Press.

Barber, Joseph. 1986. "The Case of Superman." In *Case Studies in Hypnotherapy*, ed. E. T. Dowd and J. M. Healy. New York: Guilford.

Belli, Melvin, and Allen Wilkinson. 1986. *Everybody's Guide to the Law*. New York: Harper and Row.

Berne, Eric. 1964. *Games People Play*. New York: Ballantine.

Biddle, W. G. 1988. "Child Victims as Witnesses." *Law and Psychology Review* 12: 151.

Blau, G. L., and R. L. Pawewark. 1994. "Statutory Changes and the Insanity Defense: Seeking the Perfect Insane Person." *Law and Psychology Review* 18: 43.

Bloomfield Psychological Services. 1996. "Custody Issues." *Psychology and Law* (June 30).

Bork, Robert J. 1996. *Slouching Towards Gomorrah: Modern Liberalism and American Decline*. New York: ReganBooks/HarperCollins.

Boyll, J. R. 1991. "Psychological, Cognitive, Personality and Interpersonal Factory in Jury Verdicts." *Law and Psychology Review* 15: 117.

Bradshaw, John. 1988. *Bradshaw On: The Family: A Revolutionary Way of Self-Discovery*. Deerfield Beach, Fla.: Health Communications.

Brannon, L., and C. W. Christine. 1994. "The Trauma of Testifying in Court for Child Victims of Sexual Assault V. The Accused's Right to Confrontation." *Law and Psychology Review* 15: 423.

Briere, John N. 1992. *Child Abuse Trauma: Theory of the Lasting Effects*. Newbury Park, Calif.: Sage Publications.

Briere, J., and J. Conte. 1993. "Self-Reported Amnesia for Abuse in Adults Molested as Children." *Journal of Traumatic Stress* 6: 21–31.

Buckhout, Robert. 1975. "Nearly 2000 Witnesses Can Be Wrong." *Soc. Act. & L.* (May).

Burke, D. D., and M. A. Nixon. 1994. "Post-Traumatic Stress Disorder and the Death Penalty." *Howard Law Journal* 38: 183.

Burtt, Harold E. 1931. *Legal Psychology*. New York: Prentice-Hall.

Cairns, Huntington. 1904. *Law and the Social Sciences*. London: K. Paul, Trench, Trubner. (Reprint, 1935. New York: Harcourt, Brace.)

Campagne, Henriette. 1996. "Court Rejects Fired Professor's Claim." *Massachusetts Lawyers Weekly* (June 24).

Campbell, Terence W. 1994a. *Beware the Talking Cure: Psychotherapy May Be Hazardous to Your Mental Health*. Boca Raton, Fla.: SSRI/Upton Books.

Campbell, Terence W. 1994b. "Challenging Psychologists and Psychiatrists as Witnesses." *Michigan Bar Journal* (January).

Caplan, Paula J. 1995. *They Say You're Crazy: How the World's Most Powerful Psychiatrists Decide Who's Normal*. Reading, Mass.: Addison-Wesley.

Casey, John M. 1994. "From Agoraphobia to Xenophobia: Phobias and Other Anxiety Disorders Under the Americans with Disabilities Act." *Puget Sound Law Review* 17: 381–416.

Ceci, Stephen J., and Maggie Bruck. 1995. *Jeopardy in the Courtroom: A Scientific Analysis of Children's Testimony*. Washington, D.C.: American Psychological Association.

Ceci, Stephen J., Michelle Leichtman, and Maribeth Putnick, eds. 1992. *Cognitive and Social Factors in Early Deception*. Hillsdale, N.J.: Lawrence Erlbaum.

Chesler, Phyllis. 1991. *Mothers on Trial*. San Diego: Harcourt Brace Jovanovich.

Cooper, W. E. 1993. Review of J. Monahan and L. Walker, *Social Science in Law: Cases and Materials*. New York: Foundation Press.

Crnich, Joseph, and Kimberly Crnich. 1992. *Shifting the Burden of Proof: Suing Child Sexual Abusers—A Legal Guide for Survivors and Their Supporters*. Lake Oswego, Ore.: Recollex Publishing.

Davidson, M. J. 1988. "Post-Traumatic Stress Disorder: A Controversial Defense for Veterans of a Controversial War." *William and Mary Law Review* (Winter).

Davis, Robert, and Barbara Smith. "Domestic Violence Reforms: Empty Promises or Fulfilled Expectations?" *Crime and Delinquency* 4: 541–52.

Dawes, Robyn. 1994. *House of Cards: Psychology and Psychotherapy Built on Myth*. New York: Free Press.

Dershowitz, Alan. 1994. *The Abuse Excuse*. Boston: Little, Brown.

Developments in the Law: Legal Responses to Domestic Violence. 1993. "Battered Women Who Kill Their Abusers." *Harvard Law Review Association* (May).

Diamond, B. L. 1974. "The Psychiatric Prediction of Dangerousness." *University of Pennsylvania Law Review* 123: 340.

Dietz, Park. 1996. "The Quest for Excellence in Forensic Psychiatry." *Bulletin of the American Academy of Psychiatry and Law* 24: 153–63.

Dix, G. E. 1981. "Mental Health Professionals in the Legal Process: Some Problems of Psychiatric Dominance." *Law and Psychology Review* 6.

Doro. 1958. "The Brandeis Brief," *Vanderbilt Law Review* 11: 796–99.

Ehrenreich, Barbara, and Deirdre English. 1978. *For Her Own Good: 150 Years of the Experts' Advice to Women*. New York: Doubleday.

Eisikovits, Zvi, and Jeffrey Edleson. 1989. "Intervening with Men Who Batter: A Critical Review of the Literature." *Social Service Review* 63: 385–414.

Ellison, W. J. 1987. "State Execution of Juveniles: Defining 'Youth' as a Mitigating Factor for Imposing a Sentence of Less than Death." *Law and Psychology Review* 11.

Engler, Jack, and Daniel Goleman. 1992. *The Consumer's Guide to Psychotherapy*. New York: Simon and Schuster.

Erdelyi, M. H. 1990. "Repression, Reconstruction and Defense: An Examination of Sixty Years of Research." In *Repression and Dissociation: Implications for Personality Theory, Psychopathology and Health*, edited by J. L. Singer. Chicago: University of Chicago Press.

Erdelyi, M. H., and B. Goldberg. 1979. "Let's Not Sweep Repression Under the Rug." In *Functional Disorders of Memory*, edited by J. F. Kilhstrom and J. Evans. Hillsdale, N.J.: Lawrence Erlbaum.

Falk, P. J. 1995. "Novel Theories of Criminal Defense Based upon the Toxicity of the Social Environment: Urban Psychosis, Television Intoxication, and Black Rage." *North Carolina Law Review* (March).

Fauman, Michael A. 1994. *Study Guide to DSM-IV*. Washington, D.C.: American Psychiatric Press.

Faust, David, Kathleen Hart, and Thomas Guilmette. 1988. "Pediatric Malingering: The Capacity of Children to Fake Believable Deficits on Neuropsychological Testing." *Journal of Consulting and Clinical Psychology* 56: 578–82.

Faust, David, and Jay Ziskin. 1988. "The Expert Witness in Psychology and Psychiatry." *Science* 241 (July).

Flanagan, Catherine. 1986. "Legal Issues Between Psychology and Law Enforcement." *Behavioral Sciences and the Law* 4: 371–84.

Foster, W. L. 1897–1898. "Expert Testimony—Prevalent Complaints and Proposed Remedies." *Harvard Law Review* 11.

Frances, Allen J., ed. 1995. *Diagnostic and Statistical Manual of Mental Disorders*. Washington, D.C.: American Psychiatric Press.

Frankfurter, Felix. 1882–1965. *Law and Politics*. New York: Harcourt Brace.

Freud, Sigmund. 1963. *Therapy and Techniques*. New York: Collier.

Freud, Sigmund. 1966. *The Basic Writings of Sigmund Freud*, ed. by A. A. Brill. New York: Modern Library.

Furby, L., L. Blackshaw, and M. R. Weinrott. 1989. "Sex Offender Recidivism: A Review." *Psychological Bulletin* 105.

Garbarino, James. 1995. "Growing Up in a Socially Toxic Environment: Life for Children and Families in the Nineties." In *Nebraska Symposium on Motivation*, 42: 1–20, edited by Gary B. Melton. Lincoln, Nebr.: University of Nebraska Press.

Gardner, M. R. 1976. "The Myth of the Impartial Psychiatric Expert." *Law and Psychology Review* 2.

Gardner, Martin. 1989. *Science: Good, Bad and Bogus*. Buffalo, N.Y.: Prometheus.

Geller, Shari. 1996. *Fatal Convictions*. New York: ReganBooks/HarperCollins.

Gelles, A. 1973. "Child Abuse as Psychopathology: A Sociological Critique and Reformulation." *American Journal of Orthopsychiatry* 43: 611.

Gerbasi, K. C., M. Zuckerman, and H. T. Reis. 1977. "Justice Needs a New Blindfold: A Review of Mock Jury Research." *Psychological Bulletin* 84, no. 2: 323–45.

Gilligan, Carol. 1982. *In a Different Voice: Psychological Theory and Women's Development*. Cambridge, Mass.: Harvard University Press.

Gilligan, Carol, Annie Rogers, and Deborah Tolman, eds. 1991. *Women, Girls and Psychotherapy: Reframing Resistance*. New York: Harrington Park Press/Haworth.

Gordon, R. I. 1976a. "The Application of Psychology to the Law." *Law and Psychology Review* 2.

Gordon, R. I. 1976b. *Forensic Psychology: A Guide for Lawyers and the Mental Health Professions*, vol. 2. Chicago: Nelson Hall.

Graham, E. S., and R. E. Kabacy. 1990. "Expert Testimony by Psychologists: Novel Scientific Evidence." *Law and Psychology Review* 14: 71.

Graham, J. R. 1993. *MMPI–2 Assessing Personality and Psychopathology*. 2nd ed. New York: Oxford University Press.

Hacking, Ian. 1995. *Rewriting the Soul: Multiple Personalities and the Sciences of Memory*. Princeton, N.J.: Princeton University Press.

Hagen, Ann M. 1991. "Tolling the Statute of Limitations for Adult Survivors of Sexual Abuse." *Iowa Law Review* 76: 355–82.

Hagen, Margaret A. 1980a. *The Perception of Pictures: Alberti's Window: The Projective Model of Pictorial Information*. New York: Academic Press.

Hagen, Margaret A. 1980b. *The Perception of Pictures: Dürer's Devices: Beyond the Projective Model of Pictures*. New York: Academic Press.

Hagen, Margaret A. 1986. *Varieties of Realism: Geometries of Representational Art*. New York: Cambridge University Press.

Hall, Calvin. 1963. *A Primer of Freudian Psychology*. New York: New American Library of World Literature.

Hall, G. C. N. 1995. "Sexual Offender Recidivism Revisited: A Meta-Analysis of Recent Treatment Studies." *Journal of Consulting and Clinical Psychology* 63, no. 5: 802–8.

Hallisey, R. J. 1995. "Experts on Eyewitness Testimony in Court—A Short Historical Perspective. *Howard Law Journal* 10: 237.

Hathaway, Stark R., and Paul E. Meehl. 1951. *An Atlas for the Clinical Use of the MMPI*. Minneapolis: University of Minnesota Press.

Henderson, J. A. 1995. "A Square Meaning for a Round Phrase: Applying the Career Offender Provision's 'Crime of Violence' to the Diminished Capacity Provision of the Federal Sentencing Guidelines." *Minnesota Law Review* (June).

Herman, Judith. 1992. *Trauma and Recovery*. New York: Basic Books.

Higgins, Robert B. 1988. "Child Victims as Witnesses." *Law and Psychology Review* 12: 151.

Higgins, S. A. 1991. "Post-Traumatic Stress Disorder and Its Role in the Defense of Vietnam Veterans." *Law and Psychology Review* 15: 259.

Hilgard, Ernest. 1965. *Hypnotic Susceptibility*. New York: Harcourt, Brace and World.

Hoffman, P. B. 1981. "Mental Health Professionals in the Legal Process: A Plea for Rational Applications of the Clinical Method." *Law and Psychology Review* 6: 21.

Holmes, David. 1990. "The Evidence for Repression: An Examination of Sixty Years of Research." In *Repression and Dissociation: Implications for Personality Theory, Psychopathology, and Health*, ed. Jerome L. Singer. Chicago: University of Chicago Press.

Holmes, Oliver Wendell. 1963. *The Common Law*, ed. Mark De Wolfe Howe. Boston: Little, Brown.

Hopkins, Carol Lamb. Prepared Testimony for the U.S. Senate Committee of Labor and Human Resources, Subcommittee on Children and Families, May 25, 1995.

Hothersall, David. 1986. *History of Psychology*. New York: McGraw-Hill.

Huber, Peter W. 1993. *Galileo's Revenge: Junk Science in the Courtroom*. New York: Basic Books.

Interface, course and workshop catalog, Cambridge, Massachusetts, 1993.

Jacobson, Neil. 1995. "Reevaluating Therapeutic Effectiveness." *Family Therapy Journal*.

Jendrek, M. P., and M. F. Kaplan. 1987. "Social Science Evidence and the Discrepancy in the Federal Rules of Evidence on Character Testimony." *Law and Psychology Review* 11: 39.

Kalman, L. 1996. *The Strange Career of Legal Liberalism*. New Haven, Conn.: Yale University Press.

Kaminer, Wendy. 1992. *I'm Dysfunctional, You're Dysfunctional: The Recovery Movement and Other Self-Help Fashions*. Reading, Mass.: Addison-Wesley.

Kaminer, Wendy. 1995. *It's All the Rage: Crime and Culture*. Reading, Mass.: Addison-Wesley.

Kassin, Saul M. 1988. *The American Jury on Trial: Psychological Perspectives*. New York: Hemisphere.

Kendall-Tackett, Kathleen, Linda Meyer Williams, and David Finkelhor. 1993. "Impact of Sexual Abuse on Children: A Review and Synthesis of Recent Empirical Studies." *Psychological Bulletin* 113: 164–80.

Kihlstrom, J. F. 1996. "Williams Study." *SSCP Network* (July 8).

Kirk, Stuart A., and Herb Kutchins. 1992. *The Selling of DSM: The Rhetoric of Science in Psychiatry*. New York: Aldine de Gruyter.

Klatzky, Roberta. 1980. *Human Memory: Structures and Processes*. New York: Freeman.

Klein, A. J. 1994. "Forensic Issues in Sexual Abuse Allegations in Custody/Visitation Litigation." *Law and Psychology Review* 18 (Spring): 189.

Kolb, L. C. 1988. "Recovering of Memory and Repressed Fantasy in Combat-Induced Post Traumatic Stress Disorder of Vietman Veterans." In *Hypnosis and Memory*, edited by H. M. Pettinati. New York: Guilford.

Koocher, G. P., and P. C. Keith-Spiegel. 1990. *Children, Ethics, and the Law. Professional Issues and Cases*. Lincoln.: University of Nebraska Press.

Koszuth, Ann M. 1991. "Sexually Abused Child Syndrome: Res Ipsa Loquitur and Shifting the Burden of Proof." *Law and Psychology Review* 15: 277–96.

Lees-Haley, P., and R. S. Dunn. 1986. "Pseudo Post Traumatic Stress Disorder." *Trial Diplomacy* (Winter): 17–20.

Loftus, Elizabeth. 1979. *Eyewitness Testimony*. Cambridge, Mass.: Harvard University Press.

Loftus, Elizabeth, and Katherine Ketcham. 1991. *Witness for the Defense: The Accused, the Eyewitness, and the Expert Who Puts Memory on Trial*. New York: St. Martin's.

Loftus, Elizabeth, and Katherine Ketchum. 1994. *The Myth of Repressed Memory: False Memories and Allegations of Sexual Abuse*. New York: St. Martin's.

Loh, W. D. 1981. "Psycholegal Research: Past and Present." *Michigan Law Review* 79: 659.

Lower, J. S. 1978. "Psychologists as Expert Witnesses." *Law and Psychology Review* 4: 127.

McCahill, Thomas W., Linda C. Meyer, and M. Fischman. 1979. *The Aftermath of Rape*. Lexington, Mass.: Lexington Books/D.C. Heath.

McCarty, Dwight Gaylord. 1960. *Psychology and the Law*. Englewood Cliffs, N.J.: Prentice-Hall.

McCary, J. L. 1955. "The Psychologist as an Expert Witness in Court." *American Psychologist* (February).

McDonald, James J., and Francine Kulick, eds. 1994. *Mental and Emotional Injuries in Employment Litigation*. Washington, D.C.: Bureau of National Affairs.

Maguire, Kathleen, and Ann Pastore, eds. 1994. *Sourcebook of Criminal Justice Statistics, 1993*. Bureau of Justice Statistics, Office of Justice Programs, U.S. Department of Justice. Washington, D.C.: Government Printing Office.

Marshall, James. 1966. *Law and Psychology in Conflict*. Indianapolis: Bobbs-Merrill.

Meehl, Paul E., Anthony C. Anderson, and Keith Gunderson. 1991. *Selected Philosophical and Methodological Papers*. Minneapolis: University of Minnesota Press.

Melton, Gary, John Petrila, Norman Poythress, and Christopher Slobogin. 1987. *Psychological Evaluations for the Courts*. New York: Guilford.

Mesmer, F. A. 1980. *Mesmerism: A Translation of the Original Scientific and Medial Writings of F. A. Mesmer*. Trans. by George J. Bloch. Los Altos, Calif.: William Kaufmann.

Miller, G. A. 1995. "Strong Medicine. Psychological Science." *American Psychological Society* 6, no. 3 (May 3).

Miller, H. L., J. S. Lower, and J. Bleechmore. 1978. "The Clinical Psychologist as an Expert Witness on Questions of Mental Illness and Competency." *Law and Psychology Review* 4.

Monahan, J. 1984. "The Prediction of Violent Behavior: Toward a Second Generation of Theory and Policy." *American Journal of Psychiatry* 141 (January): 1.

Montgomery, Imogene, Patricia Torbet, Diane Malloy, Lori Adamcik, James Toner, and Joey Andrews. 1994. *What Works: Promising Interventions in Juvenile Justice*. Program Report, Office of Juvenile Justice and Delinquency Prevention, U.S. Department of Justice. Washington, D.C.: Government Printing Office.

Munsterberg, Hugo. 1908. *On the Witness Stand: Essays on Psychology and Crime*. New York: Clark Boardman.

Myths and Realities: A Report of the National Commission on the Insanity Defense, National Mental Health Association, 1983.

Nabors, K. L. 1990a. "Selecting the Perfect Jury: Use of Jury Consultants in Voir Dire." *Law and Psychology Review* 14: 153.

Nabors, K. L. 1990b. "The Statute of Limitations: A Procedural Stumbling Block in Civil Incestuous Abuse Suits." *Law and Psychology Review* 14: 253.

Nelson, Katherine. 1933. The Psychological and Social Origins of Autobiographical Memory." *Psychological Science* 4: 7–13.

Ofshe, R. J. 1992. "Inadvertent Hypnosis During Interrogation: False Confessions Due to Dissociative State." *International Journal of Clinical and Experimental Hypnosis* XL: 125–56.

Ofshe, R. J., and Ethan Watters. 1993. "Making Monsters." *Society* 30: 4–16.

Olson, Walter. 1991. *The Litigation Explosion: What Happened When America Unleashed the Lawsuit*. New York: Truman Talley Books/Dutton.

Orr, A. W. 1989. "Expert Opinion Testimony: Experts, Where Did They Come From and Why Are They Here?" *Law and Psychology Review* 1391.

Othmer, Ekkehard, and Sieglinde Othmer. 1994. *The Clinical Interview Using DSM-IV: The Difficult Patient*. Washington, D.C.: American Psychiatric Press.

Otto, R. K. 1994. "On the Ability of Mental Health Professionals to 'Predict Dangerousness': A Commentary on Interpretations of the 'Dangerousness' Literature." *Law and Psychology Review* 18: 43.

Pardee, R., of the Psychology and Law Internet. 1996. "Daubert and Clinical Opinion Testimony." *Psychology and Law* (October).

Parker, L. Craig, Jr. 1980. *Legal Psychology: Eyewitness Testimony: Jury Behavior.* Springfield, Ill: Thomas.

Pendergrast, Mark. 1996. *Victims of Memory: Sex Abuse Accusations and Shattered Lives*. Hinesburg, Vt.: Upper Access.

Peirce, John C. 1990. "Selecting the Perfect Jury: Use of Jury Consultants in Voir Dire." *Law and Psychology Review* 14: 167–84.

Pope, Harrison. 1997. *Junk Psychology: Fact and Fallacy in Studies of "Repression" and Childhood Trauma*. Boca Raton, Fla.: SSRI/Upton Books.

Poythress, Norman. 1992. "Expert Testimony on Violence and Dangerousness: Roles for Mental Health Professionals." *Forensic Reports* 5: 135–50.

Press, M. P. 1983. "Premenstrual Stress Syndrome as a Defense in Criminal Cases." *Duke Law Journal* (February).

Rahaim, G. L., and S. L. Brodsky. 1982. "Empirical Evidence Versus Common Sense: Juror and Lawyer Knowledge of Eyewitness Accuracy." *Law and Psychology Review* 7.

Robinson, Edward Stevens. 1937. *Law and Lawyers*. New York: Macmillan.

Robinson, L. L. 1989. "Hypnotically Enhanced Testimony: Its Role and Admissibility in the Legal Process." *Law and Psychology Review* 13: 119.

Rogers, Richard. 1987. "APA's Position on Insanity Defense: Empiricism Versus Emotionalism.: *American Psychologist* 42.

Rosen, Gerald. 1996. "Post Traumatic Stress Disorder, Pulp Fiction, and the Press." *Bulletin of the American Academy of Psychiatry and the Law* 24: 267–69.

Rovee-Collier, Carolyn. 1993. "The Capacity for Long-Term Memory in Infants." *Current Directions in Psychological Science* 2: 130–35.

Russell, Diana E. 1983. "The Incidence and Prevalence of Intrafamilial and Extrafamilial Sexual Abuse of Female Children." *Child Abuse and Neglect* 7: 133–46.

Sales, Bruce. 1995. "Suggestibility of Child Witnesses: The Social Science Amicus Brief in State of New Jersey v. Michaels." *Psychology, Public Policy, and Law* 1.

Schacter, D. L. 1987. "Implicit Memory: History and Current Status." *Journal of Experimental Psychology: Learning, Memory and Cognition* 13: 501–18.

Schmidt, Janell D., and Lawrence W. Sherman. 1993. "Does Arrest Deter Domestic Violence?" *American Behavioral Scientist* 36.

Schneider, Elizabeth. 1995. "Particularity and Generality: Challenges of Feminist Theory and Practice in Work on Woman-Abuse." *New York University Law Review* 5: 535–39.

Scholder, M. H. 1982. "The Argument Against the Use of Hypnosis to Improve or Enhance the Memory of Courtroom Witnesses." *Law and Psychology Review* 7: 53.

Schopp, Robert, and Michael Quattrocchi. 1984. "Tarasoff, the Doctrine of Special Relationships and the Psychotherapists' Duty to Warn." *Journal of Psychiatry and the Law* 12: 23.

Schopp, R. F., B. J. Sturgis, and M. Sullivan. 1994. "Battered Woman Syndrome, Expert Testimony, and the Distinction Between Justification and Excuse." *University of Illinois Law Review*, 45: 91–113.

Scotford, R. 1995. "Lancet Commentary." *Lancet* 346 (October 21).

Shepard, Melanie. 1992. "Predicting Battered Recidivism Five Years After Community Intervention." *Journal of Family Violence* 7: 167–78.

Sherman, Lawrence, and Richard Berk. 1984. "The Specific Deterrent Effects of Arrest for Domestic Abuse." *American Sociological Review*, 49: 261–72.

Smith, Susan. 1995. *Survivor Psychology*. Boca Raton, Fla.: SSRI/Upton Books.

"Spivack Background." May 1994. *The Hartford Courant.*

"Spivack Testimony." May 25, 1995. *Federal Document Clearing House Congressional Testimony.*

Stark, E. 1973. "Symposium on Reconceptualizing Violence Against Women by Intimate Partners: Critical Issues: Re-Presenting Woman Battering: from Battered Women Syndrome to Coercive Control." *Albany Law Review* 58: 973.

Steadman, H. J. 1993. *Before and After Hinckley: Evaluating Insanity Defense Reform.* New York: Guilford Press.

Sullivan, J. T. 1995. "Psychiatric Defenses in Arkansas Criminal Trials." *Arkansas Law Review*, 48: 439–509.

Tapp, June Louin, and Felice J. Levine. 1977. *Law, Justice, and the Individual in Society: Psychological and Legal Issues.* New York: Holt, Rinehart and Winston.

Taub, Sheila. 1996. "The Legal Treatment of Recovered Memories of Child Sexual Abuse." *Journal of Legal Medicine* 17: 183–214.

Terr, Lenore. 1990. *Too Scared to Cry.* New York: Basic Books.

Terr, Lenore. 1994. *Unchained Memories: True Stories of Traumatic Memories, Lost and Found.* New York: Basic Books.

Thoennes, N., and J. Pearson. 1988. "Summary of Findings from the Sexual Abuse Allegations Project, Sexual Abuse Allegation in Custody and Visitation." *Golden Gate University Law Review* 15: 513, 516.

Tolman, Richard, and Larry Bennett. 1990. "A Review of Quantitative Research on Men Who Batter." *Journal of Interpersonal Violence* 5: 87–118.

Tomlin, C. W. 1994. "The Trauma of Testifying in Court for Child Victims of Sexual Assault v. the Accused's Right to Confrontation." *Law and Psychology Review* 18: 423.

Udolf, Roy. 1983. *Forensic Hypnosis: Psychological and Legal Aspects*. Lexington, Mass.: Lexington Books.

Umakantha, Abha. 1989. "Hypnotically Enhanced Testimony—Its Role and Admissibility in the Legal Process." *Law and Psychology Review* 13: 119.

Unger, Rhoda, and Mary Crawford. 1996. *Women and Gender: A Feminist Psychology*. New York: McGraw-Hill.

Usher, JoNell, and Ulric Neisser. 1993. "Childhood Amnesia and the Beginnings of Memory for Four Early Life Events." *Journal of Experimental Psychology: General* 122: 155–65.

van der Kolk, Bessel, and Mark Greenberg. 1987. "The Psychobiology of the Trauma Response: Hyperarousal, Constriction, and Addiction to Traumatic Reexposure." In *Psychological Trauma*, ed. Bessel van der Kolk. Washington, D.C.: American Psychiatric Press.

van del Kolk, Bessel, and Alexander McFarlane. 1996. *Traumatic Stress: Effects of Overwhelming Life Experience on Mind, Body and Society*. New York: Guilford Press.

Wade, James. Prepared Testimony for Senate Committee on Labor and Human Resources, Subcommittee on Children and Families, May 25, 1995.

Walker, Lenore. 1979. *The Battered Woman*. New York: HarperPerennial.

Watkins, Ludlam, and Stennis. January 1996. "Insurance Policy Does Not Apply to Harassment Claim." *Mississippi Employment Law Letter.*

"Weber Testimony." May 25, 1995. *Federal News Service.*

Weisz, John R., Bahr Weiss, Mark Alicke, and M. L. Klotz. 1987. "Effectiveness of Psychotherapy with Children and Adolescents Revisited: A Meta-Analysis for Clinicians." *Journal of Consulting and Clinical Psychology* 55: 542–49.

Weisz, John R., Bahr Weiss, Susan Haan, Douglas Granger, and Todd Morton. 1995. "Effectiveness of Psychotherapy with Children and Adolescents Revisited: A Meta-Analysis of Treatment Outcome Studies." *Psychological Bulletin* 117: 450–68.

Wesson, Marianne. 1985. "Historical Truth, Narrative Truth and Expert Testimony." *Washington Law Review* 60: 331–54.

Whipple, G. M. 1909. "The Observer as Reporter: A Survey of the Psychology of Testimony." *Psychological Bulletin* 6, no. 5 (May 15).

Whipple, G. M. 1910. "General Reviews and Summaries. Recent Literature on the Psychology of Testimony." *Psychological Bulletin* 7, no. 2 (November 15).

Whipple, G. M. 1911. "The Psychology of Testimony." *Psychological Bulletin* 8.

Whipple, G. M. 1912. "Psychology of Testimony and Report." Ed. by A. H. Pierce, H. C. Warren, J. B. Watson, and J. R. Angell. *Psychological Bulletin* 9.

Whipple, G. M. 1913. "Psychology of Testimony and Report." Ed. by A. H. Pierce, H. C. Warren, J. B. Watson, and J. R. Angell. *Psychological Bulletin* 10.

Whipple, G. M. 1914. "Psychology of Testimony and Report." Ed. by S. I. Franz, H. C. Warren, J. B. Watson, and J. R. Angell. *Psychological Bulletin* 11.

Whipple, G. M. 1915. "Psychology of Testimony." Ed. by S. I. Franz, H. C. Warren, J. B. Watson, and J. R. Angell. *Psychological Bulletin* 12.

Whipple, G. M. 1917. "Psychology of Testimony." Ed. by S. I. Franz, H. C. Warren, J. B. Watson, and J. R. Angell. *Psychological Bulletin* 14.

Wigmore, John. 1935. *Wigmore's Code of the Rules of Evidence in Trials at Law*. Boston: Little, Brown.

Wigmore, John. 1937. *The Science of Judicial Proof: As Given by Logic, Psychology and General Experience*. Boston: Little, Brown.

Williams, Linda Meyer. 1994. "Recall of Childhood Trauma: A Prospective Study of Women's Memories of Child Sexual Abuse." *Journal of Consulting and Clinical Psychology*, 62: 1167-1176.

Williams, Linda Meyer. 1995. "Recall of Childhood Trauma: A Prospective of Study of Women's Memories of Child Sexual Abuse. A Correction." *Journal of Consulting and Clinical Psychology*, 63: 343.

Winner, Karen. 1996. *Divorced from Justice: The Abuse of Women by Divorce Lawyers and Judges*. New York: ReganBooks/HarperCollins.

Wood, James, M. Teresa Nezworski, and William Stajskal. 1996. "The Comprehensive System for the Rorschach: A Critical Examination." *Psychological Science* 7: 3–17.

Woodward. 1952. "A Scientific Attempt to Provide Evidence for a Decision on Change of Venue." *American Sociological Review* 17.

Worrell, Claudia. 1987. "Psychiatric Prediction of Dangerousness in Capital Sentencing: The Quest for Innocent Authority." *Behavioral Sciences and the Law* 5: 433–46.

Wright, Lawrence. 1994. *Remembering Satan*. New York: Knopf.

Young-Bruehl, Elisabeth. 1990. *Freud on Women: A Reader*. New York: Norton.

Ziskin, Jay. 1995. *Coping with Psychiatric and Psychological Testimony*. 5th ed. 3 vols. Los Angeles: Law and Psychology Press.

NEWSPAPER AND MAGAZINE ARTICLES

"Air Force Cites Lapses in Murderous Spree." August 13, 1994.

Allee, R. February 8, 1995. "State Joins Sex-Harassment Case; West Milford Cop Accused of Stalking Women." *Record* (Bergen County, N.J.).

"Amish Man Found Guilty of Manslaughter in Grisly Slaying and Mutilation of His Wife." March 27, 1994. *Napa Valley Register.*

"Analysis, More Than a Pretty Face." September 1996. *Esquire.*

Anand, Geeta. October 8, 1995. "Brockton Mayor Rethinks Hiring of Officer." *Boston Globe*.

Anderson, J. May 31, 1995. "Westmead Hospital." *Listing of Australi.*

Arena, S. October 6, 1995. "Eatery Big in a Soup for Slap." *Daily News* (New York).

Benning, Victoria. June 21, 1992. "Therapist Who OK'd Release 'Shocked.'" *Boston Globe*.

Berkow, Ira. October 1, 1995. "An Athlete Dies Young But by His Own Hand." *New York Times*.

Boodman, Sandra. March 17, 1992. "Does Castration Stop Sex Crimes? An Old Punishment Gains New Attention, but Experts Doubt Its Value." *Washington Post*.

Booth, W. April 17, 1996. "Suffer the Little Child." *Washington Post.*

Brod, E. May 26, 1996. "Psychotherapist Has Duty to Maintain Privacy." *Boston Globe*.

Butterfield, Fox. March 2, 1996. "Dispute over Insanity Defense Is Revived in Murder Trial." *New York Times*.

Campagne, Henriette. June 24, 1996. "Court Rejects Fired Professor's Claim." *Massachusetts Lawyers Weekly*.

Ceci, Stephen, and Eduardus de Bruyn. January 1993. "Child Witnesses in Court." *Children Today*.

"Charges Are Lifted for a Boy, 6, in the Severe Beating of a Baby." July 14, 1996. *New York Times.*

Clark, Kenneth, and Michael Myers. April 1, 1995. "Separate Is Never Equal." *New York Times.*

Cortez, A. August 1, 1996. "Slaying Puts Attention on Mental Illness." *Denver Post.*

Curtius, Mary. July 3, 1996. "Man Won't Be Retried in Repressed Memory Case." *Los Angeles Times.*

Delfiner, R. September 25, 1996. "Woman Files 'Cur'ious Suit." *New York Post.*

Dembner, A. July 15, 1996. "Lawsuit by BU Professor Fired for Sex Harassment Is Dismissed." *Boston Globe.*

Dohert, Brian. July 16, 1995. "Disabilities Act: Source of Unreasonable Accommodations." *San Diego Union Tribune.*

Dowdy, Z. H. June 5, 1996. "Man Held in Killing Got Probation in Ex-Girlfriend's Beating." *Boston Globe.*

Ellement, J. March 16, 1995. "Beverly Man Off His Medication Cleared in Attack on Black Officer." *Boston Globe.*

Ellement, J. July 19, 1996. "Court Suggests Twins Should Be Reunited." *Boston Globe.*

Ellement, J. July 19, 1996. "Sex-Offender Registry Legal, Says High Court." *Boston Globe.*

Ellement, J. October 14, 1996. "Suspect May Argue 'Urban Psychosis.'" *Boston Globe.*

"Equal Coverage for Mental." September 29, 1996. *Boston Globe.*

"Erna H. Gill, 67, of Newton; Led Effort to License Social Workers" (obituary). May 26, 1996. *Boston Globe.*

"Family Injustice in B.C." May 7, 1995. *The Province.*

Ferdinand, P. August 23, 1996. "Specialists Offer Theories on Why Youths Might Rape." *Boston Globe.*

Francke, Caitlin. August 27, 1996. "Man Held Not Criminally Responsible in Slaying; Judge Orders Moncarz Held in Mental Institution." *Baltimore Sun.*

Freking, K. September 3, 1994. "City Lawyer Tells Board to Demolish Shaky Home." *Arkansas Democrat-Gazette.*

Freyd, P. August 30, 1994. "Newsletter." *FMS Foundation Newsletter* 3, no. 8.

Freyd, P. February 1, 1995. "Noah Background 2." *FMS Foundation Newsletter* 4, no. 2.

Freyd, P. May 2, 1995. "Newsletter." *FMS Foundation Newsletter* 4, no. 5.

Freyd, P. June 1, 1995. "June's Newsletter." *FMS Foundation Newsletter* 4, no. 6.

Freyd, P. May 1, 1996. "Crime Victims' Compensation and Repressed Memory." *FMS Foundation Newsletter*, revised.

Fried, Joseph. December 17, 1996. "Plea Deal in Killing of Woman on the Subway Is Criticized." *New York Times.*

Gaines, J. May 2, 1996. "One Mother's Gain Leaves Brighton Couple at a Loss." *Boston Globe.*

"Girl, 13, Charged in R.I. Killing." September 13, 1996. *Boston Globe.*

Goldberg, C. April 26, 1996. "Six-Year-Old Charged with Trying to Kill Baby." *New York Times.*

Grady, Bill. March 15, 1988. "Felde Executed for Cop-Killing in 1978." *Times-Picayune* (New Orleans).

Grunwald, M. June 17, 1996. "Family Values, at the Child's Expense." *Boston Globe.*

Hayward, Ed, and Tom Mashberg. December 6, 1995. "The Fells Acres Case: Justice on Witch-hunt?" *Boston Herald.*

Houston, Eric. August 22, 1995. "Saleswoman for KVI Wins Discrimination Suit." *Seattle Post Intelligencer.*

Hunger, K. June 21, 1996. "Freetown Officer Wins $263,500 for Race Bias." *Boston Globe.*

Impellizzeri, L. April 1994. "Teen-ager's Trial Hears Psychiatrist." *Boston Globe.*

Jackson, O. June 1, 1985. "Librarian Sex Case Detailed; an Affair Grew from Platonic Beginnings, a Teen Testifies." *Tampa Tribune.*

Jacobs, Sally. April 4, 1993. "Sex Abuse Memories in Question." *Boston Globe.*

"Judge Decreases Amount of Award to USC's Cobb; Courts: A Problem with the Form Given to Jurors Leaves Him to Receive $1 Million Less in Damages from the School." July 16, 1994. *Orange County* (Calif.) *Register.*

"Jury Rejects Defense That Blamed City Life." November 13, 1994. *New York Times.*

"Kee McFarlane." July 14, 1993. *Chicago Tribune.*

Kennedy, Randy. September 18, 1996. "Officials Find Plenty of Blame to Cast in Borough Park Siege." *New York Times.*

King, W., and S. Gilmore. March 17, 1994. "Rare Illness Could Bring Murder Charges for Mother." *Seattle Times.*

Knox, R. A. September 16, 1996. "Changing World, Changing Ailments." *Boston Globe.*

Langner, Paul. May 17, 1995. "Doctor Testifies Moved Funds a Mystery." *Boston Globe.*

Langner, P. April 30, 1993. "Judge Orders Man Away from All Children." *Boston Globe.*

Langner, P. February 8, 1996. "Psychiatric Evaluation Sought for Rosenthal." *Boston Globe.*

"Legislative Panel Begins Study of Child Protective Services." June 2, 1995. *Associated Press.*

Lieberman, P. July 11, 1996. "Ex-Guard Seeks Share of Heiress's Fortune." *Los Angeles Times.*

Lindsay, S. July 14, 1995. "Confidential Settlement Ends Suit over Molestation." *Rocky Mountain News* (Denver).

Loftus, E. June 3, 1995. "MSF Newsletter." *FMS Foundations Newsletter* 3, no. 8.

Lorch, Donatella. April 25, 1994. "Rwandan Refugees Describe Horrors After a Bloody Trek." *New York Times.*

Lyons, Kim. October 27, 1996. "Nine-Year-Old Is Cleared in Providence Arson." *Boston Globe.*

McNamara, Eileen. September 30, 1995. "A Judgment Call Ending in Death." *Boston Globe.*

McQuiston, J. T. September 2, 1994. "Confession Is Admissible in Rifkin's 2d Murder Trial: Judge Says Police Upheld Suspect's Rights." *New York Times.*

"Man Freed in Repressed-Memory Case." July 4, 1996. *Boston Globe.*

"Man Is Found Not Guilty in Killing of Nuns." October 17, 1996. *New York Times.*

Mangan, P. December 29, 1995. "Residents Can Condo on Toilet Explosions." *Daily News* (New York).

Martin, J. June 13, 1996. "Mister Boffo." *Boston Globe.*

Mello, M. June 4, 1995. "Did Tainted Testimony Doom Man? As Joseph Spaziano Nears Execution, a Lawyer Questions the Evidence That Sealed His Fate." *Orlando Sentinel.*

"Morton Testimony." May 25, 1995. *Federal News Service.*

"Mother Accused of Infecting Son." February 15, 1995. *Boston Globe.*

Mulvihill, Maggie. June 30, 1994. "Flashback Defense Wins Rape Acquittal." *Boston Herald.*

Nathan, Debbie. April 1996. "The Teacher Hurt Me: Why Children Don't Always Tell the Truth About Sexual Abuse." *Redbook.*

"National News: Cross-Dressing School Punishment Basis of Suit." May 25, 1995. *Legal Intelligencer.*

Nealon, P. January 27, 1994. "SJC Overturns Conviction of Man for Killing Wife." *Boston Globe.*

Nealon, P. January 30, 1996. "Murder Suspect May Have Quit Mood Medication." *Boston Globe.*

"A Needless Mental Health Tragedy" (editorial). February 29, 1996. *New York Times.*

Nirode, J. July 28, 1996. "Freed Women and Acceptance Hard to Come By." *Columbus Dispatch.*

Nordheimer, Jon. November 8, 1994. "Youth, 14, Draws 9 Years to Life in Killing of 4-Year-Old." *New York Times.*

O'Brien, E. December 29, 1995. "Evaluation Sees Hope for O'Brien." *Boston Globe.*

O'Brien, E. September 25, 1996. "Victim Had Tried to Appease Husband; Asked Judge to Let Officer Carry Gun." *Boston Globe.*

"An Offender's Right to Treatment" (editorial). June 2, 1992. *Boston Globe.*

"Parents Win Suit Against Psychiatrist in Sex Case." December 16, 1994. *New York Times.*

Patterson, M. J. August 7, 1994. "Fatal Flaw Sex Offenders 'Max Out' and Avoid Treatment." *Star-Ledger* (Newark).

"Prosecutors Say Mother Injected Son with Bacteria." February 15, 1995. *Orlando Sentinel.*

"Psychiatric Exam for Dog." September 29, 1996. *New York Times.*

Quindlen, A. December 10, 1994. "The Good Mother." *Boston Globe.*

Rabinowitz, D. January 30, 1995. "A Darkness in Massachusetts." *Wall Street Journal.*

"Rarely Used Law Catches a Killer Who Went Free." August 21, 1994. *New York Times.*

Reid, S. M. March 26, 1996. "USC Confirms Its Pursuit of Controversial Recruit: The Trojans Are Interested in Richie Parker, a Former High School All-American, Who Was Convicted of Sexual Assault." *Orange County* (Calif.) *Register.*

Restak, Richard. September 1996. *Esquire.* (Quoted in "Reality Check").

Robey, R. December 12, 1994. "Student Sues in Accident; Woman Who Killed Peer Cites Distress." *Denver Post.*

Sciacca, Joe. May 2, 1996. "Disabled System Socks Taxpayers." *Boston Herald.*

Scott, J. May 9, 1994. "Multiple-Personality Cases Perplex Legal System." *Boston Globe.*

Sennott, Charles. February 20, 1994. "Finding Four Generations Sustained by Welfare." *Boston Globe.*

Shalit, R. June 17, 1995. "Out of Thin Air; Accusations of Child Abuse Destroy Innocent Family." *Ottawa Citizen*.

Slattery, R. June 6, 1996. "Gay Janitor Wins $150,000 in Sex Bias Suit." *Boston Globe*.

Smith, D. June 3, 1995. "Scholar Who Says Jung Lied Is at War with Descendants." *New York Times*.

Smith, K. July 2, 1995. Letter About Bunbury Case. *The Australian*.

Smith, P. May 24, 1996. "Art Creates New View of Life." *Boston Globe*.

Stevens, D. G. July 16, 1996. "Dad Has Choice in Fight to See Daughters: Judge Drops Lisle Mom's Contempt Charge." *Chicago Tribune*.

Sweeney, A. June 22, 1995. "Woman Sues Ex-Nun for Alleged Abuse." *Detroit News*.

"Sympathy for Killer Claiming Post-Vietnam Stress." February 14, 1993. *New York Times*.

Talbot, D. June 3, 1995. "Fells Acre Retrial Considered; Judge Mulls Request in Day-Care Molest Case." *Boston Herald*.

Talbot, D. November 8, 1996. "Psychiatric Experts Cost State Big Bucks." *Boston Herald*.

Tavris, Carol. January 3, 1993. "Beware the Incest-Survivor Machine." *New York Times Book Review*: 1, 16–17 and subsquent Letters to the Editor. (February 14, 1993). "Real Incest and Real Survivors." *New York Times Book Review*: 3, 27.

Terry, Don. January 30, 1996. "Sentences for Boy Killers Renew Debate on Saving Society's Lost." *New York Times*.

"Therapists Take on California on the Issue of Their Oversight." August 14, 1996. *Boston Globe*.

Tizon, Alex. March 18, 1994. "Man Charged in Benefits Scam Among Refugees." *Seattle Times*.

"Two Who Taped Children's Fight, Charged Michigan Parents to Be Tried on Abuse, Extortion Counts." July 3, 1996. *Boston Globe*.

"'Urban Survival' Mistrial Declared." April 21, 1994. *Newsday* (Long Island, N.Y.).

Vachss, Andrew. November 3, 1996. "If We Really Want to Protect Children." *Parade*.

Vaillancourt, M. September 27, 1996. "Addiction Experts Say Weld Ad 'Misleading.'" *Boston Globe*.

Verhovek, S. H. November 8, 1996. "In Texas, Pistol Packers Must Know Psychology." *New York Times*.

"Victim's Mom Files Wrongful Death Suit." August 9, 1996. *Seattle Post Intelligencer*.

Vigue, D. I. October 2, 1996. "Caring Therapist Had Fake Credentials." *Boston Globe*.

Weiss, K. July 14, 1996. "Judge Suspends Prosecution of Boy, 6, in Infant's Beating." *Los Angeles Times*.

Weizel, Richard. December 10, 1993. "Families of Slain Women Fear Release of Connecticut Murderer." *Boston Globe*.

Wells, P. August 2, 1995. "Very Sad Smith Trial Was Psychiatrist's Toughest." *News and Observer* (Raleigh, N.C.).

Wildermuth, J. July 4, 1996. "Quick Hearing Sends Franklin to Freedom; Dad Leaving State—and Repressed Memory Case." *San Francisco Chronicle*.

Will, George. April 5, 1996. "Government's New Kick: Protect Social Misfits in the Workplace." *Boston Globe*.

Woo, Junda. April 27, 1993. "Urban Trauma Mitigates Guilt, Defenders Say." *Wall Street Journal.*

"Youth Sues After He Is Left on Plane." July 31, 1995. *Boston Globe.*

CASES

American Airlines, Inc., Crandall, R. L., Shannon, W. P., Jacob, J. R., Treiber, C. I., and Zurlo, R. J., Defendants–Appellants–Respondents. Supreme Court, Appellate Division, First Department. *Westlaw* (October 14, 1993).

Anonymous, E. K., v. Anonymous. Proceeding No. 1. In re Nassau County Department of Social Services o/b/o Anonymous, M. K., v. Anonymous, S. K. Proceeding No. 2. 90–00196, 90–00214. Supreme Court of New York, Appellate Division, Second Department. 176 A.D.2d 326; 574 N.Y.S.2d 767; 1991 N.Y. App. Div. *Lexis 12335* (argued May 13, 1991; decided, September 30, 1991).

Bailey v. American General Insurance Company. 279 S.W. 315, 316–17 (Texas, 1955).

Barefoot v. Estelle. No. 82-6080. Supreme Court of the United States, 1983 U.S. *Lexis.*

Betty J. W., Dorothy N. W., James E. W., Sandra K. W., and Cassie, A. W. No. 17482. Supreme Court of Appeals of West Virginia. 179 W. Va. 605; 371 S.E.2d 326; 1988 W. Va. *Lexis 97* (July 1, 1988).

Brown v. Board of Education [of Topeka, Kansas]. 347 U.S. 483, 495, 1954.

Brown, S. R. S., et al., v. Hartford Life Companies, et al. 91–CA–443. Court of Appeal of Louisiana, Fifth Circuit, 593 So. 2d 1376; 1992 La. App. *Lexis 158* (January 31, 1993).

Cobb, M., v. University of Southern California. No. B087275. Court of Appeal, Second District, Division 5. *Westlaw* (May 23, 1996).

Commonwealth of Massachusetts v. Hunter, A. J. E–6105, Supreme Judicial Court of Massachusetts, 416 Mass. 831; 636 N.E. 2d 873; 1994. *Lexis 15* (argued, December 7, 1993; decided, January 27, 1994).

Commonwealth of Massachusetts v. Perry P., A Juvenile. No. 93–P–307 Appeals Court of Massachusetts 36 Mass. App. Ct. 914; 628 N.E. 2d 32; 1994 Mass. App. *Lexis 179* (February 22, 1994).

Cooper, B. K., v. Oklahoma. No. 95–5207. Supreme Court of the United States. 116 S. Ct. 13373; 1996 U.S. 2649; 134 L. Ed. 2d 498; 64 U.S.L.W. 4255 (argued, January 17, 1996; decided, April 16, 1996).

Coy v. Iowa. No. 86–6757. Supreme Court of the United States. 487 U.S. 1012; 108 S. Ct. 2798; 1988 U.S. *Lexis 3033*; 101 L. Ed. 2d 857; 56 U.S.L.W. 4931.

Crabb, D., v. Shalala, C. A. No. 93–55628, United States Court of Appeals, Ninth Circuit. 1994 U.S. App. *Lexis 37281.*

Dalton, J., v. Secretary of Health and Human Services. No. 89–5774. United States Court of Appeals, Sixth Circuit. 1990 U.S. App. *Lexis 11983* (filed, July 16, 1990).

Daubert v. Merrell Dow Pharmaceuticals, Inc. No. 92–102 509 U.S. 579, 113 S. Ct. 2786.

David W. v. Julia W. No. 39953W. Supreme Court of New York, Appellate Division, First Department. 158 A.D.2d 1; 557 N.Y.S.2d 314; 1990 N.Y. App. Div. *Lexis 7268* (June 14, 1990).

Drope v. Missouri. No. 73–6038. Supreme Court of the United States. 420 U.S. 162; 95 S. Ct. 896; 1975 U.S. *Lexis 32;* 43 L. Ed. 2d 103 (argued, November 12, 1974; decided, February 19, 1975).

Eli, Janine, v. Eli., W. Docket No. V9876/92. Family Court of New York, New York County. 607 N.Y.S.2d 535; 1993 N.Y. Misc. *Lexis 567* (November 9, 1993).

Erika K. v. Steven K. Nos. 90-00196, 90-00214, Supreme Court of New York, Appellate Division, Second Department. *Lexis 12335.*

Esdale (Cohen), B. A., v. Esdale, R. No. 85–544. Court of Appeals of Florida, Fourth District, 487 So. 2d 1219, 11 Fla. *Law W. 1091.* (May 7, 1986).

Felex, M. H., v. Nevada. Francisco J. Ontiveros v. Nevada. Nos. 18960, 19191. Supreme Court of Nevada (March 18, 1993).

Foster, R., v. Globe Life and Accident Insurance Company. Civ. Act. No. CC 90–274-D-O. United States District Court for the Northern District of Mississippi, Greenville Division. 808 F. Supp. 1281; 1992 U.S. Dist. *Lexis 19451* (May 27, 1993).

Frye v. United States. No. 3968. Court of Appeals of District of Columbia. 54 App. D.C. 46, 293 F. 1013.

Gage, J. S., v. Hage, J. No. 90–04765. Supreme Court of New York, Appellate Division, Second Department. 167 A.D.2d 332; 561 N.Y.S.2d 299; 1990 N.Y. App. Div. *Lexis 13387* (argued, October 12, 1990; decided, November 5, 1990).

Goetz, L. R., v. Cans. No. 91–7761. United States Court of Appeals, Second Circuit. 967 F.2d 29; 1992 U.S. App. *Lexis 13711* (argued, November 15, 1991; decided, June 10, 1992).

Guillot v. Sentry Insurance Company. Louisiana Court of Appeals, 1987. 472 So. 2d 197, 200–01.

Harris, J.–Dissent, Maryland v. Craig. No. 89–478. Supreme Court of the United States. *Mime Format* (June 27, 1990).

Hennelly, R., Jr., v. Viger, L. 92–06359. Supreme Court of New York, Appellate Division, Second Department. 194 A.D. 2d 791; 599 N.Y.S. 2d 623; 1993 N.Y. App. Div. *Lexis 6665* (argued, June 10, 1993; decided, June 29, 1993).

Hidden v. Mutual Life Insurance Company. 217 F.2d 818 (4th Cir. 1954).

Hunio, R. A., v. Tishman Construction Corporation of California et al. No. B064811. Court of Appeal, Second District, Division 1. *Westlaw* (review granted, March 31, 1993; decided, June 23, 1993).

Irvin, J. L., and Lovato, B. A., v. Irvin, J. L. Bankruptcy No. 82 B 01368 J. Adv. No. 82 M 0933. United States Bankruptcy Court for the District of Colorado. 31 Bankr. 251; Bankr. L. Rep. (CCH) P69, 282.

Jackson, E., v. Walter Fogg. No. 421, Docket 78–2107. United States Court of Appeals, Second Circuit (argued, November 17, 1978; decided, December 19, 1978). *Westlaw* (1996).

Jaffee, C., v. Redmond, M., et al. No. 95–266. Supreme Court of the United States. 1996 U.S. *Lexis 3879*; 64 U.S.L.W. 4490 (argued, February 26, 1996; decided, June 13, 1996).

James, W. et al. v. Superior Court of San Diego, Kathleen Goodfriend. No. D017377, Court of Appeal of California, 17 Cal. App. 4th 24; 21 Cal. Rptr. 2d 169.

Johnson, T., v. Johnson, R. F. 93–07201. Supreme Court of New York, Appellate

Division, Second Department. 202 A.D. 2d 584; 609 N.Y.S. 2d 81; 1994 N.Y. App. Div. *Lexis 2730* (argued, March 1, 1994; decided, March 21, 1994).

Kostelac, S. W., v. Feldman's Inc. and Great American Insurance Companies. No. 376/91–1755. Supreme Court of Iowa. 497 N.W.2d 853; 1993 Iowa Sup. *Lexis 78* (filed, March 24, 1993).

Lafferty, R. W., v. Cook, G. No. 90–4010. United States Court of Appeals, Tenth Circuit. 949 F.2d 1546; 1991 U.S. App. *Lexis 28705* (filed, December 9, 1991).

Landau, E., v. Landau, S. 93–01707, 93–01708. Supreme Court of New York, Appellate Division, Second Department. 214 A.D. 2d 541; 625 N.Y.S. 2d 239; 1995 N.Y. App. Div. *Lexis 3524* (submitted, February 24, 1995; decided, April 3, 1995).

Larson, A. The Wade Case/Immunity Issues. James, W., v. Superior Court, No. D017377. Court of Appeal of California, Fourth Appellate District Division One. 17 Cal. App. 4th 246; 21 Cal. Rptr. 2d 169; 93 Cal. Daily Op. Service 5449; *93 Daily Journal Dar 9211* (decided, July 16, 1993).

Lobo, P. f/k/a Mutte, P., v. Muttee, R. 92–08905, 93–02088, 93–02090. Supreme Court of New York, Appellate Division, Second Department. 196 A.D. 2d 585; 601 N.Y.S. 2d 322; 1993 N.Y. App. Div. *Lexis 8073* (argued, June 24, 1993; decided, August 16, 1993).

Maryland v. Craig. No. 89–478. Supreme Court of the United States. 497 U.S. 836; 110 S. Ct. 3157; 1990 U.S. *Lexis 3457;* 111 L. Ed. 2d 666; 58 U.S.L.W. 5044; 30 Fed. R. Evid. Serv. (Callaghan) 1 (argued, April 18, 1990; decided, June 27, 1990).

Mateu v. Hagen, 91–2–08053–4, Superior Court of the State of Washington for King County, 1993.

Medina, T. Fr., v. California. No. 90–8370. Supreme Court of the United States (argued, February 25, 1992; decided, June 22, 1992). *Westlaw.*

New York v. Emick, L. A. 481 New York Supplement, 2d Series (1984).

Nir, M., v. Nir, M. No. 2451. Supreme Court of New York, Appellate Division, Second Department. 172 A.D. 2d 651; 568 N.Y.S. 2d 452; 1991 N.Y. App. Div. *Lexis 4586* (argued, May 19, 1990; decided, April 15, 1991).

Pamperin, C. L., v. Pamperin, E. No. 81–2401. Court of Appeals of Wisconsin. 112 Wis. 2d 70; 331 N.W. 2d 648 (submitted on briefs, January 30, 1983; decided, February 23, 1983).

People v. Harrison, D. Supreme Court of California. In Blank. (March 24, 1988). *People v. Lucero cit as 245 Cal. Rptr. 185* (Cal. 1988).

People v. Kay, V. J. No. F014113. Court of Appeal, Fifth District. *2 California Reporter, 2d Series*. (January 6, 1993).

People of the State of New York, Respondent v. Emick, L.A., Appellant. *481 New York Supplement, 2nd Series* (1984).

Pugh v. Georgia. No. A89A0001. Court of Appeals of Georgia. (April 25, 1989).

Rogers, M. J., v. Florida. No. 91–854. Court of Appeal of Florida, First District. 616 So. 2d 1098; 1993 Fla. App. *Lexis 3865*; 18 Fla. Law W.D. 930 (filed, April 8, 1993).

Satterwhite v. Texas. No. 86–6284. Supreme Court of the United States. 486 U.S. 249; 108 S. Ct. 1792; 1988 U.S. *Lexis 2474*; 100 L. Ed. 2d 284; 56 U.S.L.W. 4470 (argued, December 8, 1987; decided, May 31, 1988).

Shahzade v. Gregory. No. 92—12139—EFH. United States District Court, District of Massachusetts (May 8, 1996).

Sheppard v. Maxwell. No. 490. Supreme Court of the United States (argued, February 28, 1966; decided, June 6, 1996).

State v. Felde. 422 So.2d 370 (La. 1982).

State of New Jersy, Plaintiff–Respondent v. Kelly, G. Defendant–Appellant. *478 Atlantic Reporter, 2d Series* (1984).

Stegman v. Martinez. No. 94–L–67. Circuit Court for the First Judicial Circuit of Illinois, Massac County, Metropolis, Illinois.

Sturgis, E., v. Goldsmith, R. No. 83–2281. United States Court of Appeals, Ninth Circuit. 796 F. 2d 1103 (argued and submitted, February 14, 1984; filed, August 11, 1986).

Swift, M. D., v. Swift, C. No. 59880. Supreme Court of New York, Appellate Division, Third Department. 162 A.D. 2d 784; 557 N.Y.S. 2d 695; 1990 N.Y. App. Div. *Lexis 7190* (June 14, 1990).

Synakowski, J., v. Synakowski, T. No. 64984. Supreme Court of New York, Appellate Division, Third Department. 191 A.D. 2d 836; 594 N.Y.S. 2d 852; 1993 N.Y. App. Div. *Lexis 2376* (March 11, 1993).

Tennessee v. David Willard Phipps. No. 02C01–9207–CC–00152. Court of Criminal Appeals of Tennessee, at Jackson. 883 S.W. 2d 138; 1994 Tenn. Crim. App. *Lexis 298*.

Thompson v. Oklahoma. No. 86–6169. Supreme Court of the United States. 487 U.S. 815; 108 S. Ct. 2687; 1988 U.S. *Lexis 3028*; 101 L. Ed. 2d 702; 56 U.S.L.W. 4892 (argued, November 9, 1987; decided, June 29, 1988).

Tschantz v. Ferguson. No. 64115. Court of Appeals of Ohio, Cuyahoga County. *Westlaw* (September 7, 1994).

United States v. Emroyln Kae Whitetail. No. 91–1400. United States Court of Appeals, Eighth Circuit. 956 F. 2d 857; 1992 U.S. App. *Lexis 1724*; 35 Fed. R. Evid. Serv. (Callaghan) 150 (submitted, October 15, 1991; filed, February 12, 1992).

Wessel, C., v. AIC Security Investigations, Ltd., and Ruth Vrdolyak. Nos. 93–3939, 94–1018, 94–2895, and 94–3089. United States Court of Appeals, Seventh Circuit (argued, February 7, 1995; decided, May 22, 1995). *Westlaw*.

Young, E., v. Young, S. 94–09240. Supreme Court of New York, Appellate Division, Second Department. 212 A.D. 2d 114; 628 N.Y.S. 2d 957 N.Y. App. Div. *Lexis 7102*.